Racial Resentment
in the Political Mind

Racial Resentment in the Political Mind

DARREN W. DAVIS
AND DAVID C. WILSON

THE UNIVERSITY OF CHICAGO PRESS   CHICAGO AND LONDON

The University of Chicago Press, Chicago 60637
The University of Chicago Press, Ltd., London
© 2022 by The University of Chicago
All rights reserved. No part of this book may be used or reproduced in any manner
whatsoever without written permission, except in the case of brief quotations in critical articles and reviews. For more information, contact the University of Chicago Press,
1427 E. 60th St., Chicago, IL 60637.
Published 2022
Printed in the United States of America

31 30 29 28 27 26 25 24 23 22   1 2 3 4 5

ISBN-13: 978-0-226-81467-4 (cloth)
ISBN-13: 978-0-226-81484-1 (paper)
ISBN-13: 978-0-226-81470-4 (e-book)
DOI: https://doi.org/10.7208/chicago/9780226814704.001.0001

Library of Congress Cataloging-in-Publication Data

Names: Davis, Darren W., author. | Wilson, David C. (David Christopher), author.
Title: Racial resentment in the political mind / Darren W. Davis and David C. Wilson.
Description: Chicago : University of Chicago Press, 2022. | Includes bibliographical
    references and index.
Identifiers: LCCN 2021021096 | ISBN 9780226814674 (cloth) | ISBN 9780226814841
    (paperback) | ISBN 9780226814704 (ebook)
Subjects: LCSH: Race awareness—United States. | Whites—United States—Attitudes. |
    African Americans—Attitudes. | Resentment—Social aspects—United States. | United
    States—Race relations.
Classification: LCC E185.615 .D3857 2022 | DDC 305.800973—dc23
LC record available at https://lccn.loc.gov/2021021096

♾ This paper meets the requirements of ANSI/NISO Z39.48-1992 (Permanence of Paper).

Contents

Prologue

As reported in the major headlines and bolstered by public opinion data, there is a growing sentiment among Whites that they are losing ground, being left behind and overlooked, and "cut in line" by undeserving racial and ethnic minorities. Increasingly, Whites perceive that the "American way of life" is changing in such a way that their privilege and status are being threatened, and African Americans and other minorities are benefiting unfairly by circumventing generally accepted rules of the game and eschewing traditional values. Such sentiments are not exclusively grounded in racial prejudice, hate, or anti-Black affect; rather, Whites' sense of threat is connected to beliefs about justice, fairness, and legitimizing racial myths. Many refer to this growing sentiment as *racial resentment*, which we believe is the correct terminology but based on the wrong reasoning. Racial resentment and its measurement were introduced over 30 years ago, becoming the most identifiable and available indicator of racial prejudice. It is extremely limited as an analytical framework and incapable of explaining politics and political appeals today because it rests on the notion that racial prejudice is the main ingredient driving political and social attitudes when what is really happening involves a reaction to the loss of status and privilege. Nevertheless, racial resentment, properly conceived and measured, offers the most valid analytical framework for understanding such perceptions.

We argue that racial resentment may *also* stem from a justice motive, in which people have an expectation for and belief in an orderly and just world where people get what they deserve and deserve what they get. A sense of uncertainty, discomfort, and dissonance occurs when positive outcomes are perceived to be awarded randomly, or when people are perceived to be rewarded or advantaged when they have ostensibly not met the criteria for deservingness. Racial stereotypes, prejudice, and other information facilitate an appraisal of deservingness concerning what relief African Americans and other minorities receive. While racial resentment may be influenced by both racial and non-racial information, it is not itself wholly prejudice; instead, resentment is conceivably an outgrowth of this process when African Americans and other minorities are perceived to be rewarded undeservingly, threatening broader systems of merit. And because this process begins with a justice motive or expectation of fairness, the sense of justice in the racially resentful person needs to be restored. Until it is restored (if it ever can be), racial resentment festers—creating a desire for retribution in order to restore a belief in a just world. Retribution takes the form of psychological desires like schadenfreude and political preference like opposition to ameliorative policies. In a nutshell, people can develop beliefs about race that are only partially, if at all, based on racial prejudice or antipathy. Racial resentment may stem from broader non-racial motives applied to racial groups when considering politics.

Whites perceive that African Americans are seeking to use different means to benefit more than everyone else when there is no evidence they have specifically been harmed by racism or slavery, and expect Whites to remain silent when they have legitimate questions about racial issues. Such racial information and beliefs become important aspects of how Whites appraise African Americans' deservingness. And so, decisions may be racial because they involve an implicit or explicit reference to African Americans and other minorities without necessarily being racist.

Although the classic racial resentment measure has been broadly accepted and legitimized in political behavior and public opinion research (i.e., codified in the American National Election Studies [ANES] since 1986 and replicated in numerous surveys), there have been questions related to whether it measures what it purports to measure. Researchers may be surprised to learn that the technical concept of racial resentment began as a renaming of symbolic racism, which at that time was embroiled in its own measurement controversy. Using the same survey measures and theory as symbolic racism, classic racial resentment was simply a new name for an existing idea; the new label was intended to capture both Black affect (or racial prejudice) and perceptions of Blacks' violating traditional norms. Without any other available measures of racial prejudice, classic racial resentment became accepted as a measure of racial prejudice. Perhaps due to its grounding in symbolic racism, its explicit connection of policy attitudes and race, and its being located on the canonical survey of political attitudes (i.e., the ANES), classic racial resentment became the go-to measure of racial prejudice in political science and other disciplines. While there were carry-over controversies from debates related to symbolic racism—which was simultaneously being developed by other researchers—the classic racial resentment concept and measurement were privileged without much debate. In fact, it took almost 30 years for classic racial resentment to undergo a rigorous validation, though those same items under the umbrella of symbolic racism were seriously scrutinized as ideological. Make no mistake, the rebranding of racial resentment was broadly accepted by researchers and proved to be a quite powerful predictor of political attitudes and behavior. Our assessment is that because of deep racial polarization in the American public, classic racial resentment captures "something" correlated with anti-Black affect, as do nearly all measures of racial attitudes—and some measures of non-racial attitudes (e.g., social dominance, conservatism, and authoritarianism)—but that the measure captures neither racial resentment nor racial prejudice.

With a new conceptualization and measure of racial resentment, this book examines the meaning and consequences of racialized resentment, how it explains and structures political attitudes and behavior, and how it aids in understanding political appeals today. It provides a new framework for thinking about race, but it is robust in its conceptualization, such that it can be applied to other group resentments. Our analyses employ alternative racial resentment measures we developed over the course of a decade, and our scale of Whites' resentment toward African Americans is highly valid and reliable, distinct from classic racial resentment and modern racism, and has desirable scaling properties. In short, we are seeking to lay the theoretical and empirical groundwork for resentment in politics in general, and racial resentment in particular.

Origin of Racial Resentment

Racial resentment, in its current formulation, is commonly thought to stem from the 1960s, when the government began to respond to African Americans' demands for equality and fair treatment. We disagree, as Whites' sense of injustice due to African Americans' demands, perceived as reducing their power and status, dates to periods much earlier, and has reoccurred at various points when the status quo is under threat. As far back as the Reconstruction era, racial resentment stems from perceptions of racial advancement and progress. Whites generally perceive a zero-sum allocation of rights, power, and status in which the extent to which they perceive Blacks are advancing diminishes or threatens their rights. Following the Civil War and the formal emancipation of slaves, the Reconstruction era was the first period when African Americans were bestowed the same rights as Whites to create an integrated society. The slavery amendments (13th, 14th, and 15th Amendments to the US Constitution) were passed during this time, and African Americans enjoyed unprecedented access to voting and property ownership. Whites' resentment grew out of the challenges to the existing social hierarchy as African Americans were perceived as undeserving of equal status because they were less than human and had not proved themselves worthy of civil interaction. This relatively tranquil period for African Americans did not last long as Whites reasserted their dominant and privileged status through Supreme Court decisions (e.g., *Plessy vs. Ferguson* in 1896), Jim Crow laws, violence, and flat-out disregard for existing laws and the US Constitution. It would not be until the 1950s, with the beginning of the civil rights movement and certain Supreme Court decisions (*Brown vs. Board of Education*), that African Americans would begin to reclaim a semblance of power and again threaten Whites' status.

For all of US history, Whites dominated American society and politics, but following the successes of the civil rights movement, Whites had to compete for jobs, access, resources, and prerogatives (i.e., statuses and privilege). They could no longer be assured a level of prosperity by the existing rules of the game because there were new competitors to contend with—ones who were once easily eliminated from competition merely due to skin color. Instead of thinking about how African Americans could integrate to become closer to the "perfect union," many Whites felt the union should involve only Whites and be a reference to states. The civil rights movement intended to alter the power distribution and social hierarchy of society, and in many ways it did. African Americans may not have been perceived as equal after the movement, but they at least had a basis by which they could make claims of maltreatment and injustice. Whites continue to feel the threat of the civil rights movement agenda decades later with discussions questioning the imposition of political correctness, African American voter turnout, diversity and inclusion, multiculturalism, the need for a social safety net, the overreach of government in private lives, and the dismantling of Civil War statues and monuments.

Racial Resentment in the Current Era

This book is more than just a criticism of the measure of classic racial resentment. We propose a new way of thinking about racial resentment and how it enters politics. We offer a general theory and necessary constructs to explain how Whites and African Americans employ similar concepts of justice and fairness to form attitudes about dominant groups that seek to defend their status and subordinate groups that seek to change their status. A central theme of this book advances the idea that racial prejudice is extremely narrow and limited in analyzing politics today, while racial resentment, properly conceived, offers a more useful and robust analytical framework. Racial prejudice is fundamental to human wiring, and it will probably never disappear. This is a point on which we cannot be clearer—racial prejudice, hate, and antipathy toward African Americans and other minorities will always be a component of political and social attitudes. But there are other motives, like justice and deservingness, with less obvious racial content, that are just as powerful as racial prejudice. The election of President Obama signaled to many Whites what they had suspected since the civil rights era: they were in fact losing ground to African Americans and other minorities. The American way of life—in which Whites dominated governance roles, did not have to compete with other groups for jobs, received status and privileges ostensibly by hard work and not complaining, and did not have to constantly address their racial past—had changed forever. Whites' status and power were eroding because civil rights–era legislation had emboldened African Americans and women to assert their rights, and it was the federal government, not states, and the Democratic Party, not Republicans, that allowed such a change to take place.

It was not only racists who perceived an acute threat with the election of President Obama; it was also everyday people who held no particular malice or hate toward African Americans. Everyday citizens clung to the belief that Whites' status—which included their values, courtesies, traditions, and sizable presence—needed to be preserved. Whites' status is based on a system that provides certainty and security, and thus provides justice. Therefore, Whites perceive that when there is a threat to the system and the values that support Whites' dominant status, there is a threat to justice. Under threat, individuals target their concerns to the source of the threat. In the context of racial resentment, the sources of threat and recipients of the threat are racial groups contending with competing desires for change.

Summarily, classic racial resentment—including "new racisms" like symbolic racism or modern racism—became relevant because it was the most useful and valid concept to describe Whites' reactions to the threat imposed by racial minorities who wanted to change society so that they too could prosper. Racial resentment acknowledged the threat Whites perceived in undeserving African Americans and other minorities who were taking advantage of "their" (Whites') resources, not abiding by the established societal norms and values, and not playing by the rules of the game. Since the outcome of these perceived threats is racial progress, it usually elicits strong negative reactions among Whites, and the election of Obama was no different. Thus, we were witness to a period in which racial resentment constantly guided political discourse and motivations, even when news media and experts rejected or ignored such a claim.

The discourse of this period included coded language, like political correctness, that conveyed a racial threat to Whites. President Trump would pick up on and expand the meaning of political correctness in 2016, but under Obama, political correctness was a cooperation—an often tense one, but a cooperation nonetheless—between White liberals and the Black civil rights establishment that was intended to delegitimize any criticism of their post–civil rights agenda by labeling the criticism racist. Principled objections to affirmative action programs, immigration policy, and social welfare were seen as racist, and once they were labeled as such, any further discussion was circumvented. Diversity, multiculturalism, and identity politics were now valued over free speech rights, further signaling to Whites a change in status quo rules (i.e., social unacceptability of racial critique). The reaction was resentment, and Whites holding higher levels of it deemed the election of President Obama to be illegitimate and a response to political correctness (e.g., believing that people voted for Obama only because of his race and because they did not want to be perceived—even by their own minds—as racist (see Wilson and Davis 2018). Because people could not really say what they meant without being accused of being racist, Obama would be spared legitimate questions by the media and other political candidates.

Political correctness meant dismissing or obscuring facts about Obama's policies and positions. Thus, racial resentment began to fester. Not only was the American way of life changing, as African Americans were seen as benefiting unfairly, but people now had to watch what they said about politics even if they felt their concerns were legitimate. It could be said that the Obama presidency shifted many Whites into a constant state of perceived injustice that could be resolved only by retribution against the sources of unfairness: Obama, Democrats, and African Americans.

In the 2016 presidential election, Donald Trump openly exploited Whites' racial resentment and anger. Trump railed against political correctness incessantly, furthering the efforts Republicans had already made to racialize political correctness and convey racial diversity and multiculturalism as a threat to Whites' status. However, no campaign appeal communicated a greater threat to the American way of life and White status than *Make America Great Again*. Without mentioning race, this slogan subtly communicated to Whites that their ways of thinking, doing, and leading were in decline and that they needed to return to an era when Whites were more dominant and people, especially African Americans, knew their place. The slogan spoke volumes to Whites who were already concerned about their loss of status and privilege as a consequence of diversity and multiculturalism, and it spoke volumes to African Americans, who recognized that a return to a previous era would be perilous for them. Racial resentment, as well as racial prejudice, was the appeal, and this is why it resonated with ordinary citizens.

African Americans' Racial Resentment

It may be a significant challenge to many researchers that Whites are not the only group that can express racial resentment. We come down somewhat hard on the dearth of research on African Americans' racial resentment toward Whites. It is astonishing, especially with regard to the topic of racial resentment, that no one has yet asked whether African Americans hold racially motivated resentments, how their resentment differs from Whites, and how it informs a general theory of racial resentment. Is it inconceivable that one of the most aggrieved and oppressed groups in society might know something about resentment? Is it impossible for African Americans to believe White discrimination protects the status quo and keeps them in a disadvantaged position? Equally important, is this not an important question for scholars?

The absence of research on African Americans' racial resentment is shameful. We do not mean simply asking African American respondents the same resentment questions, as this would be extremely insulting and borders on violating effective survey design practice—crushing trust and rapport among Black respondents who must continue to endure a survey after having to answer questions about their group alone. Instead, the shame is that scholars have simply avoided, for whatever the reason, crafting new measures that take African Americans' experiences and different viewpoint into consideration when studying political behavior.

We did just that, creating and analyzing a set of items to uncover African Americans' racial attitudes, and this book reports on the meaning of their resentments. African Americans have legitimate reason to be resentful toward Whites, but their resentment stems from Whites' defense of the status quo, which places Blacks at a disadvantage. The crucial difference is that African Americans, as a whole, are in less powerful positions and the existing social hierarchy benefits them less than it benefits Whites. African Americans are resentful toward Whites because Whites defend their status and privilege by denying the derogatory racial experiences of Blacks, dismissing their racism claims and blaming Blacks for their lower status, and constantly creating new ways (i.e., voter suppression tactics, unfair loans, dismantling of civil rights laws and protection) to keep them unequal and relegated to lower status positions. Discrimination, the objection to ameliorative racial policies, and the denial of voting rights are intended to keep African Americans at the bottom of the social hierarchy, and African Americans are resentful because of it.

And so, this book is an attempt to restart the conversation on racial resentment and advance the understanding of racial attitudes by moving beyond mere hate and dislike of African Americans as an explanation for politics today. We have learned a lot about racial resentment over the past decades, and we are not arguing that these lessons should be disregarded, nor are we seeking to quarrel with the scholars who have produced these lessons. Instead, we are seeking to ground racial resentment in *resentment*, and to examine how it becomes racialized. We are taking Whites at their word when they say they are "not racist," and then examining their ostensibly non-racist views on race to understand the extent to which being racist or not actually matters. We are pushing the discipline to think about racial politics beyond broadly categorizing all things racial as prejudice, just as all things partisan are not ideological, and vice versa. And, we are seeking to give students of racial attitudes—academic and non-academic—pathways to discussing race by broadening the motivations for describing how one feels about race, rather than describing whether one is racist or not, which is often erroneous.

"I'm Not a Racist, but . . ."

The Problem

With the growing sentiment among Whites that they are "losing out" and "being cut in line" by African Americans and other minorities—as reflected in an emphasis on diversity and inclusion, multiculturalism, trigger warnings, and political correctness, as well as the projected majority-minority shift in the composition of the US population, an increase in African Americans occupying powerful and prestigious positions, and the election of Barack Obama as the first African American president—there is a perception that the "American way of life" that has advantaged them is being threatened. These perceived threats come in the form of attacks on the status quo and social hierarchy, defiance of traditional political and societal values, and a contestation of White entitlement and privilege.[1] Perceptions that they are falling behind culminate in a belief in reverse discrimination. A vast majority of Whites (72 percent) believe their group is discriminated against, while substantially less (28 percent) report experiencing discrimination personally.[2] The culprits, as they see it, are undeserving and contemptible African Americans, as well as other minorities, who are perceived to benefit unfairly from, and take advantage of, resources that come at Whites' expense (Crawford et al. 2019; Mayrl and Saperstein 2013; Wilkins and Kaiser 2014).[3] This perceived reallocation of unearned resources to undeserving African Americans challenges the status quo and the "rules of the game," especially as they relate to justice and deservingness. Such reactions do not stem exclusively from racial prejudice or hatred toward African Americans; instead, they may result from threats to Whites' sense of justice, entitlement, and status. This sentiment is occurring among everyday citizens who may not subscribe to hate-filled racial or nationalistic ideologies but rather seek to treat everyone respectfully and equally, even those who are different, and understand that reject-ing others because of racial prejudice is offensive. They may not think of themselves as racially prejudiced and indeed readily insist that they are not (Dovidio and Gaertner 1986), but they adhere to beliefs that place them in the same bucket with racists.

People do not have to hate or subscribe to racist ideologies to commis-erate with racists (Bonilla-Silva 2006; Federico and Sidanius 2002; Snider-man and Piazza 1993). Principled and race-neutral motivations, such as political conservatism (McClosky 1958), authoritarianism (Adorno et al. 1950; Altemeyer 1981), perceived group conflict (Blumer 1958; Bobo 1999), dogmatism (Rokeach 1960), and social dominance (Sidanius and Pratto 1999),[4] assert that everyday people can do and say things that pro-duce the same outcomes as those who are racially prejudiced but with-out the racially demeaning rationalizations. In plain terms, race-neutral and principled people base their decisions on values, like justice, fair-ness, or defense of the status hierarchy, that do not require a belief in the inferiority of African Americans or antipathy toward African Ameri-cans and other minorities (Gibson 2008, 2009). Rigid and inflexible ad-herence to a set of values can make one virtually indistinguishable from racists, however. Conservatives may object to policies like affirmative action, like racists do, because they believe in self-reliance and that peo-ple should pull themselves up without any help from others. Authoritar-ians may defend the police killing of unarmed black men and women, like racists do, because they respect law and order, and obedience. And individuals high in social dominance may oppose policies designed to aid in the welfare of African Americans, like racists do, because they think the social divisions are acceptable and should be preserved.

This literature teaches us that racial prejudice is neither a necessary nor sufficient explanation for understanding racial politics. Yet, the cur-rent conceptualization and measure of classic racial resentment, the dominant analytical framework available to political scientists in under-standing racial politics introduced over 30 years ago, superimposes ra-cial prejudice and hatred on explanations of behavior (Kinder and Sand-ers 1996). The current conceptualization of classic racial resentment has failed on several grounds; chief among them are presumptions that its measurement reflects racial prejudice and violations of individualism. More importantly, as an analytical framework, the current conceptualization of classic racial resentment suggests that the denigration of President Obama and the rise of President Trump can be explained only in terms of racial prejudice.

Our contention parallels the arguments made by Lawrence Blum (2002), who referred to the tendency to label racial discourse as racist as "conceptual inflation." Blum (2002) asserts,

> Not every instance of racial conflict, insensitivity, discomfort, miscommunication, exclusion, injustice, or ignorance should be called "racist." Not all *racial* incidents are *racist* incidents. We need a more varied and nuanced moral vocabulary for talking about the domain of race. We need to articulate the range of values and disvalues implicated in race-based beliefs and attitudes, actions and interactions, institutions and practices. . . . If someone displays racial insensitivity, but not racism, people should be able to see that for what it is. (p. 2)

We agree wholeheartedly with Blum (2002) on this point. We contend in this book that Whites' resentment toward African Americans, properly conceived and measured, is not necessarily racial prejudice, but rather it may stem from a just-world motive and an appraisal of deservingness along with legitimizing racial myths (i.e., negative racial information and stereotypes). The major problem, as we see it, is that the only analytical framework available to political scientists for understanding politics today is seriously flawed and sees everything racialized as being motivated by racial prejudice or anti-Black affect. Researchers overlook so many other values among ordinary citizens and fail to hold them accountable for beliefs that have the same consequence as racial prejudice.

This book separates racial resentment from racial prejudice. Considering the recent political messaging suggesting that undeserving African Americans and minorities are threatening the status quo and the "American way of life," this task has a special urgency. Stemming from an internal sense of justice, which we all possess, racial resentment contends that it is objectionable, discomforting, and antithetical for African Americans and other minorities to benefit from unearned resources that ultimately are perceived as disadvantaging Whites or altering the status quo. Thus, unlike racial prejudice, racial resentment is motivated by the feeling that people *should* get what they deserve and deserve what they get. When this fundamental expectation is disrupted, one's sense of justice or fairness is violated, and resentment toward an "undeserving" individual ensues. By definition, resentment is anger over the unjust receipt of positive outcomes, and the sense of injustice stems from a negative appraisal of the means used to gain the outcome (Feather 1999). Injustice also occurs when deserving individuals are *not* rewarded.

While racial prejudice and race-neutral beliefs, like conservatism, authoritarianism, social dominance theory (SDT), and many others, are relevant in understanding recent presidential elections (Hutchings 2009; Tesler and Sears 2010; Valentino and Brader 2011), we believe that racial resentment toward African Americans is a more valid analytical framework within which to understand political sentiments today. When Whites perceive that they are losing ground to African Americans because of concerns over racial equality and amelioration, they become resentful and seek to preserve their status and privilege (Wetts and Willer 2018; Wilkins and Kaiser 2014). This has been evident throughout American history.

By raising the relevance of racial resentment as an analytical framework, we are in no way suggesting that racial prejudice is disappearing or that it is being replaced by race-neutral sentiments. We are suggesting that, at least in political science, little is known about how everyday citizens who cling to values like justice and racial resentment thus perpetuate racial inequality (Gibson 2008, 2009). Moreover, the attention devoted to racial prejudice and racists ignores other motivations that produce the same effects and that implicate a broader swath of people who think they bear no responsibility for the perpetuation of racial inequality.

Goal of the Book

We contend that racial resentment, defined as a belief that undeserving African Americans and other minorities are taking advantage of resources that challenge Whites' status and privilege, is a prevalent and extremely potent sentiment driving political and social attitudes today. By treating racial resentment as a serious and important emotion-laden belief, this book highlights the adverse effects of just world rationalizations about African Americans. Race-neutral individuals operate under just world expectations, acquiescing to racially prejudiced arguments and appeals, but this occurs through socialization processes that most would view as normal. Thus, when Whites assert they are not racially prejudiced toward African Americans and other minorities it may actually be true because racial resentment sentiment does not stem only from racist motivations. Just world expectations, fairness, and deservingness produce adverse racial effects, just as racial prejudice does.

As we already have stated, racial prejudice, by itself, cannot explain expressions of racial intolerance today. Rather, appeals to racial resentment may be more obvious in our current political and social discourse. The notion that only racists can feel threatened by the perceived advancement of African Americans and other minorities is an extremely low standard to explain how inequality gets perpetuated, and it ignores other pathways in which individuals can arrive at the same racialized political preferences. It is quite common nowadays to attribute support for candidates who espouse a defense of the status quo and the social hierarchy as prima-facie evidence of racism and racial prejudice, but we hope to show how such a position overlooks the overwhelming majority of ordinary citizens who are racially resentful toward African Americans but do not endorse necessarily racist views.

We are not the first to question the role of racial prejudice and hatred in structuring political and social attitudes. Over 20 years ago, Sniderman and Piazza (1993) in *The Scar of Race* asserted:

> Prejudice has not disappeared, and in particular circumstances and segments of the society it still has a major impact. But race prejudice no longer organizes and dominates the reactions of whites; it no longer leads large numbers of them to oppose public policies to assist blacks across-the-board. It is . . . simply wrong to suppose that the primary factor driving the contemporary arguments over the politics of race is white racism. (p. 5)

As a finer point, Sniderman and Piazza (1993) stated further:

> Arguments over race now cut at new angles. To treat the politics of race as though it is only about race and not about politics misrepresents the nature of contemporary disagreements over issues of race. (p. 5)

It is fair to say that these provocative statements have been largely overlooked, as we cannot recall any research following up on this claim.

However, as important as Sniderman and Piazza's proposal is to our thinking about racial resentment, their argument that beliefs about the role of government dominate Whites' racial policy attitudes does not help us very much in understanding racial resentment in this new era. Beliefs about the proper role of government will always resonate, but how helpful is such an approach when political campaigns exploit Whites' fear of being left behind?

The questions we address are varied and straightforward. We begin by revisiting the core aspects of resentment, explaining how it stems from a justice motive and appraisals of deservingness. This is important at the outset because classic racial resentment is currently situated in much of the political science literature as a form of racial prejudice or anti-Black affect; the crux of our argument is that Whites' resentment toward African Americans is not necessarily racial prejudice nor does it require racial hatred. Thus, we must correct a mischaracterization of racial resentment that has ensnared a generation of scholars, including us.

Following this review, we propose a new measure of Whites' resentment toward African Americans, steeped in our own theory—as opposed to one based on symbolic racism and prejudice—and based on a rather voluminous literature. Measuring Whites' resentment toward African American is no simple matter nowadays, as visceral, knee-jerk reactions to race and racial polarization make it difficult to distinguish among racial belief systems. Nevertheless, we assess the psychometric properties of the measure and explore its predictive validity. As it turns out, our concept and measure is quite powerful in predicting and structuring other attitudes, and explaining a host of political issues, racial and non-racial. And we don't mean powerful in just a correlational sense—our conceptualization and measurement speak to how Whites are motivated to construct a false reality that leads them to support antidemocratic values like inequality. Our conceptualization of racial resentment performs similarly to partisanship in that it aids in deciding what is meaningful and discordant to one's politics. Whites' resentment toward African Americans facilitates motivated reasoning whereby individuals seek to maintain (i.e., defend) a set of system-legitimizing beliefs that align with their beliefs about justice and deservingness. The incorporation of justice provides a means for individuals to rationalize opposition to racial amelioration, minority candidates and their policies, and other issues that ostensibly call for actions that disrupt the status quo.

Because Whites' resentment toward African Americans stems from an appraisal of deservingness based on one's sense of justice, it is not the conclusion or end of a social psychological process, like the way scholars think about racial prejudice. It may instead be the beginning of a process in which individuals seek to resolve the injustice, at least in their minds. To the extent that a perceived injustice goes unresolved, resentment can grow and fester. Although people move on with their lives, resentment from perceived injustice produces a desire, and a certain amount of pleasure, in seeing people suffer from their transgressions. Thus, when racial groups are perceived to benefit undeservingly from resources that challenge the status quo, thereby violating notions of justice, the resulting racial resentment creates a desire to see those racial groups fail. This leads to what we will later call *racial schadenfreude.*

Bandura's (2016) moral disengagement becomes relevant to our theory of racial schadenfreude because it enables people to retain their positive self-regard while doing harm. Bandura (1999, 2002) describes how individuals are able to avoid distress and self-condemnation after committing immoral acts against others. Moral disengagement further rationalizes racial schadenfreude and racial resentment with minimal self-condemnation and moral self-sanctions. According to the theory, when individuals violate moral standards of harming another individual, they typically experience self-condemnation and negative emotions such as shame. However, by using a variety of strategies to disengage moral self-sanctions, individuals are able to behave inhumanely while avoiding self-condemnation and distress. In this way, moral disengagement allows "good" people to support "cruel" deeds by making those "cruel" deeds seem acceptable or moral (Bandura 2002).

Moral disengagement has been found to be a powerful motivation in rationalizing bullying in children (Bandura et al. 1996, 2001; Gini, Pozzoli, and Hymel 2014), killing during war (Aquino et al. 2007; McAlister, Bandura, and Owen 2006), cruelty against animals (Vollum, Buffington-Vollum, and Longmire 2004), and the death penalty (Vollum and Buffington-Vollum 2010).

Figure 1.1 introduces our theoretical model of racial resentment. Most apparent is that racial resentment is neither the beginning nor the end of a theoretical process and it is not fueled by racial prejudice or hatred. Racial resentment begins with a just-world motive, which is a belief in fairness and an expectation that people get what they deserve (Hafer

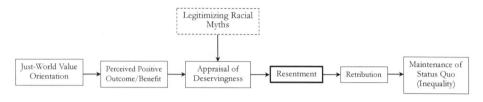

FIGURE I.I. Theory of Racial Resentment

and Rubel 2015; Lerner 1980a, 1980b). If a just-world value system is perceived to be violated or if a group receives an unearned or unjustifiable benefit, an appraisal of deservingness ensues.

Appraisals of deservingness are shaped by legitimizing racial myths, which are widely shared beliefs and stereotypes about African Americans and other minorities that justify their mistreatment and low status. Legitimizing myths are any coherent set of socially accepted attitudes, beliefs, values, and opinions that provide moral and intellectual legitimacy to the unequal distribution of social value (Sidanius, Devereux, and Pratto 1992). Beliefs about African Americans not taking responsibility for what happens in their lives make them appear less deserving of special treatment and place more of the blame on them for their status in society. Such beliefs are hierarchy-enhancing as they help maintain or increase group-based inequalities.

With such racial myths and racial stereotypes, resentment is triggered when one perceives African Americans and other minorities have received a benefit they do not deserve. African Americans may be perceived to be unfairly advancing by circumventing the traditional values and established rules of the game to which others adhere. When people who believe in the fundamental fairness of the world are challenged by a system or African Americans whom they perceive to be acting unjustly, they aim to restore balance. Among the various solutions to restoring this balance (Darley and Pittman 2003), punishing the perpetrators becomes an obvious sanction.

African Americans also possess a strong justice motive, but experiences with racial discrimination (and their group) produce different views of justice and fairness. For African Americans, racial discrimination is perceived as unjust and unfair because it serves to protect Whites' advantage. Resentment toward Whites arises from a belief that Whites are undeserving of their advantage because it is obtained at African Americans' expense.

Evolution of Racial Resentment

Racial resentment is predicated on the belief that African Americans and other ethnic minorities are undeserving of equal treatment, special considerations, or special protections.[5] Because African Americans historically were considered less-than-human and inferior, they were not entitled to the same rights and treatment enjoyed by Whites, as outlined in the original US Constitution. In chattel slavery, Blacks were not a threat to the status quo and therefore appraisals of deservingness did not stem from a justice motive. We identify four time periods in which intensified racial resentment toward African Americans flourished. Each period coincides with a significant identifiable event that expanded African Americans' status and power and by extension challenged Whites' dominance. Alternatively, racial prejudice should be thought of as a constant, activated regardless of whether a group is threatening the status quo or not.

The first period of intensifying racial resentment was during Reconstruction (1863–1867). There was no greater threat to White hegemonic status than when Blacks were deemed eligible for the same rights as Whites. The constitutional amendments during Reconstruction established, at least on paper, Blacks' full rights as citizens. The 13th Amendment abolished slavery; the 14th Amendment granted citizenship to former slaves and guaranteed all citizens equal protection of the laws; and the 15th Amendment granted the right to vote to Black men. During this period when Blacks received legitimate claims to racial equality, equal protection, and the right to vote, the seeds of racial resentment began to germinate. With the assistance of Northern protection, Blacks challenged White status and power by exercising voting rights, winning elections, owning property, and racially integrating. It was during this period that Blacks were first elected to political office, including 147 Black members elected to the US House. Beliefs about racial inferiority were not altered, however, and Whites perceived these advances as unjust and illegitimate, fostering anger and resentment.

A desire to restore White supremacy following Reconstruction resulted in the birth of the Ku Klux Klan, systematic violence directed toward Blacks, and the establishment of Jim Crow laws—laws enacted by state legislatures to legally segregate the races and impose second-class citizenship upon African Americans. Enforced by criminal penalties, these laws created separate schools, parks, waiting rooms, and other segregated public accommodations. Supreme Court decisions such as *Plessy vs. Ferguson* (1896), which legalized segregation, and the Civil Rights Cases ruling of 1883, which struck down the prohibition of racial segregation in public accommodations, reinforced Whites' status and privilege.

For the next 50 years following the turn of the century, America changed in significant ways as it negotiated industrialization, the Great Depression, an influx of ethnic immigrants, and the Great Migration, which brought Blacks in greater contact with Whites beyond the South. Racial prejudice and resentment during this time were expressed directly through violence, lynchings, and discrimination in jobs and housing. Government took on greater responsibility for social welfare and security. Whites did not have to compete against Blacks in the workplace, and they benefited from laws that sustained their status.

A second period that fostered racial resentment was the civil rights era (1950–1970). The status quo and social hierarchy were not seriously challenged until the Supreme Court decision in Brown vs. Board of Education (1954) and the civil rights movement. The Brown vs. Board of Education decision was a landmark United States Supreme Court case in which the Court declared state laws establishing separate public schools for Black and White students to be unconstitutional. Dealing a significant blow to White supremacy, segregation, according to this decision, was inherently unequal, and Blacks were entitled to the same facilities as Whites. The Court supported desegregation in both public facilities like bus stations and in privately owned establishments like hotels and cafes. From a broader perspective, the Court's decisions reflected a significant and successful challenge to the White social hierarchy, which led to intense resistance from Whites seeking to maintain their status and power.

As the civil rights movement picked up steam, three legislative enactments became chief among the outcomes challenging White dominance. First came the 1964 Civil Rights Act, which banned segregation in public places (e.g., bus stations, shops, and restaurants), made employment discrimination on the basis of race (and other categories) illegal, and created the Equal Employment Opportunities Commission

(EEOC) to investigate complaints and enforce the laws. The Equal Protection Clause of the Civil Rights Act of 1964 allowed for the implementation of ameliorative racial policies, like affirmative action programs intended to protect and give preference to African Americans. Second, the 1965 Voting Rights Act protected the voting rights of African Americans by creating legal mandates for states, and rendering discriminatory eligibility practices illegal. Third, the 1968 Civil Rights Act made it illegal to discriminate in jobs and housing.

While perceptions of the inferiority of Blacks have changed over time, appraisals of deservingness in this era still hinged on racial stereotypes. Although many Whites viewed these ameliorative racial programs as unfair and unjust on non-racial grounds tied to the role of government (Sniderman and Piazza 1993) or nuances about outcomes versus opportunities (Bobo and Kluegel 1993), the lion's share of opposition seemed to be rooted in appraisals of symbolic values, especially merit and deservingness (Kinder and Sears 1981; Kinder and Sanders 1996; McConahay, Hardee, and Batts 1981). Whites considered the policies a transference of power and resources to a group of people who were lazy, violent, lacking in self-discipline and family values, and disobedient, and who did not want to work for what they got. This was perceived as a direct threat to Whites' beliefs about how the distribution of rewards in society, and the political system more generally, should work. It was also seen as a violation of norms of fairness and equality of opportunity, as it granted special advantages to some and not others. Thus, many Whites viewed the ameliorative policies of the era as violating standards of merit and legitimate processes for achieving equality. The policies were deemed unjust.

A third period that fostered racial resentment is the current era of politics, which we call the Obama/Trump Era, ranging from 2008 to 2020. The 2008 election saw the ascendency of Barack Obama, a little-known, first-term senator from Illinois, who was considered a rising star in the Democratic Party at the time. Obama, a great orator with an Ivy League education, excelled at connecting with people; he was considered compassionate, articulate, and hip. Yet, many also viewed him as inexperienced and unwilling to wait his turn, playing a race-card to advance his political agenda. The racial divisions were clear even before his election (Hunt and Wilson 2009). People worried that, as an African American, Obama would be narrowly focused on race and his inexperience would make America look bad (or weak).

Obama's victory crystalized Whites' sense of power-loss to undeserving African Americans and other minorities (Jardina 2019), perhaps due
to the belief that, as an African American president, Obama would advantage his own racial group over Whites—that he would enact policies and support legislation to improve the status and position of African Americans at the expense of Whites. From Trump's vantage point,
America was greatest when there was no pressure toward political correctness and Whites did not have to filter what they said or how they
said it to accommodate others. Accordingly, a theory of racial resentment suggests that political correctness and the social sanctions on derogatory and offensive expressions were additional ways that American
society had changed for the worse under President Obama because any
political commentary about Obama, racial or not, might be viewed as
racist. This placed Whites at a disadvantage: their speech freedoms were
limited, but African Americans—and Obama—could lash out at Whites,
even though many Whites may have done nothing to harm them.

Just to be clear on this point, Republicans have routinely criticized
political correctness to express discomfort with liberal censorship, especially the limiting of conservative speakers on college campuses.
Trump's attack on political correctness in 2016 was a continuation of the
Republican view, but it also became a protest against Whites' inability
to speak plainly or disagree with the problems facing the country under
President Obama's administration. Trump himself was targeted on numerous occasions as he attacked the idea that Obama was a legitimate
citizen and president. Even if Trump saw his birth-certificate campaign
as non-racial, and a legitimate service to the country, he was largely ridiculed as racist and bigoted. Thus, like a coded message, Whites perceived a threat in the restrictions on their ability to speak their minds
and to express differing viewpoints, restrictions that had run amok under President Obama's leadership.

Trump supporters believed that, with the right president, not only
could their racial resentments receive a fair hearing, but they could actually change America back to a period where people knew their place
and would not disrupt the status quo (i.e., reverse political correctness).
We empirically explore Trump's messaging and reactions to it in later
chapters.

A fourth period of intense racial resentment will most likely occur
with the forecasted change of majority-minority. According to published
reports by the US Census Bureau (2012), a seismic shift in American

demographics is predicted to alter the future distribution of racial-ethnic groups. For the first time, current racial-ethnic minorities make up more than half of the under-five age group, which means that as early as 2044, if the current growth rates continue, Whites will no longer be the majority group. The share of the White population is predicted to significantly decline as older Whites die more quickly than they replace themselves, the Baby Boom generation dies off, and younger child-bearing-age cohorts immigrate. The Census Bureau reported that the minority population would increase from 38 percent in 2014 to 56 percent in 2060, a non-trivial difference. As might be expected, the projected decline in the White population has caused some consternation; many Whites see it as a threat to their way of life, culture, and the comfort they have long enjoyed (Bai and Federico 2019; Craig and Richeson 2014; Danbold and Huo 2015).

In short, racial resentment is activated and promulgated in reaction to the belief that Whites are losing ground to African Americans and other minorities. This is coupled with the notion that that such groups benefit unfairly and that they are undeserving of the benefits.

Contemporary Appeals to Racial Resentment

Beyond the obvious racist messages, language, and associations, Donald Trump's *Make America Great Again* slogan is a prime example of the activation of racial resentment. As part of his 2016 election campaign, it implicitly conveyed a popular sentiment that Whites' position and status were in decline. Although he used it most provocatively, Trump actually did not coin the slogan; Ronald Reagan repeatedly promised to "make America great again" during his 1980 presidential campaign, and the slogan was also batted around by Bill Clinton during his 1992 campaign. Trump first used it in 2012 in reference to President Barack Obama's "failed" administration and policies, and continued to use it effectively in the 2016 presidential primaries and general election. The slogan quickly became a popular rallying cry for Trump's supporters, appearing on baseball caps, placards, banners, and t-shirts. After securing the Republican presidential nomination, and well into his first term as president, Donald Trump continued to use *Make America Great Again* in speeches and in his social media exchanges. The use of the *Make America Great Again* slogan was extremely effective, but it had taken on additional meaning than when it was first used. While Trump was defiant and unapologetic in his expressions of racist and derogatory sentiments—for example, refusing to disavow the Ku Klux Klan and White national-ists—a lot of his racial references were interlaced with beliefs about the threats racial minorities posed to the American way of life.

Though labeled racist by many individuals—like actor Samuel L. Jackson, who remarked in an interview that the slogan "reminded him of growing up during apartheid," and actress Alyssa Milano, who tweeted that the "red MAGA hats are the new white hood"—*Make America Great Again*, in our view, is not overtly racist, but it exploits the anxi-ety of racial anguish through the use of the word "again" (Davis, Wil-son, and Moy 2019). While most citizens would like to see their coun-try aspire to greatness, "again" is an explicit comparison to the past, and Whites and African Americans interpret the past very differently (Grif-fin and Bollen 2009). References to the past, for Whites, elicit nostalgic memories of how good life used to be for them—a time when Whites as a group enjoyed greater power and status, and people knew their place (ac-cepted the racial hierarchy), but also a time when people did not have to bite their tongue on matters of race and other sensitive subjects. Accom-panied by Trump's inflammatory comments, this single word "again" implicitly suggests that the America of today is not as good as the Amer-ica of the past (though the specific past era is left intentionally vague). For Whites, the points of reference accessed by the word "again" may include the greater availability of jobs, lower taxes, and more affordable living costs; it may conjure a time when people respected and obeyed the law, had morals and self-discipline, and did not have to be politically cor-rect and could say what they wanted. In 2016, it also triggered a sense that people, specifically African Americans and other minorities, had forgotten their place. In other words, African Americans were no lon-ger playing by the rules of the game, and were instead rejecting the tra-ditional values of society and challenging the racial hierarchy. Thus, the *Make America Great Again* slogan effectively engaged racial resentment because it raised awareness of existing or burgeoning latent threats to Whites' status and privilege—hence a need to halt the encroachment and return to a state of promise. This interpretation is reflected in a sug-gestion by Westacott (2016):

> Underlying these political agendas is a real preference for a world in which everyone "knew their place" and behaved accordingly: when children obeyed

their parents or felt the back of a hand; when men earned bread while women kept house; when white privilege and power went largely unchallenged. (para. 5)

African Americans likely have a different interpretation of the past, and therefore of the *Make America Great Again* slogan. African Americans find little nostalgic or pleasant about an America of the past; the word "again" instead invokes a more perilous era in which racial prejudice and discrimination were more pervasive. Among the thoughts triggered by references to the past: Jim Crow practices and legal discrimination, lynchings, racial segregation, and the acceptance of the status quo and the existing racial hierarchy. In other words, the slogan was likely interpreted among African Americans as a threat to their progress (i.e., the status quo), and as an accusation that they had forgotten their "rightful" place in society, when America was greater for Whites and Blacks were not protected by social desirability norms and government overreach into state's rights. Perhaps the African American interpretation is best summarized by former PBS host Tavis Smiley's remark about the slogan:

To what specific period of American greatness are you wanting us to return? When black folk suffered segregation after slavery? When women had no right to vote or control their own bodies? When gay brothers and lesbian sisters felt ceaseless hate? When we stole land from the Native Americans? When we sent Japanese families to internment camps? When America lynched Mexicans? I just need Trump to give me some clarity on the time period he wishes to travel back to. (McGirt 2016)

In short, political appeals and messaging during the 2016 campaign framed to Whites the threat to their "American way of life" and status quo and reflected the existing racial resentments of everyday citizens. While racial prejudice will probably never disappear and will remain a strong element motivating political and social attitudes, the problem that no one seems focused on is this one: how non-racists end up commiserating with racists.

Several recent books have reinvigorated the concern about racial resentment. In *The Politics of Resentment: Rural Consciousness in Wisconsin and the Rise of Scott Walker*, Cramer (2016) observed a rise in resentment among rural residents in Wisconsin who perceived they were not getting their fair share of governmental resources, which were being channeled instead to urban areas like Madison. Cramer (2016) contends that, although Wisconsin is a predominantly White state and its urban areas are largely segregated, racial considerations were embedded in rural residents' resentment. As Cramer states, "Given the way arguments against government redistribution in the United States have historically been made by equating deservingness with whiteness," the threat driving rural residents' concerns about losing-out alludes to race even if race is not mentioned. Rural residents perceived they were being disadvantaged because "urban areas" were getting more than they deserved (i.e., paying fewer taxes but receiving more government services such as better schools and infrastructure).

In *Dying of Whiteness*, Metzl (2019) highlights the mortal consequences of racial resentment. He argues that many Whites have become racially resentful to the point where they now justify their opposition for certain policies, such as Obamacare, on the basis that it would benefit African Americans and thereby threaten their status and privilege. Ironically, Whites object to these programs even though they themselves would benefit from them as well. Yet, many Whites would be willing to "literally die" rather than support policies that would benefit undeserving minorities. We are encouraged by this type of work because it helps to establish the potency of racial resentment and the desire to defend White privilege.

In *Strangers in Their Own Land: Anger and Mourning on the American Right*, Hochschild's (2016) qualitative interviews link the contradiction in eschewing governmental regulation despite widespread suffering from the ill effects of pollution, or what she refers to as the "Great Paradox," to Whites' loss of status. According to Hochschild (2016), Whites perceive African Americans, ethnic minorities, women, refugees, and immigrants to be unfairly cutting in line ahead of them in pursuing the American Dream—aided by President Obama, who is perceived as a line-cutter himself. Whites are angry and resentful that others are being advantaged and given opportunities while they are being forgotten. Rather than enforcing a fair and equitable process, government is perceived as aiding and abetting these line-cutters, which ultimately makes Whites less trustful and more suspicious of government. Whites in this situation began to identify with those who are better off to detach themselves from those below. Compounding the problem, those who object to line-cutters are ridiculed by the media as rednecks and racists, even though they may not harbor antipathy toward African Americans and other minorities. Individuals with such attitudes naturally gravitated toward Donald Trump in 2016 because he articulated their sense of anxiety about the changing American way of life.

Hochschild (2016) acknowledges that racial resentment is an outgrowth of feeling passed over and betrayed in favor of African Americans and other minorities. But it is also easy to imagine that these resentful individuals would desire minority groups to suffer in some way for not playing by the rules.

Taken together, the commonalities of these works parallel our contention in several important ways. First, these works describe in detail the relevance and application of racial resentment among Whites as it relates to a fear of being left behind and disadvantaged while African Americans and ethnic minorities move ahead (Parker 2021). The studies explicate how Whites are angry and bitter about the perceived changing American way of life due to liberal policies that redistribute material resources, economic opportunities, and social prerogatives to the less deserving. These views were exacerbated by the election of President Obama, who, ostensibly due to his racial background, is perceived as facilitating an attack on Whites. Second, the subjects in these works are presented as neither bigots nor members of hate groups. From rural Wisconsin to Missouri to Lake Charles, Louisiana, the subjects reflect average everyday Whites (though hardly representative). Their expressed concerns are intended to reflect typical or "run of the mill" people who have no ill will but are just trying to have a fair shot at the American Dream. It would be easy to dismiss these subjects' concerns as simple racial prejudice, but their beliefs may involve more than racial prejudice. Third, anecdotally, none of these works connect the rise in racial resentment to racial prejudice or hatred toward African Americans. If, as Allport (1954) states, racial prejudice is group antipathy (i.e., hate) based on faulty inflexible generalizations, then by itself racial prejudice cannot explain what is occurring among the subjects of these studies. Racial resentment matters, not just because it penalizes African Americans and other minorities for behavior attributed to their group, but also because it is a manifestation of a deeper value system that we all possess.

Racial Resentment as a Measurable Concept

Classic racial resentment, as a politically relevant and powerful concept in political behavior research, grew out of the discourse on the measurement of symbolic racism. The concept of symbolic racism was developed by David Sears, Donald Kinder (Sears and Kinder 1971), and John Mc-Conahay (Sears and McConahay 1973); it derived from surveys collected in the late 1960s in Los Angeles, after urban riots plagued parts of the city. Originally, the symbolic racism concept was explicitly called "racial prejudice"; it maintained that contemporary racial prejudice had transi-tioned to a more covert form where Whites' anti-Black affect was shaped by perceptions that African Americans were violating traditional val-ues like discipline, hard work, and personal responsibility. In the words of Kinder and Sears (1981), "symbolic racism is a form of [Whites'] re-sistance to change in the racial status quo based on moral feelings that blacks violate such traditional American values as individualism and self-reliance, the work ethic, obedience, and discipline" (p. 416). The items that were used to measure symbolic racism were characterized as having abstract symbolic character unrelated to respondents' per-sonal lives, but closely connected to their moral code and social ideals (Sears 1988).

Yet, many scholars found symbolic racism controversial because its conceptual underpinnings did not seem to mesh with its measure, which tended to reflect aspects of individualism and conservatism blended with anti-Black affect (see Carmines, Sniderman, and Easter 2011; Snider-man 2017). Later, Kinder and Sanders (1996) in *Divided by Color* re-cast the concept and measure of symbolic racism as "racial resentment," maintaining the same basic operational terms that Whites harbored an-tipathy and disdain toward African Americans for violating traditional values. The name change was driven primarily by a desire to place more emphasis on values. Kinder and Sanders (1996) state:

> What should we [Sears and Kinder] have called the moralistic resentments that Los Angeles suburbanites expressed toward blacks that figured so prom-inently in their votes in 1969? Not symbolic racism, but racial resentment. The new terminality acknowledges the point that as open expressions of bi-ological racism have declined, prejudice has become more difficult to docu-ment. . . . We intend racial resentment to take on the characteristics normally attributed to symbolic racism. (p. 293)

Kinder and Sanders (1996) observed appeals critical of African Ameri-cans that were different than traditional racial stereotypes (e.g., African

Americans as violent); instead they depicted African Americans as not trying hard enough to overcome their difficulties and instead choosing to rely on government resources. These assertions resonated with many Whites who considered effort and hard work to be important components of success and broadly accepted values. Presumably, Whites harbored antipathy toward African Americans because of deep-seated resentment stemming from their taking advantage of a benevolent system to gain cherished prerogatives (e.g., public benefits, educational opportunities, jobs, and housing) that were unearned or undeserved. African Americans were perceived as disrupting the rules of the game, redefining "merit" as mere racial identification rather than hard work and cultural discipline, and allowing their own failures to be excused by past tribulations of slavery and discrimination. Thus, by emphasizing the violation of traditional values Whites could skirt appearing racist and legitimize their reasonable political arguments as ideologically principled (Sniderman and Carmines 1997).

Along this vein, Kinder and Sanders (1996) maintain that the core of racial resentment involves a stereotype, "the contentions that blacks do not try hard enough to overcome the difficulties they face and that they take what they have not earned" (p. 106). To be resentful, a person has to believe that another person has not earned some benefit, a belief which could be based on information obtained through actual observations or perceptions, rumors, and stereotypes. People are less willing to extend benefits to those who they think are undeserving. Research consistently finds that Whites perceive African Americans as lazy, less intelligent, and violent (Devine 1989; Devine and Elliot 1995; Peffley, Hurwitz, and Sniderman 1997). African Americans are therefore likely to be considered unworthy of resources and certain benefits because their perceived behaviors are not in line with the rules and expectations that Whites believe are important for society.

Our conceptualization of Whites' resentment toward African Americans considers several of these existing elements outlined above—in particular, negative racial information acquired through stereotyping, attribution error, and illusory correlations (Cikara and Fiske 2012). Negative racial information activates beliefs about a just world (Dalbert 2001, 2009; Furnham 2003; Lerner 1965, 1980; Lerner and Miller 1978) and, then, an appraisal of deservingness (Feather 1999, 2006; Smith 2013).

We will flesh out our own theory of Whites' resentment toward African Americans in the following chapters, but, in brief, a belief in a just world is the tendency to believe that people should get what they deserve (i.e., an evaluation of outcomes) and should deserve what they get (i.e., an evaluation of actions). Because people are motivated to believe that the world is fair, they will look for ways to explain or rationalize injustice, often erroneously blaming the person or group who is actually the victim in a situation. This belief also leads people to think that when good things happen to people it is because those individuals are good and deserving of their happy fortune. Because of this, people who are extremely fortunate are often seen as more deserving of their positive outcomes. Rather than attributing their success to luck or circumstance, people tend to ascribe their fortune to the intrinsic characteristics of the individual. This is a form of confirmation bias and attribution error that tends to occur for social groups with automaticity and regularity (Ross, Amabile, and Steinmetz 1977; Pettigrew 1979a, 1979b).

Motivated by an internal sense of justice, individuals will appraise the deservingness of a group, for example calculating whether African Americans and other minority groups deserve to benefit from governmental resources given their negative stereotypes and perceptions (Feather 1999; Smith 2013). On the basis of the work by Feather (1999, 2006) and others, appraisals of deservingness occur when there is an inconsistency between the valence (positive or negative) of the outcome and the valence (positive or negative) of the behavior that led to it; low effort would generally be judged as less positive and less appropriate behavior in an achievement context than high effort, and success would be positively valued. Thus, individuals prefer and are motivated toward consistency; success following low effort would be seen as less deserved than success following high effort (Feather 1999). Negative perceptions of African Americans, violating the rules of the game and traditional values, should lead to negative outcomes. By contrast, evaluations of deservingness occur when the outcome fits or is consistent with the behavior. If the behavior is positive, such as hard work, self-discipline, and respecting the rules of game, this leads to positive outcomes.

For a substantial percentage of Whites, the perception that African Americans abandon or refuse traditional values, reject the existing racial order and structure, and reject Whites' claims of entitlement justifies and warrants African Americans' mistreatment and lower status. In order to safeguard the status quo and protect Whites' status and privilege, they reason African Americans are better left to their own devices, outside of the system that ostensibly relies on Whites' resources. Their lack of effort, self-discipline, and perseverance—values that many perceive necessary to the system's function—cannot be rewarded and must be thwarted, lest the system become corrupted by an unjust arrangement of resource distribution. The fact of the matter is that most Whites do not see African Americans as overwhelmingly held back or punished by racial discrimination or decades of slavery (e.g., Huddy and Feldman 2009; Pew Research Center 2019), and, thus, most Whites believe Blacks are deserving of their lower status, poor treatment, and social, political, and economic circumstances.

This is the injustice of it all. Because the current political system protects and insulates Whites' status, power, and privilege, Whites perceive it as unjust for undeserving racial and ethnic minorities to benefit from resources they have not earned, and they see the ameliorative policies that advance the unearned outcomes as rampant and unchecked. As a result, Whites come to reason that special considerations based on race are a slippery slope that lead to the destruction of the American way of life. The fear of injustice is enough to create legitimizing myths about African Americans that counter facts and even good reason. For instance, African Americans might be blamed for taking jobs from Whites, even if the real culprit is multinational corporations outsourcing jobs abroad, using cheap foreign labor to displace American workers. Entitlements, on which a disproportionate number of African Americans rely, might be blamed for rising national debt, but tax-avoidance by corporations and the wealthy has a greater impact. Even more troubling is the belief that the election of America's first African American president could be due to electoral malfeasance or other illegitimate reasons as opposed to sound policy proposals and good political strategy (Wilson and Davis 2018; Wilson and King-Meadows 2016).

An appraisal of deservingness is based on one's existing information about African Americans and other racial minorities. Such information may stem from racial stereotypes, attribution errors, and illusory correlations in which African Americans are seen as not playing by the rules of the game and as violating traditional values, such as hard work, self-reliance, delayed gratification, perseverance, and obedience. All this information, regardless of its accuracy, figures into appraisals of deservingness. Because African Americans are usually perceived to be at the low end of these values, they are seen as undeserving and not warranting special consideration. More than that, because this is a violation of justice and fairness, African Americans and ethnic minorities may also be viewed as deserving of sanctions (e.g., supporting extreme criminal punishments or other injustices for the group) in order to restore a sense of justice.

We borrow a great deal from social dominance theory (SDT). SDT begins with the principle that all societies tend to be organized in systems of group-based social hierarchies. These social structures are established with one (or a small number) of powerful groups at the top of the structure, and a larger number of weaker or subordinate groups at the bottom of the social structure. Powerful or hegemonic groups at the top of the structure contain and strive to maintain a disproportionate share of what they refer to as *positive social value*. While the dominant group is enjoying the luxury of positive social value, the subordinate group is left with what the theorists termed *negative social value* (Sidanius and Pratto 1999). Negative social value can include low social status, high-risk jobs or disrespected occupations, and severe negative sanctions (Sidanius and Pratto 1999). SDT outlines the mechanisms working behind the maintenance of this division of values.

Among the two types of hierarchies, in the one focused on the individual (and their unique characteristics), one's own characteristics are used to achieve prestige or wealth within society (Sidanius and Pratto 1999). Group-based social hierarchy, on the other hand, allows an individual to achieve prestige or wealth by "virtue of his or her ascribed membership in a particular socially constructed group" (Sidanius and Pratto 1999, p. 32). The suggested group memberships can include race, religion, linguistic group, or social class. The two hierarchies can work side by side and be interrelated.

SDT suggests the notion of the arbitrary-set system: a system filled with "socially constructed and highly salient groups based on characteristics such as clan, ethnicity, race, social class . . . and any other socially relevant group distinction that the human imagination is capable of constructing" (Sidanius and Pratto 1999, p. 33). In essence, membership to join the criteria for the "in-group" is both socially and contextually constructed, formed and maintained by certain societies. Sidanius and Pratto (1999) describe the arbitrary-set system as being associated with a higher degree of violence throughout history. Most forms of group conflict and oppression (e.g., racism, ethnocentrism, sexism, nationalism, classism, regionalism) can be regarded as different manifestations of the same basic human predisposition to form group-based social hierarchies.

Sidanius and Pratto suggest that group dominance is expressed in terms of social dominance orientation (SDO) (Sidanius and Pratto 1999). SDO is defined as a "very general individual differences orientation expressing the value that people place on nonegalitarian and hierarchically structured relationships amongst social groups" (Sidanius and Pratto 1999, p. 61). SDO is the value individuals place on domination of certain groups within society. In developing the SDO scale, the theorists constructed value scales from 18,741 respondents living in 11 countries (Sidanius and Pratto 1999). The SDO scale places greater emphasis on group-based dominance (Sidanius and Pratto 1999). The scale was designed to capture the essence of an individual's dominance toward social groups.

Our theory departs from social dominance theory (SDT) in that our theory rests on beliefs in the fundamental fairness and justness of the status quo and that those beliefs work in conjunction with legitimizing myths to create feelings of resentment.

The research by Bonilla-Silva (2018) is extremely influential in our work. Bonilla-Silva (2018) argues that the racial structure (the totality of the social relations and practices that reinforce white privilege) is reproduced to maintain the racial status quo. Racial ideology is created to justify Whites' dominance or challenge subordinate races. The frameworks of the dominant race tend to become the mast framework upon which all racial actors ground (for or against) their ideological positions. Part of the racial ideology, according to Bonilla-Silva (2018), contains language and beliefs that attribute responsibility to deficiencies of African Americans and other minorities themselves for their second-class status. Whites or racial discrimination are not to blame.

For Bonilla-Silva (2018), there are common frames, styles, and racial stories that "bond together a particular racist ideology." We refer to these as racial myths. Racist positions can be rationalized by non-racist motivations that he calls *abstract liberalism*. Bonilla-Silva considers abstract liberalism as most important, which is interpreted to mean "using ideas associated with political liberalism" (e.g., "equal opportunity, the idea that force should not be used to achieve social policy and economic liberalism [e.g., choice, individualism] in an abstract manner to

explain racial matters," p. 36). Thus, Whites are able to "appear reasonable and even moral" while African Americans are perceived as immoral. Bonilla-Silva (2018) uses "Why should we use discrimination to
combat discrimination? Two wrongs does not make it right."

While Bonilla-Silva (2018) makes a big leap forward in explaining the
individual dynamics of color-blind racism, we assert that Whites, particularly those who do not think they are racist, possess certain values and
believe the political system and other systems (e.g., education and employment systems) are fundamentally fair and just. This component is
critical for us because while some racists may operate to protect White
privilege (or what Bonilla-Silva calls the racial structure) directly, we
argue that everyday Whites may support other values—such as justice
and fairness—that ultimately do the same thing. Individuals may support abstract liberalism because of their beliefs in justice, fairness, and
a just world.

In addition to the need for theoretical reconsiderations, a seemingly
intractable problem with the measurement of classic racial resentment
arises from the fact that, early on, it shared the same measurement items
as symbolic racism, which has been criticized on a number of fronts. Despite the measurement criticism, the prevalence of the symbolic racism/
racial resentment measure on prominent studies like the General Social Surveys (GSS) and American National Election Studies (ANES) led
many researchers to use the measure out of convenience and necessity.

Despite our criticisms, we have a very favorable view of the generalized concept of classic racial resentment, and consider it to reflect more
closely the nature of racial appeals in politics today. However, we jet-
tison the classic measure and strict interpretation as prejudice or racism because the aforementioned criticisms muddy their quality. For
the past ten years, we have developed and tested different racial resentment measures that we think capture the essence of racial resentment and avoid the confounding relationships with individualism and
conservatism. We believe the evidence herein shows our scale's consequence through proper alignment with the sentiment of resentment, excellent psychometric properties, and empirical consistency. Additionally, we desire to show that while racial prejudice, or hate, and racial
resentment will overlap in the sense that individuals who hate African
Americans are also likely to resent them, it also plausible that individuals need not harbor racial hatred to be resentful. Racial hatred is not a
necessary condition for racial resentment, and we argue that racial re-

sentment can be based on other beliefs, such as perceptions of threat to the status quo.

Supporting Theory

Whites become resentful toward African Americans and other minorities because they perceive race as an illegitimate basis for reward, celebration, or influence. For Whites, racial politics emphasizing ameliorative policies and appeals, whether implicit or explicit, disrupt the status quo system that protects majoritarian dominance, and thus race threatens the "American way of life" and the existing structure that benefits Whites. Perceptions that African Americans are taking advantage of unearned resources and the threat it presents to the current system and values are at the core of racial resentment, not necessarily racial prejudice and hatred. This perceived injustice threatens Whites' prerogatives—status, power, and privilege—activating intolerance. If racial minorities' perceived behaviors were no threat to Whites, there would be little need to be intolerant or resentful—perhaps dismissive or pitying, but not threatened. The resentment over race from Whites signals that they perceive the progress made by African Americans and other racial groups is unearned, and at Whites' expense. This is certainly a racial threat, but it does not necessarily indicate that Whites are racist because they sense the threat.

Later in the book we will also examine African Americans' racial resentment toward Whites, showing that racial minorities can also perceive a justice-motivated threat to their status quo. In the case of African Americans, it is a threat to their current state of racial progress, and a desire to not return to periods of the past where they faced explicit subjugation merely because of their skin color. African Americans want to eliminate racial inequality and inequity, and policies and appeals to advance their status have substantive political consequence. We argue that African Americans hold legitimate resentment over Whites' denials of the prevalence and consequence of racial discrimination, and believe that Whites unjustly benefit from a system that rewards them for simply being White. In the end, African Americans' quest for civil rights and social justice is resented by Whites, and Whites' maintenance of their group dominance is resented by African Americans. Thus, several theories related to threats, uncertainty, and the status quo are core components of racial resentment and help to guide our framework. We outline the theories here.

System Justification Theory

Jost and colleagues (Jost 2020; Azevedo, Jost, and Rothmund 2017; Jost, Banaji, and Nosek 2004; Jost and Banaji 1994) contribute to our assumption about the role of perceptions of threat to the status quo. Stemming from a belief in the instrumental function of racial stereotypes in preserving different systems (Jost and Banaji 1994), system justification is a fully developed belief system postulating that individuals are motivated "to defend and justify the status quo and to bolster the legitimacy of the existing social order" (Jost, Banaji, and Nosek 2004). The underlying notion is that people want to hold favorable attitudes about themselves (e.g., ego-justification) and their group (e.g., group justification), but they also want to hold favorable attitudes about the social and political systems that affect them (e.g., system justification). This third component leads to social and psychological motivations to see the status quo as not only legitimate but also good, fair, natural, and desirable. As Azevedo, Jost, and Rothmund (2017) assert, "Because the social system on which human beings depend provides a sense of safety, security, familiarity, predictability, and solidarity, it is psychologically painful to regard them as irredeemably awful or unjust."

While a major contribution of this theory has been its use in explaining how subordinate groups adhere to motives that go against their self-interest or develop "false-consciousness" (Jost and Banaji 1994; Jost, Burgess, and Mosso 2001), expectations regarding the behavior of dominant groups' defense of the status quo are critical to our assumption underlying racial resentment.

In applying system justification to racial motivations, Whites, as a dominant group, may rationalize and consider the status quo as legitimate because the system works in their favor and they benefit most from it. Whites' status, privilege, and power come from the existing structures, institutions, and values that they want to preserve and expand. (This is a commonality with Blumer's [1958] group position expectations theory, explained below.)

It is easy to imagine challenges to the status quo and privileges that might trigger Whites' hostility. Such reactions need not arise from racial hatred, though racial hatred may be operative for many Whites.

For instance, many African Americans desire equal job opportunities, which may threaten the dominant prevalence of White workers. Certainly, African Americans may wish their children to receive a good education and attend high-performing schools, which may threaten resources allocated for White schools. Moreover, the disproportionate violent crimes committed by African Americans may threaten resources that could be used in other places and undermine the traditional values of society. Outside of policy, African Americans may simply wish to be treated fairly and have their status as equal citizens respected, which may threaten Whites' desire to openly criticize African Americans for their social behaviors. At the most insidious level, African Americans may desire to date, love, marry, or have children with Whites, which may threaten Whites' belief that their majority "cultural values" will be subordinated to minority values. Another framing of this latter example is that Whites may be concerned that their group members will turn against other Whites and White traditions. All of these actions have the potential reaction of uncertainty, anxiety, and fear. Thus, Whites' hostility toward African Americans and other minorities might plausibly come from the perception that African Americans constitute a threat to their group's status, traditions, privilege, and general dominance.

Group Position Theory

Blumer's (1958) theory of group position was the first to suggest that intergroup hostility or intolerance emanates from socialization processes or individual learning of negative feelings, beliefs, and orientations toward out-group members. Through historical processes, social discourse, and interactions, dominant groups come to believe that they are superior to out-group members; that out-groups are different, which elicits stereotyping; that the dominant group has proprietary claims over certain rights, resources, and privileges; and that desires for a greater share of rights and privileges are warranted (i.e., they deserve and are entitled to them). These beliefs form the core of the dominant group's "position," and it is from these components that other behaviors (e.g., discrimination) emanate.

Hostility toward racial groups emerges from perceived challenges to the dominant group's position. If dominant group members who possess a sense of entitlement and deservingness to all of the rights, resources, and statuses of society perceive a threat to these prerogatives and the related "livelihood" that prospers from them, the result may be hostility and intolerance. The dominant group is considered to have more of a stake or interest in maintaining the existing racial order.

Bobo and colleagues strengthened Blumer's theory and its credibility by incorporating and extending the psychological aspects of group position. Blumer had focused primarily on "realistic" and material threats, ones which were evidenced (Bobo 1983; Kinder and Sears 1981). Bobo (1999) extended the threats to a "sense" of encroachment, where the threats could simply be perceived or felt. This helped to explain the attitudes of not only Whites but racial minorities as well. For instance, Bobo and Hutchings (1996) show that group position provides the greatest leverage for understanding intergroup hostility among Whites; neither self-interest, racial prejudice, nor individualism could account for their perceptions of group hostility. Research from Bobo (1999) and Bobo and Tuan (2006) on the Chippewa Indian treaty study found that when enough people perceive themselves and others with whom they identify as losing ground to a racial minority, it can serve as a powerful trigger for racial prejudice.

White Victimization

Norton and Sommers (2011) argue that Whites now view racism as zero-sum. In other words, decreases in perceived anti-Black racism over the past six decades are associated with increases in perceived anti-White racism. The irony is that "Whites think more progress has been made toward equality than do Blacks, but Whites also now believe that this progress is linked to a new inequality—at their expense" (p. 217). This zero-sum belief among Whites fuels racial resentment, promoting the belief that even though racial minorities are worse-off economically, they are in such a position by their own making and therefore do not deserve to take resources from others who are subjectively more deserving. Such beliefs restore, or balance, the scales of justice and rationalize continued inequality.

Racial resentment relies on a judgment of undeservingness and is predicated on the system-legitimizing myth that African Americans specifically, and racial minorities in general, are job-taking, under-qualified, lazy, unintelligent, violent, disobedient, arrogant, and irresponsible. Because we are motivated to believe in a just world in which people get what they deserve and deserve what they get (Lerner 1980a,

1980b), we are also motivated to believe that people who lack good character and personality, who are also hindered by their culture, should be allowed to suffer. Safety-net and ameliorative policies are perceived in zero-sum terms, depriving Whites of resources and awarding them to African Americans. Affirmative action has been the most obvious policy used by politicians to convey reverse discrimination and the persecution of Whites. For people with the mindset that Whites are somehow losing out to people of color, the evidence that White people are being discriminated against often lies in college admissions and in job hiring and promotion and firing.

An overwhelming number of Whites say discrimination against them exists in America today, according to the 2016 American National Election Study; 72.38 percent say that they believe there is at least a little discrimination against White people in America today. As an indicator that this may be more symbolic than real, but nonetheless powerful, 28 percent of Whites say that they have experienced at least a little discrimination personally. Regardless, such a belief is now a critical part of Whites' reality that can be readily exploited to fuel racial resentment.

Research by Wilkins and Kaiser (2014) shows that racial progress—or racial minorities more frequently occupying high-status positions traditionally held by Whites, such as the election of President Obama—is one of the reasons why Whites believe they are being discriminated against. In Study 1, Wilkins and Kaiser showed that Whites who believed in the fairness of the existing social hierarchy or status quo were more likely to perceive more anti-White bias (for example, agreeing with the statement: "Reverse racism, where racial minorities are favored over Whites, is pervasive") when assigned to a racial progress treatment (e.g., "Racial minorities now occupy high-status positions traditionally held by Whites") than subjects assigned to a control. In Study 2, which experimentally manipulated racial progress, they found that subjects in the higher racial progress condition perceived more anti-White bias, but only among those who endorsed the status hierarchy. In Study 3, subjects were reminded of racial progress and were randomly assigned to either a self-affirming or non-affirming condition to protect self-integrity. When buffered from threats to the self, Whites did not seem to be threatened by racial progress. Wilkins and Kaiser (2014) suggest that racial progress causes Whites who view the status hierarchy as fair to react by perceiving more anti-White bias.

We are encouraged by this research, as it helps to clarify Whites' zero-sum responsiveness and defensiveness to racial progress. Racial progress is thus perceived as a threat to the status hierarchy and challenges the status quo from which Whites benefit.

African Americans' Resentment toward Whites

African Americans' absence from the literature gives the impression that, even though they are among the most aggrieved and targeted groups in American society, their attitudes and beliefs are not meaningful and studying them does not contribute to existing theory. This book corrects this oversight; African Americans' resentment against Whites is just as important, albeit for different reasons. Furthermore, because of different justice concerns and motives, asking African Americans the same racial resentment questions as Whites, as others have routinely done, means something very different. Accordingly, just as our assessment of racial resentment for Whites prompts a new measure, so does our assessment of racial resentment for African Americans.

African Americans and Whites have different reasons to be resentful toward each other, and each group requires a unique set of measurement items to capture resentment. For instance, African Americans are not threatened by the same challenges to the status quo as Whites. While Whites have benefited from their dominant group racial position, African Americans and other racial minorities have been hampered by targeted structural policies and practices designed to keep them in a subordinate position. African Americans have not benefited from the current status quo like Whites. If anything, African Americans perceive that racial discrimination, which maintains the status quo and racial hierarchy and keeps them from succeeding, is unjust and unfair. Therefore, African Americans' resentment toward Whites involves a different support for the status quo, one based not on race, but on rules. African Americans actually express broad support for the rules of the game, including hard work, discipline, personal responsibility, and fair play. What they resent is that Whites seemingly go to great efforts to deny their racism and prejudice, as well as consistently tout the mantra of democratic equality and freedoms, but seemingly ignore the claims brought forward by African Americans when the system, or individuals, are not following the rules.

A Word about Racial Prejudice

Paradoxically, many analyses of racial prejudice attitudes do not define racial prejudice, and leave it open to interpretation (Bonilla-Silva 2018; Kinder and Sanders 1996). To avoid confusion, we rely on Gordon Allport's (1979 [1954]) seminal definition of prejudice, as most definitions stem from his conceptualization. Allport defines prejudice as "thinking ill of others without sufficient warrant" (p. 6). Further, he stated that prejudice is an "antipathy based upon a faulty and inflexible generalization . . . directed toward a group as a whole or toward an individual because he is a member of that group" (p. 9). Antipathy is faulty because people do not usually possess "sufficient warrant," as such groups are too large for anyone to have valid personal grounds for reacting to the entire group.

Furthermore, Allport believed that prejudice stemmed from a process of social categorization. In the process of categorizing people into different groups, people typically classified themselves into in-groups and out-groups. Attachment and loyalty to one's in-group and group norms reinforced hostilities to out-groups. This social categorization and the need for positive self-identity would become more explicit two decades later with the work by Tajfel and Turner (1979).

Despite broad acceptance, we are mindful that Allport's definition has been criticized for being tailored toward devalued groups (Eagly and Diekman 2005) and that newer definitions have moved the focus beyond the most extreme forms of racism (e.g., Dovidio, Gaertner, and Pearson 2005), and that more general definitions of prejudice exist. For instance, while hate is an explicit feature of prejudice for Allport, Jackman (2005) maintains that prejudice can stem from a variety of motivations, such as the desire to maintain structural constraints and social organization. Dovidio, Gaertner, and Pearson (2005) emphasize that prejudice may be motivated by "individual needs, standards, and beliefs" (p. 212) beyond hate, and that Allport neglected the violent discrimination (i.e., behavioral aspects) in his definition. *The Cambridge Handbook of the Psychology of Prejudice* (Sibley and Barlow 2016) also broadly defines prejudice as "ideologies, attitudes, and beliefs that help maintain and legitimize group-based hierarchy and exploitation" (p. 4). This expanded definition does not specify intent and opens the does for almost any group belief to border on prejudice.

Ultimately, we agree with Badaan and Jost (2020), who propose that prejudice should be measured on hatred, subjugation, and desired discrimination. In their words, "[prejudice] is not a term to be used lightly or a phenomenon to be trivialized or equated simply with dislike or distrust . . . with the hold of lukewarm attitudes or a process of critical discernment" (p. 231). While the classic conceptualization of racial resentment—and its measurement—is characterized as a form of prejudice, we disagree.

Plan of the Book

The importance of racial resentment as a political and social construct is developed over several chapters. Correlational and experimental evidence are used in various ways to examine theoretical expectations underlying racial resentment. Chapter 2, much like this chapter, describes the current concept of racial resentment and its usefulness as an analytical framework in understanding current political appeals. Racial resentment may come not only from racial prejudice or antipathy toward African Americans, and as long as it is allowed to be treated as racial prejudice, we will ignore the power of Whites' race-neutral concerns regarding the threat to privilege and status. This is problematic because principled and race-neutral beliefs enable racists.

Chapter 2 focuses on racial resentment as a theoretical construct. A surprising amount of research has been done on resentment, which we use to model racial resentment. We contend that Whites' resentment toward African Americans begins with an expectation of justice, which leads to an appraisal of deservingness. In other words, people expect an orderly and just distribution of rewards and punishments in society, and racial resentment occurs when African Americans and other minorities appear to benefit from circumventing the rules of the game—for example, not working for what they get or lacking self-discipline—thereby violating this sense of justice. This is seen as a challenge to the status quo and the values upon which the system operates, which incidentally insulate Whites' status and privilege. The goal of chapter 2 is to show theoretically that racial prejudice is not a prerequisite for racial resentment and intolerance. This is an extremely important point as racial prejudice and racial resentment have tended to be conflated.

Chapter 3 focuses on the measurement of Whites' resentment toward

African Americans and its validity. Over the past ten years, we have developed and tested a series of items and amassed a wealth of data on these new racial resentment items. Given that measurement-related issues have raised questions about racial resentment, this chapter seeks to establish the validity and reliability of our new measure. We begin with a discussion and theory about resentment and apply it to racial resentment. Individual items are derived from this theory. Then, we examine the performance and predictability of our racial resentment measure, addressing whether the measure is related to political and social attitudes. Of particular concern in this chapter is examining our assumption regarding the extent to which racial resentment is simply a measure of racial prejudice. This is admittedly difficult to test for our measure given that it should be related to a host of attitudes, like conservatism, social dominance, and authoritarianism; it is also complicated by the fact that racial polarization and knee-jerk answers to racial items may make them difficult to distinguish. Ultimately, we aim to discover whether racial resentment is a consideration only among racists, or is a more diffuse belief system.

Assured by the validity of Whites' resentment toward African Americans, two important and somewhat obligatory questions are raised pertaining to *who are the most racially resentful Whites in American society, and how well does our measure predict other behavior relative to other measures?* In chapter 4 we identify the traits and characteristics most common to individuals who harbor racial resentment toward African Americans. We raise the contention that people high in racial resentment do not resemble racists—for example, those who would wear white hoods and capes, attend Klan rallies and meetings, donate to extremist organizations, consume and share social media denigrating African Americans as less than human, or openly espouse racist views—but may actually resemble the average person in the community—for example, those who volunteer at their children's schools and athletic youth leagues, drink cappuccinos at Starbucks, and do not try to intentionally offend anyone. People who endorse racially resentful views may not think of themselves as racists or be aware of the racial consequences of their beliefs. We identify them in our survey data by examining the extent to which racial resentment is associated with sociodemographic and political factors.

We also examine the performance of Whites' resentment toward African Americans as it pertains to how well it predicts relevant political attitudes and behavior. Individuals possess a multitude of dispositions and beliefs that compete with, and may potentially overshadow, racial resentment. Ideology, education, social dominance, and, more recently, White identity (Jardina 2019) are among a powerful set of factors said to predict political preferences. Presumably, Trump's appeals stoked Whites' sense of solidarity and identity, which strengthened his support and propelled him to a presidential election win in 2016. Therefore, if racial resentment is to be considered a useful and powerful analytical framework, it should provide equal, if not added, value relative to standard explanations of political and social attitudes. We begin by elaborating on theoretical expectations for racial resentment, followed by a profile of racial resentment and its performance as an independent variable.

Chapter 5 explores how Whites' resentment toward African Americans makes certain campaign appeals, like President Trump's *Make America Great Again*, more appealing. We contend that while a vast majority of Americans, or anyone for that matter, would like to see their country aspire to greatness, references to the past using "again" activate sentiments about the threat to Whites' status. Because "again" references a previous era and individuals' perceptions of the past are likely shaped by race, African Americans' and Whites' interpretations of the slogan are expected to differ dramatically. This expectation stems from the notion that African Americans' recollection of the past likely reflects a more perilous era in which racial prejudice and discrimination were more pervasive. In contrast, Whites' recollection of the past likely reflects an era in which they were more dominant and benefited more from the status quo or when people knew their place and were reluctant to challenge it. Exploring the extent to which racial resentment makes one open to campaign appeals offers important insight into how seemingly benign and ostensibly non-racial expressions (or a single word) can be exploited. The 2016 presidential election will be remembered as one of the most racially polarizing elections, and the *Make America Great Again* slogan was its call to arms for President Trump.

Chapter 6 raises the question of motivated reasoning and cognitive consistency in structuring political attitudes. Recent research on spillover effects has focused attention on the association between racial resentment toward African Americans and ostensibly non-racial attitudes. Individuals appear motivated, for whatever reasons, to apply racial evaluations of President Obama to non-racial policies, like the performance of the national economy and, more recently, to beliefs about climate change. Presumably, individuals who express greater resentment toward

African Americans are more likely to reject the occurrence of climate change because it is associated with President Obama. The discourse among political elites—as reflected in the media—frames or structures the expressions of racial resentment toward African Americans to President Obama's agenda, at least with regard to his efforts on climate change. Several scholars have suggested that motivated reasoning or a racial cognitive consistency might underlie the willingness to perceive the economy differently under President Obama's leadership. That is, individuals may align their evaluations of President Obama's agenda and performance not with their dislike of him but rather with their racial resentment toward African Americans. As spill-over effects take on greater seriousness as an explanation for the correlation between racial resentment toward African Americans and other non-racial attitudes, the underlying motivations connecting these seemingly unrelated attitudes require a more serious examination. Grounding spill-over effects in "race" or "racial prejudice," which may or may not be attributed to President Obama, ignores the functionality of racial resentment. Thus, by examining the relationship between climate change and racial resentment, we offer an alternative explanation for the spill-over effects of racial resentment. As opposed to elite framing of the issues, we argue that system-justifying beliefs or defensiveness against perceived challenges to the status quo—perhaps exacerbated under the Obama administration—connect racial resentment toward African Americans and the denial of climate change.

Chapter 7 introduces racial schadenfreude to the analysis of Whites' resentment toward African Americans. Going beyond the mere reporting of attitudes and preferences, racial schadenfreude allows us to question how much Whites want to see African Americans succeed or how much joy they receive from seeing African Americans fail. This is new and uncharted territory in racial attitudes. Racial schadenfreude suggests that individuals are not dispassionate in their racial beliefs and attitudes toward African Americans. One of the consequences of racial resentment is that individuals who perceive the most threat to the racial status quo from African Americans are more likely to take joy in their failure than individuals who are least threatened.

Because a justice motive and deservingness, facilitated by legitimizing racial myths, are at the heart of racial resentment, racial resentment reflects the continuation of a process rather than the end. If African Americans are perceived as violating traditional values and effort, thwarting established societal norms, and taking advantage of unearned resources—all of which threaten the status quo—this challenges Whites' sense of justice, creating a need to restore justice through a desire to see African Americans and other minorities fail. We contend that feelings of racial resentment do not dissipate, instead they fester to the point where they affect other emotions, like pleasure from seeing African Americans suffer from their poor choices and behavior. People also lash out by joining hate groups, expressing hurtful and denigrating epithets, and, for ordinary citizens, gravitating toward political messages that promote harsh and punitive treatment of African Americans and other minorities (i.e., death penalty, stop-and-frisk, and separating families at immigrant detention centers).

Chapter 8 turns racial resentment inside out through the analysis of African Americans. Although this is also uncharted water, we proceed with the argument that African Americans should not be required to respond to negative items about their own group, as is frequently done in public opinion research. Because African Americans' responses to the classic racial resentment items would mean something entirely different than Whites' responses and we are not interested in their resentment toward other African Americans, a new battery of items pertaining to their resentment toward Whites is examined. African Americans' resentment toward Whites is likely fueled by the perception that Whites use discrimination to hold them back. The status quo, traditional values, and the racial hierarchy are thus not appealing because they serve to insulate Whites' status and privilege at African American's expense. The threat underlying racial resentment for African Americans likely comes from greater oppression and hopelessness. This chapter examines how African Americans' racial resentment toward Whites operates and manifests itself in their political and social attitudes.

In the concluding chapter, we return to the race-neutral features of racial resentment. In light of the ground covered and our analyses, we are prepared to be more assertive in our claims that racial prejudice and hate are unnecessary for racial intolerance.

CHAPTER TWO

Resentment Is Not Prejudice

In this chapter, we explore the meaning of resentment and how it is derived, with a keen interest in whether hatred, antipathy, and dislike are necessary motivating factors. The classical form of "racial resentment," at least in its conventional conceptualization and measurement, is thought of as synonymous with racial prejudice, and the two terms are often used interchangeably. This is mainly because classic racial resentment derived from the measure and theory of symbolic racism (Kinder and Sears 1981). The concept was relabeled from symbolic racism to racial resentment, not as a way to tout a new theory or measure, but to steer clear of the pejorative wording of "racism" in the name, and to give greater emphasis to the symbolic "values," such as the individualism and the Protestant work-ethic, articulated in the theory of symbolic racism, as well as modern racism (McConahay 1986). Thus, classic racial resentment is virtually the same in concept and measurement as its predecessors symbolic racism and modern racism, and scholars today continue to use these terms interchangeably (Sears et al. 1997; Henry and Sears 2002; Feldman and Huddy 2005; Tarman and Sears 2005; Tesler 2012a, 2012b). As a result, today, classic racial resentment equates to the hatred, malevolent affect, and hostile oppressiveness of racism and prejudice (Kinder and Schuman 2004; Cramer 2020). However, we argue that resentment as a form of political anger over the use of race is a more apt conceptualization than resentment as a form of racism and prejudice. In addition, the current four-item classic racial resentment scale certainly measures some form of racial attitudes, but recent research questions its ability to accurately measure either prejudice or resentment (Wilson and Davis 2011; Kam and Burge 2019; Sides, Tesler, and Vavreck 2019).

Given that most contemporary research requiring some measure of racial prejudice utilizes a form of classic racial resentment—coupled with the fact that racial resentment has become the most identifiable, available, and replicated indicator of racial prejudice in the discipline of political science, and arguably across the social sciences—the current state of affairs in the study of racial attitudes is untenable. The classic concept and measure of racial resentment need revisiting.

The challenge with the current conceptualization of classic racial resentment is that one is compelled to classify all racial motivations as racist or prejudiced regardless of whether those labels fit or not. Within the realm of politics, there must be space for racialized antagonism and disagreement without an instant labeling of racism or prejudice, and we contend that racial resentment, properly conceived and measured, offers the most valid analytical framework and language for understanding Whites' perceptions of a changing "American way of life." Thus, the extant literature on resentment—free of racial mention—is the most appropriate place to begin to understand the underlying components of the concept of racial resentment, to develop a criteria evaluating the existing concept, and, ultimately, to establish a more valid conceptualization and theory.

A clarification of terminology is necessary at this point. First, we refer to the current concept and measure used in political science and elsewhere, initially developed by Kinder and Sanders (1996), as "classic racial resentment" or "Kinder and Sanders' racial resentment." This term applies to its initial measure as well as to survey items added to the measure and its abbreviated form. Second, we refer to our new concept and measure as simply "Whites' resentment toward African Americans." We are sympathetic to the view that concepts like resentment should explicitly connect to the principal, especially since we will later argue that African Americans, although subordinate in the racial hierarchy, can be resentful toward Whites for basically the same motivating reasons. We assert that the perceiver (e.g., Whites) and the object (e.g., Blacks) of resentment should be explicit. Although the book is mostly about Whites' racial resentment toward African Americans, we develop a measure of African Americans' resentment toward Whites in chapter 8. To distinguish it from Whites' racial resentment, we refer to this measure as "African Americans' resentment toward Whites." Our intention is to provide a useful shorthand reference to similar concepts.

Opening Arguments: Putting Classic
Racial Resentment on Trial

In its most basic conceptualization, resentment results from an appraisal of whether an individual or group receives an undeserved positive or valued outcome. In concert with information about the exchange, such as how the benefit was obtained and whether the benefit levels were appropriate, the appraisal stems from a set of values and beliefs regarding justice and fairness. Although many informational factors can influence one's thinking, these values of justice and fairness are the main criteria that the appraisal uses to determine deservingness. Resentment, in our conceptualization, occurs when a reward is felt to be undeserved, and something is undeserved when an observer disagrees with the means used to gain the outcome. From this we can conclude that any form of racialized resentment must involve a belief that race is an unfair criterion for reward, and therefore when race is factually used, or perceived to be used, as a means for reward, or status maintenance or advancement, it serves as an injustice. Justice and fairness are moral concerns for people, and adherence to them is so fundamental to one's judgments that threats to their standing create powerful motives that support conformity, order, and certainty. Most people reject that rewards and punishments are best handed out indiscriminately, choosing to instead believe what people get in society should be proportionate to what they deserve. Melvin Lerner calls such motivated reasoning "Belief in a Just World" (BJW) or "Just-World Hypothesis" (Lerner 1965, 1980). This just-world belief orientation is the foundation of our framework of resentment and its racialized form, and we are not alone in arriving at the connection between racial attitudes and justice motives (e.g., Carney and Enos 2017; Hunt 2000).

Justice Motives and Affect

The belief in a just world asserts generally that the world in which we live and operate is a fair place where people get mostly what they deserve and deserve mostly what they get (Lerner 1980a, 1980b). Most people hold this belief in some form; it helps individuals adapt to their environment, providing comfort and certainty by enabling them to see the world as stable and orderly (Lerner 1980a, 1980b; Lerner and Miller 1978).

While justice is the general value identified with the belief, it is actually injustice that produces resentment.

When appraisals of a distributional result (e.g., free health care for all low-income persons) conclude that an outcome is undeserved, the injustice of unearned reward activates strong negative reactions that can be inwardly (e.g., shame and guilt) or outwardly (e.g., anger and resentment) directed (Cropanzano and Folger 1989; Goldman 2003; De Cremer, Wubben, and Brebels 2008). The outward emotions like anger can produce defensive states that serve to protect one's values, including the withholding of help. These oppositional, and often antipathetic, situations buffer the pains of injustice (Barclay, Skarlicki, and Pugh 2005). Thus, the anger resulting from an injustice is more than mere emotional expression; it is functional, signaling a need to "right a wrong" (i.e., seek retribution) and restore justice in some way. Resentment is therefore an outwardly directed response to threats to justice that produces a lingering desire to retaliate, in the form of thoughts or behaviors (Skarlicki and Folger 1997; Barclay, Skarlicki, and Pugh 2005). Later in chapter 7, we discuss one of these specific retaliatory states, *schadenfreude*, which is a sense of pleasure at the misfortune of others. Resentful individuals can come to view the punishment of undeserving individuals and groups as justice served. Such a proposition shows the theoretical range of a proper conceptualization of resentment as injustice.

Smith and Lazarus (1993) define justice-related anger as that which has been provoked by "a demeaning offense"—especially when it is arbitrary, inconsiderate, or malevolent—against an individual or some relevant aspect of the individual's social world. Research also ties resentment to distributive, procedural, and interactional injustices. Distributive injustice results from a perception of unfair outcomes; procedural injustice is the perceived unfairness of the procedures used to determine outcomes; and interactional injustice results from perceptions of ill treatment from others (Skarlicki and Folger 1997). Studies show that strong feelings of anger and resentment are especially likely when individuals perceive the presence and application of unfair procedures (Cropanzano and Folger 1989; Goldman 2003; De Cremer, Wubben, and Brebels 2008). Thus, a sense of injustice due to procedural or interpersonal actions (e.g., negative treatment from authorities) can invoke strong affective reactions, and the most commonly cited emotional reaction is anger (e.g., Folger and Skarlicki 1998; Tepper 2000).

Surprisingly, there is sparse mention of justice in the classic literature on racial resentment; instead the original work focused on individualism, stating that racial resentment is a new form of prejudice "preoc-
cupied with matters of moral character, informed by virtues associated
with the traditions of individualism" (Kinder and Sanders 1996, pp. 105–
106). The classic theory asserted that Whites felt that Blacks did not
work hard enough to overcome the difficulties they faced and were taking what they had not earned. Accordingly, Whites did not appreciate
these threats to America's "civic virtue," leading to their antipathy, or
prejudice, toward African Americans specifically. Yet, there was limited theoretical focus in the literature on why the low perceived effort
was so threatening and, given the debilitating historical treatment of
Blacks in America, why these "special considerations" were not toler-
ated. We argue that the deservingness appraisal in the post–civil rights
era that was cited by Kinder and Sanders (1996) involved the same
value-concerns that always exist in America: that Whites' dominant position, and the system that maintained it, was just, and therefore any
threat to either was an injustice deserving of moral outrage and retaliation. In the minds of Whites, it is not America that needs changing to
accommodate Blacks, it is Blacks that need to change; otherwise, they
get what they deserve. Ostensibly, Whites are suggesting that Blacks deserve the inequality they have for not adhering to the rules of the dominant group.

We arrived at justice motives very early in our investigations of
resentment—free of racial influence. Every scholarly source outside of
political science viewed resentment as a legitimate moral reaction to a
perceived injustice (e.g., Montada, Schmitt, and Dalbert 1986; Feather
1999, 2006; Barbalet 2001; Turner and Stets 2005). Yet, in political science it was conceptualized as a form of prejudice. We suspect this was
due to its introduction to the discipline through racial subject matter
(cf. Cramer 2020). This divergence between resentment as a concept versus resentment as prejudice stunted our progress, but also turned our
attention to justice, just-world beliefs, and deservingness. Resentment
was indeed a negative sentiment, but at its core was an appraisal of deservingness that may or may not be due to personal attributes. In a 2009
conference paper (Wilson and Davis 2009) we proposed that, instead of
racial animus or anti-Black affect, racial resentment characterized offense due to unfair and inappropriate claims of racism and racial dis-

crimination. In the minds of Whites, their held offense was valid because from their vantage racism and discrimination are events of the past, and therefore attempts to use race for social, economic, or political advancement are simply unfair to Whites who have not necessarily done anything to contribute to the problems that beset African Americans. Essentially, Whites felt that since contemporary society did not look like the Jim Crow past, race was not a legitimate criterion for social advantage. The result is that racial justice policy benefiting African Americans violates Whites' just-world beliefs, and alternatively, Whites' opposition to policies promoting racial justice violates African Americans' just-world beliefs. Both groups can hold racial resentments based on their justice motives.

Other researchers have arrived at the connection between justice motives and racial attitudes. Hunt (2000) examined racial-ethnic differences in just-world beliefs. The beliefs consisted of agreement with assertions like the "world is a just place," that "by and large, people deserve what they get," and that "people who meet with misfortune have often brought it on themselves." Hunt found that Latinos and Whites hold stronger just-world beliefs than African Americans. His findings suggested that Whites and Latinos (who tend to identify as White as well) would be more likely to attribute inequality to individual (e.g., laziness) rather than structural (e.g., discrimination) factors. Carney and Enos (2017) examined the shared conceptual underpinnings of contemporary racial attitudes and conservative belief systems. They argued that instead of racial animus, the content of newer racism measures reflects a denial of how much Americans' racial past affects racial differences today. Denial of discrimination implies that racial inequality is due to individual attributes (e.g., work-ethic), and that there is no need to change broader social structures because the world is already just—further reflecting that if African Americans simply worked harder, they would be better-off.

Defending the Status Quo by Blaming the Victim

According to Lerner (1980), people confronted with unjust experiences or unexpected misfortunes usually employ one or more cognitive strategies to defend their sense of justice and reaffirm their belief in a just world. In other words, feelings of resentment that arise due to injustice serve as a defensive function to protect status quo beliefs. As a result, those who prefer the status quo, especially those holding dominant group status, are motivated to defend it. One of the defense strategies is victim-blaming (Furnham 2003; Jost, Banaji, and Nosek 2004; Hafer and Begue 2005; Dalbert 2009).

Victim-blaming allows individuals to maintain positive beliefs about the current system by placing the blame for outcomes on the internal character of other individuals rather than structural conditions that are a part of a favored status quo system. Victim-blaming also provides a clear target for outwardly directed emotions: namely, those individuals or groups who are ostensibly threatening the system. Thus, a belief in a just world renders notions of justice highly subjective and dependent on a host of cognitions and cognitive processes that affect the appraisals of others as deserving of what they get in society. If the world is just and people are getting what they deserve, then no fundamental changes to the system are necessary, unless they are inevitable and/or consistent with the preservation of the current system's ideas (Feygina, Jost, and Goldsmith 2010; Laurin, Kay, and Fitzsimons 2012). This is not to suggest that simply holding a just-world belief indicates support for the status quo; rather, it suggests that dominant groups are particularly motivated to defend a system that supports the current hegemony (e.g., Sidanius et al. 2004). Thus, resentment should result when any legitimate system is threatened, even in a context where racism is considered immoral and undemocratic. In addition, dominant groups, ideological or demographic, will target their resentment at the individuals and groups threatening the system, attributing their lower status to internal character flaws. Such processes help to maintain a just-world belief, even when the observer views a victim's outcomes as unfortunate (e.g., Hafer and Begue 2005; Williams 1984).

In addition to potentially blaming victims for their negative circumstances, people who believe in a just world might rationalize that victims deserve to suffer, or deserve no help, because the victims—due to their reckless behavior or flawed character—are actually the problem (Dalbert 2001; Furnham 2003). Not only are they to blame, they must pay the consequences for violating or going against the rules of the game. An impressive number of empirical studies support this basic point; a belief in a just world leads to negative perceptions of the handicapped, the poor, victims of rape, diagnoses of AIDS and other sexually transmitted diseases, and ameliorative racial policies like affirmative action (e.g., Montada, Filipp, and Lerner 1992).

Deservingness, Moral Judgment, and Justice

A just-world value orientation precipitates an appraisal of undeserving-ness, the core facilitator of resentment. Feather (2008) argues that re-sentment is anger at a perceived injustice that occurs when "an observer reacts to another person's undeserved positive outcome" (p. 1234). In a similar vein, Turner and Stets (2005) contend that resentment is anger that arises when people believe others are getting more than they de-serve (i.e., more than their fair share), and it is exacerbated when indi-viduals perceive that these gains of others are denying them what they deserve. Turner and Stets further emphasize that resentment can arise due to a relative loss of power and resources resulting from others having skewed or ignored the rules of the game, thereby gaining power unfairly. Such an appraisal implies that the newly empowered group is undeserv-ing. Similarly, Barbalet (1998) proposes that resentment arises when oth-ers are perceived as having gained power, resources, status, or material well-being by skirting established norms and cultural expectations.

Resentment involves a moral judgment. Gibbard (1992) casts resent-ment as a purely "moral emotion," proposing that, in general, such sen-timents involve a value judgment that something tangibly moral or im-moral has occurred, producing positive (e.g., pride, gratitude) and negative (e.g., guilt, resentment) sentiments respectively (see also Rawls 1971; Hoggett, Wilkinson, and Beedell 2013). According to Gibbard (1992), when individuals evaluate actions as morally wrong or not, they tie their assessments to blame, and "a person is blamed if and only if re-sentment is warranted." This reasoning suggests that when one resents another they have concluded that the actor has morally transgressed and thus deserves some penalty. Thus, when resentment is present, any ex-cuse for the targeted object's meritorious behavior or beneficiary status, legitimate or not, will have been rejected. It is possible that this inflexi-bility stems from a belief in a just world, where victim-blaming supports the maintenance of the status quo. As stated, a just world is a world that is morally correct and not corrupted by unfairness. Therefore, feelings of resentment tied to justice and fairness assume a moral positioning that supports the status quo. Such sentiment is more than mere anger. In summary, resentment is a value motivated anger theorized to occur when there is a perceived moral wrong; when another receives or enjoys an advantage in an improper and unequal way (Barbalet 1998); and when the impropriety is in contravention to values, norms, and other cultural expectations (Ortony, Clore, and Collins 1988).

The target of one's resentment is limited only by the requirement that it cannot be inwardly directed. Solomon (1993), for instance, proposes that resentment is not directed at the self; rather, it is experienced only toward other individuals or groups, and reoccurs until such feelings are resolved. Deviating slightly from this theme to include a self-evaluative dimension, Roberts (2003) asserts that resentment is an emotion directed at offenses carried out by others against one's self, one's group, or one's close associates, implying that greater social distance—but not necessarily direct contact—between one's self or in-group and "others" creates the conditions for resentful feelings.

Though resentment is never directed at the self, it can also be impersonal, targeted at inanimate objects. Roberts (2003) makes a distinction between classic resentment and impersonal resentment. *Classic resentment* exists when one is offended by another person or group, while *impersonal resentment* is not directed at any person or group, but rather against an unjust pain caused by non-human phenomena (e.g., taxes). Accordingly, individuals and groups can be resented but objects (e.g., luxury goods), events (e.g., protests), institutions (e.g., federal government), rules (e.g., public assistance policies, performance standards), and ideas (e.g., political correctness) can also be resented. Impersonal resentment may also result from historical events (e.g., the election of a Black president), social norms (e.g., political correctness over race), symbols (e.g., confederate flag), and institutional acts (e.g., the recognition of a Black history month).

Each of these definitional claims about resentment explicitly or implicitly focuses on deservingness and justice, and there is no allusion to, or a necessary condition of, prejudice, dislike, or hate toward the resented target.

Power, Status, and Resentment

When others (e.g., out-groups) are able to gain benefits and rewards in ways that are immoral, unjust, and generally undeserving, it signals they have a level of power that could threaten the existing system. Scholars have theorized how power differentials produce resentment, further clarifying the concept in a way that involves the information cues in everyday decision-making. For instance, resentment is viewed by several sociologists as arising from perceived gains or losses in power between the self, or their group, and others. These scholars (e.g., Thamm 1992, 2004; Kemper and Collins 1990; Barbalet 1998) argue that perceived power differentials shape the nature—arousal, targeting, and intensity—of one's resentment, and that levels of resentment are influenced by the extent to which the power-advantaged actors do not meet expectations but still receive rewards.

Kemper and Collins (1990) propose that when individuals maintain or increase their power, they will likely experience positive feelings like satisfaction, confidence, and security. Alternatively, when individuals lose power, they likely experience anxiety, fear, and loss of confidence. Essentially, perceived gains in power/status are associated with positive emotions, but perceived losses in power/status are more complex and motivate individuals to think about why their status has changed or will change. This Laswellean aspects of politics is especially true for dominant groups who, consciously or unconsciously, take for granted their privileged power position because it serves as the status quo. For dominant groups, an appraisal of loss gives rise to negative feelings about the causes or sources (e.g., competitive out-groups) of their placement in a less dominant position.

Some scholars have suggested that resentment may be more likely to reside among psychologically repressed, subordinate, and powerless individuals and groups, even if they hold more objective power. This is important because we argue that racial resentment, at least in American society, is a feature of both the dominant and non-dominant groups. Nietzsche refers to resentment as a "slave emotion," occurring when people feel they have to do without or give up a benefit, and have less representative power because no one will stand up for them. Lower-power group members repress their emotions because they fear retribution from authorities, both formal (e.g., laws) and informal (e.g., norms), or social sanction. With the threat of punishment for free expression, these individuals and groups are less powerful psychologically, leading them to resent the authorities that ostensibly believe they do not deserve power. Scheler (1992) refers to persons holding resentment as having a lasting "self-poisoning of the mind" (p. 17), caused by the systematic repression (e.g., social sanctions for speaking one's mind) of certain emotions that typically go unchecked as normal components of free expression. According to Scheler, the loss of freedom to express beliefs and ideas can fester and lead to psychological tendencies to indulge in value delusions and corresponding value judgments. Examples among racial groups include resentful Whites engaging legitimizing myths that African Americans' seeming rejection of personal responsibility, hard work, and discipline lessen the American way of life (e.g., Kinder and Sanders 1996); or, to take a less contemplated example, resentful African Americans engaging beliefs that their economic opportunities are harmed by Hispanics' willingness to take lower pay for jobs because they have low self-worth (e.g., Vaca 2004). In both cases, individuals and groups who perceive a loss of power, opportunity, or freedom can create a perceived reality—a delusion—motivated by the need to attribute their losses to the lack of values by others.

Summary

To summarize the points above, there are several core features that we can expect to underlie racial resentment. First, resentment involves a situational appraisal shaped by values, identity, and perceptions of justice. Second, resentment is a negative sentiment resulting from a perceived wrong; the wrong is an unfair or unjust receipt of a positive outcome. Third, resentment can be targeted at individuals, groups, or impersonal objects like policies, practices, events, or symbolic ideas. Fourth, resentment is fundamental to systems of power. It is theorized to occur more among the psychologically repressed who feel powerless in the face of authority. In addition, the relative power positioning in society (i.e., statuses) among individuals and groups makes resentment inherently political because it involves the distribution and redistribution of material resources and prerogatives. Also, higher status members (e.g., who are in power) can be resented by lower status members because the latter have met formal expectations but receive fewer rewards, and yet so-called victims are resented by non-victims because the former are seeking a benefit without having gained appropriate status.

This expanded discussion of the features of resentment is an important precursor to coverage on the existing literature examining "racial" resentment. It is noteworthy that the research on resentment never alludes to hate or antipathy as a basis for the emotion. While it is easy to imagine that hatred and antipathy cause resentment, they are not necessary conditions. However, much to our dissatisfaction, hatred and antip-

athy are assumed to be the basis for racial resentment in the extant literature. Prior to symbolic racism being renamed by Kinder and Sanders
(1996) there is little evidence that resentment is a form of prejudice or
racism. While racial resentment toward African Americans can indeed
emanate from racial prejudice, it can also arise from a variety of other
sources, such as violations of justice and fairness. To be clear, Kinder
and Sanders, Sears (1988), and colleagues (e.g., Henry and Sears 2002)
make clear statements about deservingness and the violation of values
in their scholarly accounts on symbolic racism and racial resentment,
but by linking the concept to racial prejudice and anti-black affect one
can only surmise that hatred or dislike toward African Americans as
a group is the underlying motivation. We believe this conceptualization
minimizes beliefs about deservingness and justice (fairness).

The Racializing of Resentment through Deservingness Considerations

Resentment is racialized when individuals use discerning values, legitimizing myths, and racial information, such as stereotypes and other information cues (e.g., descriptive traits, past experiences) about the quality of actions, that negatively influences their appraisal of deservingness.
People who are high in racial resentment are not likely to view African
Americans dispassionately nor are they likely to want to see them succeed with assistance. Instead, Whites' racial resentment stems from an
appraisal of the extent to which African Americans deserve what they
get based on their sense of justice and fairness.

According to work by Feather (1996, 1999), evaluations of deservingness occur when a benefit is consistent or commensurate with effort. A
reward following low effort, for example, would be seen as less deserving (Feather 1999). Consistency is important: negatively valued actions
such as laziness, irresponsibility, lack of self-discipline, cheating and
other violations of the "rules of the game," and shirking traditional values should lead to negative outcomes, such as being denied college ad-
mission, being demoted from a job, or being relegated to poor housing.
If the aforementioned negative actions (e.g., laziness, irresponsibility)
result in a positive outcome, on the other hand, such as receiving a job
promotion or recognition from peers and coworkers, then the inconsis-

tency of the result produces an appraisal of undeservingness—and then resentment.

As we stated previously, reliance on negative information, such as stereotypes, assists in the determination of deservingness; having to observe negative valence behavior is not necessary (Cikara and Fiske 2012). Indeed, negative racial stereotypes are pervasive in American society and have a powerful influence on attitudes toward African Americans (e.g., Peffley, Hurwitz, and Sniderman 1997; Peffley and Hurwitz 1998; Weber et al. 2014). Through parental socialization and the media, negative stereotypes of African Americans form in children at a very early age. African Americans are likely to be perceived as mostly undeserving based on the content of these racial stereotypes. Relative to other groups in society, African Americans are perceived as more violent, lazier, unwilling to work for what they get, lacking self-discipline, disobedient, and less intelligent (Dovidio, Evans, and Tyler 1986; Sniderman and Piazza 1993; Peffley, Hurwitz, and Sniderman 1997; Brezina and Winder 2003).

Racial stereotypes can influence deservingness judgments, but they can also lead to errors about group behaviors and subsequent outcomes (Brandt and Reyna 2011; Yzerbyt, Rogier, and Fiske 1998). The fundamental attribution error is the tendency to attribute other people's negative outcomes to their internal dispositions rather than external structural or situational explanations. People who attribute a group's failures to internal qualities like personality, intentions, or culture are more likely to blame the group member for their failings. If failures are inherently individual, there is no need to give weight to the situational or structural factors, and therefore if the group member receives a positive reward, they must have done so unfairly. The implication for racial resentment is that African Americans are not likely to be perceived as deserving of special consideration if they are blamed for having some internal character defect. This becomes an integral component of the information that people use regarding race. And this is why racial resentment has been viewed as racial prejudice or a new form of racism.

Another factor that influences deservingness appraisal is ideology. Ideology, especially conservatism, serves as a filter for evaluating deservingness by way of individualistic values as a criterion for reward. That is, individuals who prioritize specific ideological values will be more likely to use them in the appraisal of others. For example, research indicates that deservingness is at the heart of conservative ideology (Reyna et al. 2005) and the likely reason that "new racism" measures—modern racism (McConahay and Hough 1976), symbolic racism (Kinder and Sears 1981), and classic racial resentment (Kinder and Sanders 1996)—reduce support for ameliorative policies designed to help African Americans reach equality. Conservatives place a high value on merit, and in the absence of specific details about situations where racial minorities are rewarded or racial policies are at play, they may rely on racial stereotypes and other system-legitimizing myths (e.g., "racial discrimination is not widespread") to oppose racial amelioration and egalitarianism more generally (Kay et al. 2007). For example, principled conservatives prioritize values of equity and individualism through beliefs about the Protestant work ethic and the value of race. Since conservatives morally oppose race as a criterion for merit, they are more likely to scrutinize African Americans' receipt of rewards to ensure no "special considerations" are being given. For conservatives, only those who can show and prove their unassisted work ethic should be rewarded with desirable outcomes, and therefore any program or policy that goes against this philosophy will be opposed on the basis that it is unfair and ultimately un-American (Sniderman, Brody, and Kuklinski 1984; Sniderman and Piazza 1993; Reyna et al. 2005). In this way, conservatism is concerned with justice by way of deservingness.

In summary, resentment becomes racialized through the information that people have about African Americans—including stereotypes, attributions, and ideological predispositions—and in how people process that racial information. Resentment may thus be grounded more in legitimizing myths—such as the belief that the prevalence of racial discrimination is sparse and has limited effects on the prosperity of African Americans—than actual facts.

Our main argument is that a person who is high in racial resentment can be expected to value and defend the existing status quo. This somewhat agrees with Kinder and Sanders' (1996) statement that "blacks constitute a moral threat" (p. 108) to Whites' sense of civic virtue because they challenge community standards and the order that exists in the world. Such a threat is real to Whites, and it is not necessarily a faulty generalization as it is characterized by Allport's (1954) definition of prejudice.

If racial resentment is a matter of injustice, then individuals should be motivated to fix moral wrongs in order to bring about justice. This could occur in a number of ways: opposition to policy, opposition to candidates and their issue positions, avoidance behaviors, support for punitive actions, and low empathy for the undeserving recipients. Regardless of the specific approach, the natural motivation is toward justice and a positive emotional state that suggests it has occurred. In other words, injustice motivates resentment, resentment motivates a need to restore justice, and a need to restore justice motivates a desire to see the unjust recipients lose their cherished outcome or be punished in some way. This pleasure in the misfortune or pain of others is called *schadenfreude*.

Schadenfreude toward African Americans and other minorities is likely to occur when they are perceived to benefit or thrive but are not perceived to be following the expected rules of meritorious action. This perceived rule-breaking not only challenges the status quo, it also challenges Whites' privileged position in society and threatens their dominant status. Thus, schadenfreude is a retaliatory sentiment that results from a perceived injustice being righted, partially or in whole. This suggests that racial resentment is not the end of a psychological process of evaluating deservingness, it is the emotional signal that action is required to restore justice, and schadenfreude signals a return to some level of justice.

In the following section, we review the classic conceptualization of racial resentment among Whites, discussing the controversies tied to both the theory and measurement. Understanding the definitions and flaws of classic racial resentment provides a starting point to developing a more apt and robust theory of Whites' resentment toward African Americans, one that does not hinge on racial prejudice.

The Existing Concept of Racial Resentment

Now that we have outlined the major components of resentment, we are able to use them as an analytical framework for evaluating classic racial resentment. Most of the empirical research examining classic racial resentment builds off the conceptualization by Kinder and Sanders (1996) and their racial resentment scale (RRS). According to Kinder and Sanders (1996), classic racial resentment is a relatively new concept, emerging from the backlash to the civil rights movement and exacerbated by racial protests in the late 1960s and early 1970s (Sears and Kinder 1971). Governmental policies enacted to ameliorate racial discrimination and urban problems were seen as unfair because African Americans were perceived as being responsible for their own problems. In essence, African Americans were seen as unable to capitalize on the plentiful opportunities existing in America. Thus, as a backlash to governmental policies, a *new* racial "prejudice" (pp. 105–106) was created, one founded on the dual premise that Blacks do not try hard enough to overcome their problems (i.e., an appraisal of their actions) and receive benefits that they have not earned (i.e., an appraisal of their outcomes).

The notion that African Americans receive undeserved benefits has been expressed in terms of them receiving "special considerations" (or preferences), which violate the principle value of "individualism" (Kinder and Sears 1981) or "black individualism" (Sears and Henry 2003), and the negative feelings targeted at African Americans (anti-Black affect) due to their violations of individualistic norms are viewed broadly as classic racial resentment (Kinder and Sanders 1996). Thus, classic racial resentment was originally conceived of as a "blend" of anti-Black affect and beliefs about African Americans' violation of cherished values.

Resentment and Symbolic Racism: Same Coin, Same Side, Different Label

Classic racial resentment, for all intents and purposes, morphed from *symbolic racism* (Kinder and Sears 1981; McConahay and Hough 1976), as their operationalization and measurement are virtually identical. Symbolic racism is thought to be a form of racial prejudice that is expressed differently than old-fashioned racism. In symbolic racism, expressions of racial prejudice are more hidden and covert, often articulated as African Americans' violations of traditional values (Henry and Sears 2002; Sears and Henry 2005; Tarman and Sears 2005). The concept of "new racism" was broadly accepted because the changing norms of political correctness and social desirability made expressions of outright anti-Black racism taboo. The development of the original survey items that purport to measure symbolic racism actually preceded the theoretical development of the concept (see McConahay 1986); however, the survey items were valuable because they drew on the reluctance of many survey respondents to report on their biases and stereotypes of African Americans (Kinder and Sears 1981; Sears and McConahay 1973). So, as a new conceptualization and measure of racial prejudice, symbolic racism was expected to elicit more honest assessments of racial prejudice and the subtle factors substantiating it, minimizing respondent avoidance behaviors influenced by social desirability norms around race, because the items were not overt or expressive of hatred. The development of and research on symbolic racism soon spurred several other concepts and measures operating in a similar fashion, like "modern racism" (McConahay 1986), "aversive racism" (Gaertner and Dovidio 1986), and "subtle prejudice" (Meertens and Pettigrew 1997); these concepts were grouped as "new racism" (Pettigrew 1979a, 1979b; Sniderman et al. 1991).

However, controversies over the theory, measurement, and effects of symbolic racism soon came under heavy scrutiny (see Gilens, Sniderman, and Kuklinski 1998; Sniderman, Crosby, and Howell 2000; Sniderman and Tetlock 1986; Sniderman et al. 1991; Stoker 1998). One of the main concerns was that symbolic racism conflated principled ideological values and racial policy positions with racial prejudice (see Feldman and Huddy 2005; Sniderman, Crosby, and Howell 2000; Sniderman and Piazza 1993), leaving no room for non-racial individualism, and that it ignored other elements of race attitudes beyond prejudice (e.g., Bobo 1983).

Still, as Kinder and Sanders (1996) importantly state, "What's new in [our conceptualization of] classic racial resentment is not the mixing together of negative sentiment and cherished values, but rather the particular ingredients in the mix" (p. 294). This statement suggests that the substance of resentment likely changes as the "ingredients"—various political, economic, and social forces (see Bobo 1988a, 1988b)—interact with racial-ethnic currents (e.g., migration, population size, and structural gains) over time. Therefore, classic racial resentment will be shaped by different issues, events, and behaviors, yet the basis of the theory will continue to be founded on a *blend* of affective responses to race and applied perceptions of values.

Corresponding to changes in the concept, the measurement of new racism fluctuated over time. Early formulations of symbolic racism focused on beliefs about explicit policies like welfare and busing, but also attitudes toward the amount of attention from government Blacks received relative to Whites, Blacks' attainment of jobs and education via quotas, Blacks receiving more social and economic gains than they were entitled to, and Blacks encroaching on areas—both residential and societal—where they were not welcome (Kinder and Sears 1981; McConahay and Hough 1976). Later formulations included agreement with statements about Blacks getting more than they deserve, opposition to education quotas, Blacks pushing too fast into areas they were not welcome, and racial discrimination denials (McConahay 1986). The most recent measures of symbolic racism (also called the symbolic racism 2000 or "SR2K," Henry and Sears 2002) have included items that compare the work ethic of Blacks to other minority groups, asking respondents to what extent they think Black leaders are demanding too much too fast and whether they blame Blacks for creating racial tensions in the United States.

What is known about the name change at this point is somewhat esoteric. Scholars John McConahay and Donald Kinder were branching out to their respective audiences, the former in psychology and the latter in political science. And, as Kinder was developing a symbolic racism scale for the American National Election Study (ANES), the thinking about the name changed, but with little forewarning. By 1996, the symbolic racism scale had become *the* racial resentment scale. Kinder and Sanders (1996) acknowledge the similarities between symbolic racism and racial resentment but preferred the "racial resentment" label over symbolic racism because of the over-attention from critics on whether or not the items and theory tap "racism," and the under-attention scholars gave to the role of symbolic values. They explicitly state that the original conception of symbolic racism (Kinder and Sears 1981; Sears and Kinder 1971) should have been called "moralistic resentments" or "racial resentments" (p. 293). And to their credit, the scholarship prior to their 1996 book often referred to the symbolic racism items as tapping "resentments," but the resentments in those cases were a conflation of queries about policy attitudes and race. For example, Kinder and Sears (1981) presented a dimension of "expressive racism" (table 2, p. 420) that included a mixture of items assessing "symbolic resentments" about government policy (e.g., "Do you think that most Negroes/blacks who receive money from welfare programs could get along without it if they tried, or do they really need the help?"). Even with a broad focus on judgments of policy and race, Kinder and Sanders' complete renaming of symbolic racism was bold given such little justification, and also because they offered no new measurement scale or definition to distinguish "resentment" from "racism," much less the long-standing concept of symbolic racism.

A second cause for concern in the adoption of Kinder and Sanders' concept of racial resentment is the confusion it created. After their book *Divided by Color* was published in 1996, Sears and colleagues (Henry and Sears 2002; Sears and Henry 2005; Tarman and Sears 2005) came out with many studies, all still calling the newly conceived racial resentment "symbolic racism." In an article published the year after Kinder and Sanders' book, Sears and colleagues (1997) made a point of grouping the different new racism measures as a "family of concepts using very similar measurement" (p. 20), and declining to offer a distinction among them (see footnote 3, pp. 21–22). In later research, Henry and Sears (2002) stated that the new racism concepts, including racial resentment, were consequential "evolutions" that originated from symbolic racism, and that the subsequent label of "racial resentment" helped to convey that symbolic racism was not only racism, but involved beliefs about the "perceived moral transgressions and value violations of blacks" (p. 255). Even with this assessment in mind, Henry and Sears (2002) still proceeded to develop their SR2K scale of symbolic racism. The continued use of the symbolic racism label suggests disagreement or at least a lag in agreement about what to label the concept that is actually being measured, or how to measure either concept that had already been labeled.

A third concern involving classic racial resentment pertains to whether it captures the idea of African Americans' violating important values, such as individualism, broadly defined as unassisted and uncorrupted effort. Studies conducted after the pronouncement of racial resentment as the preferred term suggest that those who hold symbolic racism may not value individualism strongly after all (Sears and Henry 2003; Tarman and Sears 2005). This is important because the point of renaming symbolic racism "racial resentment" was to emphasize the central role of values, and the central value was thought to be individualism. Hughes (1997) finds no strong evidence that individualism is a component of symbolic racism/classic racial resentment. Sears and Henry (2003) find that "black individualism"—measured by individualism measures inserting "Black" descriptors to generic individualism measures (Feldman 1988)—is a key factor in symbolic racism beliefs. They characterize Black individualism as a specific belief system related to perceptions about Blacks' work ethic. However, by placing a racial label on an existing concept, Black individualism could be tapping basic stereotypes about Blacks needing special assistance or being lazy, rather than a form of "individualism" per se.[1] However, recent research by Kam and Burge (2018) that conducts qualitative interviews of respondents finds that the theme of individualism is consistently a part of how the items are interpreted by Whites and Blacks alike. Thus, the empirical results on the role of individualism are inconclusive at best. These statements about the importance of individualism have not altered the conceptualization of racial resentment, even though substantive changes have altered the conceptualization of symbolic racism. The result is a great deal of conceptual murkiness due to unresolved disagreement: there are different labels for the same concept, and similar measures for what are said to be different concepts.

Henry and Sears (2002) importantly state, "Just as updating has been necessary for earlier measures of old-fashioned racism and of symbolic racism as well as for the modern racism scale, so updating ultimately will be necessary for the SR2K scale, as attitudes and the language in which they are expressed continue to evolve in the coming years" (p. 279). Yet, the acknowledgment that symbolic racism theory and its measurement need constant revisions has not produced consistent attempts to revisit the concept of racial resentment in the same fashion (cf. Hughes 1997; Wilson and Davis 2011). Recently, Kam and Burge (2018) suggest that the 4-item racial resentment scale battery be "recast as Structural versus Individual Attributions for Black Americans' Economic and Social Status (SIA)" (p. 6), as it better encapsulates the substantive meaning of lower (i.e., belief in structural inequality) and higher (i.e., belief in individual failings) ends of the scale, as opposed to just the high end (i.e., resentment). Thus, most scholars, particularly in political science, view classic racial resentment as a valid label, concept, and theory, even though there are many strong and valid critiques of its measurement and conceptual clarity (e.g., Feldman and Huddy 2005; Sniderman, Crosby, and Howell 2000; Wilson and Davis 2011). In short, we suggest that it is time to replace the symbolic racism measure of racial resentment wholesale, and allow racial resentment to stand on its own theory.

A comprehensive list of the items measuring classic "racial resentment" (post Kinder and Sanders 1996) are provided in table 2.1. It is easy to note the overlapping nature of many of the racial resentment items with new racism measures. At the end of each item is an abbreviation to indicate that the measure has appeared in other scales or studies. In some cases these items have been pulled together in a cursory fashion for statistical enhancement (e.g., Feldman and Huddy 2005; Tuch and Hughes 2011), and in others people have simply relied on the original measures, which are now at least 35 years old (first appearing in the 1986 ANES).

The expressed rationale of the classic racial resentment theory was

TABLE 2.1. **Existing Survey Questions Used to Measure Classic Racial Resentment**

1. Irish, Italians, Jewish and many other minorities overcame prejudice and <u>worked their way up</u>. Blacks should do the same without any <u>special favors</u>? (RRS: SR: SR2K; GSS)
1b. Many other minority groups have overcome prejudice and worked their way up; African Americans should do the same without any special favors. (CCAP)
2. Over the past few years blacks have gotten less than they <u>deserve</u>. (RRS: SR: MRS [similar])
2b. Over the past few years, African Americans have gotten less than they deserve. (CCAP)
3. It's really a matter of some people not <u>trying hard enough</u>; if blacks would only <u>try harder</u> they could be just as well off as whites. (RRS: SR: SR2K)
3b. It's really a matter of some people not trying hard enough; if African Americans would only try harder they could be just as well off as whites. (CCAP)
4. Generations of slavery and discrimination have created conditions that make it difficult for blacks to <u>work their way out</u> of the lower class. (RRS: SR: SR2K)
4b. Generations of slavery and discrimination have created conditions that make it difficult for African Americans to work their way out of the lower class. (CCAP)
5. Government officials usually pay less attention to a request or complaint from a black person than from a white person. (RRS)
6. Most blacks who receive money from welfare programs could get along without if they tried. (RRS)
7. On the average Blacks have worse jobs, income, and housing than white people. Do you think these <u>differences</u> are mainly <u>due to discrimination</u>? (Feldman and Huddy 2005)
8. On the average Blacks have worse jobs, income, and housing than white people. Do you think these differences are because most blacks <u>don't have the chance</u> for education that it takes to rise out of poverty? (Feldman and Huddy 2005)
9. On average blacks have worse jobs, income, and housing than white people. Do you think these differences are (Tuch and Hughes 2011):
   (1) "Mainly due to discrimination?" (1 = yes, 2 = no)
   (2) "Because most blacks just do not have the motivation or willpower to pull themselves up out of poverty?" (1 = no, 2 = yes)

Note. RRS="racial resentment scale" from Kinder and Sanders (1996) item; SR=traditional symbolic racism scale from Kinder and Sears (1981) or Sears (1988); SR2K=Henry and Sears (2002); MRS=modern racism scale from McConahay (1986); CCAP=Cooperative Campaign Analysis Project; GSS = General Social Survey.

to "distinguish between those Whites who are generally sympathetic toward blacks and those who are unsympathetic" (Kinder and Sanders 1996, p. 106). The creation of a measure to reflect such resentment was intended to tap into the broader beliefs that promote the expression of subtle racial hostility without violating democratic norms of racial egalitarianism. Descriptively, the RRS proposed by Kinder and Sanders contained six questions (items 1, 2, 3, 4, 5, and 6 in table 2.1) characterizing Blacks as a whole, containing strong evaluative components designed to reveal racial antipathy without referencing White supremacy and to focus on adherence to values (e.g., effort, determination, and enterprise) rather than racial superiority. After much criticism about the items containing explicit references to government and policy (welfare) (e.g., Mendelberg 2001; Sniderman, Crosby, and Howell 2000; Stoker 1998), the scale was reduced to four items (1, 2, 3, and 4 in table 2.1), excluding the questions about welfare and government officials. The removal of those two items is the extent of revisions to the scale.

Where Is the Resentment in the Classic Racial Resentment Scale?

Conceptually, classic racial resentment is said to feature annoyance and fury as its central emotional themes, and these emotions are provoked by the absence of Blacks' "moral character" (p. 105), by "racial anger and indignation" (p. 294), and by a sense that "black Americans are getting and taking more than their fair share" (Kinder and Sanders 1996, p. 293). Yet, none of the RRS items seem to explicitly connect anger, indignation, fury, or even deservingness to Blacks or to the underlying notion of unfairness or special consideration. The items more or less allege that the underlying source of resentment is antipathy or prejudice. The lack of affective resentment in the items is apparent through the wording, and is likely the reason the items lean more toward individualism (or Black individualism) than resentment. Rather than merely offering a critique of the limited presence of resentment in the RRS items, we sought to test whether our claims had substance by way of a brief experiment.

Using data collected in September 2016 via an online Qualtrics panel, we randomized two different versions of the Kinder and Sanders resentment scale to White respondents (N=358). The first group (N=180) received the RRS as assertions—on a 5-point strongly agree to strongly disagree response scale—verbatim, in the classic four-item measure in studies like the ANES. The second group (N=178) received the RRS items with slight wording adjustments that include "explicit" statements about anger or resentment. We hypothesized that since resentment and anger are more explicitly affective in nature that they would give different meaning to the items in terms of a distinction between individualism and prejudice. This difference would be reflected in correlations with political ideology. We present our findings—response distributions and correlations—in table 2.2.

The first classic racial resentment item we analyzed proposes that "over the past few years blacks have gotten less than they deserve." Disagreement with this question—believing Blacks have not gotten less—is presumed to indicate racial prejudice and resentment; however, this is a questionable inference. Disagreement can come close to resentment only if one believes that Blacks have gotten more than they deserve, which is implied, not measured, by the response. Also, one could strongly

	Strongly Disagree	Disagree	Neither	Agree	Strongly Agree	Mean (SD)	% Resent
Original: Irish, Italians, Jewish and many other minorities overcame prejudice and worked their way up. African Americans should do the same without any special favors.	5.0%	11.1%	20.6%	33.3%	30.0%	3.72 (1.15)	63%
Explicit: Irish, Italians, Jewish and many other minorities overcame prejudice and worked their way up. **I resent when African Americans request special favors to do the same.**	10.7%	11.2%	26.4%	25.8%	25.8%	3.45 (1.28)	52%
Original: It is really a matter of some people not trying hard enough; if African Americans would only try harder they could be just as well off as whites.	13.9%	13.3%	33.3%	26.7%	12.8%	3.11 (1.21)	39%
Explicit: It is really a matter of some people not trying hard enough. **It angers me that African Americans do not try harder to be just as well off as Whites.**	16.3%	11.8%	29.8%	25.8%	16.3%	3.14 (1.29)	42%
Original: Over the past few years, African Americans have gotten less than they deserve. (Rev.)	18.9%	22.8%	32.8%	13.9%	11.7%	3.23 (1.24)	42%
Explicit: **I resent the notion that over the past few years,** African Americans have gotten less than they deserve.	10.7%	11.8%	31.5%	29.8%	16.3%	3.29 (1.19)	46%
Original: Generations of slavery and discrimination have created conditions that make it difficult for African Americans to work their way out of the lower class. (Rev.)	21.1%	18.3%	20.6%	26.1%	13.9%	3.07 (1.36)	39%
Explicit: **It angers me when African Americans claim that** generations of slavery and discrimination have created conditions that make it difficult for them to work their way out of the lower class.	10.1%	14.6%	12.4%	36.0%	27.0%	3.55 (1.30)	63%

Note. Results are for non-Hispanic White respondents.

disagree with the question—purportedly, a prejudiced response—and feel as though Blacks have gotten exactly what they deserve, and not necessarily more or less; such a position is neither necessarily resentful nor prejudiced. Finally, it is not clear *what* Blacks have gotten less of, or less of it relative to what. In the end, the assertion attempts to tap resentment through deservingness, yet there is a great deal of ambiguity about what the item elicits (e.g., anger, prejudice, factual knowledge) and what disagreement indicates.

When the assertion is stated with an explicit emotional tone, the meaning ostensibly changes. The explicit versions had respondents assess their agreement with the statement, "I resent the notion that over the past few years, African Americans have gotten less than they deserve." This is an imperfect wording, but the effect is consequential. The fifth and sixth rows of table 2.2 show the differences and similarities. There are no large statistical differences in the means for the original (M=3.23) and explicit (M=3.29) versions of the statement (Δ=.06), or the percentage of resentful responses (Δ=4% points); however, the original RRS item correlated (r=.212, p<.01) with self-reported conservatism (on a 5-point scale from very liberal to very conservative) and the explicit version did not (r=.051, n.s.). Thus, the content of this item provides a similar level of response, but the content associated with the response is seemingly different, with only the original version resonating with one's ideology.

A second assertion in the classic racial resentment scale asks respondents to evaluate whether "generations of slavery and discrimination have created conditions that make it difficult for blacks to work their way out of the lower class." Disagreement with this statement presumably indicates resentment, but, similar to the item above, the resentment is implicit, not explicit. There is not much annoyance or fury to be found in the item. For example, one could disagree with this statement—concluding that slavery and discrimination have not created difficult conditions—but still believe that some other (contemporary) structural, legal, or attitudinal conditions, other than slavery and discrimination, have made it difficult for Blacks to work their way out of the lower class. Perhaps the conditions that make upward mobility difficult are living in racist communities, the prevalence of biased media and reinforced stereotypes, punitive state policies and programs, and segregation, but not so much slavery *and* discrimination. Also, even if one strongly agrees that slavery and discrimination have made it difficult—a purportedly non-racially resentful response—one could still conclude that the difficulty could be overcome by hard work and determination (i.e., the Protestant work-ethic values that constitute resentment). Hence, a symbolically prejudiced person could agree with this item. Generally, this item appears to make assumptions about the factors that racially resentful Whites might view as relevant or not to upward mobility, and the responses to the item do not clearly indicate resentment or prejudice.

When the item is framed with explicit emotion, the meaning changes. Respondents evaluated their level of agreement with, "It angers me when African Americans claim that generations of slavery and discrimination have created conditions that make it difficult for them to work their way out of the lower class." The items are located in the last two rows of table 2.2. The explicit version produced statistically higher mean levels (Δ=.48, p<.01) and a significantly greater proportion of resentful responses (Δ=24% points, p<.05) than the original RRS item. Yet, even with higher levels, the explicit version of the statement did not significantly correlate with ideology (r=.108, n.s.), while the original RRS item did show a correlation (r=.216, p<.01). Connecting explicit anger with African Americans' claims about slavery and discrimination seemingly activated resentment more than offering the classic statement that is free of emotion.

A third classic racial resentment scale statement also alludes to work and effort, offering the assertion that, "It's really a matter of some people not trying hard enough; if blacks would only try harder they could be just as well off as whites." The intent of the item is clear: hard work alone is the means to racial equality for Blacks, and factors like racial prejudice and discrimination are not consequential barriers. Agreement with this item purportedly indicates resentment. However, it is difficult to see the anger or resentment in the item because it rests as a straightforward opinion (i.e., "could be just as well off"), rather than an emotionally reactive sentiment. Addressing the first part of the statement, it is conceivably true that for "some people" trying harder is valuable. Similarly, the second part of the statement asserts another potential truism that trying harder could lead to (some) Blacks being just as well off as (some) Whites. Such beliefs are neither inherently racist nor does the statement indicate that Blacks are not trying hard, just that they need to try harder. Lastly, the question arises, would a racially prejudiced (or racist) respondent actually endorse any prescription that makes Blacks as well off as Whites? The answer depends on the looseness of one's definition of prejudice, but we are given pause that the question was antipathetic. Again, the statement presumes anger, resentment, and racism, but their presence is not clear.

When this item contains an emotional tone, once again, the meaning changes. Respondents in the adjusted-wording group were presented the statement, "It is really a matter of some people not trying hard enough. It angers me that African Americans do not try harder to be just as well off as Whites." We left the first part of the assertion the same, and just changed the presumed substance of resentment. These two versions are in the third and fourth rows of table 2.2. When we compare these items, the mean levels (Δ=.03) and percentage of resentful responses (Δ=3% points) are not statistically different; however, once again, the original RRS item is correlated with ideology (r=.230, p<.01), but the explicit version is not (r=.030, n.s.). Apparently, trying harder is a core value, but African Americans' not trying harder to be just as well off as Whites did not make our respondents that angry.

One of the most troubling, but commonly replicated, classic racial resentment scale items is this: "Irish, Italians, Jews and many other minorities overcame prejudice and worked their way up. Blacks should do the same without any special favors."[2] Strong agreement with the statement supposedly signifies resentment. But, once again, the assertion does not, on its own, invoke the fury or annoyance emphasized by Kinder and Sanders; rather, it is a straightforward opinion about what Blacks should do. Certainly, believing that Blacks should work their way up without special favors is aligned with traditional Black conservatism (Watson 1998; Dawson 2003; Lewis 2005, 2013). Even if one agrees with the entirety of the statement, it does not necessarily mean that one believes African Americans do not already work their way up without special favors, just that they "should." As an indication of the low-prejudiced nature of the item, in each year of the American National Election Study (ANES) between 1986 and 2004 where the item was presented to Black respondents, only once did the percentage of Blacks agreeing with the item fall below 40 percent.[3] Thus, the content appears racially neutral, and it may simply reflect political values.

There are also a number of controversial issues embedded in this item's content. First, the item implies a factual point that Blacks do not already work their way up, or that they do not work their way up at the same level as the other groups listed in the statement. Not only do Kinder and Sanders (1996) admit the factual inaccuracy of the statement's implication, saying it is "false" (p. 109), such an assertion is arguably racist in its assumption in that it calls on the prevalent racial stereo-type that Blacks are lazy and undisciplined. The ultimate danger is that the item could influence respondents because it is presented as a fact. The initial part also states, also as a fact, that Irish, Italian, and Jew-ish groups have not received "any special favors" in their efforts to over-come prejudice, which is not a factual statement. While each of these im-migrant groups had its challenges with prejudice and discrimination, the fact that they were not brought over to America as slaves and were af-forded industrial employment opportunities because of their locations in shipping port areas (e.g., New York, New Jersey) provided a status not allotted to most Black Americans (e.g., Perlmann 1988). This digression is simply to illustrate the contentious tone of the question.

The fourth item is also problematic in that it makes multiple assertions for respondents to agree or disagree with. The first assertion asks respon-dents to judge whether Irish, Italian, and Jewish minority groups have worked their way up. The second one asks respondents their agreement on whether Blacks should do the same (as the other groups). The third one asks whether Blacks should do the same as the other groups without "any special favors." One could agree that the other groups have worked their way up, but disagree that Blacks should do the same without special considerations, or vice versa. This concern is less the fact that the asser-tion is double- or triple-barreled and more that the statements are almost independent, with one making assertions about one set of groups (i.e., Irish, Italians, Jews, and other minorities) and a second assertion about Blacks. It is also unclear who the "other" minorities are in the initial as-sertion; they could be Blacks (e.g., Haitians, Brazilians, South Asians, or Africans) who live in America, but who would not classify themselves as African Americans. Thus, the location of racial resentment, or prejudice, in this item is unclear, and in our view this item brushes against good survey practice because of its characterizations of the mentioned racial-ethnic groups relative to African Americans. It is noteworthy that the most recent versions of the item in the Cooperative Congressional Elec-tion Studies (CCES) refer to African Americans rather than Blacks, and simply refer to "other minorities" rather than a specific list.

When we present this item with explicit language, the meaning changes, just as it does for the three previous items. The altered asser-tion states, "Irish, Italians, Jews and many other minorities overcame prejudice and worked their way up. I resent when African Americans request special favors to do the same." The items are located in the first two rows of table 2.2. The explicit version produced significantly lower mean levels (Δ=.27, p<.01) and lower percentages of resentful responses (Δ=11% points, p<.05). However, the original RRS item is correlated with ideology (r=.190, p<.05) and the explicit version is not (r=.110, n.s.). The inference is that Whites value the sentiment of individualism, perhaps more so than other ethnic minorities, but they are not overwhelmingly angered by it, and when they are it does not correlate with their level of conservatism.

Beyond showing that question wording can alter levels of resentment, the most noteworthy finding from the experiment is that versions of the assertions that add explicit mentions of anger or resentment do not correlate with self-reported political ideology. Such a finding is key because it seemingly resolves the criticism that properly conceived and measured racial resentment is not a form of conservatism. Secondly, the experiment revealed that some content makes respondents angrier than others. For example, while the higher level of response in the original RRS scale came from the "work their way up without special consideration" statement (M=3.72, % resentful=63%), the highest level of response in the explicit items came from the "angers me when African Americans claim . . . slavery and discrimination . . . make it difficult" statement (M=3.55, % resentful=63%). The lowest-scoring item for both the original classic racial resentment scale (M=3.11, % resentful=39%) and the explicit versions (M=3.14, % resentful=42%) was the item about African Americans trying "harder to be just as well off as Whites." Thus, there is a great deal of ambiguity as to what content and sentiment the original items are tapping into, and, more importantly, it is unclear if the original content reliably makes Whites angry or resentful.

We suspect the differences in wording between the standard and emotional versions are signaling the need to identify acute sources of resentment that Whites hold toward African Americans. This might include more specificity about the injustices Whites claim to experience due to race, such as the whittling away of merit and the blame generalized to Whites for African American inequalities. Unfortunately, we cannot take this analysis much further due to the limited scope of the data collection, but we hope this type of experimentation leads to more scholarship challenging the traditional wording of measures. Future work might also examine whether the content changes have downstream effects on policy attitudes or other opinions strongly tied to ideology or government.

Based on our experimental results, it is tempting to conclude that simply adding the explicit emotion components to the items resolves the matters of measurement. Yet, that would assume that racial resentment is merely about how much effort and responsibility Blacks display. That is, altering the language of the scale to include an explicit emotional bent is not enough to improve the measure; it simply points out that the current measure needs more vetting. In our view, the RRS needs a complete revision, with new content and language.

Many of these observations about the classic racial resentment scale items are not new (cf. Schuman 2000; Wilson and Davis 2011). Wilson and Davis (2011) make a key distinction that resentment and prejudice are distinct concepts, even if one may influence the other. They also point out the lack of explicit resentment that we find above. They claim this basic lack of explicit mention renders the classic scale a measure of the original symbolic racism concept, rather than racial resentment. Sniderman, Crosby, and Howell (2000) and colleagues (Sniderman and Carmines 1997; Sniderman and Tetlock 1986) argue that the classic racial resentment scale and symbolic racism items have less to do with racism, and instead mainly reflect ideological preferences related to government, governing, and group values. For example, a person could believe that hard work and playing by stated rules should be prioritized in the distribution of social reward for any and all groups, but also *not* have dislike for or antipathy toward African Americans. These individuals might score high on the value-conflict aspect of racial resentment, but low on the anti-Black-affect part. Thus, the "blend" of affect and values makes for a confusing definitional statement. These concerns are further noted by Feldman and Huddy (2005), who find classic racial resentment is particularly associated with values (i.e., individualism) among conservatives, but strongly associated with measures of prejudice among liberals, who ostensibly have no ideological basis to offer resentful sentiments since they are ostensibly open to government assistance. These points about the role of ideology also speak to our findings above where the original items correlated with political ideology, but the explicit items do not.

Evaluating the Classic Racial Resentment Scale
Measurement Properties

Over the past decade, scholars have revisited the classic racial resentment scale to investigate its psychometric properties. Carmines, Sniderman, and Easter (2011) and Schuman (2000) each voiced the concern that the items in the RRS reflect the measures of racial policy attitudes instead of racial resentment; however, recent research by Roos, Hughes, and Reichelmann (2019) showed that the racial resentment and racial policy attitudes are distinct from each other and from traditional prejudice. Henry and Sears (2002) identified validity issues related to the dimensionality of the scale, finding that the four items of the classic racial resentment scale loaded statistically on three different dimensions. Pietryka and Macintosh (2017) evaluated the measurement equivalence of classic racial resentment scale in the ANES 2012 and 2016, and results showed that the RRS is multi-dimensional and conflated with political predispositions like ideology and party identification. In addition, Loose, Hou, and Berinsky (2018) concluded that even with only four items the RRS is too lengthy, and their analysis showed that a revised three-item racial resentment scale performs similarly to the original 4-item scale. These recent studies also draw conclusions similar to our already-voiced concerns related to conceptualization, but we sought to conduct additional analysis to aid our understanding of the classic racial resentment scale's value.

Our interest in the measurement of racial resentment led us to examine the most complete set of data on the subject: the American National Election Study (ANES). Since 1986, the ANES has included a core 4-item Kinder and Sanders racial resentment scale in its studies— which have been conducted at least every presidential election year. We analyzed data from approximately 14,724 non-Hispanic White respondents in the 2016 ANES Time Series cumulative data file to assess the extent to which the items in the Kinder and Sanders scale adhere to their stated measurement properties. The data contain responses to the classic racial resentment scale from 1986 to 2016, and we looked at unweighted response estimates, including descriptive (central tendency and dispersion) and measurement statistics (Cronbach alpha, factor results, and confirmatory factor fit measures). Our findings, shown in table 2.3, are somewhat surprising.

First, while the items are somewhat stable in terms of their central tendency and variability, and display decent internal consistency, there are consistent issues with how well the data fit the proposed model of racial resentment. Although statistically significant, the differences between the lowest (3.32 in 1990 and 2016) and highest (3.64 in 2012) aggregate scores on racial resentment are slight (Δ=.32). The standard deviation estimates reflect a similar magnitude of change, with the dif-

TABLE 2.3. **Measurement Statistics of Classic Racial Resentment Scale by Year ANES Cumulative Data**

	Descriptive Statistics			Reliability	EFA		CFA	
Year	M	SD	N	Cronbach's Alpha	Eigenvalue	Percent Variance Explained	CFI	RMSEA
1986	3.39	.91	816	.74	2.27	56.71%	.97	.11
1988	3.55	.87	1,333	.73	2.21	55.52	.95	.15
1990	3.32	.94	726	.78	2.41	60.22	.92	.22
1992	3.47	.93	1,694	.76	2.35	58.68	.91	.22
1994	3.56	.85	1,336	.69	2.11	52.85	.89	.21
2000	3.52	.94	1,177	.75	2.27	56.77	.95	.15
2004	3.50	.96	743	.80	2.52	63.07	.93	.22
2008	3.60	.93	1,029	.78	2.40	60.06	.87	.28
2012	3.64	.95	3,259	.83	2.63	65.82	.95	.19
2016	3.32	1.13	2,611	.86	2.84	71.10	.95	.21
Overall	3.50	.97	14,724	.79	2.47	61.73	.92	.22
F-test		24.14 **						
Eta-squared		.02						

Note. *p<.05, **p<.01. Results are for non-Hispanic White respondents. Exploratory Factor Analysis (EFA) was used to detect the number of factors underlying the RRS. Confirmatory Factor Analysis (CFA) was then conducted to confirm the exploratory model. Two goodness-of-fit indices including the Comparative Fit Index (CFI) and Root Mean Square Error of Approximation (RMSEA) were used to assess the degree of fit between the model and the sample. F-test statistics test the null hypothesis that all mean values over time are equal.

ference between the highest (1.13 in 2016) and lowest (.85 in 1994) values being modest (Δ=.28). Also, in each year, the Cronbach alpha measures of reliability (internal consistency) are very good (>.700), and the set of four items consistently accounts for as much variance in the scale as two items (unweighted by year, Eigenvalue average = 2.40, variance explained average = 60%). These are decent attributes, but their magnitudes may be influenced by a host of factors like sample size and a few items doing most of the measurement work. The more accurate test is to assess whether the model and data align by using confirmatory factor analysis (CFA). On this standard, the classic racial resentment scale never reaches a consistent threshold of excellence. There are several goodness-of-fit measures, which come in the form of indices. Two standard measures are the Comparative Fit Index (CFI; >.90 acceptable fit, >.95 excellent fit; Bentler 1990) and the Root Mean Square Error of Approximation (RMSEA; <.08 acceptable fit, <.05 excellent fit; Brown and Cudeck 1993). Across the eleven ANES studies, the classic racial resentment scale reaches excellence with the CFI only once (in 1986) and never reaches excellence or acceptability with the RMSEA. These less-than-stellar properties suggest that the actual ANES data do not align with the theoretical structure of the items, and perhaps fewer or different items would better represent a structure of racial resentment.

We also assess the predictive validity of the classic racial resentment scale by examining the bivariate correlations between the RRS and feeling thermometer (FT) scores related to race and ideology. Again, the controversy remains centered on the extent to which the items actually measure anti-Black affect, whether they actually measure resentment, and whether they conflate principled ideological values with racial prejudice, leaving no room for non-racial individualism or non-racist criticisms of African Americans as a political group. If the classic racial resentment scale is measuring prejudice toward African Americans, then anti-Black affect should play a dominant role in discriminating the respondents at the high and low ends of the racial resentment scale. Alternatively, the scale has been criticized by scholars as reflecting ideological leanings, and thus actually measuring a broader set of anti-progressive, more conservative, political positions. Figure 2.1 shows the ANES trend in correlations between the RRS and FT scores toward African Americans, Whites, Conservatives, and Liberals.

The results of this analysis are quite informative, and all estimated correlations surpass a minimum (p<.05) threshold of statistical signifi-

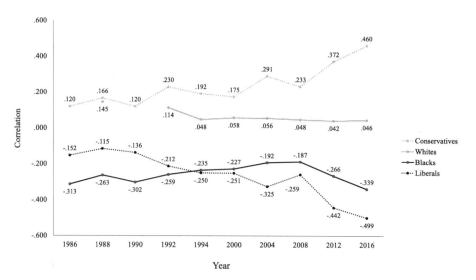

FIGURE 2.1. Correlation between Classic Racial Resentment and Feeling Thermometer Ratings, ANES 1986–2016

cance. First, the classic racial resentment scale barely registers a relationship with affect toward Whites, indicating that more negative attitudes do not influence feelings about White in-group members. Second,
the line for the FT scores toward Blacks shows a consistently negative
relationship with RRS, and this correlation is relatively flat over time
(-.313 in 1986, and -.339 in 2016; Δ=.026), with the highest correlation
of -.339—or 11.5 percent of the variance in classic racial resentment explained by anti-Black affect—registering in 2016. Third, the strongest
trend lines in the figure show a result from the relationships between the
classic racial resentment scale and warmer affect toward conservatives
(as high as .460 in 2016) and colder affect toward liberals (as low as -.499
in 2016). It appears that, over time, the meaning of the racial resentment
scale has changed for White respondents; rather than prejudice toward
African Americans, the scale appears to be primarily associated with
negative feelings toward liberals and positive feelings toward conservatives. The difference between the results for the FT scores for Blacks
and liberals suggest that the RRS now predicts partisan rather than racial affect.

What these patterns essentially signal is that the classic racial resentment scale offers a muddied picture of racial antipathy, especially
as it relates to the anti-Black-affect component of symbolic racism and
the Kinder and Sanders racial resentment operationalization. Thus,
past critiques about the role of political ideology in the symbolic racism measures, conceptually and as a scale, appear more valid now than
in the past. Additionally, some of the growing correlation with ideological groups may be due to the individualism content within the items
(e.g., subtle allusions to effort [i.e., "work"] and "deservingness") or to
the increasing racial polarization after the 2008 presidential election of
Obama. Regardless, the finding that the RRS's correlations with affect
toward ideology groups dwarf those for racial groups signals uncertainty
around what the current scale actually measures.

Conclusion

In this chapter we ground racial resentment in the larger theoretical and
research literature on resentment. Doing so establishes agreed upon or
accepted components of resentment in the existing literature, providing
a criterion for evaluating the classic theory and measure of racial resent-

ment. We found that the tenets of resentment, free of race, are not well considered in the classical conceptualization, theory, and measurement of racial resentment. Most notably, the classic racial resentment concept does not speak to justice motives, and the resentment literature does not speak to individual or group hate or dislike. We also evaluated the classic racial resentment scale in terms of its ability to tap resentment, rather than presume the agreement or disagreement with the assertions actually measure it. We found inconsistencies in whether or not the assertions that respondents review actually make them angry. We used an experiment to aid our review, finding that assertions that include explicit mentions of anger or being angry changed response distributions. For example, we found that all of the classic racial resentment items correlate with political ideology, but none of the explicitly worded versions of the items did so. Our review of the items also identified several question design problems in the current items that give pause in concluding they assess resentment or prejudice. Finally, we assessed how well the items gauge the most consistent measure of Black affect in the ANES: the Black feeling thermometer. While showing good internal consistency, we found that the classic scale items found in the ANES are not structurally sound: the theory of the measurement structure and the collected data have less than adequate fit. Also, correlational analyses over time show that the scale has come to indicate something different than anti-Black affect, and now mostly measures colder affect toward liberals and warmer affect toward conservatives. On these grounds, classic racial resentment, articulated as a form of (symbolic) racism and prejudice, falls short as an analytical framework and measure for understanding politics and racial appeals today.

Although the classic concept of racial resentment and its measurement were introduced over 30 years ago, becoming the most identifiable and available indicator of racial prejudice in political science, it has essentially fallen short on several grounds, and chief among them is the presumption that it reflects racial prejudice. As critics have claimed, it is very difficult for a single construct and measure to capture the blend of both racial prejudice and non-racial attitudes on the violation of values. That is, when classic racial resentment is used to explain the rejection of ameliorative social policies—such as affirmative action, health care, or housing—it is suggested that this is due to racial prejudice or, as Kinder and Schuman (2004) state, "defects of [African Americans'] temperament and character—that Blacks disdained hard work and re-fuse . . . the ample opportunities . . . open to them" (p. 381). When seek-ing explanations for voting decisions, such as the rejection of President Obama or the support of President Trump, or policy opinions, such as health care or even climate change (e.g., Tesler 2012a, 2012b; Benegal 2018), scholars use the scale to suggest that such positions are due to ra-cial prejudice or hatred toward African Americans. Yet, our assessment of the scale herein, and in prior work (e.g., Wilson and Davis 2011), and the comments from others (e.g., Kam and Burge 2019), conclude that the scale does not measure prejudice so much as it taps beliefs about the structural condition and subsequent behaviors of African Ameri-cans. Also, since the original theories behind both symbolic racism and classic racial resentment were developed after the scale's items (see Mc-Conahay 1986), it is not surprising that the scale has conceptual murk-iness. While symbolic racism has moved to align its theory with items seeking its measurement, the restudy of classic racial resentment has re-mained static. The static nature is evidenced by the slowness to offer re-visions to the measure (Wilson and Davis 2011; Cramer 2020), and the fact that political studies have reverted back to calling the concept sym-bolic racism (e.g., Kinder and Schuman 2004; Gomez and Wilson 2006) or using both labels interchangeably in the same study (e.g., Tesler and Sears 2010). The discipline is left to conclude that racial resentment, in its current formulation, rests on the notion that prejudice is the main in-gredient driving political and social attitudes today. We find this for-mulation extremely limiting, especially as an analytical framework for understanding politics today.

When the core elements of resentment are identified, such as deserv-ingness, justice, and power-status relationships, the racialization of the sentiment, particularly in politics, becomes clearer. If one starts with resentment as a form of anger stemming from a perceived injustice—occurring when an observer reacts to another person or group's unde-served positive outcome—the theory becomes about how individuals make sense of actions and outcomes in politics. Judgments of deserving-ness can be conditioned by a host of factors, including racial factors like stereotypes and prejudice, but also non-racial factors like beliefs about how resources should be distributed and at what level. They can also be influenced by information framing particular policies and by the errors associated with standard cognitive processes. Racism and prejudice are but one form of motivation for judgments of undeservingness, and it is unfortunate that the discipline's first foray into the study of resentment came in the context of Whites' attitudes about Blacks.

As we will show in the forthcoming chapters, racial resentment is not bound to those with high levels of prejudice, and it is not absent from those who are liberals and Democrats. As opposed to disliking or hating Blacks because of their moral defects related to effort and their receipt of benefits they have not earned, Whites are angry at how African Americans and others—including government, liberals, and Democrats—use race more generally as a way to gain power and status. What Whites, as a dominant group, perceive as unfair makes them more sensitive to issues, groups, and political figures that threaten the current power-status racial structure in America. This suggests that contemporary racial resentment need not stem from 1960s-era backlashes that reflected turbulent disagreements over policies that benefited African Americans. Today's generation is far removed from this past era, and many of the issues of that time (e.g., busing, affirmative action) are no longer salient, let alone legal. Instead, racial resentment originates in a just-world belief that deservingness and merit are important features in American culture and politics, and when there is a perceived inconsistency between what individuals do and what they have received, the resulting sense of injustice prompts an enduring and targeted anger at those who facilitated the decision and those who were unfairly rewarded. In this conceptualization, racial resentment offers a robust analytical framework for understanding Whites' perceptions of a changing "American way of life." Racial resentment toward Blacks is not the beginning of the motivation for political preferences, it is a facilitator between justice and status. Without the motivation for justice, there is not much reason to oppose racial policies or give much thought to how groups seek to achieve equality. This is a different approach to the study of race, but it is one that aligns with political decision-making and judgments. While it may seem nonsensical on first impression, ostensibly racial beliefs and behavior cannot always be attributed to racial prejudice.

CHAPTER THREE

Pressing Restart on Racial Resentment

The previous chapter revealed many of the problems with classic racial resentment and its measurement, which factor into its limitations as an analytical framework. Despite these limitations, it not only has been used as an indicator of racial prejudice, it is widely regarded as the most valid indicator of racial prejudice in politics. It has regularly appeared in the ANES since 1986, and when other national studies (e.g., Cooperative Campaign Analysis Project [CCAP] or the Cooperative Congressional Election Study [CCES]) look to identify a measure of racial attitudes, they turn to the classic racial resentment scale. As a result of this anchoring in the existing scale, scholarly attempts to advance the concept of racial resentment by way of reconceptualization, operational difference, and alternative measurement have been met frequently with doubt and resistance. Often, rather than revise classic racial resentment, defenders and opponents alike have taken stronger positions in their corners, offering very little beyond new labels for the items. Ironically, the substance of the support for and opposition to classic racial resentment is based in little more than the fact that the classic measure and concept is the status quo. We have editorial letters and reviewer comments from various prominent journals attesting to our observation.

In this chapter we develop a new measure of Whites' resentment toward African Americans. We have been experimenting with individual items and their scaling for over ten years, and this chapter reports on our effort to produce a valid and reliable scale. For such an important concept and powerful measure, our desire is to be transparent regarding its

conceptual meaning, how it is derived, and, equally important, its validity as a scale.

We approach racial resentment as a negative reaction to how racial groups threaten the status quo systems, practices, and procedures
that determine who (i.e., racial groups) gets what (i.e., cherished resources), when they get it (i.e., after showing merit), how they get it (e.g.,
government policy), and why they get it (i.e., deservingness and special considerations). To reiterate the definition developed in the previous chapters: Racial resentment originates from legitimizing beliefs
that motivate opposition to change and a defense of the status quo, and
there is no requirement that the beliefs are racist or prejudiced. Thus,
any political phenomenon, racial or otherwise, that promotes or creates
change to a system of comfort, uncertainty, or privilege will produce resentment because it threatens cherished elements that maintain justice
in society.

The research by Gibson (2008, 2009) influences our thinking about
how people utilize justice judgments. Gibson's (2008, 2009) work indicates that, "Justice judgements matter" (Gibson 2008, p. 699). First, justice judgment is a "terribly important criterion, perhaps the most important criterion, in the calculus of opinion formation" (Gibson 2008,
p. 701). People are essentially "lay philosophers" often using justice to
make sense of complex policies (Gibson 2008). Second, justice matters
because "one does not have to be a party to a dispute to care about fairness of its outcome—people care about injustices done to others" (Gibson 2008, p. 701). Third, justice judgments matter because justice may be
formed in reference to individual or group interests. "Some people draw
conclusions about justice in terms of what they think is fair to themselves, but many base their views on what is fair to their group" (Gibson
2008, p. 702). Gibson (2008) shows that justice and fairness are often intertwined with social identity. In a more extensive development of the
concept, how ordinary people apply principles of justice is incredibly important because values such as the rule of law, due process, and property
rights are often pitted against other important concerns like apartheid
and the need for a place to live for millions of people (Gibson 2009). In
our case, African Americans can be expected to possess different con-
ceptualizations of justice, fairness, and deservingness than Whites based
on the historical treatment of their group (e.g., slavery and Jim Crow)
and contemporaneous discriminatory practices (e.g., institutional rac-

ism), which will be most helpful when we argue that African Americans' resentment toward Whites cannot be measured using the same items as Whites' resentment toward African Americans.

Other scholars seeking to understand the connection between justice and political behavior have also influenced our thinking. Tyler and van der Toorn (2013) provide an extensive review on distributive, procedural, and retributive justice, and provide applications for social group politics. Hochschild (1981) examines the legitimizing norms and values of distributive justice, particularly those based on equality and differentiation in political decision-making. Finally, Peffley and Hurwitz's (2010) research on the system and racial group level beliefs about criminal justice and policing leads to an instructive conclusion: that justice is "an inherently racial concept . . . it is impossible to think about . . . justice without also thinking about race, and, contrariwise, it is essentially impossible to think about race without also thinking about justice" (p. 80). Thus, we advance our theoretical framework and subsequent analyses of racial resentment in a well-established literature on politics, groups, and justice.

A Theory of Whites' Resentment toward African Americans

Before describing our new measure, let us first lay out a theory of racial resentment as it has been developed in the previous chapters. As we are proposing a new approach to examining racializing political resentment, it is important to revisit a few key components that will guide the remaining theory and analyses in subsequent chapters. To reiterate: resentment is anger that occurs when an observer perceives that another person or group received an undeserved reward, and it stems from an appraisal of deservingness, responsibility, and a violation of justice and fairness. Applying this to racial perceptions, racialized resentment encompasses anger, bitterness, or concern related to Whites' beliefs about the deservingness of special considerations on the basis of race. The racially resentful person is offended by unfair and inappropriate claims of racism and racial discrimination because they believe that racism and discrimination are events of the past, and attempts to use them are simply unfair to Whites who have not overtly or intentionally done anything to contribute to the problems that beset African Americans. This is our theoretical and operational account of Whites' resentment toward

African Americans. We do not believe that holding such resentments over race makes someone prejudiced or racist, even if it does lead to the enabling of racial inequality or political disagreement. It should be clear that our operational framework actually expands the culpability among Whites for lingering issues of racial intolerance, inequality, and injustice.

In the context of public opinion surveys, Whites' resentment toward African Americans presents itself as a sentiment, reacting to statements about how African Americans use, and benefit (unfairly) from, race. The evaluator's reaction can arise from a range of internal (e.g., prejudice, ideology, or efficacy) or external (e.g., media reports, rules, perceived facts) factors that affect their appraisal of deservingness. Resentment involves a judgment about deservingness, a perceived injustice, and a perceived threat to the status quo: values and rules determine who should get what and when, why they should get it, and how they should get it. Thus, at the most fundamental level, resentment should occur if and only if 1) another person or group received, is likely to receive, or is perceived to receive, a positive outcome (a reward), and 2) the other's actions judged—fairly or not—to be relevant to getting the positive outcome are viewed negatively.

Just-World Motive

The first condition that makes resentment possible is a desire for justice. In fact, it is actually the injustice that produces the anger that, along with beliefs, fuels resentment. Resentment, in other words, stems from a belief that others have violated norms of fair play and justice. Justice is a powerful motive in political judgments, as it seeks to legitimize existing structures of status and influence. Psychology research (Lerner 1980a, 1980b) shows that most individuals are strongly motivated to believe that they live in a world where people generally get what they deserve, and deserve what they get. Assuming that individuals oppose racial maltreatment and inequality, the presence of systemic racism, racial prejudice, and racial discrimination—particularly as it relates to inequality—renders a just system unjust. The justice motive is so strong it elicits motivated reasoning (Lodge and Taber 2013): even when individuals are confronted with information that contradicts their just-world view, they go to great lengths to dismiss, reinterpret, distort, or forget the new information by identifying imaginary merits and or assigning blame to innocent victims, thereby justifying the status quo as legitimate (Lerner 1980a, 1980b). Instead of accepting that the world is unjust, individuals balance (Heider 1958) their psychological state by attributing negative outcomes to the group's or group member's behavior, rather than society at large (Pettigrew 1979a, 1979b). Importantly, this also suggests that racial progress in the form of removed system barriers (e.g., forced desegregation, election protections, equal opportunity, and other diversity practices) becomes a threat to the supposedly just system that works just fine in the minds of most Whites. In short, the system is not the problem; the people who cannot succeed within it that are the problem.

As we have stated, the violation of justice—or the presence of injustice—is what activates resentment. When people value justice, using it as a standard of judgment, it has both an instrumental and a terminal importance, as its perceived existence both facilitates and is an end-state to safety and security of both society and the mind. The instrumental state of justice is produced by things like liberty, autonomy, equality, morality, and fairness, while the terminal consequence of justice is peace of mind, certainty, and comfort. When people perceive their sense of justice and fairness is being violated, they also perceive greater uncertainty, challenges to the status quo, and a threat to certain values. Thus, the simple violation of an individual's sense of justice and fairness is enough to elicit resentment. When justice is violated in the context of race, it elicits racial resentment.

Deservingness and Consistency

Appraisals of deservingness are innate to politics. As an important role of governance is decision-making about the allocation of resources in society, citizens are motivated to consider whether allocations are deserved by those who benefit from them. Psychological evaluations of deservingness do not typically occur in a vacuum; they are contextualized by readily available features of the political landscape: partisanship, ideology, geographic location, media sources, and identity. It is these factors that quickly inform deservingness by assessing the consistency between the recipient and the actions used to gain benefit. Policies that seek to redress past discrimination or prejudice may elicit justice concerns about deservingness and legitimacy among both high and low status groups as they seek to enhance and maintain their statuses. Thus, deservingness is key to political preferences and racial resentment.

The appraisal of deservingness directly targets the actions—the means by which unearned positive rewards are gained—of an individual or group (Feather 1999). The evaluation of the actions that ostensibly led to outcomes, and therefore deservingness, have an emotional bent because they are closely bound up with the observer's own value preferences—those standards the observer uses to judge what is right or wrong, or good or bad (Feather 1999, 2006). For example, justice motives dictate that greater effort deserves greater reward, and lesser effort deserves lesser reward. In both instances, there is consistency between the actions and the outcomes. The state of consistency meets expectations for fairness and justice, and, thus, positive emotional reactions, such as satisfaction and pride, are more likely than negative reactions (e.g., disappointment) when consistency occurs. As a result, consistency between appraisals of actions and outcomes produces positive emotions, satisfying a sense of justice and eliciting a judgment of deservingness.

Inconsistency, on the other hand, produces a negative state in which effort does not match the perceived reward. If an observer believes another individual's actions (e.g., judged as negative) do not match their outcome (e.g., getting a reward), then they will perceive an injustice because a person is supposed to get what they deserve. Negative actions that result in any positive outcomes, and positive actions that result in negative outcomes, are inconsistent and should be judged as undeserved.

Threats to the Status Quo

When people perceive that others are getting cherished benefits they do not deserve, or those who are deserving go unrewarded (Whites themselves), it threatens people's sense of fairness and justice; but more importantly it threatens the existing system of prerogatives and material resources that support the opportunity for a "Good Life." We agree with Kinder and Sanders (1996) that Whites' resentment toward African Americans involves value-laden beliefs, such as African Americans thwarting traditional values tied to merit, having questionable Protestant work ethic and self-reliance, using slavery and discrimination as excuses for their lack of success, or taking advantage of undeserved positive outcomes that come at the expense of Whites. But simply holding these beliefs is not enough for racial resentment. Whites must also perceive a threat or actual loss, which can be symbolic or material, and they must also be angered when these beliefs are brought to mind. Thus, at a minimum, racial resentment toward African Americans involves a threat to Whites' status, power, privilege, and value system.

It is the belief in a fundamentally fair system and just world that begins an evaluation of deservingness and a need for restoration. This is why the presence of an injustice based on a lack of deservingness leads to sense of racialized anger: the perceived benefits that African Americans receive are inconsistent with the perceived means by which they are received. As a result, African Americans do not deserve to be rewarded on the basis of race because doing so threatens the values upon which the system operates. This reasoning is consistent with Blumer (1958), and later Bobo (1999), who recognized some time ago that a perceived threat—whether material or sensed—to the racial hierarchy and the system that defends it triggers a need to defend an advantaged group's power position. Subsequent research shows the connection between threat to group position and opposition to ameliorative racial policies (Bobo 1983, 1999; Bobo and Hutchings 1996). Recent scholarship on the consequence of White identity (Jardina 2019) supports this status-threat hypothesis as well, finding that Whites with more racial resentment have higher identity centrality, ostensibly due to concerns about their racial group's status in America's changing demographic landscape. Finally, Kinder and Sears (1981) suggest that Whites' "political response to racial issues is based on moral and symbolic challenges to the racial status quo in society generally rather than on any direct, tangible challenge to their own personal lives" (p. 429). Thus, African Americans and their pressures on the systems that support inequality are perceived as antagonistic to the values and structures that Whites respect and from which they benefit. We expect that individuals who express greater racial resentment seek to insulate the system from unfair demands by African Americans and preserve their dominant-group status, as well as the "just" system that supports it. Importantly, preserving one's dominant group status does not necessarily mean excluding others from joining the group; so long as the values and respect for the system among say African Americans are consistent with the dominant group, the threat will be minimal. Individuals who express lower concerns about race, on the other hand, should not perceive African Americans as threatening to Whites' privilege and status as a dominant group.

Summary

Whites' resentment toward African Americans is a racial sentiment based on system-justifying beliefs (Cassese, Barnes, and Branton 2015; Jost, Glaser, and Krugalski 2003) within which anger over African Americans' use of race, their receiving special considerations, and their unwillingness to adhere to the rules of the status quo violate Whites' sense of justice and fairness. African Americans' receipt of special treatment or considerations is perceived as unjust and unfair, and not only do such perceptions drive Whites' antagonisms toward African Americans, but also they may have associative properties. For example, the resentment toward African Americans produced by justice concerns may spill over to the groups and individuals that aid the positive political outcomes for Blacks. This suggests a racial schema that might include resentment toward the federal government, liberals, and Democrats, who are all ostensibly acting to disrupt, or threaten, the status quo with policies that advance special considerations (e.g., Tyler 2000). We explore expectations like these, and many more, in the forthcoming chapters. For now, we turn to our proposed measure of racial resentment.

A New Measure of Whites' Resentment toward African Americans

In this section, we present the items that assess Whites' resentment toward African Americans and examine the validity and reliability of the items, as well as the composite measure of racial resentment. Although in previous publications we have referred to the scale as "Explicit Racial Resentment" because we sought to make obvious what Whites resented about African Americans (Wilson and Davis 2011), we now arrive at a new name, one that provides more specificity as well as theoretical development.

The empirical work that we have conducted to fully develop our framework for racial resentment has been a ten-year journey. Throughout that period, we've consumed stacks of journal articles, book chapters, and conference papers on the subject, fielded numerous surveys, and presented as frequently as possible in professional and academic settings. We are pleased with the framework birthed from the journey, as it has been about the scientific understanding of racial attitudes. In this way, we are as proud of the journey as we are the destination.

After all is said and done, our new measure correlates highly with the classic measure of racial resentment, and other racial attitudes more generally. It was never our claim that the classic measure was unhelpful or useless, or that aspects were unserviceable, just that ours exhibits stronger validity and reliability and is grounded in the same framework it proposes to measure. The classic measure possesses overlapping content, namely agreement that Blacks should not "receive special consideration" or "more than they deserve," which taps into aspects of justice and deservingness. But in our measure, there is no requirement that such content must indicate racism or prejudice, which is where our journey departs from the classic conceptualization. Therefore, expecting independence among items measuring racial attitudes presents too narrow a view of survey methodology and scaling that precludes alternative ways of operationalizing and measuring key concepts.

Despite similarities with classic racial resentment, our conceptualization of racial resentment is grounded in a different theory of resentment, one based on just-world beliefs and deservingness criteria, as opposed to symbolic racism or prejudice, and more specifically the presence of anti-black affect. We appreciate that respondents can arrive at the same conclusions using our items as they do with the classic racial resentment items.

We began with the assumption that any measure of racial resentment must go beyond merely stating how people feel about a racial-ethnic group and should clearly identify the basis of the annoyance (Wilson and Davis 2011). Building off theories of justice and deservingness discussed earlier, we began to experiment with various survey items in 2007. Like many survey scales that came before ours, the items are assertions or statements—not questions—that respondents have to think about and determine the extent to which they agree with them. The studies we used to test our items contained different samples (i.e., convenience, state, and national) that were collected at different times (i.e., between 2007 and 2018) and across different modes (e.g., in-person phone, face-to-face, self-administered). As our intent was not to assume that we had discovered a perfect or conclusive scale, we intentionally altered items and wordings to assess the robustness of the content. As a result, the specific items and sometimes the wording in the scale vary from year to year, and from study to study. In this way, we were able to understand better the relevant dimensions of racial resentment, especially the ways in which the assertions capture nuances in the legitimizing beliefs that might invoke emotion. The wordings for the items are listed in table 3.1.

TABLE 3.1. **Survey Questions Used to Measure Whites' Resentment toward African Americans**

I. Whites Losing Out

1. I resent all of the special attention/favors that African Americans receive, other Americans like me have problems too. (MURAP; CCAP; UALR)
2. How concerned are you that the special privileges for African Americans place you at an unfair disadvantage when you have done nothing to harm them? (MURAP; UALR)
3. The special privileges for African Americans place me at an unfair disadvantage when I have done nothing to harm them. (CCAP)
4. What upsets me most about some successful African Americans is that they had advantages and opportunities I did not have. (CCES10; CATH)
5. Special considerations for African Americans place me at an unfair disadvantage because I have done nothing to harm them. (CCES10; CCES12a; CCES12b; CPC; CCES16a; CCES16b; CATH)
6. If had the advantages that African Americans have today, I would be much better off. (CCES10; CATH)
7. I resent any special considerations that Africans Americans receive because it's unfair to other Americans. (CCES10; CCES12a; CCES12b; CCES16a; CCES16b; GSS; CPC; CATH)
8. I don't understand why race is any different from what other people have to deal with. (CCES10; CCES 18; CATH)
9. Racial discrimination is no different from other everyday problems people have to deal with. (CCES12a; CCES12b; CCES18)
10. African Americans bring up race only when they need to make an excuse for their failure. (CCES10; CCES12a; CCES12b; CPC; CCES16a; CCES16b; CATH)

II. African Americans Exploiting Race

11. For African Americans to succeed they need to stop using racism as an excuse. (MURAP; CCAP; CCES10)
12. For African Americans to succeed they need to stop using racism and slavery as excuses. (GSS; UALR; CATH)
13. For African Americans to succeed they need to stop using past racism and slavery as excuses. (CCES12a; CCES12b; CCES16a; CCES16b)

III. System Support for Special Considerations

14. African Americans should not need any special privileges when slavery and racism are things of the past. (MURAP; CCAP; UALR)
15. African Americans do not need any special consideration because racism is a thing of the past. (CCES10; GSS; CATH)

Note. MURAP = 2008 Multi-University Racial Attitudes Project; CCAP = 2009 Cooperative Campaign Analysis Project; CCES(YR) = Cooperative Congressional Election Study (CCES). Within the CCES years, the letter "a" denotes Team A module, and the letter "b" denotes Team B module; GSS = 2010 General Social Survey; CPC = 2010 Center for Political Communication; UALR = 2011 Racial Attitudes Survey of Pulaski County; CATH = 2011 National Black Catholic Survey.

Readers should note that in several items we explicitly mention the words "resent" and "special" considerations or privileges. These instances help to make an obvious connection between the source of the resentful feelings and race, or between resentment and African Americans as an undeserving group. In addition, we undertook changes in item-wording that adhered to several primary dimensions we thought were critical to racial resentment, such as a belief that special considerations due to race are unfair, that African Americans are not deserving of special consideration or treatment, that African Americans use race to their advantage, that race is an improper explanation for shortcomings, and that special racial considerations place Whites at a disadvantage. We consciously avoided the contamination of other highly correlated constructs, such as racial prejudice or antipathy, perceptions of government, conservatism, and a justice motive, which is a separate concept and deserving of its own measure.

An important ingredient in Whites' resentment toward African Americans is a belief that African Americans are exploiting race to gain an advantage that ends up costing Whites. Many of the items involved in our experimentation in table 3.1 touched heavily upon this sentiment in the form of perceived excuses. We argue that this matters for Whites because such perceptions violate the rules of the game that protect their opportunities to succeed. African Americans are not necessarily seen as passive, but they are perceived as making illegitimate and unjustifiable claims based on race.

Another important set of beliefs that underlie Whites' resentment toward African Americans is the perception that race is a special consideration primarily for African Americans or that they receive some form of benefit because of it even when they are not explicitly mentioned in a policy or program. This is conveyed through deeply held perceptions that African Americans are being given privileges and special considerations because of slavery and racism. In our view, these items capture pressures on the status quo and the political system that rewards African Americans more than they capture how African Americans benefit from the system.

The last dimension of Whites' resentment toward African Americans we sought to capture is Whites' perception that they are being penalized because of special considerations for African Americans or that they are losing out to African Americans. This was conveyed through the sentiment that special considerations regarding race placed them at an unfair disadvantage.

Many of the item-wording trials were included in collaborative surveys like the CCES, which allows teams of researchers to propose questions and take advantage of common content. Several surveys were original surveys pertaining to a variety of content, such as the National Black Catholic Survey. In a few surveys, such as the GSS, we were limited to a subset of our items. As indicated by the assessments reported in table 3.2, the Likert formatted items result in a valid and reliable scale.

TABLE 3.2. **Summary of Whites' Resentment toward African Americans and No. of Items Included in Various Data Sets**

Title	Alpha	M (SD)	EFA λ (Pct σ2)	N	Sample
2007 Univ. of Delaware Student Data – (4 Items)	.752	.53 (.20)	1.76 (44%)	520	UD Student Sample (CAPI)
2008 CCAP (Wave 1) – (4 Items)	.894	.66 (.25)	2.75 (68%)	556	Knowledge Networks Panel (CASI)
2008 CCAP (Wave 2) – (4 Items)	.908	.68 (.25)	2.86 (71%)	546	Knowledge Networks Panel (CASI)
2010 CCES (Pre-Election) – (8 Items)	.911	.60 (.23)	5.30 (67%)	966	YouGov Panel (CASI)
2010 GSS – (3 Items)	.751	.62 (.24)	1.54 (51%)	1160	US Adults (CAPI)
2011 Religion & Politics Study – (8 Items)	.904	.55 (.20)	5.30 (66%)	1070	Knowledge Networks Panel (CASI)
2011 Univ. of Arkansas Little Rock Study – (3 Items)	.715	.62 (.26)	1.39 (46%)	772	Arkansas Adults (Pulaski County) (CATI)
2012 CPC – (3 Items)	.795	.44 (.30)	1.70 (56%)	580	US Adults (CATI)
2012 CCES – Team A (Pre-Election) – (5 Items)	.874	.61 (.24)	2.98 (59%)	532	YouGov Panel (CASI)
2012 CCES – Team A (Post-Election) – (5 Items)	.900	.62 (.26)	3.27 (65%)	358	YouGov Panel (CASI)
2012 CCES – Team B (Pre-Election) – (5 Items)	.909	.61 (.26)	3.38 (67%)	1092	YouGov Panel (CASI)
2012 CCES – Team B (Post-Election) – (5 Items)	.910	.60 (.27)	3.40 (68%)	332	YouGov Panel (CASI)
2016 CCES (Pre-Election) – (4 Items)	.922	.62 (.30)	3.00 (75%)	1077	YouGov Panel (CASI)
2018 CCES (Pre-Election) – (6 Items)	.938	.51 (.31)	4.30 (72%)	743	YouGov Panel (CASI)
Averages	.863	.59 (.26)			

Note. All sample statistics are based on unweighted data for White adult (18+ years) respondents. CAPI=Computer assisted personal interview; CASI=Computer assisted self-interview; CATI=computer assisted telephone interview. Team A=Wilson and Davis; Team B=Center for Political Communication. Alpha = Cronbach's alpha statistics; M = mean, SD = standard deviation; Scale = number of responses for the items in the scale; EFA = Principal Axis Exploratory Factor Analysis; λ = eigenvalue for the set of items, Pct σ2 = Percentage of variance in items explained by the scale.

The far left of table 3.2 provides Cronbach's alpha statistics; descriptive information like the mean (M), standard deviation (SD), and sample size (N); and survey design details, such as the number of items in the scale, response scale categories, and mode of data collection for each study. The mean "Whites' resentment toward African Americans" scores range from .44 (2012 CPC) to .68 (2008 CCAP-Wave 2) with an average score of .59, and the variability (SD) statistics range from .20 (e.g., 2008 student sample, and the 2011 Catholics study) to .31 (e.g., 2018 CCES) with an average SD of .26.

The Cronbach's alpha statistics in the table serve as a standard measure of the internal consistency of a scale, and its values range from 0 to 1 (Cronbach 1951). Internal consistency describes whether several items that propose to measure the same general construct produce similar scores (Furr and Bacharach 2014). The acceptable values for internal consistency are those alpha statistics equal to .70 or higher. The alpha statistics for our measures are consistently strong (above .70), ranging from .715 (2011 Arkansas state sample) to .938 (2018 CCES) with an average reliability of .863. In the more recent years, upon which our forthcoming analyses are strongly based, the reliability coefficients are .94 in the 2018 CCES, .92 in the 2016 CCES, and .87 and .91 in the 2012 CCES team A and team B studies respectively. Based on this reliability statistic alone, we are confident in the coherence of our racial resentment scale, but we wanted to go further to assess validity.

Table 3.2 also contains results from principal axis exploratory factor analysis (EFA), which produced assessment measures like component eigenvalues (λ) and the percentage of variance ("Pct σ^2"). The EFA results indicate the scale is also marked by good validity. EFA procedures explore the possible underlying factor structure of a set of observed variables without imposing a preconceived structure on the outcome (Child 2006). The technique hypothesizes that there are a typical number of common latent factors to be discovered in the data set and enables researchers to find the smallest number of common factors that will account for the correlations among a set of items. EFA then analyzes the variances among the items to produce commonalities between variables, and the commonality is the variance in the observed variables that are accounted for by a common factor (Child 2006; Yong and Pearce 2013). Generally, the percentage variance tells us how much each factor contributed to the total variance. The acceptable variance explained in the EFA for a construct to be valid is 60 percent or above (Hair et al. 2012). We meet this criterion in nine out of fourteen studies and in nearly every study with a national sample—those that do not meet the criterion are based on student samples or those with a smaller complement of items than our four core measures. The variance-explained metrics range from 44 percent (University of Delaware Student Sample) to 75 percent (2016 CCES) of the variance in the items.

Table 3.2 also shows the variation in the modes of data collection (e.g., phone, in-person, computer-assisted self-administered), the different sampling frames (e.g., state, national, convenience), and the number of items composing each scale.

Over time, our analyses have revealed that four items do an exceptional job of capturing racial resentment, and thus we have selected them as a core measure. Feedback from conferences, invited lectures, and manuscripts on this topic figured prominently in our assessment of face validity and in the selection of the items. The following four items constitute our core measure of Whites' resentment toward African Americans (WRTA):

African Americans do not need any special considerations because racism is a thing of the past.

For African Americans to succeed they need to stop using past racism and slavery as excuses.

Special considerations for African Americans place me at an unfair disadvantage because I have done nothing to harm them.

African Americans bring up race only when they need to make an excuse for their failure.

These are the recommended items for scholars seeking to utilize the racial resentment scale. Together, the items have excellent psychometric properties and predict a host of political behaviors and issue positions.

Now that we have identified a set of items that best capture racial resentment toward African Americans, our next task is to assess their coherence. We expect our racial resentment scale to be characterized by strong validity and reliability, and to have strong associations with other known correlates of system-justifying beliefs.

Is the Scale Different from Prior Scales?

The 2016 CCES included new racism measures like McConahay's (1986) modern racism scale (MRS) and the classic measure of racial resentment (RRS). One difficulty in asserting that our Whites' resentment toward African Americans measure is different from other racial attitudes measures is that they are all correlated. This is expected since most questions pertaining to race tend to identify a specific group and place the group in a negative evaluative condition by referring to their shortcomings (e.g., stereotypes), lower status (e.g., racial inequality), or interpersonal transactions (e.g., amounts of discrimination they face), which all tend to be highly correlated. Thus, many respondents evaluate survey items about race with little regard for the item's substance because they already understand that race is polarizing. That is, race is an "easy issue" for most people driven by low information, political symbols, and identity shortcuts (Carmines and Stimson 1980).

People who are averse or ambivalent to issues of race or appraisals of African Americans will often express their feelings regardless of the substantive content of the question. This response tendency has the effect of bolstering their correlation. The time-pressured and content-diverse nature of surveys makes it difficult to capture small nuances between questions, which necessitates more sophisticated methodologies. If our measure of racial resentment is synonymous with any other racial attitudinal measures, we believe that modern racism and classic racial resentment would arguably be the most difficult test of validity to overcome. Thus, in addition to its own scaling properties, we examine the extent to which racial resentment is different from the measures of modern racism and classic racial resentment.

To do so, we ran a series of analyses on the 2016 CCES to assess the extent to which the scales have discriminating qualities. The question wordings for the scales are presented in table 3.3. The three scales were located in different parts of the 2016 CCES questionnaire, and all responses were collected on a 5-point agree-disagree scale with final scores rescaled to range from 0 to 1, and higher values indicating a higher level of the construct.

We first analyzed each scale independently from one another. Our results reveal that the three scales are indeed highly correlated—intraclass correlation (ICC) is .914 (95% CI [.91, .92])—but appear to be measuring different aspects of racial attitudes. For instance, the mean values are not equivalent (Hotellings T^2 [2, 1048]=1325.6), nor are the scales' reliability statistics or measurement properties. Table 3.4 shows that respondents scored highest on our measure of racial resentment (WRTA) (M=.62), then RRS (M=.57), and lowest on MRS (M=.41). The 95 percent confidence intervals for the scores do not overlap, indicating statistical differences. Table 3.4 also contains the Cronbach alpha statistics for each of the scales, along with their 95 percent confidence interval values (Feldt,

TABLE 3.3. **Question Wording for Whites' Racial Attitudes Scales–2016 CCES**

White Racial Resentment toward African Americans (WRTA)

UNFAIR	I resent any special considerations that Africans Americans receive because it's unfair to other Americans (WRTA1)
STOP	For African Americans to succeed they need to stop using past racism and slavery as excuses (WRTA2)
DISADVANTAGE	Special considerations for African Americans place me at an unfair disadvantage because I have done nothing to harm them (WRTA3)
EXCUSE	African Americans bring up race only when they need to make an excuse for their failure (WRTA4)

Modern Racism Scale (MRS)

DISCRIMINATION	Discrimination against African Americans is no longer a problem in the United States (MRS1)
UNDERSTAND_r	It is easy to understand the anger of African Americans (MRS2)
DEMANDING	African Americans are too demanding in their push for equal rights (MRS3)
PUSH	African Americans should not push themselves where they are not wanted (MRS4)
DESERVE	Over the past few years, African Americans have gotten more economically than they deserve (MRS5)

Classic Racial Resentment Scale (RRS)

OVERCOME	Other minorities overcame prejudice and worked their way up. African Americans should do the same (RRS1)
DIFFICULT_r	Generations of slavery and discrimination created conditions that make it difficult for African Americans to work out of lower class (RRS2)
DESERVE_r	Over the past few years, African Americans have gotten less than they deserve (RRS3)
HARDER	It's really a matter of some people not trying hard enough; if African Americans would only try harder they could be just as well off (RRS4)

Note. All items have 5-point strongly agree to strongly disagree response categories. "_r" = reverse coded.

Woodruff, and Salih 1987). Statistical tests (Diedenhofen and Musch 2016) comparing the Cronbach alpha values indicate that our racial resentment scale (WRTA) has significantly higher reliability than both the MRS (χ^2 [df=1]=51.8, p<.01) and RRS (χ^2 [df=1]=62.6, p<.01), with the latter two scales having statistically similar reliability (χ^2 [df=1]=0.81, p=.37).

The far right side of table 3.4 contains results from CFA models for each scale. CFAs offer a more rigorous assessment of a scale's validity by testing a specific hypothesis about how the items correlate (Suhr 2006). The corresponding fit statistics evidence whether the observed and theorized data structures match. We evaluate the Comparative Fit Index (CFI; >.90 acceptable, >.95 excellent; Bentler 1990) and Root Mean Square error of approximation (RMSEA; <.08 acceptable, <.05 excellent; Brown and Cudeck 1993). Our CFA results show stronger,

TABLE 3.4. **CFA Scale Descriptive and Measurement Statistics—2016 CCES**

Scale	Descriptive Statistics			Measurement Statistics		
	M [95% CI]	SD	N	α [95% CI]	CFI	RMSEA
White Resentment toward African Americans (WRTA)	.62 [.60, .63]	.30	1,077	.92 [.91, .93]	1.00	.06
Modern Racism (MRS)	.41 [.40, .43]	.23	1,071	.86 [.84, .87]	.97	.12
Classic Racial Resentment (RRS)	.57 [.55, .58]	.25	1,077	.85 [.83, .86]	.92	.28

Note. CFI, Comparative Fit Index; RMSEA, Root Mean Square Error of Approximation.

as well as more acceptable, fit for the racial resentment scale (CFI= 1.00 / RMSEA=.06) than the MRS (CFI=.97 / RMSEA=.12) and RRS (CFI=.92 / RMSEA=.28) scales. In fact, the racial resentment scale is the only scale among the three to show acceptability for both fit measures.

We further compared our Whites' resentment measure to the modern racism and classic racial resentment measures with a simultaneous CFA. This allowed us to assess the hypothesized structure for all three measures at once. The models are illustrated in figure 3.1.

The top section of figure 3.1 shows the set-up of the CFA models with the underlying traits predicting response levels for the observed variables. The unidirectional arrows indicate the direction of the effect, curved bi-directional arrows indicate a correlation, circles represent unobserved variables (e.g., underlying traits and unexplained errors), and the rectangular shapes indicate observed variables in the data. The CFA produces fit indices that indicate how well the hypothesized interrelationships shown in the visual models at the top of figure 3.1 match the actual relationships in the 2016 CCES data. The bottom section of figure 3.1 shows a table with five fit measures, including the CFI and RMSEA, but we have also included the normed fit index (NFI), relative fit index (RFI), and Chi-squared statistic for a more full assessment of the models. These indices tell us which model best explains our data, and the criteria for acceptability are a non-significant (p > .05) Chi-squared ($\chi2$) statistic; CFI, NFI, and RFI fit indices of > .95, > .90, and > .90 respectively; and a RMSEA < .08 (Tabachnick, Fidell, and Ullman 2007).

In model 1, we hypothesize that a single factor structure provides a best fit for the data, or in other words that all the items measure the same latent construct. Our analysis does not support this conclusion. The

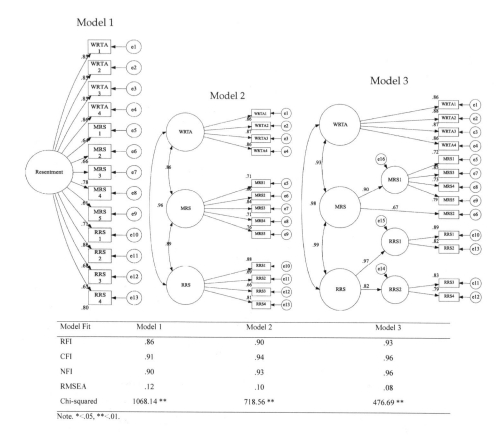

FIGURE 3.1. Confirmatory Factor Models

three scales do not form a singular dimension of resentment (or whatever it might capture), and the goodness-of-fit indices, such as RFI, CFI, RMSEA, and Chi-square, all fall below acceptable levels. In addition, the factor loadings show a great deal of variability suggesting that resentment predicts some items better than others. Thus, there is no basis for the suggestion that the differences between RRS, MRS, and racial resentment are minor, even if the items are correlated.

In model 2, we hypothesize that the items measure three distinct factors, and that this is the best fitting model for the data. The results of this model indicate an improvement in fit compared to the previous model, though there is some cause for concern. For instance, the RFI and NFI measures surpass the acceptable threshold, but the CFI, RMSEA, and

Chi-squared statistics do not. An important takeaway from this model is that there are at least three individual latent constructs in the data.

Model 3 builds off model 2 in that we hypothesize multiple dimension structures for modern racism and classic racial resentment based on factor loadings from model 2, though we continue to represent the racial resentment measure as a single-dimension construct. Model 3 maintained the correlations among the latent traits, but also created separate dimensions within the modern racism and classic racial resentment scales where the factor loadings for model 2 were less than .80. Since the loadings for our racial resentment measure had no lower loadings, we did not alter its structure. We created two secondary dimensions for the modern racism measure, one with a single item (MRS2: *It is easy to understand the anger of African Americans*) serving as its own dimension, and the remaining items serving as a second dimension. We also divided the classic racial resentment measures into two dimensions, with RRS1 (*African Americans should work their way up*) and RRS2 (*Conditions make it difficult for African Americans*) as one dimension, and RR3 (*African Americans have gotten less than they deserve*) and RRS4 (*African Americans should try harder*), as a second dimension. The model asks whether relaxing the single-dimension assumptions about the MRS and RRS measures will improve how well the model explains what is in the data, thereby improving the fit. With these modifications, model 3 provides the best-fitting model; all fit statistics, except for the sample sensitive Chi-square statistic, surpass the thresholds for good fit.

Taken together, there are two important conclusions based on our CFA. First and foremost, our racial resentment measure stands as the only unidimensional trait among the three scales. The factor loadings for the racial resentment items hardly changed as we modified the models, and when considered with the independent model results (table 3.4), the final combined CFA model bolsters our confidence in the validity of our racial resentment measure. Second, while our Whites' resentment measure is correlated with both modern racism ($r=.93$) and classic racial resentment ($r=.98$) measures, they are clearly not measuring the same dimension of racial attitudes. Our CFA results suggest that the racial resentment measure cannot be seen as another version of the modern racism scale or classic racial resentment.

Even with these strong results, we took one final step to understand the properties of our items, employing an Andrich rating scale Rasch modeling technique designed for polytomous responses (Andrich 1978).

Rasch models (Rasch 1960) measure latent traits underlying a set of items. They show the probability of an individual getting a correct response on a test item. In the case of our items, a correct response is a more resentful response. Rasch modeling produces a comprehensive picture of the association between observed item responses to scale items and an individual's overall levels on a latent variable. We have three main areas of interest for our Rasch models: item difficulty, scale reliability, and scale separation.

In Rasch modeling, the statistical difficulty of an item represents the point on the latent variable at which the highest and lowest categories of response for an item have an equal probability of being observed. When applied to survey-rating scale data, the Rasch approach considers that a person endorsing a more difficult statement should also endorse all less difficult statements, and an easy-to-endorse item is always expected to be rated higher by any respondent (Wright and Masters 1982). With regard to our racial resentment measure, for example, easier questions require less resentment to endorse than difficult questions. The difficulty of an item relative to others assists researchers in determining whether an item adequately contributes to the variability in an overall scale. In a given sample, items that are too easy—having extremely high item means—or too difficult—having extremely low item means—to endorse are likely to have low variability, and thus contribute very little to correlations necessary for acceptable validity and reliability.

The item difficulty score (IDS) measures the extent to which an item aligns with its latent construct—the extent to which an item was harder or easier to agree with. The Rasch analysis reports item difficulty estimates with a logit (log odds unit) scale. IDS scores can range from negative (lower) to positive (higher), with higher values indicating more difficulty for respondents. More specifically, a lower IDS means that respondents do not need much of the trait (e.g., resentment) to endorse the item, because it is easy to endorse; and a higher IDS means that respondents need a higher level of the trait to endorse the item. Table 3.5 provides the item difficulty measures for each of the scale's items. The scores should be balanced with roughly equal proportions of low and high IDS scores.

The Rasch polytomous model results show good measurement quality for our racial resentment measure and the modern racism scale, but only moderate quality for classic racial resentment. Racial resentment and the modern racism scale have good balance with their difficulty

TABLE 3.5. **Rasch Model Item Difficulty, Reliability, and Separation Statistics**

Item	IDS	Person		Item	
		Reliability	Separation	Reliability	Separation
Racial Resentment		.89	2.85	.99	11.26
UNFAIR	.29				
STOP	−.88				
DISADVANTAGE	−.15				
EXCUSE	.74				
Modern Racism		.81	2.06	.98	7.58
DISCRIMINATION	.34				
UNDERSTAND_r	−.29				
DEMANDING	−.47				
PUSH	.30				
DESERVE	.12				
Classic Racial Resentment		.80	1.99	.99	10.83
OVERCOME	−.73				
DIFFICULT_r	.36				
DESERVE_r	.07				
HARDER	.29				

Note. Rasch models were estimated using the Ministep Rasch model computer program. IDS, item difficulty score.

scores, but classic racial resentment has one item that is very easy to endorse and the others are more difficult. For the racial resentment items, EXCUSE (*Bring up race only as an excuse for failure*) is the most difficult item to endorse and STOP (*Stop using past racism and slavery as excuses*) is the easiest item to endorse. Interestingly enough, the content for both items is "excuses." Whites find it easier to agree that African Americans should not use excuses, but find it more difficult to agree that the group only bring up race to excuse their failures. For the modern racism items, the most difficult item to endorse is DISCRIMINA-TION (*Discrimination . . . no longer a problem*) and the easiest item is DEMANDING (*African Americans are too demanding in their push for equal rights*). Among the RRS items, the most difficult to endorse is DIFFICULT_r (*Slavery and discrimination . . . make it difficult for African Americans to work out of lower class*) and the easiest to endorse is OVERCOME (*Other minorities overcame prejudice and worked their way up. African Americans should do the same*).

The Rasch model also produces scale reliability and separation indices for respondents and the items. Person separation indices reveal how well a set of items separates those who were measured on a trait, while item separation indices reveal how well a sample of respondents explains the validity of the items (Wright and Stone 1999). Low person separation (< 2) and person reliability < 0.80) suggests that the scale may not be not sensitive enough to distinguish between those with less and more negative racial attitudes, sometimes indicating that more items may be needed. The racial resentment scale has higher person reliability and separation than the modern racism scale and classic racial resentment. The classic racial resentment's person separation is below the acceptability range, and its person reliability is at the boundary of the reliability threshold. Low item separation (< 3) and item reliability (< 0.90) implies that the sample is not large enough to confirm the item difficulty hierarchy of the instrument. The item reliability and separation scores for all of the measures are above the threshold of acceptability.

To summarize the Rasch model results, our racial resentment measure outperforms, or is as good as, the modern racism scale and classic racial resentment. The racial resentment items have good discrimination properties, reliability, and separation.

Reliability of Whites' Resentment toward African Americans Scale

The overwhelming conclusion from the validity tests indicates that the Whites' Resentment toward African Americans measure is valid and coherent, more so than the classic racial resentment and modern racism measures. Another useful indicator of measurement quality is reliability—the extent to which individuals respond to survey items consistently over time. We turn to the 2012 CCES to take advantage of the pre-election and post-election panels in which the same individuals were interviewed twice at different points in time. We participated on different research teams (indicated as team A and team B), though we used the same racial resentment items in each study. For the team A study, only a random half of the sample received the items, in each of the waves. For the team B study, the full sample received the racial resentment items in the pre-election wave, but only a sub-sample of respondents received the items in the post-election study.

The results reported in table 3.6 reveal a great deal of consistency and stability for the items across T1-T2 waves. The T1-T2 differences in the item means are slight, ranging from .03 to .04, and .00 to .03, in the team A and team B studies respectively. This indicates that the level of racial resentment reflected in the item was not substantially affected by the events of 2012 between the data collection periods (e.g.,

TABLE 3.6. **Analysis of Whites' Resentment toward African Americans Items Pre- and Post-2012 Election**

Panel I. Team A

Racial Resentment Items	Pre-election		Post-election		Item Correlation T1-T2
	M	SD	M	SD	r_{t1-t2}
UNFAIR	.62	.29	.66	.28	.71** (N=169)
STOP	.71	.26	.74	.26	.71** (N=169)
DISADVANTAGE	.62	.31	.65	.29	.67** (N=169)
EXCUSE	.56	.30	.59	.31	.76** (N=169)
Overall WRTA Scale	.62	.25	.66	.25	.80** (N=163)

Panel II. Team B

Racial Resentment Items	Pre-election		Post-election		Item Correlation T1-T2
	M	SD	M	SD	r_{t1-t2}
UNFAIR	.60	.32	.61	.32	.70** (N=334)
STOP	.70	.30	.71	.30	.67** (N=335)
DISADVANTAGE	.62	.32	.62	.32	.66 ** (N=332)
EXCUSE	.55	.32	.58	.33	.66** (N=332)
Overall WTRA Scale	.62	.28	.63	.28	.75** (N=328)

Note. *p<.05, **p<.01. UNFAIR: *I resent any special considerations that Africans Americans receive because it's unfair to other Americans*; STOP: *For African Americans to succeed they need to stop using past racism and slavery as excuses*; DISADVANTAGE: *Special considerations for African Americans place me at an unfair disadvantage because I have done nothing to harm them*; EXCUSE: *African Americans bring up race only when they need to make an excuse for their failure.* The "Overall WTRA Scale" is the mean of a 4 item composite scale calculated for each respondent.

the presidential election contest between Barack Obama and Mitt Romney). In total, the T1-T2 item correlations for both studies range from .66 to .71, and the correlations between the racial resentment scales are .85 and .75 for the team A and team B studies respectively. Thus, the 2012 CCES data indicate that at least 43.5 (r=.66) to 57.8 (r=.76) percent of the variance in T2 item response can be explained by the T1 item response. For the overall racial resentment scale, the T1 variance explain between 56.2 (r=.75) and 72.2 (r=.85) percent of responses in T2. These high correlations evidence the consistency in response and interpretation from the items, even with meaningful events occurring in between. Most certainly, our racial resentment measure captures a meaningful sentiment, one that is theoretically sound and empirically robust.

Construct Validity

The more a scale shows an empirical relationship with known correlates of the theory that underlies it, the more the scale is said to have
construct validity. Our theory of Whites' racial resentment is grounded
in the idea that racial considerations, including those that are special
in the form of offering merit or status, threaten the status quo of social position that Whites hold in society. These threats produce uncertainty about the future, and ultimately the way of life, for a dominant
group. System justification and uncertainty avoidance theories (Jost
2020) hypothesize that system-dominant groups, and their members,
are motivated to defend the existing social system against instability,
threat, and attack, prompting more conservative views (Jost, Burgess,
and Mosso 2001) and support for authoritarian leaders and institutions
and for stricter rules that can offer more security, stability, and structure (e.g., Altemeyer 1981). Importantly, this fear of change and preference for closed systems can exceed preferences for, and actions in
support of, equality (e.g., Johnston, Lavine, and Federico 2017). Thus,
holding racially resentful views toward racial minorities hinders racial
progress and defends inequality. As a result, we expect that our racial
resentment will be correlated with preference for the status quo (versus
social change), support for inequality via social dominance orientation
(SDO), support for strict leadership due to uncertainty, and less egalitarian positions. We use data from several CCES studies to examine
these relationships.

We first examined the correlations between status quo threat and
racial resentment. In the 2012 (team B) and 2016 CCES interviews,
we measured perceived status quo threat by the level of support—on a
5-point scale—for the following assertions: "The American way of life
is under attack," "Things are really out of control in the United States,"
"The United States of the past is a much better place than the United
States of the future," and "The United States is changing too fast." The
items were examined individually and were also combined to form a
composite scale (alpha=.863); higher values indicate greater perceptions
of threat. The results are presented in table 3.7.

Across both studies racial resentment correlated with status quo
threat in the expected directions. Increases in racial resentment are associated strongly with increased levels of perceived threat. Notably,
among the items, racial resentment is most strongly correlated with the

TABLE 3.7. **Correlates of Whites' Resentment toward African Americans—Beliefs Signaling Threats to the Status Quo**

	2012 CCES (Team B)		2016 CCES	
	r	N	r	N
Pre-Election: Status Quo Threat				
SQT1. The American way of life is under attack.	.57**	1,088	.64**	1,072
SQT2. Things are really out of control in the United States	.45**	1,092	.52**	1,071
SQT3. The United States of the past is a much better place than the United States of the future.	.48**	1,088	.61**	1,070
SQT4. The United States is changing too fast.	.42**	1,091	.51**	1,072
Status Quo Threat Scale	.56**	1,084	.67**	1,075
Post-Election: Status Quo Threat				
SQT1. The American way of life is under attack.	.62**	714		
SQT2. Things are really out of control in the United States.	.56**	716		
SQT3. The United States of the past is a much better place than the United States of the future.	.56**	716		
SQT4. The United States is changing too fast.	.54**	714		
Status Quo Threat Scale	.64**	712		

Note. *p<.05, **p<.01.

assertion that "the American way of life is under attack," signaling that our scale is very sensitive to the perceived threats to civic and social culture.

Next, we examined the empirical relationship between Whites' resentment toward African Americans, and egalitarianism and support for authoritarianism. We collected measures of egalitarianism and authoritarianism in the 2012 CCES (team A) study. We determined levels of egalitarianism with support for the following items: "The United States would be better off if we cared less about how equal all people were," "In America, some people are just more deserving of success than others," "If people were treated more equally we would have fewer problems in America" (reverse coded), and "It is probably a good thing that in America certain groups are at the top and other groups are at the bottom." For authoritarianism, we gauged support for the following items: "To compromise with our political opponents is dangerous because it usually leads to the betrayal of our own side," "In the long run the best way to live is to pick friends and associates whose tastes and beliefs are the same as one's own," "In this complicated world of ours the only way we can know what's going on is to rely on leaders or experts who can be trusted," and "There are a number of people in this world who I have come to hate because of the things they stand for." Again,

TABLE 3.8. **Correlates of Whites' Resentment toward African Americans—Beliefs about Equality, Authority, and Social Desirability Norms**

2012 CCES (Team A) Views on Equality	r	N
Egal1. The United States would be better off if we cared less about how equal all people were.	−.44**	534
Egal2. In American, some people are just more deserving of success than others.	−.30**	535
Egal3. If people were treated more equally we would have fewer problems in America.	−.35**	535
Egal4. It is probably a good thing that in America certain groups are at the top and other groups are at the bottom.	−.33**	533
Egalitarianism Scale	−.47**	532
Support for Authority		
Auth1. To compromise with our political opponents is dangerous because it usually leads to the betrayal of our own side.	.33**	535
Auth2. In the long run the best way to live is to pick friends and associates whose tastes and beliefs are the same as one's own.	.30**	534
Auth3. In this complicated world of ours the only way we can know what's going on is to rely on leaders or experts who can be trusted.	.01	535
Auth4. There are a number of people in this world who I have come to hate because of the things they stand for.	.19**	535
Authoritarianism Scale	.33**	534

Note. *p<.05, **p<.01

higher values for the items and the composite scales indicate greater support for equality (alpha=.723) and authority (alpha=.444). The results of our analysis are in table 3.8.

    The correlation statistics in the table show that increases in Whites' resentment toward African Americans are associated with lower support for equality and greater support for authority, although the findings on the latter are not as strong as those for the former. All of the egalitarianism items were negatively associated with racial resentment, with the strongest association coming with agreement that, "The United States would be better off if we cared less about how equal all people were." This provides evidence of our scale's sensitivity to preferences for inequality. For the most part, the correlations with the authoritarianism items support good construct validity, although the totality of relationships were not as clear-cut as the egalitarianism items. Three of the four authoritarianism items were positively associated with racial resentment, and the strongest relationship occurred with agreement with the statement: "To compromise with our political opponents is dangerous because it usually leads to the betrayal of our own side." This item speaks directly to the idea of a competitive "us and them" and the dangers of compromise, perhaps suggesting that support for racial equality is a betrayal and that any known corroborators of racial equality (e.g., liberals, Democrats, African Americans) are political opponents, or enemies. We also found that the authoritarian item concerning the need to "rely on experts who can be trusted" as the only way to know what's going on did not resonate with racial resentment. Additional analysis of the relationship shows that those who agree or strongly agree with the statement have roughly the same statistical mean racial resentment scores (M=.64, SD=.25) as those who disagree or strongly disagree (M=.63, SD=.27). Thus, levels of Whites' resentment toward African Americans are unmoved by this component of authoritarian views.

Finally, we assessed the relationship between social dominance orientation (SDO) and Whites' resentment toward African Americans, but took a somewhat novel approach. We randomized two different versions of the traditional SDO scale to respondents, one that makes reference to equality for people in general (e.g., "everyone" or "people"), and another that references "racial groups." For example, one general item read, "Our society should do whatever is necessary to make sure that [everyone] has an equal opportunity to succeed," while a racialized version read, "Our society should do whatever is necessary to make sure that [racial groups] have an equal opportunity to succeed." In another example, the general SDO item asserted, "This country would be better off if we worried less about how equal [people] are," while the racialized version read, "This country would be better off if we worried less about how equal [racial groups] are." The point of the randomization was to assess the extent to which the racial resentment scale was sensitive to group dominance relative to racial group dominance. We expected the racialized SDO items and their composite scale (alpha=.882) to have stronger correlations with the racial resentment scale than the general SDO items and its composite scale (alpha=.878). The remaining question wordings for the items, and results of our analysis, are presented in table 3.9.

With nearly every item, we find that the correlations between the racialized SDO items and the Whites' resentment toward African Americans scores were statistically stronger in magnitude than those for the general SDO items. The rightmost column in table 3.9 provides the z-test

TABLE 3.9 **Correlates of Whites' Racial Resentment toward African Americans and Social Dominance Orientation (SDO)**

2016 CCES Post-Election Data	General SDO		Racial SDO		Difference
	r	N	r	N	z-test
SD1r. Our society should do whatever is necessary to make sure that **[everyone vs. racial groups]** has an equal opportunity to succeed. (Rev.)	.42**	372	.55**	362	2.26**
SD2. We have gone too far in pushing equal rights **[for racial groups]** in this country.	.60**	371	.73**	362	3.21**
SD3r. One of the big problems in this country is that we don't give **[everyone vs. racial groups]** an equal chance. (Rev.)	.54**	372	.74**	362	4.60**
SD4. This country would be better off if we worried less about how equal **[people vs. racial groups]** are.	.63**	372	.72**	362	2.16**
SD5. It is not really that big a problem if some **[people vs. racial groups]** have more of a chance in life than others.	.47**	371	.47**	360	.090
Social Dominance Orientation Scales	.66**	370	.79**	360	3.80**

Note. *p<.05, **p<.01. Items SD1r and SD3r were reverse coded ("Rev.") such that higher values indicate more disagreement with the item and more SDO. Correlation test is a one-tailed z-test.

statistic signaling the results from a hypothesis test of equality (no difference), with the presence of asterisks indicating a rejection of this hypothesis. The only item that showed no difference is the one asserting, "It is not really that big a problem if some [people/racial groups] have more of a chance in life than others." Among the racialized SDO items, this one had the lowest mean level of support, as well as the lowest correlation with the racial resentment scale. Among the general SDO items, it had the second lowest mean and correlation for the general SDO scale items, behind the assertion stating, "Our society should do whatever is necessary to make sure that [everyone] has an equal opportunity to succeed." Beyond this item, our expectations are confirmed: not only is SDO strongly correlated with our racial resentment scale, racialized SDO is generally a stronger correlate of the Whites' resentment toward African Americans scale than non-racial SDO. The totality of our results signal that the scale has strong construct validity, supporting our conceptualization and measurement of Whites' resentment toward African Americans.

Is White Resentment Racial Prejudice? Lessons from the 2010 General Social Survey

In the preceding sections, we established our theory and measure of Whites' resentment, and provided evidence of how well the WRTA scale correlates with other ostensible measures of closed racial beliefs—like classic resentment, modern racism, social dominance, and authoritarianism. We believe our measure stands alone in terms of its psychometric properties and theory as an indicator of political resentment toward African Americans. Still, there may be lingering questions about the extent to which our Whites' resentment measure is different from other measures of racism and prejudice.

In earlier chapters, we have argued that the current conceptualization of classic racial resentment offers a limiting framework for understanding racial politics today because it proposes that "prejudice is expressed in the language of American individualism." This makes classic racial resentment's primary causal force Whites' judgments about African Americans' effort and work ethic.

Our theory of Whites' resentment is similar to the classic version of racial resentment in that effort matters, but other values matter too. Justice raises a host of questions about fairness through equity, equality, and need, and therefore how Whites come to their deservingness appraisal. We posit that Whites resent race as a method for social advancement, and therefore any attempts by African Americans to use race to get ahead are unfair. If African Americans blame Whites today for sins of the past, it is unfair. If African Americans want to talk about racial inequality, Whites view it as unfair. If African Americans want to talk about White privilege, Whites view it as unfair. None of these ideas is about individuals or effort per se; instead they are about how race disrupts the calm of social relations. Whites would prefer that African Americans simply move on from past evils and do their best by taking advantage of what is available, without complaint. When African Americans push back because of issues like racial discrimination, White supremacy, or slavery, Whites become more entrenched in their attitudes. Thus, we suspect that our measure of Whites' resentment will correlate with perceived effort, but also a host of other non-prejudiced attitudes. Thus, rather than simply disliking African Americans because of their work ethic, Whites' resentment originates with appraisals of non-deservingness for positive rewards (i.e., injustice due to an equity violation), which activate justice motives and prompt practices of retribution that restore one's belief in a just world. The retribution comes in many forms including those which are sentimental (e.g., schadenfreude) and behavioral (e.g., opposition to amelioration).

The General Social Survey Data

In this section, we provide evidence to support the contention that our measure is tapping a host of attitudes about race. We use data from the 2010 General Social Survey (GSS). The GSS is one of the seminal social indicator studies in the United States. The National Opinion Research Center (NORC) has conducted the survey annually from 1972 to the mid-1990s, and then biennially beginning in 1994. The GSS studies replicate common questionnaire items and wording for analyzing trends, but also incorporate periodic topic modules for in-depth analysis. The 2010 GSS featured a topic module on intergroup relations that included items constituting our WRTA scale, but also measures of racial identity, colorblind identity, racial apathy (see Forman and Lewis 2006, 2015), social distance from racial groups, racial stratification beliefs (e.g., Kluegel and Smith 1986), racial stereotypes, concerns about intergroup relations, and opinions about the government's role in amelioration. The appendix contains the question wording for these items. The working data file consists of 1,122 self-reported non-Hispanic Whites.

We began our analysis by examining how our Whites' resentment measure correlated with select items with explicit racial content, and a few that alluded to the role of government in providing amelioration. We estimated the semi-partial or "part" correlations—the correlation between Whites' resentment and other items controlling for the effects of other factors; in our case: age, gender, family income, education, party identification. We use the part correlations rather than zero-order bivariate estimates to ensure our relationships are not spurious to other factors; thus, any correlation we present is more conservative than the standard bivariate statistic. In addition, we ran the same part correlation analyses for prejudice (Blacks' laziness), ideology (conservatism), and White identity (stronger), since we want to compare and contrast Whites' resentment to other proposed explanations. We refer to Whites' resentment, laziness stereotypes, conservatism, and White identity as the "Core Beliefs" group of variables.

Racial Prejudice and White Resentment

In sequential order are racial stereotypes about work ethic, intelligence, and socioeconomic status, whose correlations are provided in the uppermost portion of table 3.10. The cell values are estimated part-correlations; asterisks indicate whether the correlations are statistically different from zero; and the cells with a superscript "z" indicate that the estimates are statistically different from the Whites' resentment coefficient, based on Fisher's z-test.

The results reveal several noteworthy relationships. We coded the stereotypes such that higher values indicate negative attitudes—lazy, unintelligent, and poor. We find that Whites' resentment is associated with stronger beliefs that Blacks are lazier and wealthier, but not associated with unintelligence. These suggest that the WRTA scale is tapping into equity concerns about Blacks' inputs, but also into need: Blacks are undeserving of special consideration because they are lazier but also wealthier, and therefore the society is just and Blacks do not need additional help. Among the other correlates, ideology is not associated with the racial stereotypes; stronger White identity has a weak but significant association with perceived laziness; and perceived laziness is associated with perceptions that Blacks are unintelligent and poor. The laziness stereotype appears to be the strongest indicator of prejudice. Overall, Whites' resentment appears to capture those with higher levels of racial prejudice, but what about other racial attitudes?

Next, we examined Whites' resentment's association with racial group social distance with Blacks and Whites, colorblind ideology, and White identity. Among the group, Whites' resentment only correlated with greater distance from Blacks; however, this relationship was not strong. Among the Core Beliefs, racial prejudice registered significant correlations with greater distance from Blacks and lower colorblind ideology. In addition, White identity registers its strongest relationship in the entire analysis, with a -.200 (p<.01) relationship, with lower colorblind ideology. What we learn from this second analysis is that Whites' resentment is weakly associated with social distance, racial identity, and colorblindness; but also that colorblindness seems to reflect lower prejudice and lower White identity.

TABLE 3.10. **Correlations between White Resentment toward African Americans and Other Racial Attitudes, 2010 General Social Survey**

	Core Beliefs			
	White Resentment (Higher)	Racial Prejudice (Lazier)	Political Ideology (Conservatism)	White Identity (Stronger)
Racial Stereotypes				
Laziness	.236**	—	.053** ^{z}	.081* ^{z}
Unintelligence	.046	.186** ^{z}	.013	.020
Poor	−.108**	.295** ^{z}	−.003 ^{z}	.068 ^{z}
Social Distance: Closeness to Blacks	−.092**	−.122**	−.022	−.105**
Social Distance: Closeness to Whites	−.011	.028	.021	.068
Color-Blind Ideology: "For the most part, I am colorblind; that is, I do not care about what race people are." (Agreement)	.021	−.118** ^{z}	.026	−.204** ^{z}
White Identity: "How important is your racial identity (being White) to you" (More important)	.047	.081*	−.007	—
Stratification Beliefs: Racial differences . . .				
due to discrimination	−.255**	−.099** ^{z}	−.138** ^{z}	−.025 ^{z}
due to inborn ability	.076*	.175** ^{z}	−.006	.007
due to lack of good education chances	−.294**	−.134** ^{z}	−.150** ^{z}	−.018 ^{z}
due to lack of will	.295**	.277**	.095** ^{z}	.053 ^{z}
due to upbringing	.049	.084*	.041	−.001
Racial Apathy Attitudes				
White privilege: Whites treated better than other groups. (Agreement)	−.367**	−.104** ^{z}	−.194** ^{z}	.033 ^{z}
Racial indifference: Racial minority unfair treatment is not my business. (Agreement)	.328**	.166** ^{z}	.072** ^{z}	.106** ^{z}
Racial fatigue: Tired of talk about racial problems. (Agreement)	.462**	.139** ^{z}	.190** ^{z}	−.002 ^{z}
Concern about race relations (Concerned)	−.234**	−.028 ^{z}	−.080** ^{z}	.106** ^{z}

Note. Non-Hispanic White respondents (minimum N=604). Table entries are part-correlation coefficients estimated in a model with age, sex, education level, household income, and partisanship. Superscript "z" indicates two coefficients are different from the White Resentment coefficient at the p<.05 level, based on Fisher's z-test. Asterisks indicate whether part-coefficients are statistically different from zero: *p<.05, **p<.01.

Moving down table 3.10, we find strong patterns of association between Whites' resentment and racial stratification beliefs. The items—known as the RACDIF items in the GSS—begin with the statement, "On the average African Americans have worse jobs, income, and housing than white people. Do you think these differences are . . . ?" Then respondents indicate "yes" or "no" to the set of reasons: discriminate, innate features, lack of opportunities, and upbringing. Our results show that Whites' resentment is negatively associated with structural concerns like discrimination and lack of educational opportunities, and positively associated with individual features like lack of will and inborn ability. These effects mirror those for racial prejudice in terms of statistical significance and direction; however, the effects for the structural explanations are stronger for Whites' resentment. Racial prejudice has stronger effects than Whites' resentment in predicting the inborn ability explanation, but equal effects for the lack of will explanation. These results suggest that Whites' resentment operates the same as racial prejudice in terms of how Whites think about status differences. What is also interesting is that political conservatism's correlation sizes are more similar to White prejudice on the structural explanations (discrimination and education opportunities), but different on the two major individual explanations. This suggests that when examining structural explanations conservative views can mirror racial prejudice. It is also noteworthy that White racial identity does not significantly correlate with any explanations of racial stratification. Perhaps White identity is a standalone racial identity unencumbered by dominant or subordinate group status. To summarize, Whites' resentment tends to have stronger correlations with explanations of racial inequality than racial prejudice and conservatism; however, we can begin to see how Whites' resentment can emulate antipathy toward Blacks and individualism.

The bottom-most portion of table 3.10 examines how Whites' resentment toward African Americans correlates with other racial belief measures that mostly reflect racial apathy. According to Forman and Lewis (2006) indifference to, and low concerns with, issues of race and especially racial inequality characterize racial apathy. Indicators of racial apathy include denial of White privilege, agreement that racial discrimination is a matter for others to deal with, fatigue with discussions about race, and a general lack of concern with race relations. Individuals high in racial apathy tend to reject responsibility for racial inequality, and believe that racial issues are so complex that society is better off being colorblind. Forman and Lewis (2015) state that racial apathy is a "new kind of racial prejudice" but also that it does not necessarily embody "active and explicit dislike of racial minorities" (p. 1397). We agree that racial apathy can have prejudice motivations, but disagree that the items reflect a new form of prejudice. We interpret the racial apathy measures as system-justifying motives that support status quo positions about race. They reflect a frustration and withdrawal with race as a political subject, rather than prejudice as characterized by Allport (1954) or classic racial resentment (e.g., Kinder and Sanders 1996). It is here that we begin to see the discriminating role of Whites' resentment.

Of the core beliefs, only Whites' resentment toward African Americans has correlations above .200 (indicating an $R^2 \geq .04$ even after controlling for other variables in the model). Higher Whites' resentment correlates with stronger White privilege denial ($R^2 = .134$), higher levels of racial indifference ($R^2 = .107$), being more tired of hearing talk about racial problems ($R^2 = .213$), and lower concern about race relations ($R^2 = .054$). The White privilege, racial indifference, and racial fatigue variables all have correlations larger than those seen for the traditional racial stereotype measures. In addition, three out of four of the correlations between the core racial belief measure of racial prejudice and the additional attitudes about race are significant from zero; however, they are also much lower than those for Whites' resentment toward African Americans. The same pattern exists for political conservatism, and to a lesser extent for White identity. In general, Whites' resentment is distinguished from the other core beliefs by racial attitudes that reflect a justification of the status quo: Whites are just like everyone else, racial issues are not their problem, they are less interested in hearing about racial problems, and they are less concerned about them. Thus, resentment likely comes about because politics and policies that advance equality for African Americans push against these apathetic beliefs, prompting a defensiveness among Whites.

Amelioration and White Resentment

Are there downstream effects due to resentment? Our theory posits that Whites' resentment would produce retribution that could come in the form of policy beliefs that take on anti-amelioration positions. Alternatively, a prejudice explanation would suggest that policy opposition would be due to stereotypes about Blacks being lazy; an ideology explanation would suggest individuals are thinking about core principles about the role of government; and a White identity explanation would suggest that big events like the economic recession should lead to stronger group interests in terms of help and support. We examined the extent to which Whites' resentment and our set of additional Core Beliefs

TABLE 3.11. **Correlations between White Resentment toward African Americans and Ameliorative Policy, 2010 General Social Survey**

	Core Beliefs			
	White Resentment (Higher)	Racial Prejudice (Lazier)	Political Ideology (Conservatism)	White Identity (Stronger)
Political Ideology: Conservatism	.229**	.062** ᶻ	—	−.008 ᶻ
Amelioration				
(Federal Government [should])				
Help "Blacks"				
(vs. no special treatment)	−.487**	−.193** ᶻ	−.181** ᶻ	.017 ᶻ
"Improve standard of living for the				
poor" (vs. people help themselves)	−.186**	−.120**	−.210**	.029 ᶻ
"Pay for Medical Care"				
(vs. people help themselves)	−.221**	−.079** ᶻ	−.231**	.012 ᶻ
Affirmative Action				
"Preference in hiring Blacks" (Favor)	−.252**	−.125** ᶻ	−.130** ᶻ	−.031 ᶻ

Note. Non-Hispanic White respondents (Minimum N=714). Table entries are part-correlation coefficients estimated in a model with age, sex, education level, household income, and partisanship. Superscript "z" indicates two coefficients are different from the White Resentment coefficient at the p<.05 level, based on Fisher's z-test. Asterisks indicate whether part-coefficients are statistically different from zero: *p<.05, **p<.01.

correlated with ameliorative ideologies and policies. Among these variables are conservatism—now also on the row side of the model—and beliefs about the role of government, and support for affirmative action (i.e., preferences in hiring Blacks). The results are presented in table 3.11.

Whites' resentment correlates significantly and at moderate to strong levels with all of the ameliorative beliefs and affirmative action policy. Higher Whites' resentment is associated with more conservatism; lower government assistance to help Blacks, poor people, and those who need help with medical expenses; and opposition to affirmative action. These correlations are not only significant from zero, but for all but one variable—help for the poor—they are also larger than the correlations for racial prejudice and White identity. Conservative political ideology has correlations similar to Whites' resentment for government helping the poor and those in need of medical expense support, but conservatism's effects are much lower than Whites' resentment with regard to government helping Blacks and preferences for hiring Blacks. In fact, the Core Belief table correlations for political conservatism are relatively consistent across the items, ranging from −.130 (p<.01) to −.231 (p<.01), and they are all statistically equal to or greater than the correlations for racial prejudice. From these data we infer that Whites' resentment powerfully predicts opposition to amelioration, especially for Blacks, and especially when they are perceived to receive special treatment. Once again, the data show that the WRTA scale taps into deservingness and justice motives, more than racial prejudice.

"Special" as a Racial Force

In a final analysis, we sought to assess whether the racial resentment scale and our criteria related to "special considerations" around race have empirical strength with a topic that is independent of the scale wording. We created a simple question-wording experiment that combined the concepts of amelioration and special considerations, as they apply to racial and non-racial group information.

As we have alluded to in the prior chapters, the racial-ethnic population changes in American society have been accompanied by both subtle and overt hostility and resistance. Higher status groups may be threatened by the activism of historically marginalized groups like African Americans. We hypothesize this threat stems from the belief that full inclusion of racial-ethnic groups, and others, will change the status quo, forcing Whites, as a dominant group, to change their way of life with little ability to be competitive because existing rules privilege a racial-ethnic "New Deal" that ostensibly excludes them. As a result, Whites may come to feel an overwhelming sense of injury over the role of "special" considerations that not only do harm to their interests, but reshape their existing prerogatives, including their statuses and power.

As we have outlined in our theory of racial resentment, people tend to resent others when they view the process by which the other has attained positive outcomes or rewards as unfair and unjust. Special considerations are viewed as unjust because they are not available for all to take advantage of; they are viewed as an imbalanced privilege that benefits only those trying to skirt the rules of merit and deservingness.

In the 2012 CCES (team A), we presented a sub-sample of respondents with a 2 × 2 experiment randomizing two different frames about protecting voting rights for two groups. In one setting we asked respondents about their support for "laws" that protect voting rights, and in the second condition we asked about "special laws" that protect voting rights. We also randomized several different group targets for the item, including "Americans" and "African Americans." "Americans" is considered the baseline condition because it is a neutral group. "African Americans" represent the politically relevant racial-ethnic group as they relate to power and status in America. The "laws" condition is a stripped version of the question, and the "special laws" condition is the treatment that would raise concerns related to justice. The specific wording is:

Stripped/Baseline Condition

How much do you support or oppose LAWS to protect the voting rights of [INSERT GROUP]?

Treatment Condition

How much do you support or oppose SPECIAL LAWS to protect the voting rights of [INSERT GROUP]?

In all, there are four versions of the question, taking into consideration the two groups as well as the framing of laws as special or not. Response options included "strongly support," "support," "oppose," and "strongly oppose," with higher values indicating stronger support. We are primarily interested in the conditional effects of racial resentment, which was asked only of non-African American respondents. We analyzed the experimental data for Whites (N=350), and the results of the analysis are presented in figures 3.2 and 3.3 below.

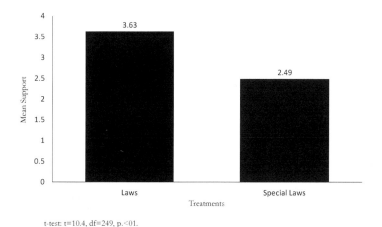

t-test: t=10.4, df=249, p.<01.

FIGURE 3.2. Mean Support for Protecting Laws vs. Protecting Special Laws, CCES 2012

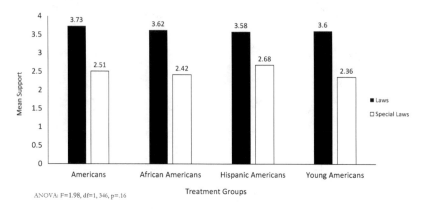

ANOVA: F=1.98, df=1, 346, p=.16

FIGURE 3.3. Mean Support for Protecting Laws vs. Protecting Laws for Various Groups

Figure 3.2 considers the first treatment of special labeling, and it re-veals that the "special" label significantly lowered support for voting pro-tections (t=13.8, p<.01). Whites express lower support for special voting laws (M=2.49) than laws with no mention of "special" (M=3.68). With re-gard to the second treatment (not shown in the figure), respondents re-ported the same level of support (t=.60) for laws regardless of whether the protected group was "Americans" (M=3.09) or "African Americans" (M=3.03). There is no significant interaction between the framing of the laws as special or not, and the group being protected (F=1.98, ns). The fig-ure included "Hispanic Americans" and "Young Americans," categories that are part of the experiment but not included in our subsequent analy-ses. Overall, we find that regardless of the group being considered, White respondents are less supportive of special laws to protect voting rights.

The survey experiment results provide initial support for the sensi-tive nature of "special" considerations in society, but they do not show any specific group targeting on the part of respondents. This suggests that the "special" laws evaluation is principled and not specific to Af-rican Americans. But, what about the role of Whites' resentment in the principle? It is one thing to see that the framing of laws as "special" de-creased support, and that these levels do not vary across groups, but it is another thing to see the consequence of Whites' resentment on support under the different conditions. Thus, we examined a saturated model of the predictive relationship between WRTA and responses to the support for voting protections item while also considering the combination ex-perimental groups. This analysis provides some insight into the extent to

TABLE 3.12. **Whites' Resentment toward African Americans and Special Voting Rights Protections for Americans and African Americans, 2012 CCES**

	b (se)	b (se)	b (se)
Intercept	4.47 (.17)**	3.67 (.26)**	3.75 (.30)**
Laws (Special=1)	−1.10 (.12)**	.10 (.32)	−.06 (.41)
Group (African Americans=1)	−.29 (.12)*	.22 (.32)	.05 (.44)
WRTA	−1.26 (.24)**	−.03 (.41)	−.17 (.47)
Laws x Group		−.34 (.24)	−.00 (.61)
WRTA x Laws		−1.77 (.47)**	−1.51 (.64)**
WRTA x Group		−.54 (.47)	−.23 (.70)
WRTA x Laws x Group			−.56 (.94)
Adjusted R-squared	.421	.470	.468
SEE	.783	.752	.751
N=164			

Note. *p<.05, p<.01

which the different experimental categories elicit resentment and predict opposition to protective rights. If our measure of racial resentment is racial prejudice, then at a minimum we should see it have stronger predictive effects under the African American condition than the baseline of Americans. We provide results from the analysis in table 3.12.

Table 3.12 shows the ordinary least squares (OLS) results for the interactive effects of Whites' resentment and the experimental treatments. The results confirm our expectations about Whites' resentment—it lowers support for ameliorative voting protections (b=-1.26, p<.01)—but it also interacts with the "special" frame. WRTA predicts stronger support when voting protections are labeled as "special" (b=-1.77, p<.01) than when the label is absent (b=.10, ns). This is an important finding because it reflects the psychological connections respondents make between their resentments over fairness and the very subtle, but relevant, "special" framing that characterizes the protections. Second, surprisingly, we find no stronger correlation between Whites' resentment and support when considering the "group" framing—for Americans (b=.22, ns) than African Americans (b=-.54, ns). This could mean that the concern over special considerations is not specific to African Americans; that respondents took "Americans" to mean mostly African Americans; or that Americans—mostly White people—especially, do not need any protections, special or not. A third finding is that racial resentment does not significantly correlate with support for "laws" regardless of whether the target group is "Americans" or "African Americans." This is reflected

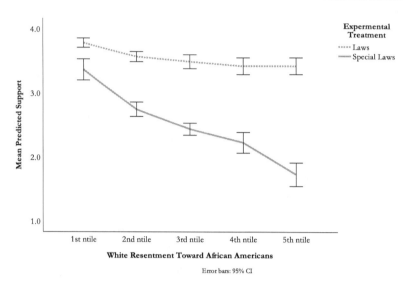

FIGURE 3.4. The Relationship between Support for "Special" Voting Laws versus Laws Experiment and White Resentment toward African Americans (WRTA)

by the non-significant 3-way (WRTA × Laws × Group) interaction term in table 3.12. This finding reinforces the idea that equity concerns related to ameliorative voting laws may not be necessarily racial, until they are triggered by coded language that violates fairness or justice. Overall, the most notable aspect of the experiment is that across all of the results, Whites' resentment is a stronger predictor of support when the word "special" is present than not. Figure 3.4 shows the clear pattern in our CCES data. These results provide additional evidence of criterion validity: racial resentment is fundamentally tied to an aversion of special considerations, which appear to heighten concerns over fairness and justice.

Conclusion

In this chapter, we sought to explain our theory and measurement of Whites' resentment toward African Americans, paying close attention to the rules of special considerations, justice, and deservingness. We posited that Whites' resentment toward African Americans is not entirely racial prejudice, but rather a predisposition that has strong emotional underpinnings tied to justice and fairness and deservingness. If Whites' resentment is not essentially prejudice, then we should not use traditional measures of classic racial resentment because they have been defined as a form of prejudicial antipathy. Thus, we created and tested new items to form a measure of Whites' resentment toward African Americans, one that is aligned with a coherent theory that incorporates elements of resentment and the specific considerations that Whites point to when appraising deservingness for African Americans. This new scale turns out to be quite robust in terms of its psychometric measurement properties. Factor analyses reveal that our measure of Whites' resentment toward African Americans is not the same as classic racial resentment or modern racism, and the racial resentment validity and reliability metrics are superior to those for the latter two concepts. Our results should not be interpreted to mean that the classic racial resentment and modern racism scales are not valuable or are invalid; rather, they are different, and the difference is consequential, particularly in terms of conceptualization and theory. Lastly, we found that our Whites' resentment scale exhibits good construct and criterion, or predictive, validity. Our Whites' resentment scale strongly correlates with status quo threat, antiegalitarianism, authoritarianism, and both racial and non-racial forms of SDO. On matters of predictive validity, we showed that Whites' resentment could predict very subtle differences in framing. When the term "special" described voting laws, Whites expressed lower support for them, and did not change their support for laws/special laws based on whether they considered Americans or African Americans. This showed that the "special" label mattered significantly for White respondents. Thus, we conclude that our WRTA measure offers great promise as a measure that captures racial, but also non-racist, sentiment.

In all, the work in this chapter provides a foundational concept, theoretical framework, and operational variable for our forthcoming analyses and arguments related to racialized resentment in general and racial resentment in particular.

The Profile and Performance of Racial Resentment

With the assured validity of our new measure of Whites' resentment, two important and somewhat obligatory questions are now raised: Who are the most racially resentful Whites in American society, and how well does our measure explain racial attitudes and behavior? In this chapter we are interested in identifying the traits and characteristics most common to individuals who harbor racial resentment toward African Americans, which helps to evidence the power of racial resentment as an analytical framework. Identifying those who are racially resentful is a straightforward task. We raise the contention that people high in resentment toward African Americans do not only resemble racists—for example, those who would wear white hoods and capes, attend Klan rallies and meetings, donate to extremist organizations, consume and share social media denigrating African Americans as less than human, or openly espouse racist views—but may actually resemble the average person in the community—for example, those who volunteer at their children's schools and athletic youth leagues, drink cappuccinos at Starbucks, and do not try to intentionally offend anyone. People who endorse racially resentful views may not think of themselves as racists or be aware of the racial consequences of their beliefs. We identify such people in our survey data by examining the extent to which racial resentment is associated with sociodemographic and political factors.

We also examine racial resentment's ability to predict relevant political attitudes and behavior. Individuals possess a multitude of dispositions and beliefs that compete with, and may potentially overshadow, Whites' resentment toward African Americans. Ideology, education, social dominance, and, more recently, White identity (Jardina 2019) are among a powerful set of factors said to predict political preferences. Presumably, former President Trump's political appeals stoked Whites' sense of solidarity and identity, which strengthened his support and propelled him to a presidential election win in 2016. Therefore, if racial resentment is to be considered a useful and powerful analytical framework, it should provide equal, if not added, value relative to standard explanations of political and social attitudes. We begin by elaborating on theoretical expectations for racial resentment followed by a profile of racial resentment and its performance as an independent variable.

Profile: Explanations of Whites' Resentment toward African Americans

Because Whites' resentment toward African Americans reflects a closed belief system, involving a sensitivity to threat, protectiveness of the status quo, and adherence to traditional values such as self-discipline and individual effort, it should be related to factors that shape other closed or conservative belief systems. For instance, higher levels of classic racial resentment have been found among older age cohorts, among those with lower levels of income and education, and among men more than women (Federico and Aguilera 2019; Oliver and Mendelberg 2000). As might be expected, these are similar to factors associated with other closed belief systems (Reyna et al. 2005). Moreover, the underlying theory behind age effects is that older individuals, more so than younger individuals, tend to be more sensitive to threats to the status quo, more rigid and dogmatic in their thoughts about justice and deservingness, and more likely to possess system-justifying beliefs. Similarly, White men should be more likely than women to express racial resentment toward African Americans because they are more sensitive and most affected by challenges to the status quo, are protective of traditional values and norms, possess more rigid views of justice and deservingness, and tend to react more negatively to racial information and stereotypes. Individuals with higher levels of education, despite their affluence connecting them to system-justifying beliefs, should be less racially resentful because they are not as sensitive to threats to the status quo, are better able to see biases in the status quo and the implications on African Americans, and are less likely to operate off negative racial information and stereotypes.

Several questions arise from this literature regarding the extent to which the factors related to classic racial resentment, and closed racial belief systems in general, are evident in our data. In other words, is the profile of those high in racial resentment consistent with theoretical expectations? Instead of presenting tables of means across several data sets, we summarize the effects of sociodemographic factors by analyzing them simultaneously in ordinary least squares (OLS) models predicting racial resentment. The results of these models are reported in table 4.1.

Consistency is an important theme in this analysis. Across the three years of data, we find that, everything being equal, individuals with higher levels of education are less resentful toward African Americans than individuals with lower levels of education. Through a variety of mechanisms, education is extremely important in influencing levels of racial resentment. Individuals with higher levels of education possess a more open belief system, which makes them less sensitive to threats to the status quo, and they are better situated to understand the adjudication of justice and fairness (Johnston, Lavine, and Federico 2018). Similarly, research shows that older Whites have higher levels of classic racial resentment than younger Whites. While this may relate to the conservatizing effects of the aging process (e.g., sensitivity to threat, defense of the status quo, and resistance to change), older individuals tend to also be more likely than younger individuals to adhere to racial stereotypes.

Also among the sociodemographic measures, gender is a significant predictor of higher racial resentment, but only in 2016 and 2018. Indeed, the correlation between gender and racial resentment loses significance when political factors are included, meaning that the difference between men and women may be a function of their ideological differences. Social status, as indicated by income level, is statistically insignificant. Regardless of income level, Whites' level of resentment toward African Americans is statistically identical. This suggests Whites at higher levels of income are not more or less sensitive to threats to their economic status from undeserving African Americans as Whites at lower levels of income.

More directly than sociodemographics, ideological conservatism reflects a dogmatic and rigid defense of the status quo, greater sensitivity to threat, stronger belief in individual merit over special considerations, and the adherence to traditional values such as self-discipline and effort (McClosky 1958; Reyna et al. 2005). Conservatism closely aligns with racial resentment in that individuals who strongly identify as conservative

TABLE 4.1. **OLS Coefficients Predicting Whites' Resentment toward African Americans, CCES**

	2012			2016			2018		
	Model 1	Model 2	Model 3	Model 4	Model 5	Model 6	Model 7	Model 8	Model 9
Constant	5.50** (.29)		5.06** (.31)	3.74** (.14)	3.33** (.09)	3.52** (.19)	3.34** (.27)	2.87** (.11)	3.07** (.27)
Education	-.20** (.04)		-.11** (.03)	-.25** (.04)		-.14** (.03)	-.22** (.04)		-.13** (.04)
Age	-.00 (.00)		-.01* (.00)	.01** (.00)		.00* (.00)	.01** (.00)		.15** (.05)
Income	-.04* (.01)		-.04* (.02)	-.07 (.04)		-.06 (.03)	.01 (.02)		-.01 (.01)
Gender (1=male)	-.05 (.11)		.01 (.09)	.20** (.07)		.12 (.07)	-.22* (.10)		-.12 (.08)
Liberal		-.87** (.12)	-.74** (.13)		-1.12** (.08)	-1.08** (.08)		-1.25** (.09)	-1.10** (.10)
Conservative		.81** (.11)	.84** (.11)		.59** (.07)	.53** (.08)		.70** (.09)	.67** (.09)
Political Interest		-.26** (.05)	-.11 (.06)		-.12* (.04)	-.12* (.04)		-.15** (.04)	-.17** (.05)
R²	.10	.32	.35	.07	.34	.36	.10	.43	.44
Root MSE	1.14	.98	.97	1.15	.98	.96	1.18	.96	.94
N	471	520	459	1,065	989	977	568	726	554

Note. **p<.01; *p<.05. Values in parentheses are standard errors. MSE, mean squared error; OLS, ordinary least squares.

are more likely to express greater support for effort as a means for de-servingness or fairness (Reyna et al. 2005). There is considerable over-lap between the two concepts. Political interest is included in the model to capture a general sense of political engagement and awareness (Goi-del, Parent, and Mann 2011). Because individuals who are more politi-cally engaged are more likely to have a realistic sense of the threat to the status quo and because they seek out and consume politically relevant information, they could be less sensitive to threat and challenges to it—assuming that they consume information that aligns with their existing beliefs. Alternatively, low interested persons may rely on their gut, ste-reotypes, or rumors for their politics, making them more susceptible to system-legitimizing information. Thus, it could be that individuals who are least informed and engaged are more likely to perceive threats from African Americans.

As reported in table 4.1, liberals and conservatives are consistently significant and distinct in their beliefs about racial resentment.[1] While liberals are consistently less resentful toward African Americans com-pared to moderates (the reference category), conservatives are consis-tently more racially resentful. This is consistent with the idea that con-servatism reflects a higher level of sensitivity to threat and a greater commitment to traditional values of effort, individualism, and deserv-ingness. Higher political interest is associated with lower racial resent-ment scores across the 2012, 2016, and 2018 data, suggesting that higher interest might lead to the consumption of more factual information that signals African Americans are not threatening the status quo.

In short, the profile of those higher in Whites' resentment toward Af-rican Americans parallels those who possess a more closed racial belief system. In a strong and consistent fashion, higher levels of racial resent-ment are associated with lower education, older age cohorts, conserva-tism, and low political engagement.

Belief in a Just World and System Justification

A belief in a just world, as a framework for understanding human behav-ior, captures the extent to which people believe in fairness and whether people get what they deserve (Lerner 1980a, 1980b). People want to be-lieve that the world is fair, and they will therefore look for ways to ex-plain or rationalize away injustice, often blaming the person in a situ-ation who is actually the victim. This belief also leads people to think that when good things happen to people it is because those individuals are good and deserving of their fortune. Rather than attributing the success of the most fortunate among us to luck or circumstance, people tend to ascribe good fortune to intrinsic characteristics of the individual, believing, for example, that they are more intelligent and hardworking than less fortunate people. Conversely, the just-world belief system helps explain why people sometimes blame victims for their own misfortune, even in situations where people had no control over the events that fell on them.

We assert that Whites' resentment toward African Americans stems from a belief in a just and fair world. A belief in a just world is the primary basis for determining who should benefit from contested resources and how much. All societies have some form of belief system for deciding how to distribute resources. The perception that African Americans and other minorities are undeserving and benefiting unfairly violates these principles that support just-world beliefs. Thus, we expect that racial resentment should be highly correlated with a belief in a just world and political preferences that support justice principles (e.g., anti-amelioration, support for candidates who are conservative, positions in favor of freedoms over regulation).

Another belief system we consider important in racial resentment is system justification. According to system justification theory (Jost and Banaji 1994; Jost 2020), people are motivated to defend, bolster, and justify aspects of existing social, economic, and political systems. They defend the status quo because they think it is just and fair, and because they benefit from it. Thus, systems that align with one's world-view should be maintained and those that do not should be changed—to become more just. In theory, there is little reason to staunchly oppose a system that benefits oneself or one's group. System justification serves a palliative function (e.g., reducing uncertainty and anxiety) by increasing satisfaction with status quo systems that appear to hold no threat.

System justification—that is, support for system-legitimizing beliefs, such as "the system is fair"—obviously should be correlated with a belief in a just world because both beliefs defend the status quo, albeit for different reasons. But they should also be correlated with racial resentment. If a person believes the status quo benefits them and their in-group, they should be more likely to think it benefits other groups as well. Therefore, resentment should lead to a defense of the system and offense at those who are perceived to threaten it, like African Americans who are per-

TABLE 4.2. **Standardized OLS Coefficients Predicting Racial Resentment toward African Americans, CCES 2018**

Independent Variables	Model 1	Model 2
Just-World Belief	.15**	.12**
System-Justification	.35**	.33**
Liberal	−.32**	−.26**
Conservative	.07*	.12**
Political Interest		.09**
Education		−.11**
Age		.07**
Income		−.03
Gender		−.03
R²	.55	.58
Root MSE	.84	.82
N	735	660

Note. **p<.01; *p<.05.

ceived to violate principles of deservingness and justice by seeking, even demanding, more than they deserve.

These relationships are examined simultaneously in a full model in table 4.2 predicting Whites' resentment toward African Americans; the relative importance of each favor is determined by their standardized regression coefficients.[2] If there were any questions about the connection between racial resentment and beliefs that the world is just, or racial resentment's connection to a desire to defend the status quo, those questions can be confidently quashed. Holding other variables constant, a belief in a just world and system justification are significantly related to higher racial resentment toward African Americans. Individuals who hold stronger beliefs in a just world are more likely to be more racially resentful toward African Americans. Similarly, individuals who hold stronger system-justification beliefs are more racially resentful. Considering the relative weight of the coefficients, a great deal more weight is attached to system justification (beta=.37) than just-world motive (beta=.11) in explaining racial resentment.

Performance: Assessing the Significance of Whites' Resentment toward African Americans

In this section, Whites' resentment toward African Americans is appraised as an independent variable, and we evaluate its strength in explaining other political and social attitudes relative to other predictors. The relative predictability of our Whites' resentment scale is a standard for determining its usefulness as an analytical framework or lens for understanding the political world.

Racial Attitudes and Policy

Classic racial resentment, in its initial formulation and its progenitor, symbolic racism, have been linked to a variety of racial attitudes and policy attitudes, such as affirmative action (Feldman and Huddy 2005; Tuch and Hughes 2011; Stoker 1998), evaluations of President Obama (Redlawsk, Tolbert, and McNeely 2014; Tesler 2012a, 2012b; Valentino and Brader 2011), and paying college athletes (Wallsten et al. 2017). People could be expected to react to these political preferences simply on the basis of their hatred toward Blacks and their beliefs that Blacks were not adhering to traditional values of individualism and effort. While the effects of classic racial resentment are indisputable, our conceptualization and measure of racial resentment toward African Americans must overcome a very high hurdle. As opposed to being motivated by racial prejudice, our measure of racial resentment stems from the belief that African Americans are using race to dismiss their lower level of effort and are gaining advantages through unfair special considerations, violating notions of justice and fairness.

We have several data sets on which to examine the relationship between Whites' resentment toward African Americans and racial attitudes. Table 4.3 reports OLS regression coefficients for racial resentment predicting a range of racial attitudes. Only the OLS coefficients for racial resentment from full models are reported.

As a start, the correlations between Whites' resentment toward African Americans and policy positions are robust and in the expected direction. Higher levels of racial resentment are associated with greater anti-ameliorative preferences. This is obviously the case on measures targeting African Americans, such as on affirmative action, whether African Americans are viewed as too demanding for equal rights, whether African Americans should not place themselves where they are not wanted, and whether Whites can understand African Americans' anger. In short, Whites high in racial resentment do not sympathize with African Americans, and they do not support special considerations for African Americans. Moreover, when the survey items target Whites' sense of

TABLE 4.3. **Whites' Resentment toward African Americans Predicting Racial Attitudes, CCES 2010 to 2018**

2010 CCES	b	$s.e.$
Support for affirmative action (CC327)	−.43**	.02
Grant legal status to immigrants (CC322_2)	−.11**	.02
Increase border patrol (CC22_4)	.08**	.02
Allow police to question (CC322_5)	.16**	.02
Obama approval (CC308a)	.30**	.04
Support for Tea Party (teaparty)	.15**	.05
2012 CCES		
Support for Affirmative Action (CC327)	−.36**	.03
Support felon voting rights (WIL14)	−.11**	.03
Support legal status to immigrants (CC322_1)	−.11**	.02
Allow police to question illegal immigrants (CC322_3)	.11**	.02
Support automatic citizenship to people born in US (CC322_6)	.14**	.02
Obama approval (CC308a)	.31**	.04
Support Tea Party (CC424)		
2016 CCES		
Discrimination is no longer a problem (MR1)	.56**	.04
Understand the anger of African Americans (MR2)	−.37**	.04
African Americans too demanding for equal rights (MR3)	.71**	.03
African Americans should not put themselves where they are not wanted (MR4)	.56**	.04
Grant legal status to immigrants (CC16_331_1)	−.09**	.02
Identify and deport all illegal immigrants (CC16_331_7)	.14**	.02
2018 CCES		
Provide legal status to children of immigrants (CC18_322b)	−.12**	.02
Imprison deported immigrants who reenter (CC18_322f)	.15**	.02
White people have advantages because of the color of their skin (CC18_422a)	−.56**	.05
Racial problems in the US are rare, isolated situations (CC18_422b)	.40**	.05
President Trump Approval (CC18_308a)	.70**	.03

Note. **p<.01; *p<.05. The b's are unstandardized coefficients based on a multivariate model including ideology, political interest, Obama approval in 2010, 2012, and 2016, education, age, income, and gender. See appendix for specific question wording, though in 2018 we use Trump approval.

privilege, high racial resentment becomes associated with a lower willingness to acknowledge this privilege and with the denial of racial prejudice and discrimination. In other words, Whites high in resentment are less likely to believe that they have advantages because of the color of their skin while being more likely to believe that racial problems in the US are rare, isolated situations.

But the effects of Whites' resentment toward African Americans extend beyond perceptions of African Americans and racial discrimination. A series of questions in the CCES inquired into various aspects of immigration—tolerance issues that are not ostensibly racial. Whites who are high in racial resentment have a certain disdain for immigration; they are not willing to grant legal status to immigrants, are supportive of increasing border patrols, and are supportive of allowing the profiling of immigrants. This is an important result, suggestive of the notion that Whites' sense of justice and deservingness extends to others who are perceived as threatening to the status quo and undeserving. It suggests that the just-world beliefs about deservingness are over-arching, and that they are applied to race, giving the appearance of racism. However, since legitimizing beliefs about African Americans also apply to other ambiguous groups—immigrants are not a single racial-ethnic group—then it also suggests racial resentment is about more than hate or dislike. Thus, despite referencing African Americans, measures of racial resentment are likely to be sensitive to other groups as well. Clearly, racial resentment is a major analytical framework for understanding various aspects of race.

White Identity

Although White identity and consciousness have been thought of as an invisible and ubiquitous identity (Delgado and Stefancic 1997; Lipsitz 1998; McDermott and Samson 2005), recent research uses it as an analytical framework through which Whites perceive the political and social world (Jardina 2019; Perry 2007). Like any other dominant identity, Whites seek to differentiate, to gain esteem and positive distinctiveness, and, ultimately, to maintain superiority over out-groups (Tajfel and Turner 1979). According to Jardina (2019), not only was White identity triggered during the 2016 election through racial appeals criticizing racial and ethnic minorities, but also the threat to their in-group became a powerful analytical framework motivating Whites' political behavior. White identity is presented as an analytical framework for understanding reactions to President Obama and the rise of President Trump. Jardina (2019) argues that

> monumental social and political trends—including an erosion of whites' majority status and the election of America's first black president—have signaled a challenge to the absoluteness of whites' dominance. These threats, both real and perceived, have . . . brought to the fore, for many whites, a sense of commonality, attachment, and solidarity with their racial group. (p. 3)

While we heartily agree that Whites could perceive a threat to their interests under President Obama and that President Trump capitalized on appeals that framed racial and ethnic minorities as threatening the status quo, we contend that the 2016 election triggered thoughts about justice, deservingness, and racial resentment as much, if not more than, White identity. We test such a contention by comparing both measures, White identity and racial resentment, in the same model predicting political attitudes. We ask, what carries the greatest weight in explaining political attitudes and behavior in the age of Obama and Trump: White identity, Whites' racial resentment, or some other explanation?

Table 4.4 reports the standardized coefficients for a model including White identity and our Whites' resentment scale predicting Trump approval, background checks on firearms, the repeal of Obamacare, and support for DACA in 2018. These issues were prominent in the 2016 election and well into the first two years of the Trump Administration, and to a certain degree they all trigger Whites to think about the importance of their racial group identity. But contrary to current assumptions, the results show that White identity is inconsequential and makes a meager contribution to understanding prominent political issues. Where White identity would be expected to be most meaningful, such as in the approval of Trump and the repeal of Obamacare, it does poorly. Thus, we find no evidence in our analysis to sustain White identity as a significant predictor.

TABLE 4.4. **OLS Standardized Coefficients Predicting Trump Approval and Various Policies, 2018 CCES**

Independent Variables	Trump Approval	Firearms Background Check	Repeal Affordable Care Act ("Obamacare")	Immigration (Support DACA policy)
Racial Resentment	.37**	−.19**	.16**	−.33**
White Identity	.02	.03	−.00	−.02
Liberal	.49**	.05	−.11**	.01
Conservative	−.98**	−.07	.19**	−.06**
Trump Approval		.09**	−.34**	.18**
Political Interest	.09**	.08**	.03	−.02
Education	.05*	−.11**	.02	−.08*
Age	−.03	.07**	−.04	.05
Gender	.04	.16**	−.06	.08*
Income	−.02	.05*	.01	.02
R^2	.61	.13	.47	.26
Root MSE	.83	.30	.36	.38
N	664	661	664	664

Note. **p<.01; *p<.05.

On the other hand, Whites' resentment toward African Americans is the most consistent predictor of political preferences across the board. Whereas the effects of other predictors vary across the issue areas, racial resentment is significant in every dependent variable and in the expected direction. Neither ideology, support for Trump, nor demographic factors are as robust as Whites' resentment toward African Americans. Risking some exaggeration here, Whites' resentment toward African Americans is an important and indispensable analytical framework. The way that people view politics and political issues is not necessarily based on racism or racial prejudice toward African Americans, but it is racial to the extent that perceptions of African Americans reflect broader values about who should get what (i.e., politics), and the extent to which political actors, institutions, and policies facilitate or violate justice and the maintenance of the status quo.[3]

Social Dominance

There are other race-neutral values (e.g., anti-egalitarianism) that underlie frameworks that explain politics, specifically the denigration of President Obama and the rise of President Trump. Trump stands unique because he is the first president with no public sector leadership experience, but he is also unique in that his tenure as a nominee and president have been ripe with allegations of corruption, the denigration and mocking of racial-ethnic groups and vulnerable populations (e.g., the disabled), misogynistic commentary, and low transparency.

Social dominance orientation is a concept related closely to Whites' resentment toward African Americans that reflects a preference for the established social order and the maintenance of group-based hierarchies (Sidanius and Pratto 1999). People who score high on SDO lack empathic concern for others and are unsupportive of ameliorative racial programs (Pratto et al. 1994). Social dominance orientation is linked to the attainment of power, dominance, self-reliance, and superiority (see also Weber and Federico 2007). Individuals higher (vs. lower) in SDO are particularly attuned to threats against dominance and superiority. Therefore, independent of racial resentment and ideas that African Americans and other minorities are challenging the status quo and justice, President Trump's campaign appeals may have been viewed as emphasizing hostility and aggression, attracting those who are higher in social dominance orientation (Choma and Hanoch 2017; Crowson and

TABLE 4.5. **Logit Coefficients Predicting 2016 and 2012 Presidential Vote, 2016 and**
2012 CCES

	2016	2012
Independent Variables	Trump vs. Clinton	Obama vs. Romney
Social Dominance	1.67** (.27)	.07 (.25)
Racial Resentment	.52** (.20)	−1.34** (.24)
Liberal	−1.80** (.47)	3.37** (1.09)
Conservative	2.40** (.41)	−3.19** (.45)
Political Interest	.24 (.17)	−.09 (.18)
Education	−.24 (.17)	−.20 (.16)
Age	−.00 (.01)	−.01 (.01)
Gender	−.09 (.36)	.04 (.42)
Income	−.25 (.18)	−.14* (.07)
Constant	4.89** (1.29)	8.65** (1.98)
R^2	.65	.62
Prob > X^2	.30	.000
N	278	337

Note. **p<.01; *p<.05.

Brandes 2017; Pettigrew 2017; Womick et al. 2019; Van Assche, Dhont, and Pettigrew 2018). At the same time, however, people high in social dominance have been shown to support Obama because his election was seen as the culmination of racial prejudice (Knowles, Lowery, and Schaumberg 2009).

We rely on vote intentions in 2016 and in 2012 measured in those years to assess the relative importance of social dominance and racial resentment. The standardized regression coefficients are reported in table 4.5. On the basis of the two years of data, racial resentment is significant and in the expected directions. Whites' resentment influenced the support for Trump in 2016 in a positive way and it detracted from the support for Obama in 2012.

While social dominance theory (SDT) is a powerful analytical framework for understanding the support for President Trump, it is less prominent in 2012. Social dominance and racial resentment measure different things, but they tap into a similar sense of threat (r=.74) to the status quo, one aspect of which is racial inequality. While both are facilitated by legitimizing myths, the threat in racial resentment toward African Americans comes from a perceived violation of justice and an appraisal of deservingness by a specific target, and the threat in social dominance orientation comes from threats to anti-egalitarianism values among groups in general. In both concepts, out-groups can be perceived as seeking benefits and statuses they do not deserve, forgetting their place in a social hierarchy, and not exerting sufficient energy to achieve their share. Certainly, more data is needed to disentangle the relationship between the two concepts, their origins of threat, and how they become racialized, but if racial resentment is motivated by justice as well as racial prejudice, there is a theoretically consistent pathway to improved understanding.

Political Institutions

Political institutions come into our purview in the analysis of racial resentment because they allocate coveted resources through governance, policy, and legal decision-making. As with social dominance (Sidanius and Pratto 1999), individuals high in racial resentment are more likely to value institutions and institutional decisions that contribute to the increase or maintenance of the status quo or group-based hierarchical relationships. In other words, institutions that protect and defend White privilege and status, punishing individuals who violate their civic obligations to responsible behavior, should find favor among those who are racially resentful. Such institutions are perceived as legitimate, trustworthy, and fair to the extent that they allocate resources without privileging race or oppose them for undeserving racial and ethnic minorities and ameliorative policies. Examples of such institutions might include conservative control of Congress and the Supreme Court, though other institutions might include police departments and other elements of the criminal justice system. However, institutions that defend and promote the minority, egalitarian interests, justice, and fairness are viewed more negatively by those with higher racial resentment. Examples of such institutions might be a Democrat-controlled Congress and Supreme Court as well as civil rights organizations, women's rights groups, human rights groups, and charities. Thus, Whites' resentment toward African Americans influences the evaluation of political institutions, those public-serving components of the system that allocate rules and resources in society on behalf of the citizenry. Be that as it may, it is rather easy to connect racial resentment toward African Americans to organizations and institutions like NAACP on one end and White nationalist groups on the other end, but it is a different task linking racial resentment to political institutions.

We do not have an extensive battery of questions with which to examine the connection between Whites' resentment toward African Americans and their evaluation of political institutions, but we are able to capitalize on the context regarding the time of our data collection. First, we have a measure of the evaluation of Congress during a time when Republicans controlled both houses. In the wake of the 2016 election, the Republican Party retained its majorities in the House of Representatives and in the Senate. Controlling the House and the Senate, President Trump would presumably be enabled to enact many of the policies he campaigned on, such as curtailing immigration and repealing Obamacare. As a result of this conservative alignment, those high in racial resentment should evaluate Congress more positively than those low in racial resentment because of its ability to enact policies they favor.

Second, we have a measure of the evaluation of the Supreme Court. Context matters here as well. President Trump had a Supreme Court nominee in Neil Gorsuch in early 2018, after the death of Justice Antonin Scalia in 2017, and another nominee in Brett Kavanaugh in 2018, with the retirement of Justice Anthony Kennedy. Both nominees were considered extremely conservative individuals who would strengthen an already conservative Court. With a strongly conservative Court, which would seek to uphold cases that would protect the status quo, those higher in Whites' resentment toward African Americans should evaluate the Supreme Court more positively than those lower in Whites' resentment.

Table 4.6 shows the influence of racial resentment on evaluations of Congress and the Supreme Court. Our expectations regarding racial resentment are supported in our 2016 and 2018 data. The coefficients for Whites' resentment toward African Americans are quite strong and in the expected direction, suggesting that Whites with higher levels of racial resentment toward African Americans viewed Congress and the Supreme Court more positively than those with lower levels of racial resentment. We attribute this relationship to a belief that the status quo, which benefits and insulates Whites' advantage, would be better protected under conservative control of Congress and the Supreme Court. Thus, Whites' resentment toward African Americans is more than an analytical framework for analyzing racial policy and campaign appeals; it extends to the evaluations of and support for non-racial entities like standard political institutions. Racial resentment's correlation with support for political institutions, such as the Supreme Court, has always been thought of as stemming from a commitment to broad political

TABLE 4.6. **OLS Coefficients Predicting Approval of Congress and the Supreme Court, CCES**

	2018		2016	
	Approval Congress	Approval Supreme Court	Approval Congress	Approval Supreme Court
Racial Resentment	.23**	.22**	.15**	.11**
	(.04)	(.03)	(.04)	(.04)
Liberal	−.09	−.34**	−.07	−.11
	(.12)	(.13)	(.10)	(.11)
Conservative	.73**	.62**	.25**	−.52**
	(.11)	(.12)	(.09)	(.10)
Political Interest	.09	−.13**	.21**	−.11
	(.05)	(.05)	(.05)	(.06)
Education	−.06*	.01	.01	.00
	(.03)	(.03)	(.04)	(.04)
Age	−.00	.01	−.01	−.00
	(.00)	(.00)	(.00)	(.00)
Gender	−.11	−.12	−.16*	−.09
	(.09)	(.09)	(.08)	(.08)
Income	.02	.01	.04	.09*
	(.01)	(.02)	(.04)	(.04)
Constant	2.53**	3.19**	1.84**	4.56**
	(.31)	(.35)	(.25)	(.28)
R^2	.26	.26	.13	.07
Root MSE	1.04	1.14	1.10	1.22
N	665	665	977	977

Note. **$p<.01$; *$p<.05$.

values (Caldeira and Gibson 1992); however, our findings suggest that the extent to which institutions can also defend the status quo and Whites' privilege is an important source of support, especially among those who are racially resentful and sensitive to undeserved racial minorities taking advantage of unearned resources. Institutions may not be designed to insulate and protect Whites' interests, but their make-up can effectively do the same thing (Brand 1994; Lublin 1999; Pratto, Stallworth, and Conway-Lanz 1998).

Belief in the American Ethos

A component or myth in the American democratic ethos is that anyone can become president—overcoming disadvantage and mediocrity to achieve success.[4] Since the election of President Trump, an entrepreneur with no prior experience who seemed to defy all norms of decorum and conventional wisdom while campaigning, the idea that anyone can be elected president has been a common refrain. Trump is the fifth president to be elected with no prior electoral experience, but three of the others (Zachary Taylor, Ulysses Grant, and Dwight Eisenhower) were military heroes. Trump's challenger, Senator Hillary Clinton, was the first female nominee of a major political party and came very close to securing the presidency by winning the popular vote. As former first lady, New York senator, and secretary of state, Clinton's experience in office suggests she would have been an effective president. Barack Obama, to whom Clinton lost in the 2008 presidential primaries, became the first African American president. Similarly, Obama's Republican challenger in 2012 was Mitt Romney, former governor of Massachusetts and the first Mormon to be nominee of major party.

Thus, while it remains true that the American presidency is certainly not replete with diversity, recently the American myth that "if one works hard and believes in oneself, one can accomplish anything one sets one's mind to, even become president" has added several exemplars. Setting politics and personal biases aside, if possible, one might be able to take a sense of pride and satisfaction in the American political system adhering to its ethos. That is, one does not have to like Trump, Obama, Clinton, or Romney personally or like their politics to appreciate that they were able to overcome challenges to achieve a measure of political success. And, it's the ability of individuals to overcome those challenges, we believe, that taps into the American spirit. Looking at these candidates as a reflection of part of the American ethos, racial resentment may either enhance or detract from this view.

We designed a small survey-based experiment embedded in the 2016 CCES to assess whether people thought it was a good or bad thing for political candidates to overcome their challenges to succeed in politics. In this experiment, respondents were randomly assigned to four different questions pertaining to "Is it good or bad that someone like [Anyone, Obama, Clinton, Trump, or Romney] can be elected president?"

Figure 4.1 shows the percentage of respondents agreeing that it is a good thing that each listed candidate can be elected president. In the abstract, an overwhelming 80.6 percent agree that the fact "anyone" can be elected president in America is good. People seem to endorse this component of the American ethos, as it reflects ideas about equality and fairness. However, like most abstract democratic ideals, they tend to disintegrate when they are framed in more specific terms. While there is a slight increase in the percent saying that it was good that Mitt Romney

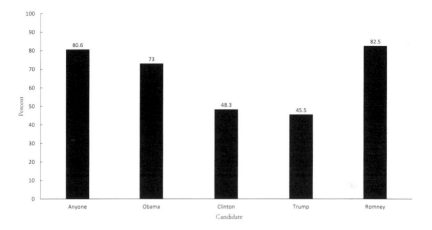

FIGURE 4.1. Percent Saying It Is Good for Someone like the Candidate to Be Elected President

(82.5 percent) can be elected president, a lower percent (73 percent) express the same regarding President Obama. Indeed, the possibility that an African American and a Mormon can be elected president reflects positively on the American political system. The numbers decline when respondents are asked about Hillary Clinton (a "woman") and Donald Trump (who had "no elected experience"); 48.3 and 45.5 percent respectively say that it is good that they can be elected president. Respondents find it more difficult to view Hillary Clinton's and Donald Trump's campaigns as objectively as they do the general norm.

An important question is whether Whites' resentment toward African Americans prevents respondents from viewing these candidates as objectively good. Table 4.7 contains our standard model and uses racial resentment to predict whether respondents viewed their campaigns as good. While racial resentment does not influence how people perceive "anyone," Clinton, and Romney, those high in racial resentment are more likely to think it was bad for someone like Obama to be elected president. The perception is that Obama, as the first African American president, was a threat to Whites' status and privilege and that he sought to advantage African Americans over Whites. On the other hand, those high in racial resentment are more likely to think it was good for someone like Trump to be elected president. The perception here is that Trump would defend, if not expand, Whites' status and privilege. Although Clinton and Romney represent different political parties, and

TABLE 4.7. **OLS Coefficients Predicting Whether It's Good Obama, Clinton, Trump, and Romney Can Be Elected President, CCES 2016**

Is it a good thing that someone like [*the following*] can be elected president?

	Anyone	Obama	Clinton	Trump	Romney
Racial Resentment	−.04 (.03)	−.23** (.07)	−.14 (.08)	.34** (.07)	.04 (.08)
Political Interest	.07 (.05)	−.05 (.07)	.04 (.09)	−.12 (.08)	−.04 (.08)
Liberal	−.00 (.09)	.38* (.19)	.71** (.21)	−.37 (.19)	.13 (.21)
Conservative	.03 (.09)	−.75** (.19)	−.73** (.19)	1.02** (.19)	−.03 (.17)
Education	.03 (.04)	−.05 (.08)	.12 (.09)	−.03 (.08)	.01 (.08)
Age	.00 (.00)	.00 (.00)	.01 (.00)	.00 (.00)	.01 (.00)
Gender	.10 (.07)	.02 (.15)	−.16 (.15)	−.08 (.16)	.05 (.16)
Income	.02 (.01)	.02 (.15)	.06** (.02)	.01 (.03)	.01 (.02)
Constant	2.48** (.24)	3.92** (.15)	1.96** (.54)	.96* (.42)	2.57** (.51)
R^2	.12	.43	.45	.56	.04
Root MSE	.36	.82	.90	.85	.79
N	119	142	158	145	135

Note. **$p<.01$; *$p<.05$.

political parties' platforms have drastically different racial implications, those high in Whites' resentment did not see it that way.

Is Racial Resentment a Feature Only of the Political Right?

Now that Whites' resentment toward African Americans has proven its worth as an analytical framework for understanding a range of racial and race-neutral issues, we return to its profile. Specifically, we explore whether racial resentment is a motivation among those exclusively on the political right or whether racial resentment also occurs among the political left. How are liberals who score high in racial resentment different from liberals who score low in racial resentment? And similarly for conservatives: how are those low in racial resentment different from conservatives who are high?

We maintain that Whites' resentment toward African Americans should not be dismissed as simply a motivation of the political right. Liberals, albeit at different levels, also utilize deservingness criteria that activate a sense of justice and fairness. They also possess racial information and stereotypes—all ingredients of racial resentment. In other words, like conservatives, liberals may also be considered enablers and supporters of positions that align with the most contemptible in society. Research by Conway et al. (2018) suggests that individuals on the political left are just as likely to be dogmatic authoritarians as those on the political right, and those left-wing authoritarians can be just as prejudiced, dogmatic, and extremist as right-wing authoritarians.[5] However, the targets of left-wing racial prejudice were not racial or ethnic minorities. Feldman and Huddy (2005) show similar effects of classic racial resentment on affirmative action programs (e.g., providing special college scholarships) among liberals and conservatives. Whereas increasing levels of classic resentment among liberals were associated with a steep decline in support for scholarship programs for Black but not White students, conservative support for the scholarship program declined regardless of the race of its intended beneficiary. From this viewpoint, we expect racial resentment toward African Americans among liberals to operate similarly to conservatives. The difference in magnitude for racial resentment's effect is a matter of degree, where liberals may exhibit larger effects on political preferences than conservatives because of the lack of variance in both resentment and policy views among conservatives, and larger variance in both among liberals.

As previous analyses in this chapter reveal, the effects of both racial resentment and ideology are largely dependent on the issue under consideration. While this is understandable given that no two issues activate the same sense of justice and deservingness, it means that racial resentment and ideology may not operate in a uniform pattern. This is indeed the case in the predicted probabilities and means on a range of issues illustrated in figures 4.2 to 4.5. On the issue of granting immigrant children legal status (i.e., DACA), liberals, moderates, and conservatives are virtually indistinguishable at lower levels of racial resentment, but as racial resentment increases, the support for granting legal status declines, though less so among liberals (fig. 4.2). Conservatives and moderates remain indistinguishable.

On an explicitly racial issue, such as whether one believes racial problems are rare, liberals are indistinguishable from conservatives and moderates at the higher levels of resentment (fig. 4.3). Here, too, liberals look a lot like conservatives. It is only at the lowest level of racial resentment that liberals and conservatives are discernible. Perhaps it is on explicitly racial issues that racial resentment compels greater similarities between liberals and conservatives. On an explicitly politically-contested race-neutral issue, such as the repeal of Obamacare, racial resentment is not as powerful in blurring ideological stripes (fig. 4.4). Liber-

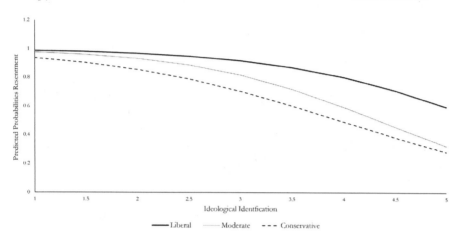

FIGURE 4.2. Predicted Probability of Support for Granting Immigrant Children Legal Status by Racial Resentment and Ideological Identification, CCES 2018

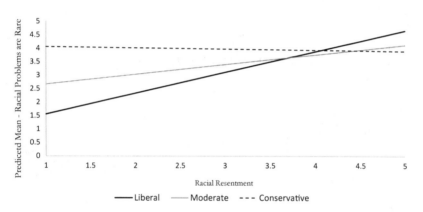

FIGURE 4.3. Predicted Mean Racial Problems Are Rare by Racial Resentment and Ideological Identification, CCES 2018

als and conservatives maintain their distinctiveness on this issue. Figure 4.5 shows the predicted level of approval for the Supreme Court due to racial resentment and ideological identity. While conservatives' support for the Supreme Court is virtually flat, unaffected by the level of racial resentment, liberals and moderates show greater approval of the Supreme Court at lower levels of racial resentment. As racial resentment increases, approval in the Supreme Court declines significantly. In a dif-

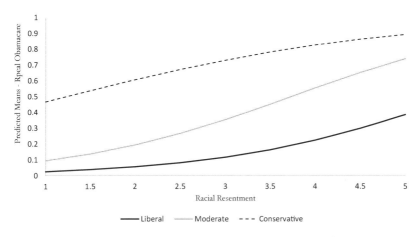

FIGURE 4.4. Predicted Means for Repeal Obamacare by Racial Resentment and Ideological Identity, CCES 2018

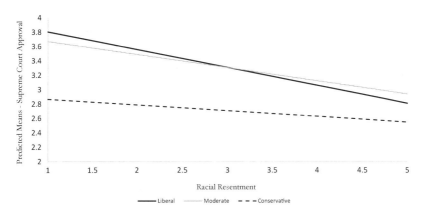

FIGURE 4.5. Predicted Means for Supreme Court Approval by Racial Resentment and Ideological Identity

ferent way not captured by the other issues, racial resentment among liberals and moderates decreases approval of the Supreme Court.

In short, liberals at higher levels of racial resentment look like conservatives on explicitly racial issues, but on non-racial issues, racial resentment may not be powerful enough to offset ideological leanings, perhaps due to the overlap in sensitivity to threat that conservatives and higher racially-resentful persons are both more likely to have.

Conclusion

Whites who show higher levels of resentment toward African Americans parallel those who possess a closed racial belief system. Higher levels of racial resentment are functions of lower levels of education, older age cohorts, conservative identity, and low levels of political engagement. Individuals with such features are not assuredly racially resentful, but on average they are more likely to express racial resentment than individuals without those features. Other features normally associated with a closed racial belief system, such as male identity and lower social status, were not evident with racial resentment.

Holding these and other factors constant, Whites' resentment toward African Americans performed in an extremely robust and predictable fashion in explaining political attitudes and behavior. Across a range of explicit racial issues, racial resentment explains why individuals support inegalitarian positions toward African Americans, and it is often the most powerful predictor. The same holds true for more subtle and race-neutral issues.

Relative to other predictors, Whites' resentment toward African Americans is a consistent and powerful predictor. The only area where racial resentment as a measure appears weakened is when it juxtaposes another race-neutral motivation, like social dominance orientation or conservatism, which overlap with values related to deservingness and justice appraisals, as well as defense of the status quo. Whites' resentment toward African Americans and social dominance are both significant and meaningful when they are in the same models, but social dominance is often the more powerful predictor. Nevertheless, on the basis of different analyses and issues, our new conceptualization and measure of racial resentment should be taken seriously as an analytical framework.

CHAPTER FIVE

Racial Resentment and the Susceptibility to Campaign Appeals

W hile many memorable and inspiring slogans have appeared in political campaigns and elections, no political slogan in recent memory has created as much consternation as Donald Trump's slogan, *Make America Great Again*. Though he did not coin the slogan (Ronald Reagan repeatedly promised to "make America great again" during his 1980 presidential campaign), Trump first used it in 2012 in reference to President Barack Obama's administration and also used it heavily in the 2016 presidential primaries. The slogan quickly became a popular rallying cry for Trump's supporters, appearing on baseball caps, placards, banners, and t-shirts. After securing the Republican presidential nomination, and well into his first term as president, Donald Trump continued to use *Make America Great Again* in speeches and rejoinders in his social media exchanges. But, how was this slogan interpreted?

Several political commentators interpreted *Make America Great Again* as a reference to restoring America to a period when economic prosperity, law and order, security, and traditional values dictated the American way of life (Soffen and Lu 2016). However, others interpreted the slogan as implicitly racial, invoking thoughts about returning to a Jim Crow era in which African Americans held lower status and racial prejudice was more pervasive (Phillips 2017). In addition to these two interpretations, the slogan elicited both non-racial and racial interpretations. As former President Bill Clinton noted in a 2016 speech,

> If you're a White southerner, you know exactly what [the slogan] means. I'm old enough to remember the good old days. And they weren't all that good in

many ways. . . . What it means is I'll give you the economy you had 50 years ago and I'll move you back up the social totem pole and other people down. (Haines 2016, para. 3)

Whatever message the slogan was intended to convey, what ultimately mattered was how individuals chose to interpret it.

Though minimal research has been conducted on political slogans, they are considered integral in political advertising and campaigns (Denton 1980; Sherif 1937).[1] With slogans, candidates seek to encapsulate their political identity into efficient and memorable expressions, allowing individuals to bypass cumbersome campaign information and policy details in favor of affective cues that aid judgment and decision-making (Sherif 1937). Thus, political slogans—short, catchy, authoritative, and ambiguous—are designed to tap into human motivations by activating deep emotional reactions that connect candidates and individuals around common values and beliefs (Sherif 1937; Vaes, Paladino, and Magagnotti 2011). Slogans also serve as a brand extension for candidates, helping to convey persuasive information beyond the candidate or policy details (Boush 1993). Instead of having to sift through the tedium of campaign information, party platforms, and media messages, individuals, with minimal cognitive effort, can draw upon information conveyed in campaign slogans.

This chapter examines the extent to which Trump's *Make America Great Again* slogan resonates with Whites who are racially resentful toward African Americans. We contend that while a vast majority of Americans, or anyone for that matter, would like to see their country aspire to greatness, references to the past through the use of "again" activate sentiments about the threat to Whites' status (DeBell 2017; Griffin and Bollen 2009).[2] Because "again" references a previous era and because individuals' perceptions of the past are likely shaped by race, African Americans' and Whites' interpretations of the slogan are expected to differ dramatically. This expectation stems from the notion that African Americans' recollection of the past likely reflects a more perilous era in which racial prejudice and discrimination were more pervasive. In contrast, Whites' recollection of the past likely reflects an era in which they were more dominant and benefited more from the status quo or when people "knew their place" and were reluctant to challenge it.[3]

Exploring the extent to which Whites' resentment toward African

RACIAL RESENTMENT AND THE SUSCEPTIBILITY TO CAMPAIGN APPEALS   139

Americans makes one open to campaign appeals offers important insight into how seemingly benign and ostensibly non-racial expressions (or a single word) can be exploited. The 2016 presidential election will be remembered as one of the most racially polarizing elections, and the *Make America Great Again* slogan was its call to arms for President Trump.

The Nature of Slogans

Slogans have existed since the formation of language and been employed as a means of focusing attention and exhorting action, historically as a rallying cry for war and violent conflict (Denton 1980; Sherif 1937). Slogans are often used as instruments of popular persuasion in advertising and political campaigns. A great deal of the research on slogans focuses on their definition or on specifying how slogans differ from other expressions. In one of the earliest examinations of slogans, Sherif (1937) defined slogans as "phrases, a short sentence, a headline, a dictum, which, intentionally or unintentionally, amounts to an appeal to the person who is exposed to it to buy some article, to revive or strengthen an already well-established stereotype, to accept a new idea, to undertake some action, to imply a value judgement" (p. 32). As for the most effective slogan, Sherif added that it is "one that appeals to a particular appetite, need, or other demand with a shortcut, simple expression whose features—such as rhythm, alliteration and punning—make its recurrence or repetition easy" (p. 32).

Shankel (1942) expanded on this term by suggesting that a slogan is "some pointed term, phrase, or expression, fittingly worded, which suggests action, loyalty, or which causes people to decide upon and to fight for the realization of some principles or decisive issue" (p. 7). Denton (1980) proposes that slogans are more than simple declarative statements; rather, they are unique rhetorical devices that may be utilized in persuasive ways. Namely, slogans function to "simplify complicated ideas, issues or ideology of a group or movement," "create attention or raise consciousness about an issue or group," "activate or increase the level of activity of one's supporters," and "aid in the creation of strong interpersonal identification" (pp. 13–14). More succinctly, slogans are designed to be short statements that contain implicit references that create alternative meanings.

Make American Great Again as a Political Slogan

On its face, *Make America Great Again* does not explicitly refer to race
or an attack on White privilege, making it easier to refute its divisive intent. Like most political slogans and phrases, its meaning becomes less
subjective as it passes through the political environment and is used by
different persons holding different identities. As Ceccarelli (1998) wrote
about polysemous messages, "distinct meanings exist for a text, and they
are identifiable by the critic, the rhetor, or the audience" (p. 398). For example, Ronald Reagan used the slogan in the 1980 presidential election
to invoke patriotism and a return to economic prosperity (Azevedo, Jost,
and Rothmund 2017; Halmari 1993). Bill Clinton also used the phrase in
disparate speeches, though it never became a full-fledged slogan.

Donald Trump used the slogan consistently in the 2016 presidential
primaries, though his gravitation toward the slogan dates to 2012, a day
after the reelection of President Obama. Tumulty (2017) suggests that it
was in the context of Obama's reelection that Donald Trump began to
consider a more serious involvement in politics and how to brand it. According to Donald Trump, *Make America Great Again* "meant jobs. It
meant industry and meant military strength. It meant taking care of our
veterans," referring to the turn of the twentieth century and the post–
World War II years (Tumulty 2017, para. 36). Despite Trump's application of the slogan to numerous issues, none of which were explicitly
racial,[4] it was perceived by many as a disparagement of the status quo.
While references to the past reflect a statement about the status quo, political cues can either exacerbate or dampen people's interpretations.
That the slogan favors a bygone era is undisputed.

Make America Great Again as an Appeal That the Status Quo Is under Threat

The *Make America Great Again* slogan can be perceived to have a negative racial undertone for several reasons. First, as instruments of popular persuasion, slogans reflect the sentiments and personas of politicians
who wield them. For example, given that presidential candidate Donald Trump sympathized with White nationalists and supremacists while
denigrating African Americans and other racial minorities, his use of

racially derogatory expressions to demean African Americans, Latinos, women, and Muslims during his presidential campaign may have contributed to perceptions of the slogan as an expression of racial-ethnic antagonism (Phillips 2017). Second, while political slogans are defined by politicians and their strategic marketing campaigns, individuals and groups contribute to the meaning as well. Candidates may lose control over the meaning of their slogans as other politicians and groups co-opt them for their own purposes. One example from the 2016 presidential election is when the *Make America Great Again* slogan appeared in the rhetoric of Alternative Right (alt-right) groups. In several instances, the slogan was rebranded as *Make America White Again,* a more racially explicit appeal intended to communicate a nationalistic ideology (Melton 2017). Furthermore, Donald Trump's involvement in the birther movement, which questioned Obama's citizenship and legitimacy as president, fueled racially tinged perceptions of the slogan.

Slogans are expressions embedded in larger advertising strategies, and despite the paucity of research on slogans (Aberbach and Walker 1970), a great deal of research has examined racial appeals in campaign advertising (Lopez 2014; Mendelberg 2001; Valentino, Hutchings, and White 2002). The literature on implicit racial appeals—messages that do not overtly express racial or anti-Black sentiment—offers an important contribution to the evaluation of the *Make America Great Again* slogan. Implicit racial appeals are extremely powerful because the omission of explicit racial language protects the communication from charges of racism (Lopez 2014; Mendelberg 2001).

While explicit racial appeals cannot be written off as ineffective (Huber and Lapinski 2006, 2008), the research literature has emphasized the importance of implicit racial cues in political evaluations (Mendelberg 2001; Valentino 1999; Valentino, Hutchings, and White 2002). References to non-racial cues in campaign ads, like law and order, government spending, traditional values, and raising taxes, activate racial predispositions that affect judgments and evaluations of presidential candidates (Hurwitz and Peffley 2005). On the basis of this literature, political slogans, especially the use of "again" in *Make America Great Again*, are expected to prime racial considerations, and because of their intentional ambiguity, slogans are most effective when they employ implicit racial cues.

An alternative argument can be made that *Make America Great Again* is more likely to activate a non-racial than a racial interpretation. References to the past in the slogan may activate a broader assessment of the status quo and attributions of responsibility. It may not be only African Americans who have forgotten their place, but, rather, threats to the status quo may be seen as emanating from ethnic minorities, political and social groups, governmental policies, and changing societal norms (e.g., political correctness). This interpretation is reflected in a suggestion by Westacott (2016):

> Underlying these political agendas is a real preference for a world in which everyone "knew their place" and behaved accordingly: when children obeyed their parents or felt the back of a hand; when men earned bread while women kept house; when white privilege and power went largely unchallenged. (para. 5)

Thus, we do not rule out the possibility of non-racial interpretations. It is also possible for "again" to activate ideological considerations. If, as Lammers and Baldwin (2017) suggest, conservatives are more likely to desire the past and feel nostalgia than liberals, the slogan may be viewed as exploiting ideological cleavages in the US electorate. Ideology will be an important consideration in this analysis.

In other original research employing a similar methodology, we found that individuals can reasonably infer anti–political correctness from the slogan.[5] Predating Trump, political correctness has always been defined in terms of Whites' interests being usurped by diversity and multiculturalism preferences. Beginning in the 1980s and 1990s, anti–political correctness grew out of a concern that colleges and universities harbored a hidden liberal agenda that imposed diversity and multiculturalism and circumvented free and open thought. Political correctness was seen as an "instrument of corrective justice" or "payback for the sins of all of the Dead White Males that created the racist, patriarchic and imperial West" (Orlet 2008, p. 2). White liberals and the Black civil rights establishment were viewed as driving political correctness to delegitimize as racist any criticism of their post–civil rights agenda. Principled objections to affirmative action programs, immigration policy, and social welfare were seen as racist, and thus circumvented discussion.

Political correctness was perceived as a threat to Whites' status in the 2008 election. The concern was that Barack Obama, the first Black president, would not receive a thorough vetting because of political correctness. Obama would be spared legitimate questions by the media and other political candidates for fear that any criticism would label them as racist. Political correctness meant dismissing or obscuring facts about Obama's policies and positions, and it also meant translating support for John McCain into racial insensitivity. Diversity, multiculturalism, and identity politics were now valued over free speech rights, thus signaling to Whites a change in social acceptability.

Donald Trump railed against political correctness incessantly in 2016. In addition to the threat to Whites' status, political correctness also conveyed that basic freedoms, such as the freedom of expression, were being curtailed. Political correctness, according to Trump, was the cause of America's ills, and many argue that his attacks on political correctness contributed significantly to his election. Trump was able to appeal to individuals who were sensitive to Whites' status and position.

"Again" likely signified a return to a previous era in which people were not politically correct and could say what they meant about race, racial policies, immigration, and Muslims without being penalized or their rights being curtailed. This would indeed parallel sentiments about racial resentment. For African Americans, "again" likely signified a return to a previous era in which they were not respected and were denigrated by abusive language.

An Interpretation of *Make America Great Again*

Our theory for how individuals interpret the slogan, as either a racial or a non-racial appeal, is based on two interrelated suppositions. First, while most Americans would like to see the country thrive and aspire to greatness, reference to the past or "again" in *Make America Great Again* produces the stress in the slogan. "Again" means to return to a previous position or condition, but the specific condition is often ambiguous and open to interpretation, which distinguishes political slogans from other forms of advertising strategies. Instead of moving forward on the current path to the future, the slogan implies that the status quo is unacceptable and that the past is preferable. "Again" raises the notion that certain aspects of society have gotten out of hand, though those aspects are left to individual interpretations. Thus, it is the interpretation of an ambiguous past that should lead African Americans and Whites to perceive *Make America Great Again* differently. As Griffin and Bollen (2009) suggest, "Race is one of the most important issues for which the presence of the past is both potent and sorrowful" (p. 594).

Second, because perceptions of the past differ significantly by race, the slogan likely activates different frames of reference for African Americans and Whites. While African Americans likely view the past as a time in which racial prejudice was more pervasive and they experienced more discrimination, Whites likely view the past as a time in which they were more dominant and people knew their place. With a single word activating such different frames of reference, *Make America Great Again* capitalizes on deep racial divisions in American society. While it is possible for the slogan to activate specific memories of the past, such as Jim Crow practices, it is not necessary for individuals to recall specific practices or to have directly experienced them. African Americans need to believe the past was more perilous for them, and Whites need to believe they possessed more power and privilege in the past. In sum, African Americans and Whites are expected to have drastically different interpretations of *Make America Great Again* based on the recollections activated by the word "again."

Evidence from our data indicating that Whites and African Americans interpret the past differently supports our expectations. We used the following survey question, which taps the preference for the past versus the future:

> *Please indicate how true or false you find each of the following statements. The United States of the past is a much better place than the United States of the future.*

The response scale includes five categories: *completely true*; *largely true*; *somewhat true*; *largely false*; and *completely false*.

A considerable racial discrepancy exists in views of the past versus the future. In line with our argument, Whites have a greater preference for the past than African Americans. Table 5.1 shows that only 20.9 percent of African Americans prefer the US of the past versus the future (combining *completely true* and *largely true*), compared to 42.6 percent of Whites. This 21.7 percentage point difference is not trivial. The group means also reflect how Whites (M=3.20, SD=1.24) view the past more positively than African Americans (M=2.49, SD=1.28) (t=11.0, df=1764, p<.01). African Americans likely think of a general time when racial discrimination was more acceptable, and Whites likely think of a time when they enjoyed greater privilege and higher status.

We further explore racial differences in an Ordinary Least Squares

TABLE 5.1. **Preference for the Past, Response Distribution by Race**

The United States of the past is a much *better place than the United States of the future*	**Whites**	**African Americans**
1. Completely false	14.3%	27.7%
2. Largely false	16.5	26.3
3. Somewhat true	26.6	25.1
4. Largely true	20.3	10.8
5. Completely true	22.3	10.1
Mean[a]	3.20	2.49
SD	(1.34)	(1.28)
N	1081	685

Note. In the upper portion of the table, all row proportions in the "Whites" column are statistically different from row proportions in the "African Americans" column.

[a] Racial group mean differences in "Preference for the Past" result from an independent sample t-test (t=11.0, df=1764, p<.01).

(OLS) multivariate model controlling for ideology, income, respondents' age cohort, education, and gender. As reported in table 5.2 (model 1), race, education, income, and ideology are significant predictors of individuals' preference for the US of the past. The significant negative coefficient for race indicates that Whites prefer the US of the past more than African Americans. Racial differences cannot be explained by differences in education, income, or ideology. Moreover, lower levels of education and income are associated with a greater desire for the past. Another important finding is that conservatives are more supportive of the past than liberals. This last finding is consistent with other research that suggests that nostalgia—preference for the past—and discomfort with societal change are core components of conservatism (Lammers and Baldwin 2017). This finding raises the possibility that the word "again" in the slogan may trigger a response among conservatives. Respondents' age and gender are not significantly related to beliefs about the past.

Nevertheless, this analysis may not fully explain the preference for the past over the future. Including African Americans and Whites in the same model (or as a simple control variable) may mask the differential effects of ideology, age, and other factors. Thus, we include a second OLS regression model (model 2) that includes (race × ideology) and (race × age cohort) interaction terms. While the expectations for ideology fit within our thinking about closed racial beliefs, respondents' age cohort is relevant because older individuals, especially African Americans, drawing on their experiences, are better able to determine the desirability of a bygone era than younger age cohorts.

TABLE 5.2. **Standardized OLS Regression Models Predicting Preference for the Past**

Independent Variables	Model 1	Model 2	(Whites) Model 3	(African Americans) Model 4
Racial Resentment			.49** (.03)	
Race (White=1)	.52** (.07)	−1.02** (.23)		
Ideology	.31** (.02)	.10** (.03)	.25** (.03)	.10** (.03)
Education	−.20** (.03)	−.19** (.03)	−.03 (.04)	−.33** (.06)
Age	−.00 (.00)	−.01** (.00)	−.00 (.00)	−.01** (.00)
Gender	.03 (.06)	−.02 (.07)	−.06 (.07)	−.02 (.11)
Income	−.02* (.01)	−.02 (.01)	−.03** (.01)	.02 (.02)
Race × Ideology		.33** (.04)		
Race × Age		.01** (.00)		
Constant	2.39** (.14)	3.38** (.20)	1.05** (.17)	3.51** (.38)
R²	.23	.27	.45	.09
Root MSE	1.20	1.17	1.01	1.23
N	1,500	1,500	901	573

Note. *p<.05; **p<.01. Dependent variable: "The United States of the past is a much better place than the United States of the future." Higher values indicate greater preference for the past.

The interaction effects in model 2 further clarify the influence of race on preferences for the US's past. Figures 5.1 and 5.2 illustrate the conditional effects of ideology (1=Very Liberal and 7=Very Conservative) and age (1=18 to 29; 2=30 to 39; 3=40 to 49; 4=50 to 59; 5=60+) on race. Figure 5.1 shows that racial differences in preferences for the past dramatically increase as the level of conservatism increases. At the liberal extreme, Whites and African Americans are virtually equivalent in their desire for the past. However, Whites' preference for the past surpasses African Americans' preference for the past as the level of conservatism increases. Equally important, respondents' age cohorts in figure 5.2 differ significantly by race, as expected. As the prediction line is virtually flat among Whites, indicative of no cohort differences, the prediction line declines as respondents' age cohorts increases among African Americans. In other words, older cohorts of African Americans are more sensitive to the perils of the United States' past than younger African American age cohorts and Whites.

Introducing our measure of Whites' resentment into the analysis for Whites (model 3) and African Americans (model 4) may help to corroborate the motivation for favoring the past over the future.[6] If those who are high in Whites' resentment toward African Americans are more sen-

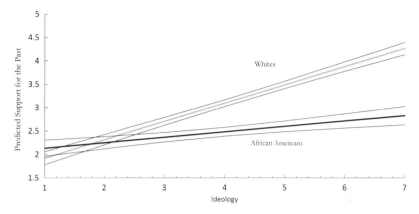

FIGURE 5.1. Predicted Mean Support for the Past by Levels of Ideology (Self-Reported) and Race (95% Confidence Intervals)

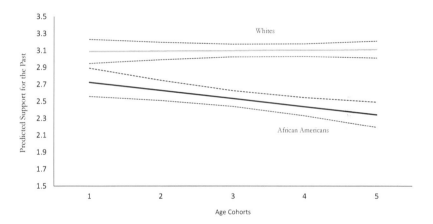

FIGURE 5.2. Predicted Mean Support for the Past by Age Cohorts and Race (95% Confidence Intervals)

sitive to violations of the justice motive by undeserving African Americans and other minorities, they should be inclined more favorably to a previous era in which Whites' status and privilege were more secure and when people "knew their place."

This is exactly what we find among Whites in model 3. Higher levels of White racial resentment are associated with greater favorability for the past, but higher African American resentment toward Whites does not produce the same effect. We take this as evidence, especially among Whites, that those high in racial resentment express a greater desire to return to a previous era because it reflects a time when Whites had greater status and privilege and when racial minorities were treated more harshly. As others have noted recently, many Whites today feel like they are losing out or being "cut in line" by African Americans. The election of the first African American president, greater concern for diversity and multiculturalism, and the rise of political correctness all signify to Whites that their concerns are secondary, if at all relevant.

In summary, these analyses of the preference for the United States' past represent direct tests of our expectations for how people interpret the *Make America Great Again* slogan, but they also show how racial differences in the interpretation have the potential to mask other effects, like the influence of ideology and respondents' age cohorts.

"Knowing One's Place" List Experiment

On the basis of the assumption that individuals might be somewhat reluctant, or find it difficult, to attribute a racial interpretation to the *Make America Great Again* slogan, we utilized a list-experiment or item-count approach—a well-known method that reduces social desirability response bias. The logic of this approach is as follows. In randomly assigned groups (at least two or three), individuals are asked to report the number of items on a list that fit a particular criterion. For example, a respondent in a control group can be given a list of three interpretations of *Make America Great Again* and asked how many of them (but not which ones) he or she thinks are correct; the average number constitutes the baseline condition. The other experimental treatment conditions involve asking the same question of participants, but with one additional interpretation option. Subtracting the average number of behaviors reported in the baseline condition from the average number of behaviors reported in the experimental treatment condition provides an estimate of the proportion of people in the experimental group(s) who identified the fourth item as an interpretation. Because respondents are aware that the researcher cannot know which of the specific interpretations they identified, their answers to this question should be undistorted by social desirability. Despite several limitations, such as not being able to distinguish individuals who are most sensitive to certain stimuli and the possibility that list experiments may not differ much from direct questions, this technique has been used extensively to address racially sensitive topics (Kuklinski, Cobb, and Gilens 1997; Kuklinski et al. 1997; Redlawsk, Tolbert, and Franko 2010; Sniderman and Carmines 1997).

We utilize a two-treatment-group list experiment, where respondents were randomly assigned to three groups—1) Control Group, 2) Treatment I: Diffuse, or 3) Treatment II: Specific. Each group was presented with a list of items and asked, *Donald Trump frequently uses the slogan "Make America Great Again." When Donald Trump says "Make America Great Again," how many of these things do you think he is referring to?* Respondents were not required to reveal which specific items she or he identified, just the number of items. The idea is to ensure the respondent's anonymity by not asking them to address each item specifically.

Each group was given the same list of three non-sensitive items from which to choose:

1. *When America held a stronger military presence in the world.*
2. *When politicians followed the voice of their constituents.*
3. *When the government was not involved in regulating business.*

One of the groups (Control Group) serves as the baseline, while respondents in the two treatment groups receive an additional sensitive item. For Treatment I: Diffuse, respondents were given the following sensitive item:

4a. *When people knew their place and accepted responsibility.*

For Treatment II: Specific, respondents were given the following sensitive item:

4b. *When African Americans knew their place and accepted responsibility.*

List experiments are valid to the extent that the baseline categories reflect reasonable alternatives and are not easily dismissed. As opposed to meaningless or vacuous items, the baseline items attempt to control for alternative perceptions of the slogan. Donald Trump himself has referred to the slogan vis-à-vis the US possessing a stronger military and military presence; he also has criticized government regulations on hindering financial and economic progress. Including hollow items in the baseline would inflate both treatments. Thus, the baseline or control items include references to actual alternative explanations of the *Make America Great Again* slogan.

We selected "knowing one's place" as the prime in the list-experiment because it conveys a sense of threat to the status quo. This prime is appropriate given that when members of a group are said to "forget their place," they are seen as challenging their lower status and the general ordering of society. Such a challenge is likely perceived as a threat to Whites, who benefit from the status quo and have a vested interest in defending it (Azevedo, Jost, and Rothmund 2017). "Knowing one's place" normally carries a negative connotation, as it conveys to someone in a subordinate position that they should be content with their situation and not try to make things better for themselves.

The racial and non-racial cues in the treatment conditions should influence the interpretation of the slogan. First, for Treatment I: Diffuse (non-racial), individuals who recognize that the past for Whites involved greater status, perhaps those with a more closed racial belief system, can be expected to view the slogan as a return to a nostalgic era of White advantage. Whites, conservatives, Republicans, the less educated, and men should show a greater propensity to perceive the slogan as non-racial because they want to deny the existence of racial prejudice.

Second, for Treatment II: Specific (racial), individuals who recognize the past for African Americans as more perilous, and perhaps those with a more open racial belief system, can be expected to view the slogan in racial terms. African Americans, liberals, Democrats, the more highly educated, and women should show a greater propensity to perceive the slogan as racial.

Factors Related to Racial and Non-racial Interpretations of *Make America Great Again*

Racial and non-racial interpretations of *Make America Great Again* are expected to vary systematically by how individuals interpret the past, racial beliefs (e.g., racial resentment and social dominance orientation), and political motivations (e.g., ideology).

Whites' Resentment toward African Americans

Key to racial resentment is the belief that racial prejudice no longer exists; it should therefore no longer be used to excuse bad behavior on the part of African Americans, and thus African Americans are undeserving of special considerations. Whites' resentment toward African Americans has been used to explain opposition to the restoration of voting rights for felons, negativity bias in evaluations of President Obama's performance on the economy, and the belief that African Americans, more so than Whites and other groups, are evaluated by racial considerations instead of objective criteria. Because Whites at higher levels of racial resentment likely reject racial explanations or justifications, they should be more likely to dispute that the slogan has a racial interpretation and instead be more accepting of a broader non-racial meaning.

Social dominance orientation (SDO) is included as a predictor of support for the *Make America Great Again* slogan because it reflects Whites' willingness to accept a non-racial interpretation. Specifically, it is support for anti-egalitarianism or a desire for Whites to maintain and increase their dominance and power over other groups (Nour, Sidanius, and Levin 2010). Thus, among individuals who score high in social dominance, the word "again" is more likely to be interpreted as referencing an era in which Whites were more dominant rather than a past that was more perilous for African Americans.

A conservative ideology, even if self-reported, is associated with beliefs that African Americans violate traditional values (i.e., self-discipline, perseverance, and delayed gratification), that they should make more individual effort rather than relying on government, and that they rely on claims of racial prejudice as an excuse for lack of effort (Sidanius, Pratto, and Bobo 1996). Beyond racial considerations, conservatives also are more likely to prefer the past and experience nostalgia than liberals (Lammers and Baldwin 2017). Because the word "again" in the *Make America Great Again* slogan references changes to a previous era, it may potentially trigger a conservative preference. For these reasons, conservatives should reject a racial interpretation of the slogan more than liberals, while moderates should fall between them (Jost et al. 2003).

Demographic Explanations

This final section considers the influence of demographic variations in the interpretation of *Make America Great Again*. How many of Donald Trump's base supporters—such as White men, less educated Whites, and older White cohorts—interpret the slogan as racial? For instance, in addition to being less racist than men, women tend to be more receptive of racially egalitarian political appeals than men (Hutchings et al. 2004; Hutchings, Walton, and Benjamin 2010). Thus, women should be more likely to interpret the slogan in racial terms than men. Individuals who are more highly educated are less willing to deny the existence of racial prejudice than the less educated. The higher educated also are more likely to distinguish between implicit and explicit racial appeals than individuals with lower levels of education. Explicit racial appeals have the same influence as implicit racial appeals on the less educated. For our purpose, then, the more highly educated should be more likely to view the slogan as racial than the less educated. Finally, because racial prejudice is more prevalent among older cohorts than younger cohorts (Firebaugh and Davis 1988; Gonsalkorale, Sherman, and Klauer 2008; Wilson 1996), the former should be more likely to deny the existence of racial prejudice. Consequently, older cohorts should be less likely to interpret the slogan in racial terms compared to younger cohorts.

What Is Learned from the List Experiment?

Table 5.3 presents the mean item-counts for the control group and the two treatment groups. As is customary in the analysis of list-experiments, the proportion of respondents who refer to the *Make America Great Again* slogan as either "people knowing their place" (Treatment I: Non-racial) or "African Americans knowing their place" (Treatment II: Racial) is derived by subtracting the mean of the item-counts for the control group from the mean of the item-counts in the treatments. An important takeaway from these results is that a majority of individuals interpret people knowing their place as both—as targeting African Americans and as a non-racial appeal. In panel I, which includes all respondents, 59 percent interpret the phrase as racial while 54 percent interpret the phrase as non-racial.

TABLE 5.3. **Response Distribution to** *Make American Great Again* **Two-Treatment List Experiment by Race**

Item Count	Control Group	Treatment I: People knew their place	Treatment II: African Americans knew their place
Panel I: All Respondents			
0 Items	27.1%	19.7%	10.4%
1 Item	18.4	18.5	22.1
2 Items	21.0	18.0	22.1
3 Items	33.5	14.5	28.0
4 Items		29.3	17.4
Total	100	100	100
N	624	619	673
Mean	1.61	2.15	2.20
SD	1.20	1.51	1.26
Difference (Effect)		54%	59%
t-test (against baseline)		6.99**	8.60**
Panel II: Whites			
0 Items	19.3%	14.2%	7.2%
1 Item	16.7	16.1	19.4
2 Items	22.2	15.7	22.6
3 Items	41.8	18.8	35.8
4 Items		35.2	15.0
Total	100	100	100
N	324	330	349
Mean	1.87	2.45	2.32
SD	1.16	1.46	1.16
Difference (Effect)		58%	45%
t-test (against baseline)		5.69**	5.14**
Panel III: African Americans			
0 Items	38.9%	26.3%	11.6%
1 Item	21.3	21.7	28.9
2 Items	20.4	20.3	21.5
3 Items	19.4	8.7	16.4
4 Items		23.0	21.6
Total	100		
N	211	217	232
Mean	1.20	1.81	2.07
SD	1.15	1.50	1.33
Difference (Effect)		60%	87%
t-test (against baseline)		4.66**	7.30**

Note. *p<.05; **p<.01.

However, this interpretive nuance comes into focus when Whites (panel II) and African Americans (panel III) are analyzed separately. Here, too, the combined analysis of African Americans and Whites masks important differences. Nearly nine in ten African Americans (87 percent) interpret the phrase as racial, compared to 45 percent of

Whites. Although considerably lower than the percentage of African Americans who think the expression refers to a period in which African Americans knew their place, a sizeable percentage of Whites accept a racial interpretation of the phrase. In contrast, a slightly higher percentage of African Americans (60 percent) than Whites (58 percent) accept a non-racial interpretation, as referring to a period when people (in general) knew their place. These results support our expectations. African Americans perceive the idiom in both racial and non-racial terms while Whites see the idiom more in non-racial terms. But, as noted earlier, considerable variability likely exists among both African Americans and Whites in the interpretation of the idiom.

White respondents who believe the past was better than the future tend to see *Make America Great Again* as having more non-racial meaning; however, African Americans who believe the past was better exhibit no experimental effects. Only African Americans who believe the past was not better exhibit any experimental treatment effects, and they do not distinguish between racial and non-racial meaning. In other words, African Americans are aware that non-racial meaning can still have racial consequences.

Table 5.4 reports the factors that influence the racial and non-racial interpretations of the "knowing one's place" idiom. Recall that "knowing one's place" is a prime used to capture the threat to the status quo in the slogan. Among African Americans, those with a greater preference for the US's future over the past interpret the slogan as racial by a sizeable margin (95 percent). African Americans who express moderate (85 percent) and low preferences for the past (62 percent) similarly perceive a racial meaning. This relationship can be seen among Whites, though at much lower levels. For instance, Whites who express a low preference for the past are more likely to endorse a racial interpretation of the slogan than those who express a moderate and high preference for the past. Equally important, a higher preference for the United States' past among Whites is associated with greater support of a non-racial interpretation, compared to low or moderate preferences for the past.

Ideology is consistent with our expectations, particularly for Whites. While African American liberals and conservatives both interpret the slogan through a racial lens, White liberals are more accepting of a racial interpretation (100 percent) relative to moderates (35 percent) and conservatives (24 percent). We noted earlier that it is plausible for references to the past to resonate with conservatives because of their fondness for

TABLE 5.4. **List-Experiment, Differences in the Interpretation of Make America Great Again by Control and Treatment Groups**

	White Respondents			African American Respondents		
Variables	Control Group Mean (SD)	Treatment I: Non-racial People forgot their place, %	Treatment II: Racial African Americans forgot their place, %	Control Group Mean (SD)	Treatment I: Non-racial People forgot their place, %	Treatment II: Racial African Americans forgot their place, %
Preference for the past						
Low	1.21 (1.15)	54	74	1.12 (1.15)	59	95
Medium	1.80 (1.13)	61	46	1.27 (1.13)	63	85
High	2.32 (.96)	76	28	1.39 (1.20)	51	62
Racial Resentment						
High	2.35 (.97)	70	28			
Medium	1.92 (1.10)	51	24			
Low	1.11 (1.11)	58	100			
Social Dominance						
High	2.35 (.97)	64	39			
Medium	1.67 (1.12)	22	46			
Low	.86 (1.04)	78	100			
Ideology						
Conservative	2.48 (.84)	75	24	1.27	94	98
Moderate	1.69 (1.11)	68	35	1.26	34	38
Liberal	1.12 (1.15)	60	100	1.17	66	91
Gender						
Female	1.91 (1.11)	43	45	1.22 (1.12)	53	95
Male	1.81 (1.21)	77	45	1.17 (1.23)	78	65
Age						
18 to 29	1.81 (1.11)	30	51	1.09 (1.15)	75	100
30 to 39	1.66 (1.15)	51	27	1.17 (1.23)	77	64
40 to 49	1.74 (1.21)	61	0	1.33 (1.13)	29	82
50 to 59	1.94 (1.16)	68	65	1.02 (1.24)	62	74
60+	1.94 (1.18)	71	56	1.35 (1.03)	58	98
Education						
High School	2.01 (1.17)	35	48	1.17 (1.28)	55	28
Some College	1.88 (1.19)	61	55	1.32 (1.16)	28	76
College Grad+	1.74 (1.11)	71	37	1.12 (1.12)	83	92

Note. Percentages adding to over 100% are rounded to 100.

nostalgic sentiments. Indeed, when presented with a non-racial prime, White conservatives are more open to a non-racial interpretation compared to moderates and liberals, though sizeable majorities of each group are open to such interpretations. Thus, the effects of ideology on the interpretation of "knowing one's place" are more uniform for Whites than African Americans. However, the relationship between respondents' age cohorts and racial interpretations of "knowing one's place" deviates somewhat from our expectations.

One discernable pattern in the results suggests that younger African Americans (roughly three-quarters of those 18–39 years of age) are more accepting of the non-racial interpretation in which "people have forgotten their place" than older African Americans (roughly six in ten of those 50 years of age and older). On the other hand, younger Whites are less supportive of a non-racial interpretation than older Whites (30–51 percent vs. 70 percent respectively).

Gender differences in the racial and non-racial interpretations reveal another significant disparity among Whites and African Americans. For instance, a larger percentage of African American women (95 percent) endorse the slogan as "African Americans not knowing their place" than White women (45 percent) and African American men (65 percent). White women (43 percent) are less likely to interpret the "people not knowing their place" as racial compared to White men (77 percent). African American women appear more sensitive to racial framing than men, and White women as sensitive to the racial framing as White men.

Closed racial beliefs, asked of White respondents only, support our theoretical expectations. That is, greater antipathy expressed toward African Americans, in the form of racial resentment and social dominance, is associated with a denial that MAGA taps racial concerns. Only about a quarter of Whites who are high in racial resentment (28 percent) interpret "knowing one's place" racially compared to 100 percent of Whites who are low in racial resentment.

Similarly, only 39 percent of Whites who are high on the social dominance scale interpret the frame as racial compared to 100 percent of Whites who are low on social dominance. The data thus indicate that individuals who are high on racial resentment and social dominance scales are not as open to racial arguments and explanations as individuals on the low end of those scales. As a result, the racial interpretation of knowing one's place is rejected in favor of a non-racial interpretation.

Conclusion

This research examined what the *Make America Great Again* slogan means to individuals, specifically the extent to which it is interpreted as racial or not. While some have suggested that the slogan is a racist dog-whistle—conveying an implicit desire to return to a nostalgic era in American history, in which African Americans knew their place and played by the rules—our research raised this contention as an empirical question to be answered by the public. Ambiguous and vague, slogans leave themselves open to interpretation and lend deniability to political candidates. The extant literature on racial priming in campaign advertising suggests that such ambiguity and implicitness make racial appeals more powerful. Our results support this point.

Utilizing a two-treatment list experiment, we considered the possibility that *Make America Great Again* taps essentially two types of beliefs—one set of beliefs views the slogan as a racial appeal regarding African Americans "forgetting their place," and another set of beliefs views the slogan as a non-racial appeal regarding "people (in general) forgetting their place." Our findings suggest that, on the whole, the slogan is understood as both racial and non-racial depending on race, perceptions of the past, and the strength of an individual's closed belief systems. We have argued that while most Americans would like their country to aspire to greatness, "again" in the *Make America Great Again* slogan seems to drive the consternation. That is, African Americans and Whites have drastically different memories and perceptions about the past. African Americans' recollections of the past likely reflect a more perilous era in which racial prejudice was more pervasive and discrimination worked to the advantage of Whites, while Whites' recollection of the past likely reflects an era in which they were more dominant and benefited more from the social and political hierarchy—when people knew their place and were reluctant to challenge it. Thus, references to the past, using "again," trigger different racial reactions.

This also means individuals who view the past as a more perilous era for African Americans and as a time of greater racial prejudice interpret the *Make America Great Again* slogan as similarly racial. On the other hand, individuals who consider the "United States of the past a better place than the future" interpret the slogan as non-racial. African Americans and Whites differ considerably on their preference for the past, and, as to be expected, this impacts their interpretation of the slogan. Similarly, individuals low in racial resentment and social dominance orientation, as well as liberals, are likely to interpret the slogan as racial, while those high in racial resentment and social dominance orientation and conservatives interpret the slogan as non-racial. In short, a variety of factors shape the interpretation of the slogan as racial or non-racial, but it is clear that even when race is not explicit, it can still matter with regard to appeals.

One caveat to the interpretation of our results is that racial interpretations of the slogan may tap into conservatism. Appeals to nostalgia and the past tend to resonate more with conservatives than liberals (Lammers and Baldwin 2017). Even as a philosophy, conservatives tend to respect the past and think that only small incremental changes, if any, are necessary for society. Put another way, racial differences in the interpretation of *Make America Great Again* may reflect conservative political beliefs more than racial beliefs. Both are very powerful explanations of the preference for the US's past versus future. Therefore, we cannot rule out the possibility that the slogan was created to exploit the ideological polarization of the electorate, and, in so doing, it exacerbated racial cleavages. The interaction between racial beliefs and conservatism requires more research.

As of this writing, Donald Trump and his broad company of supporters continue to use the *Make America Great Again* slogan, which still resonates with many voters. Our study highlights the need for a better understanding of how a single and ostensibly non-racial expression can exploit racial cleavages in American society. Racially coded language in the slogan uses a veiled term to stimulate different racial reactions. According to Lopez (2014), political strategies employing racially coded appeals stem from the 1960s, during which African Americans began to challenge the racial status quo. Politicians like Barry Goldwater, Richard Nixon, and Ronald Reagan were considered adept in the use of implicit racial appeals. Almost 40 years later, Donald Trump will be added to this list.

There is not much that can be done to counteract the effects of implicit racial coding, as long as society remains racially polarized. The use of coded racial appeals is a calculated decision, but it is important to understand that such appeals capitalize on people's worst instincts. There is a cost to employing implicit racial appeals; they do not just manipulate racial resentment toward African Americans, but they also "artificially" deepen racial divisions in society.

Racial Cognitive Consistency

Over 65 years ago, the renowned psychologist Gordon Allport (1954) recognized that beliefs like racial animus toward African Americans could become so ingrained in people's minds that they become unable to view information objectively and instead "twist the facts to serve their prejudices" (p.185). As has been shown by an extensive body of research (Festinger 1957; Gawronski 2012; Lundberg et al. 2017), individuals can misconstrue, downgrade, and outright ignore information to align with their existing biases and beliefs. While individuals seek to avoid feelings of dissonance stemming from maintaining conflicting beliefs (Festinger 1957), the ultimate danger in the "twisting of facts" is that sentiments like racial resentment have the potential to become self-reinforcing, and factual information capable of altering such biases may be minimized or rejected.

We refer to this process of aligning attitudes and behavior to be consistent with Whites' resentment toward African Americans as racial motivated reasoning (Feldman and Huddy 2018; Wilson and Davis 2018). Whites' resentment toward African Americans motivates a need for consistency. If one believes that African Americans are benefiting unfairly and undeservingly and that this threatens the status quo and Whites' advantage, then one is likely to adjust one's beliefs in a similar fashion on other attitudes that are perceived to challenge the status quo and, for example, write off President Obama and his accomplishments for no reason other than that he also reflects a threat to the White-benefiting status quo. Parallel research pertaining to the use of partisan perceptual screens (Bartels 2002; Campbell et al. 1960; Druckman, Peterson, and Slothuus 2013; Gaines et al. 2007; Leeper and Slothuus 2014), motivated reasoning (Kopko et al. 2011; Lebo and Cassino 2007; Peterson et al.

2013; Redlawsk 2002; Schaffner and Roche 2017; Slothuus and de Vreese 2010; Taber, Cann, and Kucsova 2009), and motivated skepticism (Taber and Lodge 2006) reinforces this process.

Issues most susceptible to the twisting of information to fit one's racial reality have involved evaluations of former President Obama's job performance (Lundberg et al. 2017) and his specific role in handling the economy (Wilson and Davis 2018), and attitudes about the environment and climate change (Benegal 2018). For example, Tesler (2016) and Chen and Mohanty (2018) both find a "racial spill-over" effect showing that higher levels of classic racial resentment toward African Americans are associated with more negative evaluations of the national economy during Obama's administration. Tesler (2016) maintains that more racially resentful Whites perceived poorer economic performance on unemployment under the Obama administration than those with lower racial resentment. Presumably, people who are racially prejudiced malign President Obama because he is Black and seek to discredit his policies and job performance because they do not like his racial background. Chen and Mohanty (2018) demonstrate that retrospective economic evaluations became racialized under President Obama, leading to a negative correlation between economic views and classic racial resentment. Research by Lundberg et al. (2017) found that negative explicit and implicit racial attitudes both predicted negative evaluations of the state of the nation over the course of the Obama administration, which they attributed to a form of racial cognitive consistency. People who are racially prejudiced might not want Obama to succeed, and to be consistent they denigrate his accomplishments and penalize him more for economic contractions, even when the economy is improving. Along these lines, in prior research (Wilson and Davis 2018), we show that when the national economy is framed as worsening, Whites easily attribute responsibility to Obama, but when it is framed as improving, Whites do not attribute responsibility to him. We found that Whites' racial resentment predicts this pattern for evaluations of both the state and national economy. One's prior crystallized beliefs about race are so steeped in values of deservingness that they become paramount in matters of justice, and therefore condition how people perceive others and their actions.

In this chapter, racial cognitive consistency is operationalized in three ways: a *blame pattern*, attributing responsibility for the national economy to fit one's existing racial beliefs; an *association pattern*, a connection of ostensibly unrelated attitudes between non-racial issues (e.g., the economy and climate change) and racial resentment in order to fit one's existing racial beliefs; and a *deference pattern*, the expression of contradictory attitudes that diverge from one's self-interest. All three patterns reflect actions that Whites might take to reduce dissonant attitudes, beliefs, and behaviors. We explore the extent to which attributions of blame for the national economy under President Obama were motivated by Whites' resentment toward African Americans and the extent to which racial resentment becomes intertwined with ostensibly non-racial issues, such as the denial of climate change.

Racial Cognitive Consistency

Whites' resentment toward African Americans distorts how they see the world. If a person finds political information or events uncomfortable or inconsistent with their existing beliefs, whether factual or not, the information can be either altered, minimized, or outright ignored. It has long been understood that cognitive processes enable us to form a contrived and false reality. Facts become subjective and arguable, and untruths become credible and real. People who traffic in lies, untruths, and conspiracy theories may be excused, as long as they are perceived to be supporting their worldview. One might expect that individuals making decisions will gather objective evidence and draw a conclusion based on an analysis of that evidence. But, this does not appear to be the case.

Several prominent theories in psychology and political science support this premise. First, Fritz Heider created Balance Theory to show how people develop their relationships with other people and with things in their environment. Balance Theory says that if people see a set of cognitive elements as being a system, then they will have a preference to maintain a balanced state among these elements. In other words, if we feel we are "out of balance," then we are motivated to restore a position of balance. When we are comfortable in a balanced state, we have no distress, and there is no need for us to seek a change in our relationships

Second, and perhaps most noteworthy, Festinger's (1957) cognitive dissonance theory suggests that people are motivated to maintain consistent cognitions and that the lack of cognitive consistency leads to an aversive physiological state or dissonance. Cognitive dissonance theory proposes that if inconsistency exists among our attitudes, or between our attitudes and behavior, we experience an unpleasant state of arousal called cognitive dissonance. The arousal of dissonance motivates us to change something, our attitude or our behavior, to reduce or eliminate the unpleasant arousal. Reducing the tension helps to achieve consonance, a state of psychological balance.

The need for consistency drives behavior in a variety of ways. People are prone to believe what they want to believe, and it seems counterintuitive to look for evidence that contradicts their beliefs. Individuals do tend to expose themselves selectively to, and perceive and recall more readily, that which supports their already existing cognitive set of beliefs and opinions. Also, individuals selectively deny exposure to, misperceive, and forget more readily those stimuli contradictory to their beliefs and opinions. In other words, people pick out those bits of data that make them feel good because they confirm their prejudices.

Third, consistent with the general idea of consistency, selectivity, and confirmation bias, in the political science literature individuals have been viewed as employing a partisan perceptual screen (Druckman, Peterson, and Slothuus 2013; Gaines et al. 2007; Peterson et al. 2013; Slothuus and de Vreese 2010; Taber and Lodge 2006). Building off Campbell et al. (1960), these studies suggest that partisans are motivated to confirm positive information about their party and disconfirm information that casts their party in an unfavorable light (Taber and Lodge 2006). They develop attachments toward political objects and actors, prompting directional, partisan motivations that color information processing (Druckman, Peterson, and Slothuus 2013; Gaines et al. 2007; Lavine, Johnston, and Steenbergen 2013; Lebo and Cassino 2007; Taber and Lodge 2006). Partisans seek out explanations that confirm their prior beliefs, while arguing against incongruent information. These confirmation and disconfirmation biases can lead partisan groups to interpret the same information in predictably distinct—and often divergent—ways (Druckman, Peterson, and Slothuus 2013; Slothuus and de Vreese 2010; Taber, Cann, and Kucsova 2009; Taber and Lodge 2006).

Given this literature regarding consistency and selectivity, Whites' resentment toward African Americans, as an important belief system, can also be thought of as driving consistency (Feldman and Huddy 2018; Wilson and Davis 2018). That is, once individuals form crystallized racial beliefs, they are motivated to be consistent and to confirm those beliefs or to be in balance. So, racial resentment can also be thought of as a set of "blinders" or a screen through which discordant information is minimized, to the extent it is considered at all. Racial beliefs and Whites' resentment toward African Americans intensify and become polarizing as those beliefs, no matter how factual, are confirmed. Individuals maintain consistency by attaching greater weight to racially consistent information and less weight to discordant racial information, or ignoring it altogether (Festinger 1957; Lundberg et al. 2017). This psychological process prevents information that challenges existing racial beliefs about African Americans from being fully encoded. Without perhaps knowing the full details, individuals have some awareness—due to automatic affective reactions, or an appraisal, of the information sources— that upcoming information may be inconsistent with what they have already discovered. Individuals then preclude full awareness of unwelcome information by ending the information search, or minimally processing new information that has already been rejected as wrong, nonsense, or illegitimate. Ultimately, racial cognitive consistency produces a form of biased reasoning comprising weak accuracy goals, where existing beliefs potentially supplant the value of fully vetting factual discordant information.

This is exactly what we found in an analysis of racial resentment and the readiness to blame or reward President Obama for hypothetical fluctuations in the national economy (Wilson and Davis 2018). For individuals who sought to maintain consistent views between their sense of threat from African Americans challenging the status quo and the threat of President Obama to White privilege, racial resentment was related to appraisals of Obama's performance on the economy in two important ways. First, individuals who expressed greater racial resentment perceived President Obama as less capable of managing financial crises. Second, individuals who expressed more racial resentment were less willing to give Obama credit regardless of Obama's capabilities and success. Both outcomes are punitive for Obama, and reflect the perception that he was undeserving of any credit because he was a threat to the status quo and an inadequate steward of the economy. On the other hand, individuals who expressed less racial resentment or who attributed African Americans' disadvantage to external factors (as opposed to internal factors) perceived him as a successful manager of the economic crises because it was consistent with their racial beliefs that Blacks are indeed capable.

It must be noted that research employing laboratory experiments has been most successful in identifying motivations toward reasoning or cognitive consistency (Taber and Lodge 2006; Peterson et al. 2013; Redlawsk 2002), while a great deal of the research in this area relies on a "theory" of cognitive consistency to explain the association between attitudes and behavior. The distinction is that one approach tests for the presence of consistency or effortful thinking involving incongruent information while another approach uses cognitive consistency as an explanatory mechanism. Our approach is more akin to the latter in the sense that we use how individuals interpret ostensibly "objective" events, such as the performance of the national economy, as an indicator of cognitive consistency. Hence, we are not testing for cognitive consistency but rather using the theory of cognitive consistency to account for different interpretations of seemingly objective events. Later on, when we examine climate change denial, we will use cognitive consistency to account for the association between unrelated attitudes. We continue this line of inquiry, but we ask a different question: to what extent do racially resentful Whites attribute greater responsibility to President Obama—relative to other authorities like Democrats, Republicans, former President Bush, and Wall Street—for fluctuations in the national economy?

Climate change denial is another area ripe for the study of Whites' resentment toward African Americans as cognitive consistency. Climate change denial becomes a form of cognitive consistency with Whites' racial resentment not so much because President Obama is African American and Whites hold racial prejudices against him, but, rather, through a common sensitivity to a threat to the status quo way of life that Whites appreciate. This way of life includes not being forced (through federal government rules and programs) to solve problems that disproportionately require dominant group resources, affecting them more than others. In this way, sensitivities to threats to one's way of life, civic virtues, and status tie many attitudes together.

A third area we can investigate relates to policies that affect economic self-interests, like tax policy. We examine the presence of cognitive consistency due to Whites' racial resentment as a competition between support for President Trump and support for policies that go against one's economic self-interests. In such a competition, one has to choose between changing one's support for Trump or going against one's economic interests—two subjects that are both correlated with Whites' racial resentment. We propose that those with higher Whites' racial resentment are motivated to defend the system that supports a broad racial hierarchy over opportunities for their own mobility. Thus, Whites' resentment toward African Americans allows individuals to rationalize their own inequality as well as the inequality of others.

Our analysis starts with the political issue that every president must make their highest priority: the economy. Reflecting a different approach, climate change denial becomes intertwined with racial resentment through cognitive consistency not so much because of President Obama and racial prejudice but, rather, through a common sensitivity to a threat to the status quo. Sensitivity to threat to the status quo ties many attitudes together. Self-contradictory attitudes allow us to examine the extent to which people support policies that are inconsistent with their self-interest, such as when people with lower income levels endorse President Trump's tax cuts. Here, too, we argue that the desire for individuals high in racial resentment to punish African Americans and other minorities (or defend White privilege) makes them go against their own self-interest.

An Objective Economic Reality

Leading economic indicators show that President Obama inherited an economic catastrophe. Stemming from the bursting of the housing market bubble in 2007, which many connected to subprime loans and mortgage defaults (low short-term interest rates), the resulting loss of wealth triggered cutbacks in consumer spending, collapse in financial markets, reduction in business investments, and significant job losses (loss of income and increase in poverty). By the fall of 2008, before Obama's presidential election win, four major mortgage providers and three of the largest financial institutions had declared bankruptcy. As a result of the financial crisis, the United States lost more than 7.5 million jobs, and the unemployment rate doubled. The stock market lost over 50 percent of its value, with the Dow Jones hitting 6,500 and the S&P 500 hitting 675. Just 18 months earlier, the Dow Jones had hit an all-time high of over 14,000 and the S&P 500 had peaked as well at over 1,560. The unemployment rate, which had been under 5 percent in 2007, increased to 9.5 percent in June 2009 and eventually rose above 10 percent. Making matters worse, the connected nature of the financial markets across the globe led to the collapse of many international markets and economies. These international pressures exacerbated the US recession and the government's ability to recover quickly.

After assuming office, President Obama enacted several policies to stimulate economic recovery, but those very policies turned many people against him. Through the American Recovery and Reinvestment Act of 2009—enacted less than one month after his inauguration—President Obama pumped $412 billion into banks, troubled financial firms, and struggling automobile manufacturers such as General Motors and Chrysler. Criticized for being a government bailout, the combination of President Obama's efforts fueled a conservative backlash that would propel dozens of Republicans into Congress, costing the Democrats control of the House in 2010 and bringing President Obama's economic agenda to a halt. The slow economic recovery that followed was defined by political battles over the deficit, budget cuts, standoffs over the national debt, a compromise on tax cuts, and ideological banter about what role the government should play in directing the economy. By the 2012 presidential election, the US economy had turned around, with unemployment rates below 7 percent, consistent private sector job growth, significantly lower fuel prices, and a thriving automotive industry. Thus, while there were many factors and actors that did play a role in economic performance, the political standard for responsibility appraisals is the American president, unless there is a good reason to blame prior administrations or other factors (Peffley and Williams 1985; Rudolph 2003). Everything considered, President Obama likely deserves some responsibility for the economic recovery. Our foremost concern is whether or not racial resentment affects *how much* responsibility he deserves relative to others, and why individuals make such a connection.

I. Attributing Blame to President Obama

As to be expected from cognitive consistency, individuals are highly selective in their evaluations of politicians (Bothwell and Brigham 1983). People attach less weight to negative and unflattering information concerning the candidates they like while attaching greater weight to positive information concerning the candidates they like. Racial resentment is likely to drive political evaluations in such a way that in order to be consistent people can be expected to align their evaluations of candidates to their existing resentment. What this means is that individuals who are racially resentful are more likely to diminish the accomplishments of President Obama while being more likely to attribute negativity to him.

Following Iyengar (1989), we propose that individuals use economic blame attributions to simplify their political evaluations. Thus, if economic evaluations are subjective simplifications, we expect, everything being equal, that individuals with higher levels of racial resentment will place more blame on President Obama for poor economic conditions. Also, there is a tendency for individuals to hold the incumbent president responsible for national economic conditions (Peffley and Williams 1985). We turn to two studies that included questions regarding both the attribution of blame for performance of the national economy and our racial resentment items. Through our participation on two different collaborative teams in 2012, we had access to the same core question on the attribution or blame for the state of the economy question in two different contexts in the survey questionnaire. We used the following core question inquiring who is to blame for economic conditions in the US:

Who bears most responsibility for the current state of the US economy?
1. President Obama
2. Former President Bush
3. Wall Street
4. World Economy
5. Congress

The entities listed in the questions were all, to a degree, implicated in the explanations for the collapse of the stock market. While conservative media tended to blame low-income consumers' default on mortgages and liberal media tended to blame Wall Street bankers and predatory lenders, we did not have a set of hypotheses for how individuals would respond to the various actors. Our main interest was in whether more responsibility was attributed to President Obama relative to the other actors. Respondents were asked to choose among the entities who were most responsible for the state of the economy. To retain as many respondents as possible, the response scale for each item was transformed into dichotomies for each entity, where a 1 indicates "responsibility" and a 0 indicates "no responsibility." It is quite possible for individuals to hold multiple entities responsible for the state of the economy, but this forced

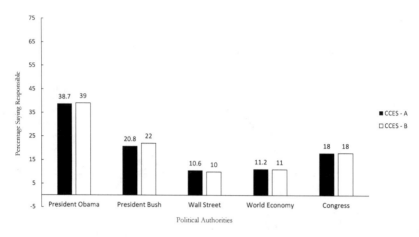

FIGURE 6.1. Responsibility for State of the Economy

choice approach does not alter the substantive results compared to asking respondents about each entity's responsibility separately.[1]

Figure 6.1 shows the percentages for the various authorities considered responsible for the state of the economy in our 2012 CCES data (A and B CCES data represent two different team modules in the same year). The response percentages in both studies are statistically indistinguishable, owing to the randomness in the selection of respondents. Substantively, President Obama was considered more responsible for the state of the economy in 2012 than former President Bush and Congress, and former President Bush was considered marginally more responsible than Congress; 39 percent and 38.7 percent considered President Obama responsible and 22 percent and 20.8 percent considered President Bush responsible. While the president can be expected to be blamed more than other authorities, people may have forgotten about the economic recession at the end of President Bush's term in office, as only one in five said he was responsible for the national economy. President Obama, on the other hand, inherited an economic crisis, and it took the better part of his first-term to show signs of recovery. His approach to economic recovery, which included a bailout of Wall Street, was indeed controversial. Wall Street and the world economy had the lowest blame attributions. Wall Street was viewed somewhat innocently, though through deregulation financial institutions engaged in subprime lending practices that ultimately led to loan defaults and the market crash. Reflecting the blame pattern we expected, the proportion of respondents holding President Obama responsible was quite high. In the following analysis of this attribution of responsibility, racial resentment and partisanship are the main foci, as both are powerful motivations toward consistency regarding President Obama. Partisan motivations to blame President Obama for the state economy, when it was not his doing, are more acceptable to racially resentful persons—for example, discrimination deniers—than the motivations about race. But it is not that race does not matter; rather, partisan motivations can mask or justify racial resentment.

It is clear from panel A in table 6.1 that attribution of responsibility for the state of the economy is filtered through a partisan lens. This is the partisan perceptual screen at work. Democrats were willing to blame President Obama less than Republicans and Independents were. Only 8.36 percent of Democrats blamed Obama, while 42.69 percent were willing to blame President Bush and 21.19 percent blamed Congress for the state of the economy. Expressing less support for Obama, 40.97 percent of the people who identify as Independent blamed President Obama and 12.89 percent blamed President Bush. A sizeable percent of Independents also blamed Congress. Reflecting greater certainty agreement and cohesiveness, 76.12 percent of Republicans blamed President Obama, but only 1.49 percent blamed President Bush. Compared to Democrats and Independents, a smaller percentage of Republicans blamed Congress. Clearly, party identification powerfully shapes evaluations of the economy and who is responsible, but the Republicans were more unified in their view that President Obama was responsible. There is not much new here in the end, but this analysis confirms a great deal of what is known about the partisan perceptual screen.

But, there can be multiple perceptual screens and lenses that on their own or through their interaction distort reality. Does racial resentment have the same effect among Republicans and Democrats? We turn to panel B in table 6.1 to help address this question. Whites with higher racial resentment blamed President Obama (64.29 percent) while those low in racial resentment did not (3.57 percent). This provides evidence of a consensus, but less so compared to party identification. Individuals low in racial resentment were more likely to blame President Bush (45.92 percent) and Wall Street bankers (39.06 percent). A sizeable percentage of individuals high in racial resentment blamed Congress, as the Democrats did have a majority of both houses of Congress during the height of the financial crisis and lost their House majority in the 2010 midterm elections. Individuals who are moderately racially resentful saw

TABLE 6.1. **Attribution of Responsibility for the State of the Economy by Partisanship and Racial Resentment**

Panel A. Attribution of Responsibility by Party Identification

Party Identification	Obama	Bush	Wall Street	World Economy	Congress
Democrat	8.36%	42.69%	20.30%	7.46%	21.19%
Independent	40.97	12.89	10.69	13.18	22.06
Republican	76.12	1.49	3.28	7.16	11.94

Panel B. Attribution of Responsibility by Levels of Racial Resentment

Levels of Racial Resentment	Obama	Bush	Wall Street	World Economy	Congress
Low	3.57%	45.92%	39.06%	20.0%	25.0%
Medium	32.14	37.76	42.19	52.0	37.50
High	64.29	16.33	18.75	28.0	37.50

Panel C. Attribution of Responsibility by Racial Resentment and Party Identification

Democrat	Obama	Bush
Low Racial Resentment	3.95%	44.74%
Mod Racial Resentment	8.0	32.0
High Racial Resentment	14.29	39.29
Independent		
Low Racial Resentment	0%	37.93%
Mod Racial Resentment	32.35	20.59
High Racial Resentment	64.20	4.94
Republican		
Low Racial Resentment	57.14%	0%
Mod Racial Resentment	75.36	2.0
High Racial Resentment	81.16	1.11

a stronger connection between the US economy and the world economy (52 percent), though many blamed Wall Street bankers and Congress. Racial resentment also structures attribution of blame for the state of the economy, but perhaps not as strongly as party identification. The remaining question that needs addressing, then, is to what degree does racial resentment interact with a partisan filter?

In panel C in table 6.1, racial resentment has an effect on partisan predispositions but it does not alter them substantially. Democrats who are high in racial resentment continue to blame President Obama less (14.29 percent) than President Bush (39.29 percent). Likewise, Republicans low in racial resentment continue to blame President Obama more (57.14 percent) than President Bush (0 percent). Republicans who are low in racial resentment do not resemble Democrats who are high in racial resentment, and Democrats who are high in racial resentment do not resemble Republicans who are low in racial resentment. More noteworthy in these results is the larger difference between high and low racial resentment among Republicans. Racial resentment has a much larger effect among Republicans than Democrats, though this does not mean that Democrats do not hold racially resentful attitudes and that it does not influence their political evaluations. In short, in attributing responsibility for the national economy, racial resentment and party identification overlap considerably but they are clearly tapping different political attitudes. Both party identification and racial resentment serve as motivations toward cognitive consistency. For Democrats, the willingness to view African Americans in non-resentful terms can be just as much a motivation toward cognitive consistency as racial resentment. Negative information about President Obama or poor performance evaluation of handling the national economy can be just as minimized. Alternatively, Democrats mirror Republicans at the highest levels of Whites' racial resentment, suggesting that partisan similarity did not protect Obama as much as it ostensibly protected Bush.

When we include other factors that are associated with the willingness to hold President Obama responsible for the economy in a multivariate model, racial resentment and partisanship are quite potent and

TABLE 6.2. **Logistic Analysis of Responsibility for Current Economic Conditions—Study I (2012 CCES): Who bears most responsibility for the current state of the US economy?**

Independent Variables	President Obama	President Bush	Wall Street	World Economy	Congress
	Model 1	Model 2	Model 3	Model 4	Model 5
Constant	−2.43** (.46)	−.50 (.51)	−.95 (.57)	−.94 (.58)	−1.75** (.47)
Education	−.08 (.06)	−.12 (.07)	.17* (.08)	.04 (.08)	.07 (.06)
Income	.01 (.03)	−.03 (.03)	−.02 (.04)	.07 (.04)	.01 (.03)
Age	.02** (.01)	.00 (.01)	−.02** (.01)	−.02* (.01)	.00 (.01)
Gender	−.12 (.17)	−.14 (.19)	.19 (.22)	.03 (.22)	.03 (.17)
Democrat	−1.49** (.23)	1.18** (.20)	.46 (.25)	−.30 (.26)	−.19 (.20)
Republican	1.59** (.18)	−2.56** (.53)	−.91* (.36)	−.69* (.29)	−1.00** (.22)
Racial Resentment	2.10** (.36)	−1.02** (.37)	−1.58** (.43)	−.76 (.44)	.40 (.36)
Pseudo R^2	.33	.29	.15	.04	.04
Prob > x^2	.000	.000	.000	.008	.001
N	986	986	986	986	986

Note. *p<.05, **p<.01.

TABLE 6.3. **Logistic Analysis of Responsibility for Current Economic Conditions—Study II (2012 CCES): Who bears most responsibility for the current state of the US economy?**

Independent Variables	President Obama	President Bush	Wall Street	World Economy	Congress
	Model 1	Model 2	Model 3	Model 4	Model 5
Constant	−5.64** (.99)	.14 (.73)	−.88 (.81)	.11 (.90)	−1.20 (.72)
Education	−.10 (.09)	.00 (.10)	.19 (.11)	−.14 (.13)	.01 (.09)
Income	.03 (.05)	.00 (.04)	−.02 (.05)	−.04 (.06)	−.00 (.04)
Age	.03** (.01)	−.01 (.01)	−.03** (.01)	−.01 (.01)	.01 (.01)
Gender	−.36 (.25)	−.08 (.27)	.30 (.30)	.62 (.35)	−.16 (.25)
Democrat	−1.00** (.32)	.79** (.28)	.50 (.32)	−1.14* (.49)	−.09 (.30)
Republican	1.66** (.27)	−2.76** (.75)	−1.83** (.56)	.05 (.39)	−.76* (.33)
Racial Resentment	3.92** (.64)	−1.61** (.59)	−.49 (.66)	−1.99* (.83)	−.70 (.58)
Pseudo R^2	.48	.29	.17	.08	.04
Prob > x^2	.000	.000	.000	.298	.055
N	476	476	476	476	476

Note. *p<.05, **p<.01.

perform as expected. The regression coefficients in tables 6.2 and 6.3 indicate that individuals high in racial resentment are more likely to hold President Obama responsible for the economy than individuals low in racial resentment. But, looking across the various authorities, racial resentment is negatively related to attributing responsibility to President Bush and Wall Street, suggesting that individuals high in racial resentment are more willing to excuse them from responsibility than individuals low in racial resentment. This finding is quite significant when controlling for partisanship because it suggests that racial resentment as a form of cognitive consistency excuses behavior of authorities who are not perceived as threatening to their sense of justice or the status quo. To be consistent with their sensitivity toward threats to the status quo, people are willing to blame President Obama because they perceive a similar threat.

Democrats and Republicans have different perceptions on who was responsible for the state of the national economy, despite the recovery. While Democrats were more likely to blame President Bush, Republicans were more likely to blame President Obama and less likely to blame Wall Street. Here, too, an objective reality does not matter on the basis of a partisan filter. Put simply, people are motivated toward consistency, and thus will believe ideas that align with their existing beliefs and desires regardless of the objective reality; to do otherwise only leads to dissonance and discomfort.

II. Whites' Resentment toward African Americans and Climate Change

The national economy was not the only area in which individuals thought President Obama was incapable and that his activities would threaten the status quo and the American way of life—mostly benefiting Whites. President Obama's policies and activities involving the mitigation of climate change have been another area in which racial resentment plays a significant and meaningful role. The connection between racial resentment and the mitigation of climate change is neither obvious nor intuitive, but we hope to make clear how the "threat" or "challenge to the status quo" underlying racial resentment sensitizes individuals to other forms of threat, such that the human drive toward cognitive consistency and dissonance reduction wed them. The wedding process is rather parsimonious in the sense that individuals are not required to know the details of climate change issues or President Obama's activities on climate change, but, rather, it requires individuals to be at least aware that climate change mitigation poses a challenge to their way of life and pushes government into areas where they think it should not go. Like attributions of responsibility for the national economy, the fact that racial resentment toward African Americans has the potential to influence non-racial and non-social-welfare issues highlights the power of threat reactions. Needless to say, it adds to the alarming aspects of racial belief systems that are influenced by pathways beyond prejudice.

There is no mistake that President Obama has been identified as a stalwart environmental advocate, though he is considered somewhat of a disappointment among environmental activists. Although climate change and the environment were not prominent themes in the 2008 presidential election, Barack Obama was characterized as out-promising John McCain on environmental stewardship (Graham 2015). Pledging to make the United States a global leader in addressing climate change, Barack Obama dared Americans to mark the day he accepted the 2008 Democratic nomination as "the moment when the rise of the oceans began to slow and our planet began to heal."[2] He campaigned for the presidency in 2008 with a clear pledge to make the United States a global leader in addressing climate change. Climate change received nearly the same importance as other scourges such as disease and poverty in his campaign. Promises to reduce carbon dioxide emissions by 80 percent by 2050 and invest $150 billion in new energy-saving technologies were consistent talking-points in campaign speeches and rally events. Actively campaigning on the mitigation of climate change, Barack Obama touted his plan to "reduce oil imports, create jobs in energy conservation and renewable sources of energy, and reverse the warming of the atmosphere."[3]

After his 2008 inauguration, President Obama's high-profile appointments to the EPA and secretary of energy, like physicist and Nobel-laureate Stephen Chu, signaled his seriousness about climate change. Faced with the greatest economic recession since the Great Depression, President Obama proposed the American Recovery and Reinvestment Act, which included $90 billion in subsidies for green energy, intended to shift as much of the economy toward cleaner and renewable energy as possible (Grunwald 2012). Seeking to capitalize on Democratic control of both houses of Congress, President Obama promoted the American Clean Energy and Security Act of 2009, which would have set limits on the amount of greenhouse gases that could be emitted nationally. Although this bill passed the House, it never made it to the Senate floor. Despite this defeat, President Obama's climate change efforts were recognized when he was awarded the Nobel Peace Prize in 2009, partly due to "meeting the great climatic challenges the world is confronting."

Following the 2010 midterm elections, which gave the Republicans control of the House and shrunk the Democratic control of the Senate, President Obama continued his legislative agenda for climate change, signing a number of executive actions increasing industrial regulations and mandating higher standards for gas mileage in cars, fuel cleanliness, energy efficiency in appliances, and emissions from new power plants. For instance, the EPA imposed new regulations on greenhouse gas (GHG) standards for power plants. In 2015, the Obama administration issued new rules regulating fracking on public lands, designed to protect against groundwater pollution. President Obama vetoed legislation authorizing the construction of the Keystone Oil Pipeline, considered extremely dangerous to the environment. In the international community, he succeeded in obtaining the 2009 Copenhagen Accord, which secured emission pledges from all major economies and China for the first time.

In 2015, President Obama entered into the 2015 Paris Agreement, in which 195 countries adopted the first-ever universal climate agreement.

President Obama received favorable public support in his handling of the nation's environment. He began his first term with a 79 percent favorability rating in handling the environment, although this approval diminished, ranging from 52 to 54 percent, in the following years. President Obama's environmental efforts were recognized, as his environmental rating ranged from 15 to 20 percentage points higher than his predecessor.[4]

Notwithstanding the criticism from environmentalists that his activities were largely ineffective, President Obama's efforts to mitigate climate change separate him from previous presidents, and identify him as a staunch, if not leading, advocate of the mitigation of climate change. We argue that this association between President Obama and the issue of climate change, along with racial cognitive consistency, contributes to Whites' reluctance to acknowledge climate change.

Climate Change as a Challenge to the Status Quo

Because of the pressure toward cognitive consistency, racial resentment alters the historical and real-time narrative of President Obama's efforts to protect the environment and slow climate change. In an era in which the truth is contested and facts are treated as negotiable, one's political reality can be contrived and artificial. The implications of individuals living in their own distorted political and social realities are problematic for effective democratic functioning, especially public opinion. A public that simultaneously values conflicting positions of a healthy environment and unregulated privilege must rationalize one side versus the other, and relying on forms of bias to reduce dissonance creates a problem for universal notions of justice. Cognitive consistency compels individuals to align their attitudes with an overarching belief system. Whites' racial resentment steeped in justice motives and deservingness provides such a worldview; it is shaped by non-racist foundations that are easily applied to political matters and that provide a framework for addressing racial and non-racial issues alike. In this way, Whites can claim that they are not racist, and that race has nothing to do with their views on the environment. Yet, Whites' racial resentment also constrains how people perceive and react to issues through justice motives. To the extent that Whites are sensitive to the threat to the status quo posed by African Americans and other minorities, they may become sensitive to other forms of threat to White privilege, including strict forms of regulation that protect the environment. In this section we explore a different threat to White privilege: specifically, climate change and global warming.

With the increasing number of environmental catastrophes, rising global surface temperatures, growing concentration of greenhouse gases, the melting of the Arctic sea ice, and rising sea levels, the vast majority of the American public now acknowledges the ravages of climate change (Brulle, Carmichael, and Jenkins 2012; Mccright and Dunlap 2011a). Research exploring attitudes toward climate change denial has identified several underlying motivations. Whites, males, and conservatives, referred to jointly as the "conservative White male effect," have been more likely to deny that climate change is occurring, less likely to attribute climate change to anthropogenic causes, and more likely to disapprove of efforts to mitigate climate change (Mccright and Dunlap 2011b). This is strikingly similar to the racial motivated reasoning tied to denials that racism and discrimination still exist and that therefore efforts to mitigate such social problems are unnecessary and opposed (e.g., Feldman and Huddy 2018). The overarching threat is a forced blame attribution to Whites, who are the dominant beneficiaries of a system of comfort and privilege as it relates to the environment. Thus, the theory underlying both racial and climate concerns relates to the preservation of the status quo (i.e., system justification theory), suggesting that the denial of climate change is a defensive reaction to a threat to the status quo and traditional values (Jost et al. 2003).

Restrictive government policies, commonly proposed to mitigate climate change, are viewed as a threat to the existing social, economic, and political system, triggering a need to defend it (Feinberg and Willer 2011; Feygina, Jost, and Goldsmith 2010; Mccright and Dunlap 2011a). The possibility that a defensive reaction to a threat to traditional values and the status quo shapes attitudes toward climate change denial among "conservative White males" invites a consideration of whether similar threats to traditional values and the status quo, such as racial resentment toward African Americans, are connected.

On the basis of system justification theory, we argue that racial resentment toward African Americans and attitudes toward climate change are perceived to threaten the status quo, which motivates individuals to defend the political system against unfair demands. Racial resentment and climate change become connected because both are perceived as a threat to a system that preserves White advantage. We ask: to what extent is racial resentment among Whites associated with a greater willingness to deny climate change and reject efforts to mitigate its effects?

System Justification Theory

According to system justification theory, people are motivated by a need for stability, for safety and reassurance, and for affiliation with others of the same social system (Jost and Banaji 1994). Thus, perceiving the status quo—the political system, the values upon which it is based, and the existing social hierarchy—as fair, legitimate, and beneficial leads to a desire to preserve and protect it, especially among those who are advantaged by the system and benefit most from it (Jost, Federico, and Napier 2009). An onerous downside to system justification is that maintaining a current system, which may not adequately or intentionally address social and economic inequalities, also leads to the rationalization and defense of inequality as well as the potentially harmful policies and institutions that preserve it (Feygina, Jost, and Goldsmith 2010; Henry and Saul 2006; Jost et al. 2003; Wakslak et al. 2007). Acknowledging discrimination and the ineffectiveness of the current system means admitting the status quo may not be entirely legitimate or fair, and it would necessitate governmental actions and a redistribution of resources to resolve those issues. Thus, the threat in System Justification not only may come from a symbolic threat to cherished traditions and values and the political order, but also the threat may come from the unfair redistribution of governmental resources to resolve (what are viewed as) illegitimate issues and to support individuals and groups (who are perceived as) undeserving.

The denial of climate change, and environmental issues more broadly, has been linked to system justification theory (Feygina, Jost, and Goldsmith 2010; Jost et al. 2003). Adherence to system-justifying beliefs downplays damaging aspects of how environmental problems adversely affect the status quo and prevent individuals from acting to correct the problems. Thus, conceding that the climate is changing, especially in response to human causes, is essentially admitting to a failure of the status quo itself. Research by Feygina, Jost, and Goldsmith (2010) shows that individuals committed to system-legitimizing beliefs were more likely to deny the existence of environmental problems. They found that system-justification beliefs were more prevalent among those most sensitive to system threats—self-identified conservatives—and were associated with the denial of environmental problems.

The idea that racial antagonisms emanate from threats to the existing racial hierarchy is not a new assertion. Blumer (1958) recognized some time ago that threats to the racial hierarchy trigger a defensive reaction to protect one's symbolic group position, and subsequent research has supported the connection between threat to one's sense of racial group position and racial policies (Bobo and Tuan 2006; Bobo 1983, 1999; Bobo and Hutchings 1996). Climate change is unique in that it does not elicit an explicit threat to the racial hierarchy and privilege like affirmative action, school busing, or charter schools. Instead, the threat comes from regulatory efforts to mitigate climate change that are already perceived as a challenge to the status quo and traditional values like freedom, individualism, and personal responsibility. Thus, racial resentment and climate become intertwined because both elicit challenges to the status quo and both activate a desire to protect the status quo from illegitimate attacks. Individuals who are more sensitive to system-legitimizing beliefs (e.g., "the climate is fine enough, we don't need to take action") are more likely to be sensitive to threats to these beliefs, be it in terms of amelioration of the climate or racial inequality. Alternatively, those who do not adhere to system-legitimizing beliefs should be less sensitive to such threats.

The expected relationships between racial resentment toward African Americans, support for a regulatory government, and the denial of climate change are straightforward. Individuals who express higher levels of racial resentment toward African Americans should be more willing to deny climate change is occurring, and thus less supportive of mitigation efforts. Also, individuals who express less support for a regulatory role of government should be less willing to acknowledge climate change is occurring and they should be less supportive of mitigation efforts.

In addition to these two hypotheses, we explore the interaction effects of gender and racial resentment on the denial of climate change. Consistent with our view that climate change denial is driven largely by a defensive reaction to the threat to the status quo (i.e., system justification theory), gender differences in climate change denial stem from defensive reactions to system justification (Feygina, Jost, and Goldsmith 2010; Flynn, Slovic, and Mertz 1994; Jost, Nosek, and Gosling 2008; Kahan et al. 2007). Women are less likely to engage in system justification than men—since, on average, women are less equal politically and economically, and therefore do not favor the status quo—and we expect this difference in system-justifying beliefs to partially account for women's greater willingness to acknowledge ecological problems and support efforts to mitigate climate change.

We rely on a survey question asking respondents their beliefs about the denial of climate change. The question wording and the response distributions are presented in table 6.4. These questions reveal low sup-

TABLE 6.4. **Mean Racial Resentment by Attitudes about Climate Change (2010 and 2012 CCES)**

From what you know about global climate change or global warming, which one of the following statements comes closest to your opinion?		2010			2012		
		%	N	Racial Resentment M (SD)	%	N	Racial Resentment M (SD)
More Urgency (5)	Global climate change has been established as a serious problem, and immediate action is necessary.	23.9	250	.58 (.23)	26.3	289	.44 (.28)
	There is enough evidence that climate change is taking place and some action should be taken.	24.1	253	.70 (.18)	27.4	301	.58 (.25)
	We don't know enough about global climate change, and more research is necessary before we take any actions.	20.8	218	.78 (.14)	22.3	245	.68 (.20)
	Concern about global climate change is exaggerated. No action is necessary.	22.9	240	.85 (.13)	17.9	197	.74 (.19)
Less Urgency (1)	Global climate change is not occurring; this is not a real issue.	8.3	87	.84 (.14)	6	66	.77 (.22)
	Total	100	1048	.73 (.20)	100	1098	.61 (.27)

Note. The mean levels of climate change are 3.32 (SD=1.29) in 2010 and 3.50 (SD=1.22) in 2012. The correlations between beliefs about climate change and racial resentment are .519 (p<.01) in 2010 and .444 (p<.01) in 2012.

port for the belief in the occurrence of climate change. Combining the top positions as an indication of acknowledging climate change and also for ease of interpretation, the survey indicates that 48 percent in 2010 and 53.7 percent in 2012 acknowledge the occurrence of climate change. This reflects a 5 percent increase in the number of respondents acknowledging climate change, and this change may also be seen in the lower percentage of CCES respondents expressing unequivocal denial of climate change. In 2010 and 2012, 8.3 percent and 6.0 percent, respectively, deny the occurrence of climate change.

Racial spillover has been proposed as an explanation for the racial relevance of climate change (Benegal 2018). According to Benegal (2018),

> While racial groups and stereotypes are not explicitly associated with climate change and its related policies, there are multiple possible pathways through which racial associations or attitudes may have spilled over into climate change discourse and opinions [. . .] many Americans' opinions on non-racial policies became tied to racial attitudes when they were unable to separate Barack Obama's personal characteristics from his policy agendas. (p. 738)

According to this theory, action on climate change (e.g., Clean Power Plan or the Paris Agreement) does not reflect a policy that benefits any racial group; however, because it is an issue supported by President Obama, who happens to be African American, it takes on an added racial dimension. In other words, non-racial issues proposed or advocated by President Obama were thought to evoke racial prejudice. Scholars typically look at the strength of correlations between racial resentment and the denial of climate change as more strongly related under Obama's presidency than Clinton's presidency as indicators of spillover. Thus, racial prejudice toward President Obama was only one source of spillover effect; another source was the challenge to the status quo.

Although we do not have longitudinal data going back to President Clinton, we are able to include Obama's approval rating as a somewhat crude indicator of racial spillover. The connection should be clear: individuals who dislike Obama should express lower approval of his performance, and also be more likely to deny the existence of climate change because he is advocating its amelioration. However, we also test a competing hypothesis, one more aligned with our theorizing about how resentment is grounded in threats to just-world beliefs and resistance to change. We propose that individuals who were experiencing a sense of threat to the status quo would be more likely to resist additional changes to their way of life through climate change regulations. System justification theory supports this reasoning, as individuals seek to protect the status quo when they are uncertain about change. By including threat and Obama approval in our model, we assess the quality of the racial spillover and our model of racial resentment being grounded in threats to a world that needs no change.

Our measure of Whites' racial resentment toward African Americans reflects a specific threat to the status quo by African Americans, but we also include a general measure of perceived societal threat to the status quo. This is a direct test of the explanation for why racial attitudes should be correlated with non-racial issues like climate change. If Whites' resentment is operating because of Obama, then its effects should be diminished by including attitudes about him into our model; however, if the effects persist, then effects of racial attitudes must be due to more than Obama. We believe that single-sourcing the type of threat as primarily racial misses the role of non-racial values like justice and the preservation of the status quo.

We created a measure (alpha = .84) of threat based on five items in our 2012 CCES survey. They were presented as follows:

Please indicate how true or false you find each of the following statements.
The American way of life is under attack.
Things are really out of control in the United States.
The United States of the past is a much better place than the United States of the future.
The United States is changing too fast.
Too many freedoms have made America its own worst enemy.

The responses to the items ranged on a five-point scale from "Completely true" to "Completely false" with higher values indicating an item was more truthful (M=3.49, SD=1.06).

According to table 6.5, the denial of climate change as a consequence of disapproving of President Obama is consistent with a racial spillover effect. Across all models, individuals who disapprove of President Obama are more likely to deny the existence of climate change, controlling for partisan identification and liberal and conservative ideology. Thus, the possibility that racial prejudice toward Obama spills over

TABLE 6.5. **OLS Coefficients Predicting Climate Change Denial (2012 CCES)**

	Model 1	Model 2	Model 3
Racial Resentment	.07** (.03)		−.05 (.03)
Obama Approval	−.27** (.04)	−.24** (.05)	−.24** (.05)
Perceived Threat		−.09** (.04)	−.07* (.04)
Democrat	−.19 (.12)	.22 (.12)	.21 (.12)
Republican	.25** (.11)	−.23* (.11)	−.23* (.11)
Ideology	.33** (.04)	−.34** (.04)	−.32 (.04)
Political Interest	.01 (.04)	.00 (.04)	.01 (.04)
Age	.00 (.00)	.00 (.00)	.00 (.00)
Gender	−.09 (.06)	.10 (.06)	.10 (.06)
Income	.00 (.00)	−.00 (.00)	−.00 (.00)
Constant	5.46** (.25)	5.42** (.26)	5.52** (.26)
R^2	.51	.51	.52
Prob > F	.00	.00	.00
N	959	956	951

Note. *$p<.05$, **$p<.01$.

into climate change denial is plausible. However, Whites' resentment is also significant in model 1 and model 2, suggesting that Whites' resentment toward African Americans continues to influence climate change denial, even with the host of political predispositions and Obama perceptions. When a general societal threat is included in the same model as Whites' resentment toward African Americans (model 3), Whites' resentment toward African Americans is no longer significant. Higher levels of a general societal threat are associated with stronger denial of climate change, even after considering the explained differences due to party, ideology, Obama, and Whites' resentment. This finding across the three models suggests that a general concern about societal threat is important in explaining climate change denial.

III. Self-Contradictory Attitudes: President Trump's Tax Breaks

Another form of consistency we can examine is a form of self-interested harmonious versus contradictory attitudes. In Metzl's *Dying of Whiteness* (2019), he describes how racial resentment toward African Americans penalizes Whites. He asserts that Whites become so concerned with denying certain benefits from what they perceive as undeserving racial minorities that they wind up suffering as well. Rather than taking advantage of programs that could improve their well-being, they oppose these programs as policies going against their values, and at the same time contradict their self-interests and group interests (e.g., as rural, lower socioeconomic status, and other vulnerable statuses). Ultimately, many Whites develop self-contradictory beliefs, motivated by their racial resentment, that prevent them from taking advantage of programs that would relieve their socioeconomic and physiological pain and suffering. Metzl (2019) applies this theory to the opposition to strict gun control laws and White suicides by gun, the objection to Obamacare and death from critical illness, and the support for tax breaks for the wealthy and the demise of public schools. The latter two issues are more amenable to examination in our data.

While self-contradictory beliefs have been explored in the past, the attractive component in Metzl's argument is that such self-contradictory behavior is triggered by racial resentment toward African Americans and other minorities. Whites become so worried that they are losing ground to African Americans and other minorities that they seek to protect their privilege by not supporting policies that would benefit those groups, giving them an advantage—even if Whites are also eligible for the same benefits. African Americans and other minorities suffer from the loss of programs that can help them, but the downside for Whites is that they also need help and could benefit just as much from such programs. But, because of their racial beliefs, translated through values, they do not.

Operationally, racial resentment may compel a person with no medical insurance, perhaps unemployed and suffering from a critical illness, to reject Obamacare, even though they would benefit from it. In a different form of self-contradictory beliefs, racial resentment may compel a person who is poor and struggling to make ends meet to support President Trump's tax cuts for corporations, even though it would end up costing them and benefiting the wealthy. In short, Whites defer their self-interests in favor of broader status quo beliefs, and they prioritize their racial group interests over their material status interests. In both cases, the focus becomes supporting what might benefit Whites as a whole and not giving anything away to African Americans or supporting liberal or Democratic candidates who are more likely to advocate for racial amelioration. This form of behavior gives a new meaning to the expression *cutting off the nose to spite the face.*

In public opinion research, there are several substantive approaches to self-contradictory behavior. While people are indeed motivated to be consistent in their survey responses, they also maintain inconsistent beliefs. For example, people may reject busing their children outside of their neighborhoods to achieve integration despite being exposed to better education and teachers; people may reject the forming of trade unions despite desiring higher wages and better benefits as unskilled laborers; or people most fearful of a terrorist attack may not allow the government to implement broad search and seizure laws to reduce the threat of terrorism. Our interest in self-contradictory beliefs, as a form of cognitive consistency (or motivated reasoning), focuses on the rejection of Obamacare among those with no health insurance and the support for President Trump's tax cuts among people with lower socioeconomic status. Racial resentment toward African Americans is expected to account for self-contradictory beliefs.

President Trump's Tax-Break Policy

Fulfilling a campaign promise, President Trump signed the Tax Cuts and Jobs Act on December 22, 2017. This tax law reduced individual income tax rates, doubled the standard deduction, and eliminated personal exemptions. The top individual tax rate dropped from 39 percent to 36 percent and the business tax rate dropped from 35 percent to 21 percent. The Trump administration and House Republicans sold the tax law as fuel for economic growth and deficit reduction. The support for the tax law in the Senate was also along party lines.

The tax plan has been criticized on basically two grounds. First, the tax breaks are considered to disproportionately benefit the rich at a time when income inequality is an economic, political, and social concern. Second, the concept of a debt-creating tax plan is unwise and counterproductive. The US budget shortfall grew by 17 percent to $779 billion in fiscal year 2018, which the Congressional Budget Office has said was partly a consequence of the tax law. In other words, Trump's tax cuts were criticized as benefiting the wealthy at the expense of the lower and middle classes. Representative Nancy Pelosi of California, the House Democratic leader, called the tax bill a scam, saying it "is simply theft—monumental, brazen theft from the American middle class and from every person who aspires to reach it."

Public opinion was divided on reducing the corporate income tax rate from 39 percent to 21 percent. The following survey question was framed around this major provision of the tax law and the part of the policy that many suggested would have the most devastating impact on the economy:

Do you support or oppose cutting the corporate tax rate from 39 percent to 21 percent?

In response to this question, 45 percent supported the tax break and 55 percent opposed it in our 2018 CCES data. But, most intriguingly, many people who would likely not receive a tax benefit or relief from the law endorsed it anyway. To examine such self-contradiction, we separated respondents into three groups based on their reported income (e.g., group 1 [lower income]: less than or equal to $49,999; group 2 [middle income]: $50,000 to $119,999; and group 3 [higher income]: greater than $120,000). To the extent that any of the groups within the income range would benefit at all from the tax breaks, the expectation was that lower income groups should be less supportive of the tax breaks because they are less likely to benefit from them.

There is some evidence that this is indeed the case, but it is not as dramatic as one might expect. For instance, 45 percent of those in lower income group, 48 percent of those in middle income group, and 54 percent of those in higher income group supported the reduction in the corporate tax. While the differences among the income groups are encouraging, the sizeable percentages within each income group suggest broad support for the tax break. That is, nearly half of the individuals who were least likely to benefit from the corporate tax cut still supported it.

A question begging to be asked is, why would individuals who were least likely to benefit from a reduction in corporate tax rate, or who would have to pay for it, support it? Obvious answers involve party identification and support for President Trump. People are likely to support the policies proposed by the president and the political parties with whom they identify. Out of allegiance or trust, or because they really believe the reduction in the corporate tax rate is best for them and the country, individuals endorse the policies of their political party. This is supported in a multivariate logit model predicting support for the corporate tax reduction in table 6.6. The columns in this table pertain to the model being run by different income groups. Thus, across all models,

TABLE 6.6. **Logistic Analysis of Support for Reducing the Corporate Tax Rate (2018 CCES): Would you support or oppose reducing the corporate tax rate from 39 percent to 21 percent?**

Independent Variables	Full Model	Income Group 1 (0 to $49,999)	Income Group 2 ($50,000 to $119,999)	Income Group 3 ($120,000+)
Education	−.01 (.07)	−.02 (.10)	−.03 (.11)	.05 (.18)
Age	.01 (.01)	−.00 (.01)	.02 (.01)	.03 (.02)
Gender	−.29 (.18)	−.40 (.28)	.01 (.32)	−.72 (.52)
Democrat	−.92** (.25)	−.60** (.34)	−1.04** (.42)	−1.20 (.66)
Republican	1.05** (.23)	1.07** (.34)	.82* (.36)	2.18** (.64)
Racial Resentment	.48** (.10)	.33** (.14)	.59** (.16)	.97* (.28)
Income	.01 (.03)			
Constant	−1.64** (.66)	−.52 (.91)	−2.68** (1.06)	−3.89* (1.76)
Pseudo R^2	.22	.15	.28	.47
Prob > x^2	.000	.000	.000	.298
N	618	276	263	149

Note. *p<.05, **p<.01.

party identification is significant in that Democratic identifiers oppose and Republican identifiers support the tax reduction.

The other part of the narrative in table 6.6 supports our expectations regarding cognitive consistency of racial resentment toward African Americans. Racial resentment is positive and significant across the income groups. This result suggests to us that individuals high in racial resentment are likely to possess self-contradictory beliefs because they know that Trump's policies or reducing the corporate tax rate would hurt African Americans and other minorities (or benefit Whites). Supporting the reduction in the corporate tax would be consistent with their concerns about protecting Whites' status and privilege.

Conclusion

With a well-established roadmap provided by cognitive consistency, this chapter explored how Whites' resentment toward African Americans affected blame for poor economic conditions during President Obama's first term, as well as the connection between racial resentment and an ostensibly non-racial issue, climate change denial. Understanding the powerful role that partisanship plays in the appraisal of political candidates and policies, the possibility that racial cognitive consistency can constrain political attitudes was inspired by two issues. First, as a result of the perceived threat to the racial status quo posed by President Obama, Whites' racial resentment became connected to issues where it has not been connected before in presidential history. The source of the connection was a perceived threat to a way of life where Whites feel privileged and where resources are distributed according to dominant group rules. Obama's message of "Change" was effective during the campaign, but once he was elected, opponents presented his policies as being the wrong type of, and too much, change. As a result, Whites' racial resentment toward African Americans became relevant to all things Obama undertook, and anything that could have earned him praise or reward was denigrated with no weight to the facts. Thus, while the economy improved from a dramatic economic recession, it was never enough improvement for his opponents. Never before have political scientists seen such a form of motivated reasoning in the face of contradictory factual evidence. Second, Whites' racial resentment is more than an expressed attitude; it guides the filtering—selection and processing—of information. The combination of these issues raised the possibility that racial cognitive consistency could be just as constraining as partisan cognitive consistency, if not even more so. The next hurdle was identifying an issue (and data) on which racial cognitive consistency might be most evident. The issue had to have some objective basis where individuals could know or contrast and compare facts. With this requirement in mind, appraisals of President Obama's performance on the economy seemed like a logical place to begin, as there were a variety of documentable accomplishments where he received minimal credit. The United States' recovery from the severe economic recession reflected the most glaring example of where individuals' racial beliefs about African Americans led to misrepresentations and skewed perspectives of President Obama and his performance.

Our analyses of whom individuals blame for poor economic conditions in the wake of the Great Recession provide strong evidence for racial cognitive consistency. We show that resentment toward African Americans increases attributions of blame toward President Obama for the poor economic conditions, even though he unquestionably inherited the economic catastrophe. Resentment toward African Americans places little blame or responsibility on persons (e.g., former President Bush, Wall Street, and mortgage lenders) who are perhaps most directly responsible. We find these effects across multiple studies, and they exist in the same direction, although at different magnitudes, for Democrats,

Independents, and Republicans alike. Given the consistency of our results, we conclude that racial resentment motivates judgments by way of
cognitive consistency, a process that biases the consumption and review
of objective facts and leads individuals to align temporal judgments with
core predispositions.

This study found that attitudes toward climate change denial are
linked solidly to racial resentment toward African Americans. This relationship is expected. On the basis of the system justification theory, we
have argued that racial resentment toward African Americans and attitudes toward climate change are inextricably linked because they both
elicit a defensive reaction to challenges to the status quo—the socio-
political order and values upon which the system is based. Individuals
who benefit most from the social and political system are likely to react defensively to various threats across different issue domains that
also elicit a challenge to traditional values, like climate change. It is this
threat to the status quo and the motivation to defend it that connect attitudes that on the surface do not appear to be connected.

Our analyses reveal that racially resentful Whites are more likely to
deny that climate change is occurring and is linked to anthropogenic
causes than those who are less resentful. Although racial resentment is
our primary focus in this research, we show through the use of a multivariate model that attitudes toward climate change are also connected to
beliefs about the role of government, approval of President Obama, partisan self-identification, and education. We find that climate change denial and efforts to mitigate the effects of climate change are inextricably
connected to the solutions, which usually involve some form of government regulation. Simply, Whites deny the existence of climate change
because of the solutions (governmental involvement) that threaten their
status quo and enduring values. Whites' advantage and progress have
been bolstered by the status quo, and any change to the status quo is perceived to come at their expense.

As long as climate change amelioration is perceived as a threat to
the status quo, the racialization of attitudes toward climate change will
likely endure, and, as a result, become another obstacle for protecting
the planet. To the extent that the election of President Donald Trump
was fueled by racial resentment and beliefs that Whites' status and traditional values needed reaffirmation, climate change will continue to be
viewed through a racialized lens due to the shared nature of the threat
to dominant values. Policies such as climate change, already perceived

as a challenge to the status quo and traditional values, are likely to be given low priority as individuals consider it necessary to recover lost resources, motivated in part by racial considerations.

Because issues like climate change become connected to other issues through system-justifying values, climate change may activate other issues, like racial resentment, and vice versa. To the extent this happens, discussions about President Obama, climate change, and racial attitudes may reflect threats to values beneath the surface of both issues. As our findings indicate, individuals may plausibly think about other challenges to the status quo and react more defensively than expected.

CHAPTER SEVEN

Racial Schadenfreude

The previous chapter revealed important downstream effects of Whites' resentment toward African Americans pertaining to the need to align social and political attitudes so that they are consistent with the willingness to defend White status and privilege. Cognitive consistency is driven by the need to reduce the discomfort and dissonance that come from holding discordant or contradictory beliefs. In this chapter, we explore another consequence of racial resentment, albeit a more pernicious one, that arises from inconsistencies between perceived actions and outcomes that violate notions of justice and deservingness.

Individuals possess a need to believe that they live in a world that, for the most part, is fair, in which people get what they deserve (Lerner 1980a, 1980b). A belief in a just world promotes the expectation that life will be stable and orderly, and that people can confront an otherwise uncertain future with confidence. When a perceived injustice occurs and the stable and orderly status quo is threatened, such as when others are perceived to benefit undeservingly (Tyler 1997), individuals are also motivated to restore their sense of justice and fairness. Whites' resentment toward African Americans occurs when the perceived injustice or violation goes uncorrected. Until there is a correction and a sense of justice is restored, individuals may desire a "pound of flesh" or to see the "undeserving" fail, from which they experience a sense of joy or schadenfreude. People are motivated to believe that only bad things happen to bad people.

Because a justice motive and evaluations of deservingness, facilitated by legitimizing racial myths, are at the heart of Whites' resentment toward African Americans, it reflects the continuation of a process rather than the end. When African Americans are perceived as violating traditional values, thwarting established societal norms, and taking advantage of unearned resources—all of which threaten the status quo—Whites' sense of justice is challenged, creating a need to restore justice and a desire to see African Americans and other minorities fail, face social penalty, and not receive additional help. We contend that feelings of racial resentment do not dissipate; instead, they fester to the point where they affect other emotions, for instance causing pleasure from seeing African Americans suffer from seemingly poor choices and behavior. People also lash out by joining hate groups, expressing hurtful and denigrating epithets, and, for ordinary citizens, gravitating toward political messages that promote harsh and punitive treatment of African Americans and other minorities (i.e., the death penalty, stop-and-frisk, and separating families at immigrant detention centers).

A surprising amount of research has been devoted to the relationship between schadenfreude and resentment, though none of it relates to race.

Deservingness, Whites' Resentment, and Racial Schadenfreude

Schadenfreude occurs when a person experiences pleasure, joy, or self-satisfaction after learning of or witnessing the troubles, failures, or humiliation of another (Heider 1958). It is usually thought of as malicious because instead of sympathy when another person is suffering, which could be considered the morally acceptable response, feelings of pleasure at the pain of another person can add to that person's suffering (Leach et al. 2003). Because schadenfreude is something that an inconsiderate, selfish, and borderline sadistic person would feel, it is typically seen as shameful, and we therefore like to pretend it does not exist (Spurgin 2015). More specifically, it is not that regular people ignore the misfortune of others, they simply deny it brings them a sense of pleasure; instead, individuals with schadenfreude engage in victim blaming through the language of just-world beliefs: "those persons are getting what they deserve." Still, there is a line of research that suggests schadenfreude helps us cope with our own private failures. Smith (2013) asserts that seeing someone else fail makes us feel better about ourselves and reminds us we are not the only one with flaws or who makes mistakes.

Schadenfreude is a fundamentally human emotion grounded in a basic drive to evaluate ourselves and to seek positive self-evaluation (self-esteem), primarily through comparisons to others (Smith 2013). It derives from social comparison, which in its theoretical form essentially states that individuals determine their own social and personal worth on the basis of how they stack up against others they perceive as somehow faring better, equally, or worse. Thus, people constantly evaluate and compare themselves to others with the hope of feeling superior to and more powerful than others. These emotions boost self-esteem and make us feel good about ourselves. Schadenfreude is this form of pleasure, and it is derived from another's failures and misfortunes because it provides us with a positive self-evaluation and a greater sense of self-worth (van Dijk et al. 2015). However, individuals with high self-esteem do not need the misfortune of others to feel better about themselves as much as individuals with low self-esteem.

The development of schadenfreude begins at a very early age (e.g., Shamay-Tsoory, Ahronberg-Kirschenbaum, and Bauminger-Zviely 2014) and can occur for several reasons, such as hate, envy, and jealousy. We are primarily concerned about schadenfreude that arises from an injustice: when we think someone or some group deserves to suffer a misfortune because they have achieved reward, or sought to, through unfair means.[1]

Schadenfreude is a useful emotion and concept for our analysis of racial resentment because resentment motivates a felt need to restore justice. Thus, people who are high in racial resentment toward African Americans are not likely to want to see them succeed in their ostensibly unjust efforts to change the social hierarchy or cherished traditional features of American society. Rather, racial resentment compels people to seek some form of justice for the policies, procedures, and outcomes that Whites view as having benefited African Americans unfairly. If African Americans do not deserve a positive outcome, then what do they deserve for having received that outcome? For those with higher racial resentment, African Americans deserve to experience punishment for their civic violations; such an outcome is just, even if it maintains and justifies inequality.

As we pointed out earlier in chapter 2, racial resentment stems from a person's need to believe in a just world. Lerner (1965, 1980) and others (Dalbert 2001, 2009; Furnham 2003; Hafer and Begue 2005; Lerner and Miller 1978) have shown that people have a fundamental desire for an orderly, certain, and just existence where people get what they deserve and deserve what they get. This motive easily applies to recipients of welfare (Williams 1984) and unemployment, but is so strong that even

victims of rape, genocide, and other atrocities are blamed for what happened to them (Hafer 2000; Hafer and Begue 2005). Resources and penalties are not distributed randomly, but rather attached to character and
effort, which is comforting to people's sense of fairness and justice. Because people want to believe that the world is fair, they will look for ways
to explain or rationalize away injustice, often blaming the other person
for their victimized (or unjust) situation. The alternative belief to a just
world is that people receive things that they do not deserve, which creates chaos and anxiety. Thus, a belief in a just world leads people to operate in a biased fashion, believing that victims deserve their fate. By extension, then, individuals who are high in racial resentment are likely to
experience a sense of injustice (and discomfort) as African Americans
are perceived to benefit unfairly and challenge the status quo; and therefore any inequality and inequity they face is not structural or systemic,
but deserved because of one or more character issues. With this reasoning, on can conclude that the rules of the world, as they exist, are fair, it's
just that people have not been successful at following them.

Regardless if schadenfreude is acknowledged, for some Whites it is
comforting and satisfying when African Americans fail or suffer because, on the basis of racial stereotypes and their perceived deficiencies,
they deserve what they get. This deservingness calculation is influenced
by attribution error, illusory correlations, motivated reasoning, personality factors (i.e., closed-mindedness or authoritarianism), or racial stereotypes depicting African Americans as lazy, unintelligent, violent,
lacking self-discipline, or failing to delay gratification. But once one is
considered undeserving, it no longer matters how the calculation was established (be it due to cheating or low effort); the injustice is done, and
restoring of justice is necessary.[2]

We argue that racial schadenfreude occurs when one believes that
African Americans, and other racial minorities, have unjustly benefited from resources that they have not earned through hard work, self-
discipline, conforming to traditional values, and playing by the rules.
Bad behavior is being rewarded and not punished. African Americans
are perceived to be circumventing the prescribed norms without suffering the consequences of their bad behavior. For Whites, who have followed the prescribed rules of the game, persevered, and worked hard,
such a perception of African Americans is discomforting because it
challenges the values upon which the social hierarchy is based and violates their sense of justice. Not only does this produce racial resentment,

but it also results in schadenfreude, because there is a need for African Americans to suffer the consequences of their perceived bad behavior. Their bad behavior does not have to be observable; it could stem from mass media, racial stereotypes, and attribution error. The bottom line is this: Whites need for African Americans to suffer the consequences of their actions to restore orderliness, certainty, and justice. This is the only way to keep society orderly and fair. Discomfort and dissonance likely occur when African Americans are not held accountable or responsible for their actions.

With the existing framework, a person who is high in racial resentment can be expected to value and defend the existing status quo or value a return to an era when Whites were more dominant and powerful (when people knew their place). Thus, people who are perceived to challenge the existing status quo (negative valence) yet thrive and take advantage of existing resources are perceived as undeserving. In this process, schadenfreude is likely to occur because the perceived benefit (positive valence) is unearned.

Meting out justice is hedonically rewarding (Chester and DeWall 2016; de Quervain et al. 2004; Singer et al. 2006; Strobel et al. 2011). Neuroscientific research shows that retribution (correcting a perceived wrong or injustice, real or imagined) activates a similar neural reward circuitry as narcotics or a drug addiction (Chester and DeWall 2016). Revenge triggers cravings (dopamine) activity in the nucleus accumbens (a brain region reliably associated with reward) in anticipation of experiencing pleasure and relief through retaliation. *Revenge addiction*, as it is referred to, helps explain why racial resentment produces racial schadenfreude and a desire to retaliate against minority groups and its members or enjoy seeing them suffer.

A lack of empathy fuels racial schadenfreude. When people have empathy with others, it is easier to treat them with dignity and respect, but empathy requires perspective taking and the ability to consciously put oneself into the mind of another individual and imagine what that person is thinking or feeling. Racial prejudice and racial resentment make perspective taking extremely difficult, and because of social distance, errors in judgment are more likely. Racial prejudice and racial resentment make it easy to exclude racial outgroups worthy of treatment as full human beings, such as in *moral exclusion*—when individuals or groups are perceived as outside the boundary in which moral values, and considerations of fairness apply (Tileagă 2016).

A particularly egregious aspect of racial schadenfreude is that it inhibits more than the support for ameliorative attitudes and policies—it also prevents empathizing with the African American community when members are murdered by the police. Racial schadenfreude obscures clear-cut deaths of innocent African Americans and it compels ordinary people to consider whether African Americans did anything to deserve or warrant such treatment, as if any benign infractions warrant death. Although we do not have survey data to capture such attitudes, we believe our theory and analyses are consistent with the notion that racial schadenfreude interrupts the empathy of the African American community. With numerous examples, such as in the killing of George Floyd (an African American man who was asphyxiated after being handcuffed and pinned to the ground by a white police officer's knee), Eric Garner (an African American man asphyxiated for selling cigarettes); Botham Jean (a Haitian man shot and killed when an off-duty officer mistook his apartment for her apartment); Sandra Bland (an African American woman asphyxiated in police custody); Breonna Taylor (an African American woman shot and killed in her house during a botched police raid on her apartment), come outrage, demonstrations, and protests. It is our belief that the language used to defend the police actions, "the police were just doing their job" or "the police were only doing what they were trained to do," triggers the deservingness of African Americans' harsh treatment and death. Notably, in nearly all of these cases, the police defendants also sought to raise issues about the victims' character, implicating the just-world reasoning. Thus, another often overlooked component of African Americans being treated harshly and murdered (punishments incommensurate with the offense) is the language used in justification of such treatment (that tends to blame them for their mistreatment), which then fuels African Americans' racial resentment toward Whites.

Bandura's (1999, 2002, 2016) Moral Disengagement Theory suggests that individuals may experience little distress from immoral behavior, such as taking joy in African Americans suffering and wanting to see them fail. Moral Disengagement Theory maintains that normal ordinary people may not experience anguish or self-condemnation from committing immoral acts against others because of their ability to disengage moral self-sanctions. Individuals, according to Bandura (2002, 2016), employ different strategies to rationalize their immoral behavior, including reframing their conduct as serving a socially worthy or moral purpose;

diffusing responsibility and obscuring their role in harmful behavior; misconstruing the negative consequences of their harmful behavior; and dehumanizing or blaming victims for bringing harm onto themselves. Moral disengagement gives people the moral latitude to harm others in ways they would not otherwise find acceptable without that psychological distancing, thereby protecting one's self-image as a good person even as one harms other people. Applying disengagement theory to racial schadenfreude, individuals high in racial resentment are likely to believe they are justified because their sense of injustice has been violated (and dissonance is produced if not restored through some form of retribution), and the tendency for them is to rationalize immoral behavior. In this way, racial resentment reflects a dynamic process in which closed minded beliefs about African Americans by normal ordinary people are justified, further enabling racial inequality and injustice. Bandura's research is also useful because the tendency to justify immoral behavior occurs among normal ordinary people and it is not a function of mental weakness. In short, individuals high in racial schadenfreude may attempt to use strategies resembling moral disengagement in their joy in seeing African Americans suffer and atone for their taking advantage of unearned and undeserved resources.

In the next section, we argue that racial resentment causes Whites to relish the failure of ordinary African Americans and to demur in their success.

Obama's Election as a Perceived Injustice

The election of an African American to our highest political office was alleged to be prima facia evidence that America had turned the corner on racial prejudice, but given the way President Obama was received and denigrated, such a belief was only wishful thinking. If anything, the election of the first African American president revealed the extent of racial polarization. Obama represented the quintessential threat to White group status and the social hierarchy.

Whites' reactions to Obama were not caused by what they might have to endure personally, but rather stemmed from a perceived threat to the status quo that protects Whites' advantage. Whites' sense of fear was more socio-tropic than egocentric, like it has always been (Davis 2007;

Davis and Silver 2001; Gibson 2013). In other words, Whites were less fearful of losing their jobs, being unable to afford groceries, or paying higher taxes, but more concerned that they would lose some of their advantage and privilege as African Americans and other minorities benefited.

Whites generally are uncomfortable with African American politicians, holding more negative stereotypes about them than comparable White politicians (Hajnal 2001; Williams 1990; Callaghan and Terkildsen 2002; Schneider and Bos 2011; Jones 2014; Weaver 2012). For instance, Williams (1990) shows that Whites view African American candidates as weaker leaders, less intelligent, less knowledgeable, and less trustworthy compared to White candidates. Callaghan and Terkildsen (2002) demonstrate that African American politicians are stereotyped as being less hardworking and less capable than White politicians. Jones (2014) shows that Whites stereotype African American politicians as more liberal and more likely to be Democrats than identical White politicians.

But Whites' perceptions may involve more nuance. Schneider and Bos (2011) argue that Whites see African American politicians as a subgroup and do not stereotype them as they do ordinary African Americans. While Whites perceive them more positively than ordinary African Americans, they are still perceived more negatively than ordinary politicians. Hajnal maintains that Whites are not all alike in their perceptions of African American politicians—Republicans view them more negatively than Democrats. For Hajnal (2001), White Republican perceptions extend beyond simple stereotypes; indeed, they view African American politicians as "a direct threat capable of disrupting the traditional balance of racial power" (p. 604). Taken together, these studies suggest that the belief that the election of the first African American president signified a post-racial America was extremely premature. It actually had the opposite effect of stoking Whites' indignation.

While there are many ways to think of operationalizing racial schadenfreude in politics, we operationalize it as a desire to see President Obama and his policies fail. President Obama, for all intents and purposes, is a polarizing political figure, even though he is no longer in office, and he is the object of extreme scorn for many Whites. During his tenure, nothing seemed off limits to Whites' scorn for Obama. And so we begin our analysis of schadenfreude by addressing the following questions: *What does President Obama represent to Whites, and why do people want to see him and his policies fail?*

Empirical Evidence of Perceived Threat

As a first step, we assess the above claim regarding the extent to which Whites perceived President Obama as a threat. In our 2012 CCES data, respondents were asked,

> "Rights and freedoms include things like free speech, voting, religious practices, and protections from unlawful searches and seizures. Do you think [___] poses an immediate threat to the rights and freedoms of ordinary citizens, or not?"

President Obama, the federal government, the US Congress, and the US Supreme Court were randomly assigned to respondents as references in this survey question. Respondents received only one of the political references, but the question was intentionally framed in broad terms to encompass aspects of the status quo.[3]

As the responses in figure 7.1 show, President Obama is among a variety of threats individuals perceive, and no institution stands out as particularly harmless. Sizeable percentages perceive the federal government,

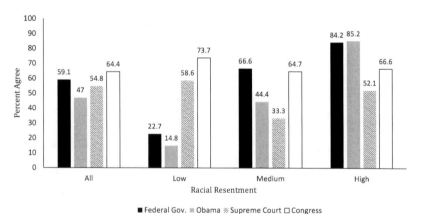

FIGURE 7.1. Percent Agreeing Target Is an Immediate Threat, CCES 2016

the Supreme Court, and Congress as immediate threats. President Obama is the lowest among them. An important question raised by this small experiment is whether racial resentment makes one more sensitive to threats, not just President Obama. Thus, to aid in the presentation of results, we divided our racial resentment measure into terciles, intended to approximate low, medium, and high levels of racial resentment.[4] With this division, the distribution of threat perceptions changes. While only 14.8 percent of those low in racial resentment perceive President Obama as an immediate threat, the percent increases to 44.4 percent among moderates and the percent skyrockets to 85.2 percent among those high in racial resentment. The federal government is the only other reference group that shows a similar increase, which is to be expected given that the federal government is frequently viewed in negative terms.

Making the Racial Threat Political

From the day he announced his run for the presidency on January 10, 2007, many Whites wanted Barack Obama to fail. Racists clearly wanted President Obama to suffer simply because he is African American. People who are not racists or don't deal in hate may also have had disdain for President Obama and desired him to fail because they perceived him to represent a significant challenge to White privilege and status. That he succeeded in being elected the first African American president and re-elected to a second term, survived reprehensible derogation, and passed significant legislation, such as the Affordable Care Act, can be seen as a challenge to a host of establishments for White privilege and status. So, it is not only the racist who might desire Obama to fail and take joy in seeing him fail, but also the ordinary citizen who is sensitive to defending their status and power.

The election of Obama challenged the just-world belief because, although the elections themselves were essentially fair and decisive, an African American was elected to the most powerful position in the world. As we have shown, a sizeable portion of Whites believed Obama would seek to empower and advantage undeserving African Americans through policies and actions that would threaten Whites' privilege and status by blaming Whites for the mistreatment of African Americans, even if they had no role in past wrongs. Such a belief is not justified, but it is discomforting. It taps a general belief that the election of African

Americans and other minorities inherently challenges the status quo. It also taps into a widely held sentiment that African Americans and other minorities are resentful toward Whites and are motivated by revenge against Whites (Norton and Sommers 2011). Conspiracy theories of African Americans, especially President Obama, seeking revenge on Whites were offered by opinion leaders.

Glenn Beck, a *Fox News* host, alleged that Obama's policies were rooted in reparations, the idea that African Americans should be compensated for slavery.

> Everything that is getting pushed through Congress, including this health care bill, are transforming America. And they are all driven by President Obama's thinking on one idea: reparations.

Similarly, Rush Limbaugh suggested as much in his comments regarding Obama's nomination of Supreme Court Justice Sonia Sotomayor,

> The president of the United States? We're talking now about a Supreme Court justice? The days of them [racial minorities] not having any power are over, and they are angry. And they want to use their power as a means of retribution. That's what Obama's about, gang. He's angry, he's gonna cut this country down to size, he's gonna make it pay for all its multicultural mistakes that it has made, its mistreatment of minorities. I know exactly what's going on.

The irony, of course, is that African Americans' status, as a whole, did not improve during President Obama's eight years in office. He simply did not seem to believe that uplifting African Americans could be achieved through race-specific programs. He was on record for stating that,

> as a general matter, my view would [be] that if you want to get at African American poverty, income gap, wealth gap, achievement gap, that the most important thing is to make sure that the society as a whole does right by people who are poor, are working class, are aspiring to a better life for their kids: higher minimum wages, full employment programs, early childhood education. Those kinds of programs are by design universal but by definition, because they are helping folks who are in the worst economic situations, are most likely to disproportionately impact and benefit Black Americans.

Objective indicators reveal the results of Obama's beliefs. For example, African Americans were hit particularly hard during the Great Recession, with many falling into poverty. By 2011, the poverty rate within the Black community reached 27.6 percent, which was almost 2 percent higher than when President Obama took office. Meanwhile, the wealth gap grew between African Americans and Whites during the Obama presidency. Based on an analysis of Federal Reserve data, wealth was eight times higher for Whites than African Americans in 2010 and increased to 13 times greater in 2013. These indicators probably should be added to examples of cognitive consistency, as perception does not reflect objective reality.

Expectations from Whites' Resentment toward African Americans and Racial Schadenfreude

Good things come to those who follow the rules, possess good personality and character, and work hard, while people with poor character and values do not succeed—and they also deserve to suffer. We want them to suffer because it restores our sense of justice. This implicates President Obama because he reflects a threat to the system just like other African Americans, and his election to the most powerful position in the world is not seen as just. There is a need for President Obama to fail. Yet, it is important to acknowledge that some Whites may have a high sense of justice but they are not resentful because they see things differently. African Americans may not be perceived as undeserving or their motivations may not be attributed to their internal qualities and character or culture, but rather to historical, environmental, and transactional factors over which they have little control. To the extent that African Americans are not viewed as undeserving, Whites' sense of resentment is not triggered. In this case, then, Obama is not perceived as a threat to White privilege and status and schadenfreude is not triggered.

Obama had significant struggles and failures; the surge in Afghanistan, the use of drones and special operations forces to chase down suspected terrorists, the mishandling of the Arab Spring, and the intervention into Libya all readily come to mind. Such failures and many more raise the question: were people also readily pleased with his failures?

Measuring Racial Schadenfreude

We measure schadenfreude toward Obama through a survey experiment embedded in the 2016 CCES study. A subsample of respondents were asked how happy or unhappy failures on the part of Obama made them feel. The following statements about Obama were considered:

Please indicate how you feel about the following items:
Barack Obama being identified as one the worst presidents in history.
Barack Obama's foreign policy failures.
The Republican Party opposition to Barack Obama.
The economic failures under Barack Obama's leadership as president.
The failures of President Obama's healthcare legislation.

The response categories for the questions ranged from *Very Happy to See* (coded 7) to *Very Unhappy to See* (coded 1). Higher scores on each of these items are associated with more happiness (i.e., more schadenfreude). An exploratory factor analysis of these items resulted in one factor (3.43), explaining 93 percent of the variance and an Alpha of .91. A composite scale was constructed using the individual items.

Racial Schadenfreude Is a Powerful Emotion

Based on the statistics in table 7.1, at least one in five respondents show pleasure at Obama failing on each of the areas under consideration. The numbers indicate that 40.3 percent are pleased with Obama's being one of the worst presidents in history; 25.7 percent are pleased with foreign policy failures; 33 percent are pleased by Republican Party opposition to Obama; 22.1 percent are pleased about Obama's economic failures; and 31.8 percent are pleased about the failure of Obama's healthcare legislation. Notably, there is lower schadenfreude for economic failures—people did not want the economy to fail. This is likely because the economy is a part of the status quo, while policies and appraisals of one's legacy are each more tied to deservingness. In general, the means and percent pleased with items listed in table 7.1 both indicate a substantial level of schadenfreude toward Obama, which aligns with the levels of White resentment toward African Americans.

TABLE 7.1. **Measuring Schadenfreude and Summary Statistics**

Question Wording	Mean	% Pleased	Correlation with Racial Resentment
Barack Obama being identified as one of the *worst* presidents in history.	4.10 (2.49)	40.29	.62**
Barack Obama's foreign policy *failures*.	3.67 (2.19)	25.73	.37**
The Republican Party Opposition to Barack Obama	3.92 (2.38)	33.00	.55**
The economic *failures* under Barack Obama's leadership as president.	3.44 (2.21)	22.10	.37**
The *failures* of President Obama's healthcare legislation.	3.77 (2.37)	31.80	.44**

Note. **$p \leq .01$; *$p \leq .05$. Percent "pleased" is based on the combined highest two response categories (i.e., "Very Pleased" and "Pleased"). Standard deviations in parentheses.

The correlations in table 7.1 also confirm, albeit in a cursory fashion, our expected relationship between racial resentment and schadenfreude. The signs and the sizes of the coefficients are particularly notable. As expected, higher levels of racial resentment are significantly associated with higher levels of schadenfreude with the items. The correlation between racial resentment toward African Americans and our schadenfreude measure is .55.

We next examine the extent to which the individual racial schadenfreude items perform as expected, when controlling for other explanations. Table 7.2 reports the bivariate relationships between the schadenfreude scale and several related factors, and it also shows the correlation between schadenfreude and Whites' racial resentment toward African Americans for each factor.

Because they inform subsequent analyses, the inferences we draw from this analysis are quite important. First, education is somewhat related to schadenfreude. With the exception of those who only completed a college education, there is a decline in the mean levels of racial schadenfreude as the level of education increases. That is, the more highly educated (i.e., those with post-college education) have lower levels of racial schadenfreude than individuals with lower levels of education. That individuals with lower levels of education, especially those with only a high school education, tend to be more racially intolerant and prejudiced is quite well known, and our analysis adds to an already voluminous body of work in this area. In addition to being exposed to

TABLE 7.2. **Bivariate Correlations to Racial Schadenfreude, 2016 CCES**

	Mean	s.d.	Correlation with Racial Resentment
Education (F=4.13, Prob>F=.006)			
High School	3.99	2.03	−.08
Some College	3.68	1.96	
College Grad	3.89	1.97	
Post-College	3.36	2.02	
Age (F=3.32, Prob>F=.010)			
18 to 29	3.75	1.76	.03
30 to 39	3.70	1.76	
40 to 49	3.88	2.92	
50 to 59	3.35	1.95	
60+	4.96	2.18	
Gender (F=5.34, Prob>F=.021)			
Male	4.09	2.04	.15**
Female	3.49	1.93	
Income (F=2.12, Prob>F=.096)			
0 to $39,000	3.75	1.97	−.02
$40,000 to $79,000	3.83	2.02	
$80,000 to $119,000	3.74	2.09	
$120,000 +	3.59	1.93	
Partisanship (F=133.90, Prob>F=.000)			
Democrat	2.40	1.54	.33**
Independent	3.91	1.90	
Republican	5.15	1.56	
Vote Intention in 2016 (F=818.69, Prob>F=.000)			
Donald Trump	5.09	1.62	−.75**
Hillary Clinton	1.98	1.03	

Note. Statistics based on 1-way analysis of variance (ANOVA). **p>.01; *p>.05.

greater information and being more capable of counteracting certain bases for intolerance, those with high levels of education are exposed to a wider range of beliefs and cultures. Such an exposure is expected to make individuals more appreciative and tolerant of differences and less racially resentful. Although not shown in this analysis, the correlations between schadenfreude and racial resentment increase as the level of education increases, suggesting that schadenfreude is more closely aligned or predictable with racial resentment among the most highly educated category. On closer examination of the data, it appears that the less uniform responses to racial resentment (or survey error) among the least educated reduces its predictive capacity. This means that we would have more difficulty in predicting racial schadenfreude by racial resentment in this education category.

Age is also weakly related to schadenfreude, with higher levels located among older individuals than younger ones. This, too, is in line with what we should expect. Younger individuals, on the whole, tend to be more tolerant and less prejudiced than older individuals. Often, this changes with the aging and maturation process as they become more conservative and have more at stake in the political system. Before such responsibilities set in and begin to change them, younger individuals see politics more liberally than older individuals. It is also possible that these indicators can be tapping into greater support for Obama among younger individuals. Younger individuals may express less racial schadenfreude because they are more likely to support to support Obama and have less to complain or be upset about.

Men and women, too, differ significantly on schadenfreude. A great deal has been made of the angry White male in the media, and the desire to get their "pound of flesh" from African Americans and from Obama is a sign of their anger. The storyline is that White men, who have historically sat at the top of the cultural and economic hierarchy, have lost more than anyone else to African Americans' demands for more civil rights and equal access, which they perceive as exacerbated under President Obama. Women may not internalize this type of threat as much as men because they were able to advance through African Americans' demand for equal rights and may have felt they would do so as well under the Obama administration.

Income, as an indicator of class status, is not as meaningful in the larger scheme of evaluations of political figures. Although the overall mean differences in schadenfreude toward Obama are not statistically significant, the means are uniform, suggesting that schadenfreude is more of an emotion among the lower income groups or class than the higher income groups. Nonetheless, income was included because we thought it might be feasible for Whites with higher levels of income or class status to feel particularly threatened by Obama. And, as a result of such threat to their well-being, they should relish the failures and demur the successes of Obama. There is some support for this in the bivariate analysis, but not as strong as other predictors.

Political Indicators

The predictability of partisanship in producing schadenfreude is strong and robust, but it does not need to be connected to racial beliefs (Combs et al. 2009). Individuals who identify as Democrat almost naturally believe that Democratic administrations have little to atone for, and individuals who identify as Republican almost naturally believe that Democratic administrations, regardless of race, have a great deal to atone for. This is just the nature of politics, and it is why partisanship is so critical to understanding schadenfreude. In other words, delight in Obama's failures and disdain in his success occurs simply because he is a Democrat. Without a more elaborate research design, we cannot really determine whether the schadenfreude experienced by Republicans is due to his race or to some other issue. But the fact remains that individuals who identify as Democrat experience the least amount of schadenfreude while individuals who identify as Republican experience the greatest amount of schadenfreude. Individuals who identify as Independent are positioned between them.

As Combs et al. (2009) show, partisan perceptions of the out-group (or the opposing party), in general, are motivated by schadenfreude. In one of their studies, Democrats were so antagonistic toward George Bush that they experienced schadenfreude on reports of American troop casualties in Iraq because the war occurred during his administration.

The correlation between schadenfreude and racial resentment is positive and in the correct direction. This means that racial resentment is not as powerful in predicting schadenfreude among Republicans (r=.15) as it is for Democrats (r=.48) and Independents (r=.53). Republicans tend to aggregate at the higher levels of Whites' racial resentment toward African Americans, but they are more dispersed in their feelings of schadenfreude. Republicans at the lower end of racial resentment register almost as high on schadenfreude as those at the higher end of racial resentment. The result is a lower predictability of schadenfreude or a lower correlation.

Partisanship is very similar to vote intention in 2016. Obviously, individuals who expressed greater schadenfreude toward Obama planned to vote for Trump in 2016, and those with lower schadenfreude supported Hillary Clinton. Nothing more needs to be said about schadenfreude and voting, as those individuals who express greater schaden-

TABLE 7.3. **OLS Regression Coefficients for Racial Resentment Predicting Various Schadenfreude, 2016 CCES**

Dependent Variables	b	s.e.	R^2	Prob > F	N
Joy in Negative Characterization of President Obama					
Obama identified as worst	.89**	.07	.54	.000	497
Obama's foreign policy failures	.52**	.09	.20	.000	497
Republican opposition to President Obama	.72**	.07	.46	.000	496
Economic failures under Obama's leadership	.53**	.09	.19	.000	455
Failures of Obama's healthcare legislation	.65**	.09	.28	.000	495

Note. These are regression coefficients for racial resentment predicting schadenfreude controlling for partisanship, education, gender, income, and age. **$p \leq .01$; *$p \leq .05$.

freude toward Obama (who is a Democrat) supported the Republican candidate.

These indicators are strong when treated sequentially, but we do not expect them to remain so when analyzed simultaneously in the same equation predicting levels of schadenfreude. Racial resentment and partisanship, due to inherent disagreement, are expected to dominate and overshadow all other explanations.

With this stated objective, we analyzed each item of schadenfreude in an OLS regression model including racial resentment, partisanship, education, income, age, and gender. Only the coefficients for Whites' resentment toward African Americans are reported in table 7.3 for ease of interpretation. However, what is not shown in the tables is the consistently significant coefficients for partisanship across all eight equations. No other predictors have nearly the level of influence on various measures of schadenfreude as Whites' resentment toward African Americans and partisanship. The remaining controls are insignificant, and thus not reported.

Nevertheless, the substantive interpretation of Whites' resentment toward African Americans remains the same in the multivariate model as it did in the bivariate analyses. Individuals who are high in racial resentment are more likely to be upset at Obama's perceived accomplishments (i.e., they express resentment) and pleased with his perceived failures (i.e., they express schadenfreude). Again, the strongest effects appear for the items referencing Obama's legacy, and the fact that it requires consistency between his inputs and outcomes suggests it is perfect for an assessment of justice concerns and deservingness appraisals. Clearly, most in the public, especially those with higher levels of Whites' racial resentment, did not believe Obama deserved such an accolade.

To recap briefly: our theory is that people experience schadenfreude when they perceive an undeserving person benefiting or being rewarded with positive outcomes. Such a state conflicts—it is inconsistent—with their view of a just world in which people get what they deserve and deserve what they get. Obama's status creates schadenfreude among Whites because he is perceived to be undeserving of accolades in his status as president because, as an African American and a Democrat, he is perceived to want to favor African Americans over Whites and to be getting special consideration (e.g., unearned awards, notoriety, and praise).

Next, we consider how partisanship interacts with Whites' resentment toward African Americans to affect levels of schadenfreude. Because partisan polarization has been partly driven by racial attitudes, there is always an open question regarding whether our findings can be explained by partisanship. To what extent is the effect of Whites' resentment toward African Americans solely due to Republicans, who have the highest levels of schadenfreude as well as the highest perceived threat from Obama?

The analysis of the relationship between Whites' resentment toward African Americans and schadenfreude can now be divided by partisanship. Doing so shows that Democrats and Republicans express their schadenfreude toward Obama differently. Take the Democrats, for example. According to table 7.4, Whites' resentment toward African Americans shows significant effects across the four negative valence questions; they are each strong in magnitude and in the expected direction, which means that Democrats who are high in racial resentment are

TABLE 7.4. **OLS Regression Coefficients for Racial Resentment Predicting Various Schadenfreude, 2016 CCES**

Dependent Variables	Democrats			Republicans		
	b	s.e.	Prob > F	b	s.e.	Prob > F
Joy in Negative Characterization of President Obama						
Obama identified as worst	.80**	.09	.000	1.22**	.15	.005
Obama's foreign policy failures	.55**	.09	.000	.72**	.15	.000
Economic failures under Obama's leadership	.50**	.09	.000	1.03**	.28	.000
Republican Party opposition to Obama	.64**	.15	.000	.72**	.15	.000
Failures of Obama's healthcare legislation	.60**	.10	.000	.92**	.16	.000

Note. These are regression coefficients for racial resentment predicting schadenfreude controlling for partisanship, education, gender, income, and age. **p≤.01; *p≤.05.

more likely to express schadenfreude toward Obama than Democrats who are low in racial resentment. Thus, highly resentful Democrats react like Republicans, but because the intercept in the equation is considerably smaller, they respond with less intensity. Whites' resentment toward African Americans among Republicans, on the other hand, is related only to schadenfreude toward Obama. This is a strong racial resentment effect, which means that there is a great distinction between Republicans with low or high levels of racial resentment. Also, as indicated by the larger intercept, they are at higher levels of schadenfreude. Thus, just like Democrats, Republicans have higher levels of retribution attitudes, in this case, schadenfreude.

Whites' Resentment toward African Americans versus Schadenfreude

Whites' resentment toward African Americans and racial schadenfreude are closely related but clearly reflect different motivational concepts that may come at different stages in the behavioral process. Once people perceive Obama as undeserving of positive outcomes, resentment is likely to occur. Then the arousal of schadenfreude can depend on a host of factors that stem from a need for retribution. If people's justice motives become activated due to Whites' resentment and the need to believe in a just world, as our theory dictates, then we should see forms of retribution attitudes across a host of opportunities related to Obama. For example, a desire to see Obama fail in the 2012 presidential election should be correlated with higher schadenfreude. We already know that Whites' resentment toward African Americans affects support for Obama (chapter 4), so the next question is, to what extent can both racial resentment and schadenfreude stand alone as important predictors of political attitudes, such as candidate support for president in 2016?

We already outlined our expectations about racial resentment, but schadenfreude may be an important component by itself in campaign appeals and in messages expressing the desire to punish African Americans and other minorities for their perceived disregard for dominant group values, disobedience toward dominant authors, and constant challenges to the status quo. Because of their need for retribution and justice, Whites may indeed gravitate toward candidates who espouse tough and harsh positions that preserve the status quo, particularly on issues such as law and order, immigration, and welfare. Of course, the implied message is that African Americans and other minorities would be treated more harshly to keep them in their place.

In the 2016 election, the contrast between the punitive appeals of Donald Trump and Senator Clinton on law and order, immigration, and welfare could not have been greater. Donald Trump conveyed a tough and boorish persona and his appeals were hard-hitting, advocating tougher prison sentences, invasive policing practices such as stop-and-frisk, and support for the death penalty. Senator Clinton was not perceived as punitive. Criminal justice reform, improving community-police relations, curtailing the use of force by the police, stricter gun control laws, and racial bias in policing were recurring themes in her political platform. Immigration was another issue where the candidates diverged. The racial implications were somewhat clear that African Americans and minorities would not be coddled but instead would be dealt with harshly. Donald Trump supported building a wall along the US and Mexico border to restrict illegal immigration and called for the deportation of immigrants living in the US illegally. Senator Clinton, on the other hand, supported immigration reform with a path to citizenship and called for an end to deportation raids. In campaign rallies, Trump advocated violence toward hecklers, and chants of "lock her up," in reference to Senator Clinton's deletion of emails from her private server, were common.

The takeaway here is that because of differences in tone and content of punitive appeals and personality in the 2016 election, people who possessed a sense of schadenfreude could find Donald Trump very appealing. His personality and messages were more likely to resonate with individuals who were seeking their "pound of flesh" from African Americans and other minorities. Therefore, independent of racial resentment, political behavior, such as voting in the 2016 election, could be motivated by schadenfreude. But schadenfreude is not limited to voting, as it is just as likely to shape punitive and retributive policies directed at minorities, such as attitudes toward the death penalty, immigration, and affirmative action.

Analyses of the individual items measuring schadenfreude can become unwieldy, as our primary focus is on the general notion of the concept. Thus, to facilitate the analysis of the general concept, we created an additive schadenfreude scale by combining the individual items. Since our initial schadenfreude items were randomly divided into two groups, by positive and negative valence, we reversed the polarity of the negative

TABLE 7.5. **Logit Estimates of Vote Intention for Trump over Clinton in 2016, 2016 CCES**

Independent Variables	Support for Trump Model 1	Support for Trump Model 2	Support for Trump Model 3
Racial Schadenfreude		.92** (.09)	.79** (.09)
Racial Resentment	1.47** (.17)		1.18** (.21)
Democrat	−2.69** (.32)	−2.06** (.33)	−2.30** (.37)
Republican	2.81** (.44)	2.81** (.49)	2.45** (.50)
Education	−.14 (.10)	−.37** (.11)	−.26* (.12)
Gender	.08 (.29)	.28 (.32)	.18 (.35)
Income	−.12** (.04)	−.15** (.05)	−.15** (.05)
Age	.03** (.01)	.02* (.01)	.02* (01)
Constant	−5.12** (.92)	5.19** (.79)	−.07 (1.17)
Pseudo R^2	.63	.68	.73
Prob >chi^2	.000	.000	.000
N	694	699	694

Note. Numbers in parentheses are standard errors. **p≤.01; *p≤.05.

valence questions and added them to their matching positive valence questions to create four items. With these four items combined, the second step was to create an additive scale to produce an overall measure of schadenfreude toward Obama. The third and final step was to settle on an appropriate dependent variable, for which the intended presidential vote in 2016 was chosen.[5]

A logit model reported in table 7.5 was run, which included Whites' resentment toward African Americans and standard control variables such as partisanship, education, age, gender, and income. The results are quite clear that schadenfreude is a stand-alone predictor. It is statistically significant, and the coefficient is in the expected direction. Substantively, individuals who are high in schadenfreude toward Obama expressed a preference for Trump over Clinton, controlling for Whites' resentment toward African Americans and partisanship. Still, racial resentment is our primary concern, and it continues to perform superbly, even with the existing control variables. We are indeed impressed with both indicators and what they contribute to understanding Trump's resonance with ordinary citizens.

Racial schadenfreude is a pleasant and natural emotion. Conditioned by justice and appraisals of deservingness, it is based on a normal process of social comparison in which individuals seek positive self-evaluation. Everyone has experienced schadenfreude, and one does not have to be racist or prejudiced to do so. But even though schadenfreude is part of human hard-wiring, it can be quite destructive. As a return to our larger theme, it is in this sense that it parallels other facets of racial resentment that implicate average citizens. So, again, if we are looking only for racists and White nationalists to support punitive policies or to be drawn to punitive campaign appeals, too many people are left unaccounted for. Schadenfreude, in its own right, need not be racist or driven by hate.

Conclusion

This chapter introduced our concept and measure of schadenfreude. Its purpose was to show that Whites' resentment toward African Americans is not the end state of holding racial attitudes, and it does not simply disappear or remain the driving motive once it is invoked. Rather, Whites' resentment toward African Americans stems from their need for justice or some sort of satisfaction of outcomes. Without retribution, a form of justice finally being served, racial resentment festers. Beginning with a sense of a just world in which people get what they deserve and deserve what they get, racial resentment stems from an appraisal of deservingness of African Americans and minorities based on a number of factors that include racial stereotypes and attribution errors. Almost invariably, African Americans, we argue, are viewed as undeserving of special considerations because they have not lived up to their side of the bargain. They are perceived to not operate under the same values and beliefs as Whites, as disobedient and lacking self-discipline, and, therefore, as undeserving. Yet, they are seen as benefiting from resources that are perceived to challenge the status quo that come at the expense of Whites, which creates resentment and schadenfreude.

Since President Obama represents the greatest threat to the status quo, we directed our attention to the desire to see him and his policies fail. Our argument is that the election of President Obama was perceived as unjust. He represented a perspective that Whites perceived would be antagonistic toward their interests, and he was also perceived as being put into office by minority voters. This provoked Whites' resentment toward African Americans and ultimately a desire to see him and his policies fail. Our analyses show that individuals who are high in racial resentment assumed that Obama was going to show racial favoritism, and that he was benefiting from his race in a period when racism was no longer relevant. These attitudes set a context where a large segment of Whites perceived him as a threat, especially relative to other political institutions. And this perception of threat was strongest among Republicans.

Across four different scenarios evaluating his legacy, foreign policy, the economy, and healthcare policy, we find that Whites reported more happiness with Obama's perceived failures than happiness with his perceived successes. These results were clear and incontrovertible. Additionally, we showed that Democrats and Republicans react similarly to Obama, with both showing positive correlations between Whites' resentment toward African Americans and schadenfreude. While the effects of schadenfreude are more consistent among Democrats, in the sense that there are larger differences between those high and low in schadenfreude, Republicans show greater intensity, particularly with regard to perceptions of Obama's legacy as the worst president in US history.

Finally, Whites' resentment toward African Americans and racial schadenfreude are both stand-alone political motivations. In predicting 2016 vote intentions, racial resentment and racial schadenfreude independently and significantly predict the vote for Trump.

CHAPTER EIGHT

African Americans' Resentment toward Whites

A lmost every analytical framework in the political behavior literature seems to impose a dominant cultural frame of reference and point of view onto African Americans. This assumed equivalence of theory and measurement often carries over to African Americans' attitudes and behavior, leaving them to be evaluated from a perspective that fails to recognize how their interactions with racial prejudice, demeaning stereotypes, discrimination, and institutional racism create divergent worldviews from the dominant group perspective (Brigham 1994).

The research on political tolerance is a prime example.[1] African Americans' willingness to tolerate the behavior of the Ku Klux Klan, a group that threatens them personally and is linked to violent activities and mass shootings, is considered virtually equivalent to groups that Whites perceive as threatening. Yet, the limits that African Americans might impose on the Klan are judged as less democratic than those imposed by Whites. Needless to say, few have considered the racial nonequivalence of political tolerance and that to be intolerant means something entirely different for African Americans (Davis 1995).

The conceptualization and measurement of classic racial resentment, as applied to African Americans, raises a similar theoretical and measurement invariance concern. When questions about African Americans' resentment are raised (Kam and Burge 2018, 2019), they are not treated as a distinct group with unique experiences within American life, particularly systemic racial prejudice and discrimination. Instead, African Americans, responding to the same survey measures that define classic racial resentment for Whites, are portrayed as antipathetic and angry toward other African Americans (Orey 2004). This leads to our core arguments. First, using measures of Whites' attitudes to evaluate African American subordinates the latter group's perspective. That is, asking African Americans to answer questions about disaffection toward their own group is a task rarely asked of other groups. Second, using classic racial resentment theory and survey items to understand African Americans' political behavior ignores their dissatisfaction with the status quo, and disregards any reason they have to be upset, angry, or even resentful toward Whites. In short, we argue that the lack of a rigorous study of African Americans' racial attitudes toward Whites has limited the understanding of racial attitudes in general.

In this chapter, we advance the scholarly study of racial attitudes using survey measures developed specifically from an African American perspective to explore African Americans' resentment toward Whites. Such resentment, we contend, is based on the same adherence to values of justice and deservingness as Whites' resentment toward African Americans. The essential difference is that whereas Whites' racial resentment stems from African Americans violating certain values that challenge the status quo, African Americans' resentment toward Whites stems from a sense of injustice from the use of racism and discrimination to protect the status quo and Whites' privilege. We begin by examining previous attempts to study African Americans' racial resentment and then proceed to the construction of our own measure.

Racial Nonequivalence: One Scale Does Not Fit All

Before elaborating on our theory and measure of African Americans' resentment toward Whites, it is important to understand the extant characterization of classic racial resentment among African Americans. As a matter of course, African American survey respondents in the ANES have been asked the same classic racial resentment questions as Whites without attention to status or cultural differences that might produce different interpretations. Instead of asking functionally equivalent questions referencing or targeting Whites' entitlement and discriminatory behavior, African American respondents are asked pejorative questions that reflect poorly on their in-group. While such an approach may be perfectly reasonable to explore African Americans' opinions about the causes of racial inequality, the meaning of those items is likely to be quite different from an African American perspective. This is particularly important in the context of classic racial resentment being theorized as a form of symbolic racism and prejudice. As a result of the measurement nonequivalence and the conceptual focus of the scale, the classic racial resentment items may measure something akin to resentment toward African Americans, among Whites, but to African Americans the items can be interpreted as attributions of structural explanations to racial inequality (Kam and Burge 2018, 2019). Yet, even if the measurement is coherent (e.g., structural attribution), the theory associated with the measure—and we now know the measure preceded the theory—is not one of racial resentment in general, or African Americans' resentment toward Whites in particular. Thus, the discipline still lacks a valid framework and measure that accounts for African Americans' racial attitudes toward Whites.

A recent example of measurement invariance is reflected in Perez and Hetherington's (2014) assessment of authoritarianism. Their research suggests that measurement invariance due to racial differences is most likely to occur when authoritarianism is based on the desirable qualities people would like to see in children, usually reflected as dependence versus respect for elders, obedience versus self-reliance, curiosity versus good manners, and being considerate versus well behaved. While the child-rearing approach to measuring authoritarianism appears valid for Whites, African Americans appear to place a higher value on certain practices (e.g., respect for elders, obedience, and good manners) because of their lower status, and not because of their authoritarianism (Perez and Hetherington 2014).

Does asking African Americans the classic racial resentment items lead to different interpretations across race? Do such attitudes reflect racial nonequivalence or measurement invariance? Kam and Burge (2018) used a "stop and reflect" cognitive response approach to explore the meaning of the classic racial resentment items. Operationally, after each classic racial resentment item, they asked both White and African American respondents this follow-up, "Thinking about the question you just answered, exactly what things went through your mind?" The intent was to allow respondents to elaborate on the cues and information they relied upon to answer the racial resentment questions. Thus, with the aid of "blind" coders, Kam and Burge (2018) were interested in whether verbatim responses referenced negative traits of Blacks, the principle of individualism, or recognition (or denial) of discrimination. Based on the verbatim follow-up responses, they suggest that classic racial resentment may not be the appropriate label for Whites. For African Americans, Kam and Burge (2018) suggest that the classic racial resentment items indicate structural versus individual attributions for African Americans, as opposed to indicating affect. Clearly, asking African American respondents the classic racial resentment items does not reflect resentment toward their in-group, and still ignores racial resentment toward an out-group.

In further research, Kam and Burge (2019) show that considerable variation exists among both African Americans and Whites on the classic racial resentment scale, and that on average African Americans score lower than Whites on attributing racial inequality to Blacks' personal failings. Among both groups, those who score higher on the scale (indicating personal failings of Blacks as a cause for inequality) are more likely to oppose ameliorative racial policies than those who score lower on the classic racial resentment scale (indicating structural explanations for inequality). Because it is reasonable for individuals, regardless of their race, to reject ameliorative racial policies, they believe that Blacks are responsible for their own situation and lower status.

Previous Attempts to Measure African Americans' Attitudes toward Whites

While some attention has been devoted to African Americans' attitudes toward Whites, such as antipathy and prejudice (Bringham 1994; Chang and Ritter 1976; Livingston 2002; Steckler 1957), research concentrating on their reactions to racial discrimination is more aligned with our interests. With varying degrees of validity, this literature helps us to understand African Americans' resentment toward Whites. Research by Wojniusz (1979), utilizing a small convenience sample of Blacks in Chicago, is perhaps the first that contains aspects of our conceptualization of African Americans' racial resentment toward Whites. Conceiving racial resentment as an outgrowth of Blacks' subordinate position in a society that extolled freedom, equality, merit, and justice for all, Wojniusz (1979) attempted to operationalize and measure a core motivation underlying African Americans' resentment toward Whites. Accordingly, Blacks' racial hostilities resulted from the nature of power differences among racial groups and from feelings of competition over scarce resources. Some groups are unfairly advantaged over others, challenging notions of justice and fairness in the distribution of rewards and resources in society. Pinpointing the injustice, Wojniusz (1979) contended that "such mechanisms as slavery, Jim Crow laws, and institutional racism have been used by whites to maintain a position of relative superiority in access to and control of scarce goods" (p. 42). Following this line of reasoning, Wojniusz (1979) developed an 8-item measure of African Americans' resentment: 1-"whether Whites owe Blacks a national guaranteed minimum income to make up for slavery and years of discrimination," 2-"whether Black people generally are now getting more, less, or what they are entitled to," 3-"whether Whites are only paying 'lip service' to the credo of equality," 4-"whether a lot of White people talk in favor of equal rights, but do not really believe in them," 5-"whether Whites try to blame a Black worker if things go wrong," 6-"whether Whites try to give all the dirty work to Blacks," 7-"whether Whites socialize with Blacks and make Blacks feel welcome," and 8-"whether Whites do almost anything to keep their children from going to schools with Blacks." All of these items have the potential to elicit negative reactions among African Americans, but it is not clear whether they specifically trigger resentment versus hostility, anger, or frustration over specific issues (e.g., school integration, minimum income, or the types of jobs Blacks hold). Still, this helps our thinking about resentment because it reminds us that racial resentment is not an automatic outgrowth of negative interactions with Whites, as such interactions can produce a range of negative emotions. As we contend early and often in this book, appraisal of deservingness is critical for triggering racial resentment. Nevertheless, we are encouraged by Wojniusz's (1979) recognition that a core component of African Americans' racial resentment toward Whites is a response to attempts by Whites to maintain their position of superiority.

With this literature in mind, we developed a measure of African Americans' racial resentment toward Whites anchored in beliefs about Whites' deservingness for their privileged position and status.

African Americans' Resentment toward Whites

Resentment, regardless of race, emanates from a justice motive and a sense of fairness, resulting from an appraisal of deservingness. Linking racial resentment to aspects of justice and fairness, rather than simply racial prejudice and hatred, allows this analytical framework to be assessed from different perspectives, such as from an African American perspective. This is sensible to us because African Americans—as one of the most aggrieved groups in American society and one that has been struggling against injustice—have to feel some resentment toward Whites, and that feeling should be recognized and respected in political science research. As we have argued elsewhere, Whites' racial resentment is driven by a belief that the status quo and the institutions that work to advantage Whites over other groups need defending. African Americans' resentment toward Whites will retain these same elements of justice and deservingness, but because of vastly different experiences, African Americans' resentment manifests very differently than that of Whites.

Because of their historical experiences with racial injustice and mistreatment, African Americans can be expected to have a more acute sense of justice and fairness. Such an integral component in their everyday perceptions stems from their socialization into a culture that emphasizes their struggle for equal rights, racial disparities in the dispensation of justice, and the ineffectiveness of the system of justice. A sense of justice and fairness is ingrained in an African American political belief system, which makes it a more highly accessible sentiment for them than Whites.

Writing about racial differences in perception of the criminal justice system, Peffley and Hurwitz (2010) contend that not only is justice a powerful motivator, suggesting that it is "almost a basic human need," but also it is impossible to think about race without considering differences in justice. Reflecting different experiences with injustice, African Americans are more likely than Whites to view the administration of justice as unfair and working to the advantage of Whites.

African Americans' expectation for a sense of orderliness and fairness is more intense. They have the same just-world expectations as Whites, stating that a person should get what they deserve and deserve what they get—they definitely are more sensitive to the injustice of racial discrimination (not getting what one deserves). The problem of course is that many believe that African Americans are not given a fair chance to succeed because they tend to live in hyper-segregated areas, areas with less well-funded public education, and areas with less adequate housing structures and lower quality-of-life facilitators (e.g., clean air and water, safe and non-congested roads, and grocery stores with fresh items). African Americans are disproportionately born into poverty and contexts in which they must struggle to thrive.

Just as Whites' resentment toward African Americans should not be attributed to disdain for them, African Americans' resentment toward Whites is more complex than simply hating Whites because of their higher status, privilege, and power. African Americans perceive injustice in how they are negatively treated and in how Whites deny the relevance of race to their mistreatment, which Blacks perceive as depriving them of equal rights and access. Whites are seen by African Americans as not taking complete responsibility for the promise of democracy and freedom, choosing instead to make excuses for the conditions they face. In effect, Whites blame African Americans for their own problems. African Americans, on the other hand, view Whites as undeserving of their privilege and status because it comes at the expense of others, in the form of racial discrimination and the maintenance of inequality. These actions and others undertaken by Whites to create, apply, and follow rules, and to adhere to seemingly cherished values in a selective (i.e., discriminatory) fashion, are what ultimately lead to African Americans resenting Whites.

Taken together, we define African Americans' racial resentment toward Whites as anger stemming from a sense of injustice that Whites use racial discrimination and other tactics to defend an "unjust" status quo and privilege, which comes at their expense and keeps them at most oppressed, and at least unequal. Racial discrimination is unjust and functional in the sense that it preserves an unjust status quo. The presence of racial discrimination, whether in hostile overt forms or unintentional disparities, means that no matter how hard African Americans work, playing by the rules established by Whites, they will never truly succeed or rise above their current position in the social hierarchy *as a whole.* That is, African Americans understand individualism very well, but they also know that, in the past, the Protestant work ethic did not lead to any additional freedom or prosperity because the challenges faced by the group had nothing to do with desire or will—they were systemic and structural. Once an individual did all that was required, they were still forced to live in the same poor communities, take lesser pay, receive lesser care, and be denied a host of prerogatives simply because of the color of their skin.

African Americans view Whites with a level of hypocrisy. Although an overwhelming majority of African Americans attempt to follow the rules of the game—working hard, going to school, finding good jobs, appreciating family values, and believing in the rights and freedoms promised by the US Constitution—they also find Whites' expectations of them naive and impractical. After centuries of racial subjugation, lack of protections from the law, the presence of norms and traditions that excluded them, and general hatred from Whites, they are expected to no longer complain simply because they live in the greatest country in the world [*sic*]. The perceived hypocrisy grows when African Americans hear Whites, for example, criticizing the federal government in vitriolic ways, wanting to deny basic freedoms of speech and expression, and claiming that guns are inherent rights to die for but due process is something that must be earned. For African Americans, not only is the status quo, which benefits Whites, stacked against them, but it is designed to keep them in their place *as a whole*. No matter how successful a single person becomes, they will still be subject to experiential (i.e., discrimination) or psychological (i.e., bias) maltreatment from Whites because they are a part *of the whole* as opposed to an individual. Such theorizing explains the exaggerated prominence of linked fate in the literature on Black political behavior (e.g., Dawson 1994). Certainly, African Americans understand society is organized racially, in a way that homogenizes Black people. This means African Americans have an awareness of racial connectedness. Yet, we argue that these perceived linkages are less vital to their politics than the surveillance of racial injustice.

What Is There to Be Resentful About?

One may ask, even if naively, what is the basis for African Americans' resentment toward Whites? Evident in just about every aspect of American political and social life, African Americans and other minorities are disadvantaged by the current racial hierarchy (inclusive of the socioeconomic) and blamed by Whites for this disadvantage. This circumstance is the source of their resentment toward Whites, who are perceived to unfairly benefit from and defend this status quo, legitimizing and reinforcing existing racial disparities by not taking full responsibility, and realizing that the penalty for long-standing racism (the injustice) must include retribution. This is where African Americans' perceptions of injustice and fairness diverge from Whites' perceptions of injustice.

Poverty and relative deprivation are important issues fostering African Americans' resentment. African Americans are twice as likely as Whites to reside in poverty; African Americans usually have double the White unemployment rate; and African Americans earn about one-third the income as Whites (Pew Research Center 2016). The wealth gap persists in such a way that Whites' wealth is 13 times that of African American households (Pew Research Center 2016). Underlying these racial disparities lies a "multidimensionality of poverty," as poverty produces further disadvantages in lack of access to health care and higher incidences of malnutrition, inadequate housing and clean water, and lower levels of education and failing schools. Ultimately, residing in poverty, earning less, and possessing lower net worth determines access to justice, social services, cultural capital, and more wealth accumulation (Shapiro 2004). When African Americans hear Whites blame them for their own poverty, it angers them. Whites tend to view poverty as simply a consequence of low effort on the part of African Americans, to be judged in temporal situations (e.g., after the fact when seeing a news story, or on the spot when considering help for someone on the street), rather than as a broader outcome of a system that maintains inequality. If lack of effort is not the cause of poverty for African Americans, it then falls to innate qualities: "they can't help themselves; it's in their culture." This is a half-truth in that of course there are elements of African American life that are self-destructive, but to claim that these elements are the main reason for poverty angers Blacks—as racism and discrimination may have actually led to the self-destructive acts. In summary, African Americans do not value poverty or desire to be unequal, so when Whites claim otherwise, it prompts resentment. But racial disparities in socioeconomic position are not the only source of African Americans' resentment toward Whites.

Equally debilitating, racial disparities in the criminal justice system also create racial resentment among African Americans. African Americans make up about 33.1 percent of the incarcerated prison population despite being only 13 percent of the total US population, compared to Whites, who make up to 30.3 percent of the incarcerated population (US Sentencing Commission 2017). African American men are six times as likely to be incarcerated as White men. African Americans also comprise 29 percent of deaths in police custody and 27 percent of those shot by the police. African American males receive 19.1 percent longer sentences for the same crimes as those committed by White males (US Sentencing Commission 2017). Alexander (2012) interprets such dire statistics as a rebirth of Jim Crow—relegating African Americans to a permanent second-class status, denied the very rights supposedly won in the civil rights movement, and effectively branding African Americans as felons and refusing the group basic rights and opportunities that would allow them to become productive, law-abiding citizens. Because Blacks and Whites have dramatically different personal encounters with the police and the criminal courts, there exists a huge gulf between the races in their general evaluations of justice in America. Personal experiences with legal authorities—the police and courts—have a profound effect on individuals' more general evaluations of the fairness of the justice system. And due to a general tendency for negative experiences to carry more weight than positive ones, the fact that Black Americans are far more likely to report unfair or disrespectful treatment by the courts and police means that they are also more likely to generalize their negative experiences to evaluations of the wider justice system. Not only does the mistreatment of African Americans by the legal system go directly to the heart of beliefs about justice and fairness (Peffley and Hurwitz 2010), but Gibson and Nelson (2018) argue that it compels African Americans to question the legitimacy of the justice system as a whole—thus making the thought of justice a fleeting desire.

Racial disparities in education, the most certain path for upward mobility, is yet another source of racial resentment toward Whites, who benefit most from higher levels of education. Although the gap in college graduates has been declining over time, the percentage of adults (25 and over) with four years of college is 35.6 percent for White adults and 22.2 percent for Blacks (Pew Research Center 2016). Even at the same levels of education, African Americans earn significantly less than their White counterparts. Below the college level, African Americans are often located in schools with less qualified and lower-paid teachers and with fewer resources compared to Whites. Within those schools, African Americans are twice as likely to be suspended as Whites due to systemic bias, and therefore spend less time in the classroom. As a result, reports show that only 77.8 percent of African Americans graduate high school, compared to 88.6 percent of Whites (*Journal of Blacks in Higher Education* 2019).

In short, such statistics describe a different and dire status quo for African Americans, who, due to structural elements and biased treatment, find it difficult to succeed. When Whites highlight stereotypical cases of irresponsible poverty, it dismisses all of the other cases where

African Americans are playing by the rules but still suffering the consequences of a status quo that limits opportunity, access, and recognition of existing effort. These are the frustrating and irritating circumstances by which African Americans must live, while still being told to simply work harder. Ultimately, Whites' egregious defense of the status quo as just and fair relegates African Americans to a life of struggle and strife. To African Americans, this is unjust and unfair, and leads to racial resentment.

Measuring African Americans' Resentment toward Whites

Taking a similar approach as the development of Whites' resentment toward African Americans, we drafted a set of survey items we thought captured aspects of African Americans' sentiments about deservingness, resentment, White privilege, and discrimination. These items are not the typical measures of African Americans' racial attitudes inquiring about whether or not racial prejudice exist, ideology, structural versus personal causes of racial inequality, or ameliorative racial policies (e.g., Allen, Dawson, and Brown 1989; Tate 1994; Ellison and Powers 1994). They were pretested in a September 2016 study collected via Qualtrics' opt-in panel, and upon further validity assessments, a subset of the items was identified as having the best scaling properties and, subsequently, included in the 2016 CCES. Table 8.1 reports the various measures tapping aspects of African Americans' resentment toward Whites. Interestingly, the items suggest that African Americans believe that Whites are "willfully blind" when it comes to the consequences of racial prejudice and how they benefit from it: African Americans overwhelmingly believe that Whites deny the existence and consequences of racism and discrimination; Whites enjoy certain privileges that are not available to them; and that Whites discount their deservingness and effort. A consequence of willful blindness is that individuals construct a distorted world around them that makes them feel safe and blinds them to harsh realities and experiences of others.

Overwhelming majorities of African Americans believe and resent Whites' obliviousness or unawareness of racism. For instance, in the 2016 CCES study, we find that 76 percent of African Americans resent that Whites deny the existence of racial discrimination; 71 percent believe Whites view African Americans in lesser terms even when they work hard to succeed; 61 percent resent Whites who claim reverse dis-

TABLE 8.1. **African Americans' Resentment toward Whites, 2016 Pilot Study and 2016 CCES**

	Percent Agree	
Survey Items	Pilot Study	CCES
I. Responsibility Denial		
I resent when Whites deny the existence of racial discrimination.	**76%**	**76%**
I resent the fact that Whites think racism does not exist.	63	74
I resent when Whites claim reverse discrimination. (Pilot: "I get irritated")	68	61
Whites tend to ignore the effects of racism and discrimination.	**80**	**56**
I believe white people are always judging me negatively.	36	30
II. White Privilege		
Whites have benefitted more from their race than they are willing to admit.	87	87
Whites are given the benefit of the doubt more than African Americans.	**87**	**85**
Whites get away with offenses that African Americans would never get away with.	**85**	**79**
Whites have many advantages that they are not aware of.	–	79
Whites do not see how their skin color gives them certain privileges that I do not have.	76	78
Generations of White privilege have created conditions that make it difficult for Blacks to work their way out the lower class.	70	65
III. Deservingness/Effort		
Even when African Americans work hard to succeed, Whites still view them in lesser terms.	**76**	**71**
Whites do not go to great lengths to understand the problems African Americans face.	**69**	**69**
Whites think they are more deserving of privileges than African Americans.	69	61
When an African American is promoted over a White person, the White claims it's due to race.	53	58
On average, Whites do not give African Americans credit for their successes.	68	56
Without working very hard, Whites have gotten more than they deserve.	–	53
Most Whites would prefer to see African Americans fail in efforts to achieve equality.	43	41
If Whites would only try harder they could make it so African Americans are just as well off as Whites.	51	42
I resent when Whites say they have worked hard for what they have.	–	31

Note. Response categories are Strongly Agree, Agree, Neither, Disagree, and Strongly Disagree. Percentages reflect the combined Strongly Agree and Agree categories, or racial resentment toward Whites.

crimination; and 56 percent believe Whites ignore the effects of racism and discrimination. Perhaps due to the tendency to view African Americans' perceptions from the dominant cultural perspective, such perceptions of Whites among African Americans have been rarely reported in the extant literature.

Several survey items capture African Americans' perceptions of White privilege. Although Whites have been said to take their privilege for granted and are reluctant to acknowledge it, African Americans see it. African Americans believe that Whites possess certain advantages that are not extended to them, and that it goes unacknowledged. For instance, the 2016 CCES data reveal that 87 percent of African Americans believe that Whites have benefited more from their race than they are willing to admit; 85 percent believe that Whites are given the benefit of the doubt more than African Americans; 79 percent believe that Whites have many advantages that they are not aware of; 79 percent believe that Whites get away with offenses that African Americans would never get away with; 78 percent believe that Whites do not see how their skin color gives them certain privileges that African Americans do not have; and 65 percent believe that generations of White privilege have created conditions that make it difficult for Blacks to work their way out of the lower class.

A final set of survey items captured African Americans' perceptions of Whites' deservingness of their advantage and whether they have earned what they have. A core component of African Americans' racial resentment is a belief that Whites are advantaged by their phenotype and not because they have invested the requisite effort. The survey items seem to substantiate this view among African Americans; 69 percent believe that Whites do not go to great lengths to understand the problems African Americans face; 61 percent believe Whites think that they are more deserving of privileges than African Americans; and 58 percent believe Whites attribute racial advantage when African Americans are promoted over a White person.

With this large battery of survey items, we were motivated to reduce these items to a more manageable and efficient measure that captures the essence of African Americans' racial resentment toward Whites. Therefore, based on exploratory factor analysis and confirmatory factor analysis, we selected six survey items to represent African Americans' racial resentment. We first used an exploratory factor model to identify items from the three main dimensions (from table 8.1) with the strongest loadings on the first factor derived, based on the largest eigenvalue and explained variance. An examination of the item-total correlations (i.e., item-reliability) led us to identify the top two items that best characterized each of the dimensions. Confirmatory factor analyses were used to evaluate our several proposed theoretical constructs of racial resentment.

On the basis of the fit of the various theoretical models, we identified six items that form our scale of African Americans' resentment toward Whites. These items are in bold in table 8.1. The appendix provides more detail of the statistical properties of the scale and the items composing it.

Expectations

African Americans who express greater resentment toward Whites should be dissatisfied with the status quo and the social-economic hierarchy because they see it disadvantaging them and advantaging Whites. As a result, African Americans should be supportive of appeals and policies that seek to redress racial injustice (and disparities), such as ameliorative racial acts. Appeals and policies that promote equality, the equal distribution of resources, and the dismantling of racist structures and practices are likely to find overwhelming support among African Americans high in racial resentment because they restore justice, and are retribution for racism, prejudice, and discrimination. From an African American perspective, the status quo is unfair and unjust because it relegates them to a permanent subservient position, due to no fault of their own other than the color of their skin. Whites are undeserving of greater advantage and privilege because many have done nothing to warrant it. Recall that this is a violation of the just-world motive and the concept of fairness. This is not resentment motivated by hatred toward Whites or racial prejudice, but by a belief in the idea that people should get what they deserve and deserve what they get. Unless racial disparities in their treatment and in the social-economic hierarchy are effectively resolved, African Americans' sense of injustice can be expected to drive their attitudes and behavior. Curiously enough, racial resentment among African Americans leads to the same predictions and expectations as other motivations like group competition and economic self-interest.

African Americans, as the statistics in table 8.1 show, overwhelmingly agree with aspects of racial resentment. Underlying the widespread agreement on racial resentment is the potential that African Americans may not be divided on other important indicators. For instance, regardless of social status, as indicated by higher levels of education and income, African Americans may perceive identical levels of racism and discrimination, and, as a result, they may possess identical levels of racial resentment. Regardless of social status, African Americans are exposed directly or vicariously through the treatment of their in-group to racial discrimination and therefore understand that Whites' privilege and status comes at their expense. To be sure, African Americans are not a monolithic group, but racial prejudice and discrimination are more systemic than other forms of maltreatment. Such perceptions of White advantage contributing to their disadvantage cut across social class boundaries. Whereas high-status African Americans tend to work in White-majority environments, which increases their exposure to racial bias, racial slurs, and offensive comments, and micro-aggressions, low-status African Americans tend to face structural racism in segregation, housing, health care, education, and employment. Racial prejudice is experienced differently in the two groups, but both can see that White advantage and defense of the status quo keep them in a system of oppression.

From a different perspective, if racial resentment varies among African Americans, higher-status African Americans may possess greater resentment toward Whites. Higher-status African Americans are quite different from lower-status African Americans. The economic success that middle-class Blacks enjoy is likely to shorten their social and physical distances from the dominant group, creating grounds for their realignment with the latter based on class interest (Banton 1987), while increasing their distance from lower-class Blacks. Owing to different social and spatial locations, higher-status African Americans are more likely to interact with Whites and more likely to be exposed to relative advantages that are denied to lower-status African Americans, which means that higher-status African Americans are more likely to be exposed to and perceive Whites' privilege and status. Lower-status African Americans are certainly able to observe White advantage and status and experience its consequences, but they perceive from a greater distance. Higher-status African Americans experience White privilege and discrimination up close and personal. Through something as simple as higher education, higher-status African Americans, for the most part, interact with Whites, compete directly with them for limited resources, and perceive a racial double standard. In *Rage of the Privileged Class*, Cose (1993) argues that high-status African Americans—educated, competent, and prosperous, who have achieved a measure of affluence—are most resentful of racial prejudice. They are angry and resentful because, as they see it, America has broken its covenant, the pact ensuring that "if you work hard, get a good education, and play by the rules, you will be allowed to advance and achieve to the limits of your ability" (p. 1).

Such a broken pact reflects the injustice and unfairness high-status African Americans experience. Similarly, in *Living with Racism*, Feagan and Sikes (1994) explore how racial discrimination targets high-status African Americans, hindering their economic and social progress. High-status African Americans, essentially following the precepts of society, are not spared the devastating effects of racial prejudice and discrimination. They are more likely to use the White middle class as their frame of reference, and, as a result, be unhappy with their present situation when discovering that they are worse-off than their White counterparts.

Profile of African Americans' Resentment

With these two different expectations in mind, we investigate the extent to which African Americans' resentment toward Whites varies by demographic factors. The critical question for us is whether African Americans' resentment is mostly a characteristic of higher-status African Americans or whether racial resentment is pervasive among all demographics of African Americans. According to the means and analysis of variance (ANOVA) statistics reported in table 8.2, African Americans' resentment toward Whites is a prevalent sentiment among African Americans that cannot be attributed to a single characteristic.[2] No particular segment or subgroup of African Americans, including high-status (e.g., more highly educated and higher income), older age cohorts, men, homeowners, or people who attend church less often, can claim to drive racial resentment. As we have mentioned already, African Americans, regardless of socioeconomic status, perceive the racial injustice and unfairness that places them at a disadvantage similarly, which ultimately fosters resentment.

African Americans' Resentment toward Whites as an Independent Predictor

A critical part of the story of African Americans' resentment toward Whites as an analytical framework, or any analytical framework for that matter, is the extent to which it is useful for understanding other political and social attitudes. Among those, we explore a range of political attitudes, policy attitudes, and attitudes toward law enforcement—a serious and important issue facing African Americans.[3]

TABLE 8.2. **Mean African Americans' Resentment toward Whites by Demographics, 2016 CCES (ANOVA)**

	Mean African Americans' Resentment toward Whites (Range=0 to 5)
Education ($F (3, 652) = 1.04, p = .374$)	
High School	4.02
Some College	4.06
College	4.15
Post	4.15
Income ($F (3, 647) = .90, p = .442$)	
≤ $39,999	4.10
$40,000 to $79,999	4.06
$80,000 to $99,999	4.06
≥$100,000	4.24
Age ($F (4, 651) = .39, p = .817$)	
18 to 29	4.04
30 to 39	4.11
40 to 49	4.08
50 to 59	4.16
60+	4.09
Gender ($F (1, 654) = 1.60 \ p = .206$)	
Female	4.12
Male	4.04
Employment Status ($F (1, 640) = .47, p = .755$)	
Full time	4.09
Part time	4.09
Unemployed	4.11
Retired	4.04
Student	4.19
Church Attendance ($F (4, 641) = 1.64, p = .162$)	
At least once a week	4.14
Twice a month	4.04
Few times a year	3.98
Seldom	4.19
Never	4.04
Homeowner ($F (3, 654) = .01, p = .922$)	
Yes	4.09
No	4.10

Democratic Norms

African Americans' resentment toward Whites is a meaningful predictor of democratic norms. While it may be easy to expect African Americans who are high in racial resentment to attribute their disadvantage
and discrimination to the social structure and political system, which

would likely lead to the rejection of certain democratic principles and values, we believe this to be invalid. To the contrary, African Americans may indeed perceive American democracy as unfair because it locks in their low status, but they are likely to think that the special efforts among Whites to keep them locked into their low status are most egregious. African Americans who are high in racial resentment are likely to see the *deviation* from democratic norms, such as equality and impartial justice, as the real problem. Thus, for African Americans, and more so among those who express racial resentment, democratic values are highly cherished. Traditionally, African Americans have usually been supportive of democratic norms, even when it was unpopular to do so. For instance, while many American citizens were willing to concede many of their rights and liberties following the September 11 terrorist attacks, one of the greatest tragedies contemporary citizens would face, African Americans were unwilling to concede their rights and liberties (Davis 2007). The commitment to civil rights and liberties was hard fought, and they are perceived as a form of protection from capricious treatment. As a result, we expect African Americans who express greater racial resentment toward Whites to be more supportive of democratic norms than those who express lower racial resentment because the adherence to democratic norms is a form of protection from racial inequality. It is the deviation from those principles that becomes problematic.

This is what we find with the three measures of democratic norms, which include support for majority rule, support for free and fair elections, and support for the "one person, one vote" rule. Table 8.3 shows a model in which racial resentment toward Whites is positive and significant across the three measures, which indicates that higher levels of racial resentment are associated with greater support for democratic norms. Clearly, African Americans are less willing to abandon their support for democratic norms compared to African Americans who are low in racial resentment.

Perceived White Privilege among African Americans

A foundational principle of African Americans' resentment toward Whites pertains to a belief that Whites, on the whole, enjoy certain resources and advantages, whether or not they acknowledge them, over African Americans and other minorities. African Americans perceive such privileges as unjust and unfair because Whites for the most part

TABLE 8.3. **OLS Analysis of Predictors of Aspects of Democracy, African Americans—2016 CCES**

Independent Variables	Support for Majority Rule	Support for Free and Fair Elections	Support for One Person One Vote
Racial Resentment toward Whites	.12**	.07*	.19**
	(.05)	(.03)	(.04)
Liberal	−.11	.09	−.05
	(.08)	(.06)	(.06)
Conservative	−.02	−.16*	.00
	(.09)	(.07)	(.08)
Education	.04	.06*	.08*
	(.04)	(.03)	(.04)
Income	−.05	−.03	.00
	(.04)	(.03)	(.03)
Age	.01**	.01**	.00**
	(.00)	(.00)	(.00)
Gender (1= Male, 0=Female)	−.14	−.05	.00
	(.08)	(.06)	(.06)
Constant	2.41** (.27)	2.95** (.19)	2.14** (.22)
R^2	.05	.07	.09
MSE	.785	.585	.680
N	496	551	534

Note. **p>.01; *p>.05. Coefficients in parentheses are standard errors.

have done little to earn or deserve them, other than being born with a certain phenotype. Because privileges are bestowed solely on the basis of race, not because Whites are deserving as individuals, African Americans come to resent Whites because their privilege is unfair. Enjoying White privilege does not make a person racist, but such enjoyment comes at the expense of African Americans who are disadvantaged.

We included several questions that capture perceptions of everyday occurrences of White privilege. The goal in drafting such questions was to determine the extent to which African Americans' racial resentment was more than an abstract construct and could explain perceptions of specific occurrences of it. The results of African Americans' racial resentment and perceptions of White privilege are reported in table 8.4. In the same model with our standard control measures, racial resentment is a significant predictor of perceptions of White privilege. Furthermore, the positive coefficients across the various measures of White privilege indicate that higher levels of racial resentment are associated with a belief that Whites have a better chance at receiving bank loans, Whites are

TABLE 8.4. **OLS Analysis of Predictors of Aspects of White Privilege, African Americans—2016 CCES**

Independent Variables	Whites Better Chance at Loans	Whites Better Treatment by Medical Providers	Whites Given Lower Sentences for Same Crime	Whites Paid Higher than Blacks for Same Job
Racial Resentment				
toward Whites	.62**	.59**	.72**	.66**
	(.08)	(.09)	(.07)	(.08)
Liberal	.06	.03	.12	−.04
	(.13)	(.15)	(.12)	(.13)
Conservative	−.12	.11	.09	.00
	(.16)	(.19)	(.15)	(.16)
Education	.04	.04	.05	.04
	(.07)	(.08)	(.07)	(.07)
Income	−.05	−.04	−.04	−.00
	(.07)	(.07)	(.06)	(.06)
Age	.01	−.00	.00	.01
	(.00)	(.00)	(.00)	(.00)
Gender (1= Male,				
0=Female)	−.05	−.03	.02	−.17
	(.13)	(.14)	(.12)	(.13)
Constant	1.05**	1.08**	1.13**	1.09**
	(.43)	(.48)	(.39)	(.42)
R^2	.18	.13	.26	.21
MSE	1.01	1.13	.91	.98
N	297	296	296	296

Note. **p>.01; *p>.05. Coefficients in parentheses are standard errors.

treated better by medical providers, Whites are given lower sentences for the same crime, and Whites are paid higher than Blacks for doing the same job. These measures are just a few of the measures we developed to measure beliefs in White privilege. Additional survey items in our data show the same consistency. African Americans who are most racially resentful do not become democratic antagonists, but rather we believe that they become more democratic supporters because they can see how deviations from those norms, through racism and discrimination, place them at a disadvantage. African Americans are supportive of democratic norms even when it is not popular to do so.

Presidential Approval

From a political perspective, African Americans who are high in racial resentment—who ostensibly believe racial inequality is driven by

Whites' defense of the racial status quo—should support candidates and policies that are perceived to redress racial inequality and disparities. Needless to say, Barack Obama and Donald Trump, the two most prominent representatives of the two political parties, offered contrasting appeals and political messaging that should trigger African Americans' racial resentment. Barack Obama, the first African American president, who campaigned on changing the political system (e.g., *Change We Can Believe In*), conveyed to African Americans that he would be more responsive toward them than previous presidents and more supportive of policies beneficial to African Americans. By contrast, in response to the perceived threat to the status quo, Donald Trump promised to return the country to a time when it was great—ostensibly to an era in which Whites had more power and privilege. African Americans high in resentment toward Whites should have gravitated toward Obama more than those low in racial resentment, and should also eschew Trump more than those low in racial resentment. This is exactly what happened according to the analysis reported in table 8.5. As represented by the positive coefficients, African Americans who expressed higher levels of racial resentment are more approving of President Obama than those who expressed lower levels of racial resentment. African Americans, particularly those with higher levels of racial resentment, expected him to challenge the social and racial hierarchy. On a certain level, being elected as the first African American president conveyed a symbolic challenge to the existing status quo, although there is not much evidence that President Obama's tenure

TABLE 8.5. **OLS Analysis of Predictors of President Obama Approval, African Americans—2016 CCES**

Independent Variables	b	s.e.
Racial Resentment toward Whites	.10**	.03
Liberal	.19**	.07
Conservative	−.23**	.07
Education	−.04	.04
Income	−.03	.03
Age	.01	.00
Gender (1= Male, 0=Female)	−.19**	.06
Constant	2.93**	.21
R^2	.22	
Prob > x^2	.000	
N	472	

Note. **p>.01; *p>.05.

in office had an appreciable influence on redressing racial inequality and racial prejudice. We argue that the election of President Obama is one of the factors that created a level of White anxiety.

An analysis of President Trump is not included in this section. African Americans are not a homogenous group, but many of their political preferences do not vary as much as Whites' political preferences. In our data, 95.8 percent of African Americans expressed a preference for Hillary Clinton and 4.2 percent expressed a preference for Donald Trump (out of an N of 289 or 12 African American respondents). As a result of the constrained variability in the preference for Donald Trump, existing methods are unable to capture any effects.

Policy Preferences

If African Americans' resentment toward Whites is grounded in a belief that Whites use racial discrimination to disadvantage them and other minorities, the effects should be seen in African Americans' policy attitudes, especially toward policies perceived to disproportionally benefit African Americans. It is through the policy process that the government allocates resources to improve education and alleviate societal problems, such as poverty.[4] Such a process is contested, of course, because groups are affected differently by those issues. In the OLS results predicting the support for various policies in table 8.6, African Americans who are high in racial resentment respond as expected to whether the state should spend more on welfare and health care. African Americans who are high in racial resentment are more supportive of welfare spending and health care spending than those who are low in racial resentment. Here, too, we find limits to racial resentment in the sense that the effects do not extend to spending on education and law enforcement. But attitudes toward law enforcement deserve more attention.

Immigration Issues

What is the role of African Americans' resentment toward Whites in the assessment of immigration policy? Do African Americans who are racially resentful support immigration or are they antagonistic toward immigrants? African Americans who are high in racial resentment might be expected to be less sympathetic toward immigrants and immigration issues because of their heightened sensitivity to their relative dis-

TABLE 8.6. **OLS Analysis of Predictors of Policy Issues, African Americans—2016 CCES**

Variables	State Increase Welfare Spending	State Increase Health Care Spending	State Increase Education Spending	State Increase Law Enforcement Spending
Racial				
Resentment	.17*	.14*	.23**	−.12
toward Whites	(.08)	(.07)	(.07)	(.08)
Liberal	.09	−.07	−.09	−.22
	(.13)	(.12)	(.12)	(.13)
Conservative	−.14	−.36**	−.47**	−.15
	(.16)	(.15)	(.15)	(.16)
Education	−.01	.00	.06	−.02
	(.07)	(.07)	(.07)	(.07)
Income	−.17**	−.07	−.00	−.03
	(.07)	(.06)	(.06)	(.06)
Age	.01	.01**	.01*	.01**
	(.00)	(.00)	(.00)	(.00)
Gender (1= Male,	−.32**	−.08	−.21	−.19
0=Female)	(.12)	(.12)	(.11)	(.13)
Constant	2.63**	3.19**	2.96**	3.82**
	(.43)	(.39)	(.38)	(.42)
R^2	.07	.06	.09	.05
MSE	1.01	.932	.910	.998
N	299	297	299	299

Note. **$p>.01$; *$p>.05$. Coefficients in parentheses are standard errors.

advantage to Whites. Put another way, broadening the groups to immigrants who claim greater access to scarce resources and benefits, who may not be deserving, may be perceived as another challenge to the status quo for African Americans, especially those who are already resentful of Whites' advantages (Tedin and Murray 1994). Thus, African Americans who express greater racial resentment may respond to immigrants and open immigration policies in similar fashion as Whites, who are concerned with justice and fairness. Racial resentment may simply heighten the hostility toward immigrants and impact their policy preferences (O'Neil and Tienda 2010; Taylor and Schroeder 2010).

From a different perspective, African Americans who express greater racial resentment might be more sensitive to the view that the advancement of their race is linked to the acceptance of universal principles of justice and fairness; the adherence to these principles makes it difficult to refuse others the opportunities to escape poverty or oppression. From this perspective, whether or not immigrants are deserving and whether this threatens African Americans' attempt to level the field with Whites is irrelevant; what matters most is adhering to American principles of justice and fairness, which bolsters African Americans' own claims.

We developed two aspects of immigration: support for granting legal status to immigrants who have held jobs in this country, and support for granting legal status to people brought to the US illegally. The latter question captures an aspect of the Deferred Action for Childhood Arrivals (DACA) controversy regarding whether undocumented youths who were brought to the US illegally and raised as US citizens should be deported or provided a path to achieve citizenship. A 2012 executive order created by former President Barack Obama shields these so-called Dreamers from deportation and provides work and study permits. The Trump administration ordered the Department of Homeland Security (DHS) to stop accepting new applications in 2017, but his second order to end renewals for DACA recipients was rejected by the Supreme Court in 2020.

According to table 8.7, African Americans' resentment toward Whites works in such a way that those who express higher levels of it are more supportive of granting legal status to immigrants. As opposed to

TABLE 8.7. **Logit Analysis of Predictors of Aspects of Immigration, African Americans—2016 CCES**

Independent Variables	Grant Legal Status to Immigrants Who Have Held Jobs	Grant Legal Status to People Brought to the US Illegally
Racial Resentment toward	.34**	.36**
Whites	(.12)	(.12)
Liberal	.27	.11
	(.22)	(.20)
Conservative	−.64**	−.65**
	(.23)	(.23)
Education	.22*	.33**
	(.11)	(.11)
Income	−.24*	−.12
	(.11)	(.10)
Age	.01	.01
	(.01)	(.01)
Gender (1= Male, 0=Female)	−.12	−.21
	(.20)	(.19)
Constant	−.94	1.68**
	(.63)	(.62)
R^2	.05	.05
Prob > X^2	.000	.000
N	588	588

Note. **p>.01; *p>.05. Coefficients in parentheses are standard errors.

viewing immigration as a threat or challenge to scarce resources, these findings suggest that African Americans who are high in racial resentment seem to be operating off of justice and fairness motives in permitting immigrants legal status.

Attitudes toward the Police

As we have stated earlier, racial disparities in the treatment of African Americans by law enforcement are more obvious and desperate, and, as a result, create a great deal of racial resentment. According to The Counted website, 266 African Americans and 188 Hispanics were killed by the police in 2016—the time during which this survey data were being collected. While 574 Whites were also killed by the police, this simply highlights the over-representation of African American deaths, given that African Americans comprise just 13 percent of the US population. We contend that such events stoke African Americans' resentment toward Whites because the killings of African Americans serve as examples of the societal injustice that preserves and defends Whites' status and privilege. Of course, this is not the only example affirming African Americans' racial resentment, but interactions with the police are a daily risk.

African Americans high in racial resentment should be less tolerant or supportive of the police than those low in racial resentment because police killings are an example of the extent to which Whites defend unjust behavior by the police. Surveying African Americans, we examined this expectation on different aspects of law enforcement and criminal justice, such as whether the police make them feel safe, grading the police, and their opinions on eliminating mandatory sentencing and increasing prison sentences for people previously convicted.[5]

According to the results in table 8.8, African Americans who are high in resentment toward Whites are less likely to believe that police make them safe and tend to give the police a lower grade than those who are low in racial resentment. These are clear and strong indicators that African Americans high in racial resentment are distrustful of the police. Equally important, African Americans high in racial resentment are more supportive of eliminating mandatory sentencing and reducing prison sentences. These results suggest that African Americans are leery of the police and the criminal justice system because they reflect an unjust system operating to protect and defend White privilege and status.

TABLE 8.8. **OLS Analysis of Attitudes toward the Police and Criminal Justice, African Americans—2016 CCES**

Variables	Police Make You Feel Safe	Grading the Police	Support Mandatory Sentencing
Racial Resentment toward Whites	−.27**	−.24**	−.14**
	(.05)	(.07)	(.02)
Liberal	−.10	.04	−.02
	(.08)	(.11)	(.04)
Conservative	−.02	.26	.12**
	(.09)	(.14)	(.05)
Education	.11**	.06	−.03
	(.04)	(.06)	(.02)
Income	.01	.11	.01
	(.04)	(.06)	(.02)
Age	.01**	.00	−.00
	(.00)	(.00)	(.00)
Gender (1= Male, 0=Female)	.08	.10	.01
	(.08)	(.10)	(.04)
Constant	3.11** (.24)	3.46** (.36)	.12 (.12)
R^2	.11	.08	.09
MSE	.834	.864	.419
N	584	299	588

Note. **$p > .01$; *$p > .05$. Coefficients in parentheses are standard errors.

African Americans' Resentment toward Whites and Linked Fate as Analytical Frameworks

The concept of linked fate was first proposed in 1994 (Dawson 1994), and it has become the dominant analytical framework for understanding African American political and social behavior. Often mistaken as an indicator of racial identity or racial consciousness, linked fate is a single-item indicator intended to capture a "black utility heuristic." Dawson (1994) argues that African Americans "use the status of the group, both relative and absolute, as a proxy for individual utility." In more practical terms, African Americans prioritize the well-being of the group over their individual interests and consider what is best for their group. In this way, political appeals, parties, and candidates that are perceived as protective of the rights of African Americans, such as through expansion of civil rights, support for ameliorative racial policies, and equal access to economic opportunity, become most attractive.

Linked fate is intended to reflect a sense of group attachment, and it is widely accepted as the dominant lens through which African Americans relate to politics. Linked fate is used to explain political behavior (Chong and Rogers 2005; McConnaughy et al. 2010; Philpot, Shaw, and McGowen 2009) and policy attitudes (Gibson and Nelson 2018), and it is now being applied to Latinos and Asian Americans (Hurwitz, Peffley, and Mondak 2015; Lien, Conway, and Wong 2003; Monforti, Lavariega, and Michelson 2014), although Sanchez and Vargas (2016) question the portability of linked fate as a measure.

Thus, another test of African Americans' racial resentment as an analytical framework is whether it carries the identical predictive power as linked fate. That is, how does African Americans' racial resentment toward Whites compare to linked fate in predicting African Americans' political behavior and attitudes? Needless to say, the two concepts have enormous consequences for African Americans' political behavior. If linked fate outperforms African Americans' racial resentment, then an in-group frame of reference remains at the center of their behavior. However, if African Americans' racial resentment outperforms linked fate, then we need to broaden our understanding of how African Americans' response to Whites' defense of the status quo and privilege, stemming from a sense of justice and fairness, contributes to their behavior.

To this end, we included linked fate in our 2016 pilot data of 500 African Americans reported in table 8.9. Our first order of business was to determine whether linked fate and African Americans' racial resentment toward Whites were tapping into similar constructs. The two measures are positively correlated (r=.27), indicating that African Americans who have a higher sense of linked fate are more racially resentful toward Whites. But they are clearly not tapping into the same construct given the moderate size of the correlation.

In separate models using a range of political indicators as dependent variables—such as the 2016 vote, whether Blacks have influence in running the country, whether Blacks should shop in Black-owned stores, and White feeling thermometer—African Americans' racial resentment and linked fate are included as independent variables. Most interesting about these analyses reported in table 8.9 is that African Americans' racial resentment is significantly related to all the measures, the coefficients are in the expected direction, and linked fate is virtually powerless. There are a few measures in our data where linked fate is significant and in the anticipated direction, but racial resentment is more pervasive. Because they offer different explanations of African Americans' orientation to

TABLE 8.9. **African Americans' Resentment toward Whites and Linked Fate Predicting Political Indicators, Standardized Coefficients, 2016 Pilot Study**

Independent Variables	Dependent Variables			
	Vote in 2016 (Clinton)[a]	Black influence in running country	Blacks shop in Black-owned stores	White Feeling Therm.
Linked fate	−.26 (.51)	.07 (.08)	.06 (.11)	−.06 (.17)
Racial				
Resentment	.75** (.01)	−.15** (.00)	.20** (.000)	−.20** (.00)
Democrat	2.17** (.00)	.15** (.00)	−.04 (.370)	−.01 (.80)
Republican	−2.71** (.00)	.07 (.11)	−.07 (.095	.02 (.69)
Liberal	1.32 (1.05)	.01 (.11)	.08 (.13)	.08 (.25)
Conservative	1.47* (.66)	−.34 (.18)	−.19 (.14)	.31 (.27)
Age	.13 (.49)	−.05 (.24)	.08 (.03)	.09* (.02)
Constant	−.15 (.90)			
R^2/Pseudo R^2	.47	.04	.06	.06
Prob > X^2	.000			
Prob > F		.000	.000	.000
N	499	613	613	613

Note. **p >. 01; *p >.05. Values in parentheses are p values.
[a]logit coefficients due to binary dependent variable.

politics, it is important to consider all relevant explanations of African American political behavior.

Conclusion

A clear outcome of this chapter is that African Americans should not be presented the same classic racial resentment survey items that Whites would answer (and perhaps vice versa); and, generally, survey items should be anchored to appropriately fit the reality of respondents and theoretical foundations, which improves measurement and data quality. When items designed on one race are automatically applied to another race under the assumption of equal meaning, it creates measurement invariance. Instead of viewing racial resentment only through the eyes of the dominant culture, African Americans express a different form, in substance, of racial resentment toward Whites, even though it stems from a similar sense of justice and appraisal of deservingness as that used by Whites. African Americans' resentment toward Whites is in need of serious scholarly attention, but it requires new measures crafted from their perspective. We found it remarkable that the literature had not yet addressed this basic equity recommendation with action at the time of our writing.

We contend that African Americans possess a similar just-world motive that leads to an appraisal of deservingness, except that racial prejudice and discrimination produce a different view of the status quo. Whereas Whites' sense of threat comes from challenges to the status quo by undeserving minorities, African Americans' sense of threat comes from Whites' defense of the status quo as it legitimizes African Americans' subservient position and mistreatment. Thus, the core of African Americans' racial resentment toward Whites is a belief that racial prejudice and discrimination are unjust and place them at a disadvantage. Moreover, when Whites claim African Americans just need to work harder, they assume that racial discrimination does not exist, which diminishes the experiences of racial minorities. Just as Whites can believe there are structural factors that matter (e.g., the federal government, too much spending, recessions, and regulation), so can African Americans have complaints about "the system" (the status quo) that are legitimate, systemic, and structural. In essence, the same model of a just world and appraisal of deservingness that guides Whites' racial resentment also guides African Americans' racial resentment.

Our new measure of African Americans' resentment toward Whites shows incredible validity and power in understanding other political and social attitudes. African Americans who are high in racial resentment can be expected to support political appeals, candidates, and efforts to redress racial prejudice and discrimination because they strive to offset the bias and disadvantage inherent in the status quo.

CHAPTER NINE

Conclusion

Political science, for the most part, has been unable to explain the growing sentiment among Whites that they are losing out and being cut in line by African Americans and other minorities. There is a growing sense among Whites that the "American way of life" is changing in such a way that the status quo—the system of values, social structures, and institutions that protect their advantage—is threatened. They point to things like the loss of jobs and greater competition, which they blame on minorities and government instead of corporations. The removal of Confederate statues, the renaming of Columbus Day to "Indigenous Peoples' Day," and the designation of a Black History Month all signify a political correctness that minimizes White cultural heritage. Growing concerns over multiculturalism, immigration and the anticipated majority-minority population shift, and promises for diversity and inclusion threaten the status quo that idealizes White culture. A sizeable percentage of Whites report experiencing reverse discrimination. Above all else, the election of President Obama and the ascension of African Americans and Latinos to positions of power and authority directly challenge Whites' political and social dominance. The tools available to political scientists assert that such growing sentiment among Whites is being driven by racial prejudice. This is our point of departure.

We contend that racial resentment stems from a just-world value system that, with the assistance of legitimizing racial myths, leads to an appraisal of deservingness. To the extent that African Americans are perceived as receiving undeserved benefits, which may violate a White individual's sense of justice and fairness, they are likely to be resented for it. Not only are they perceived to violate the rules of the game, but

African Americans' advancement challenges the status quo that protects Whites' advantage. Otherwise, why do Whites care if African Americans, a group with which they have little interaction and great social distance, receive special considerations?

Broadly shared values of justice and deservingness accompanied by legitimizing racial myths produce racial resentment toward African Americans. These racial myths are not necessarily informed or accurate beliefs but rather negative beliefs that help to justify Blacks' mistreatment and lower status. Given these negative racial myths, African Americans are not perceived as deserving of special treatment or considerations; hence, when African Americans progress or excel as a group (and individually), this triggers resentment among Whites. Racial prejudice and hate are not prerequisites.

We assert that legitimizing myths do not need to be racist or touch upon negative Black affect. Like Blum (2002) and Sniderman and Piazza (1993), we believe that people can discuss race and even express racial insensitivity without being racist or operating off hate. Thus, lumping everyone into the racist bucket ignores how fundamental values, their underlying socialization processes, and institutions contribute to the defense of White privilege and the perpetuation of inequality. Everyday people are implicated, not because they are racist but because they possess certain values that lock in disadvantage for African Americans. Such "banality" makes racial resentment frightening. While the overwhelming focus has been on the overt and blatant racists parading in hoods and capes, the ordinariness of racial resentment works in the same way as racial prejudice. As a comparison, lynchings were spearheaded by blatant racists, but thousands of everyday citizens were willing participants who cheered, posed for photographs, and departed with souvenirs as if they were state fairs.

This is our view of racial resentment, an interaction between values of justice and deservingness with legitimizing racial myths. Because everyday people can be racially resentful without displaying the outward signs of racism, their clinging to certain traditional values that align with racists can go undetected. They may not think of themselves as racists, and technically speaking, they are not racists in the sense that they do not hate African Americans, but nonetheless their values contribute to the perpetuation of privilege and inequality.

How Did We Get Here?

The story of racial resentment began over 30 years ago with the research on symbolic racism and the belief that racial prejudice was transforming from an overt or blatant expression to a more covert or subtle expression, in which African Americans were perceived to violate traditional norms and values like individualism. Underlying hatred had not changed, but social desirability norms altered the expression of anti-Black affect or racial prejudice into more coded language. While the belief in the changing expression of racial prejudice was not disputed and was broadly accepted, the measures proposed to capture the changing expression and anti-Black affect were disputed on the grounds that they conflated policy, ideology, and government attitudes. Almost overnight and adhering to some of the same measures, symbolic racism was renamed racial resentment to emphasize anti-Black affect and the threat that African Americans posed to traditional norms. Although the renaming received a great deal of criticism at the time, among political scientists racial resentment still became the dominant framework and measure for understanding racial prejudice. Indeed, it proved to be a very powerful predictor of attitudes and behavior.

Our departure from classic racial resentment stems from disagreement with its concept and measure, despite its predictive power. Because of its anti-Black affect conceptual roots, the use of classic racial resentment obliges one to view politics as motivated by racial prejudice, even when it is not. Within this framework, for example, only racial prejudice can explain the denigration of President Obama and the rise of President Trump. Thus, as an analytical framework, classic racial resentment is very limited. Additionally, as others have recognized, the measure upon which it is based seems to capture neither racial prejudice nor racial resentment.

Major Contributions

Robustness of the New Measure

Classic racial resentment was controversial because it measured neither racial prejudice nor resentment, despite its claims. If anything, the items that made up the racial resentment scale were considered to reflect a different way of measuring racial policy preferences, conservatism, and government amelioration. Mindful of the various controversies, we sought to avoid conflating racial resentment with other factors, and instead were motivated to capture items consistent with Lerner's (1980) just-world motive, deservingness, and a defense of the status quo. As we detail early in the book, we explored and tested many items across various data and years to capture racial resentment.

Through various confirmatory factor models, the items resulted in a robust fit with our theoretical expectations. Across various years of data, the fit indicators were extremely consistent. We eventually narrowed the number of items to five, which form the basis of all of our analyses. This process is noteworthy considering the evolution of the concept.

Performance of the Measure

With a valid measure of racial resentment, we connect racial resentment to political and social attitudes. The underlying theory is that people who are high in racial resentment are more likely to possess attitudes that reject special racial treatment and amelioration because they benefit African Americans and other minorities unjustly and unfairly. As a consequence of a legitimizing myth that African Americans are lazy, unwilling to work for what they get, and content with governmental handouts, African Americans are perceived as undeserving. Policies that seek to help them are therefore illegitimate and threaten the status quo. This proves to be the case across both racial and race-neutral beliefs. For instance, those who possess higher levels of racial resentment are more likely to reject affirmative action, more likely to believe that racial discrimination is no longer a problem, more likely to believe that African Americans are too demanding for equal rights, and less likely to believe that Whites have certain advantages because of the color of their skin. This is to be expected, but on questions that touch upon other minorities, racial resentment is also highly predictive. Those with higher levels of racial resentment toward African Americans are less supportive of immigration, specifically granting citizenship to children born in the US, and more supportive of the deportation of illegal immigrants and allowing the police to question them.

In direct comparison to other analytical frameworks, racial resentment outperforms White identity in explaining a variety of attitudes, such as the approval of President Trump, the repeal of Obamacare, background checks for firearms, and immigration. Relative to racial resentment, White identity is inconsequential. However, we cannot conclude the same for social dominance orientation. While racial resentment is significant and in the expected direction, it is not usually as powerful as social dominance orientation. Still, racial resentment cannot be dismissed as meaningless and insignificant.

Racial Resentment and Campaign Appeals

A particularly important finding, beyond the association between racial resentment and political and social attitudes, is that campaign appeals that convey a threat to the status quo and privilege have a special resonance. President Trump's *Make America Great Again* slogan is a prime example. References to the past reflect a return to a previous era in which Whites had higher advantage and status and African Americans and other minorities showed deference and knew their place.

In a list experiment we refer to as the "Knowing One's Place" experiment, people overwhelmingly interpret *Make America Great Again* as African Americans forgetting their place. The inference drawn from the slogan is that, unlike previous eras in which Whites had more power, African Americans are now too demanding and are circumventing traditional values, all of which challenges the status quo that benefits Whites. Individuals high in racial resentment are more likely to interpret the slogan as indicating African Americans forgetting their place.

Racial resentment is a sentiment that can be easily exploited by political campaigns and politicians with little backlash because it is not overtly racial. Political appeals to racial resentment become expressed as the defense of the "American way of life" and the values of justice. Racial resentment may reflect coded "dog whistles" stemming from legitimizing racial myths.

Racial Motivated Consistency

Racial resentment structures political and social attitudes. Because of a desire for cognitive consistency, individuals seek to align their political and social attitudes or maintain a consistency between their values of justice, deservingness, and the defense of the status quo. In other words, not only do those high in racial resentment have problems with African Americans who are perceived to violate just-world motives, but also such a framework is likely applied across a number of attitudes. This has been referred to as "spillover effects," in which people end up rejecting policies associated with President Obama because they hate African Americans. While this thesis is certainly plausible, we contend that it is a desire for cognitive consistency around the values of justice and the defense of the status quo that binds political and social attitudes.

Hence, individuals who are high in racial resentment are more likely to reject belief in global warming and that humans are causing it, not because they are racially prejudiced, but because both beliefs trigger aspects of a threat to the status quo and defense of the system. Thus, individuals who are sensitive to the threat of African Americans challenging the status quo are also sensitive to other threats to the status quo like climate change.

A similar process occurs among the highly racially resentful who refuse to credit President Obama for an expanding economy and among lower-status citizens who support President Trump's tax breaks. Those who are high in racial resentment are less likely to attribute responsibility for a good economy to President Obama, not because they are racist necessarily, but because their beliefs about an improving economy need to be consistent with the idea that President Obama poses a threat to the status quo. Racial resentment similarly compels those who would least benefit from President Trump's tax breaks to support them because they believe that President Trump is seeking to preserve and defend White privilege from undeserving African Americans and other minorities. They essentially align their attitudes to mesh with and to be consistent with their thoughts about the defense of the system.

This is another powerful aspect of racial resentment as it suggests that racial resentment contributes to a false sense of reality by distorting information.

Schadenfreude as Retribution

We introduced schadenfreude to assert that racial resentment is not a dead-end belief. Because racial resentment stems from beliefs about justice and fairness, individuals who are high in racial resentment will seek to restore a sense of justice or acquire some satisfaction that the perceived injustice has been rectified. Racial resentment does not simply disappear; rather, those feelings can be expected to fester to the point that individuals may find joy in an out-group's failure or desire to see members of the out-group fail. Such joy from the failure of the out-group is a consequence of the out-group receiving resources that are unearned and that are perceived to come at the expense of Whites.

We explored the relationship between racial resentment and schaden-freude with the reactions to President Obama. Specifically, we asked re-spondents whether they would be happy or sad regarding "if President Obama was identified as best [vs. worst] president in history"; "President Obama's foreign policy accomplishments [vs. failures]"; "economic suc-cesses [vs. failures] under Barack Obama's leadership as president"; and "success [vs. failure] of President Obama's healthcare legislation." As expected, individuals high in racial resentment expressed greater hap-piness with President Obama's failures and with him being considered the worst president in history. On the opposing side, when President Obama's successes are highlighted and he is considered the best presi-dent in history, respondents expressed greater sadness. Our interpreta-tion is that individuals with higher levels of racial resentment are more likely to express sadness in the face of African Americans' accomplish-ments and happiness in the face of African Americans' failure because they perceive African Americans as undeserving of success, and such success thus challenges their notion of justice and fairness.

Thus, feelings of racial resentment do not simply disappear. Rather, those feelings fester and linger as individuals seek to restore their sense of justice. Schadenfreude is a powerful motivation for individuals' politi-cal preferences.

African Americans' Racial Resentment

Racial resentment toward Whites among African Americans is a serious oversight in the literature. Those who have examined racial resentment among African Americans have applied the same items asked of Whites to African Americans, which produces a nonequivalent measure. In this approach, African Americans are asked about the prejudice of members of the in-group, which we consider objectionable. No groups other than African Americans seem to be asked questions about self-hate.

But, if composed correctly, racial resentment is a powerful analytical framework among African Americans. Resentment, regardless of race, emanates from a justice motive and a sense of fairness, resulting from an appraisal of deservingness. Linking racial resentment to aspects of justice and fairness, rather than racial prejudice and hatred exclusively, allows this analytical framework to be assessed from different perspectives, such as from an African American perspective. We define African Americans' racial resentment toward Whites as anger stemming from a sense of injustice that Whites use racial discrimination and other tactics to defend a status quo and privilege that come at African Americans' expense and keep them at most oppressed and at least unequal. Racial discrimination is unjust and functional in the sense that it preserves an unjust status quo. The presence of racial discrimination, whether in hostile overt form or unintentional disparities, means that no matter how hard African Americans work, playing by the rules established by Whites, they will never truly succeed or rise above their current position in the social hierarchy as a whole.

Parallel with racial resentment among Whites, we examined many items that might reflect racial resentment among African Americans. We settled on five items that show very strong internal validity. The resulting scale of African Americans' racial resentment measures the extent to which African Americans consider White advantage unjust.

Not only is this scale robust, but also it turns out to be a quite powerful analytical framework to understand African Americans' attitudes and behavior. For African Americans, higher levels of racial resentment translate into greater support for President Obama and lower support for President Trump. In terms of policy preferences, higher levels of racial resentment among African Americans translate into greater support for spending on welfare and health care, though lower spending on law enforcement.

We compared African Americans' racial resentment to a measure of linked fate, which has been the dominant framework for understanding African American political behavior. Linked fate is intended to reflect the importance of group attachment in guiding African American political behavior and preferences. In almost every instance in our analyses, linked fate is largely insignificant and meaningless while racial resentment is robust. It is clear that racial resentment is a more powerful analytical framework than linked fate for understanding African American political behavior and attitudes. On the basis of these results, we believe that considerable thought needs to go into the modeling of African American political behavior. The possibility that African Americans base their preferences and behavior on important values like justice and deservingness and react to Whites' defense of the status quo contributes a new level of sophistication. Values are just as important to African Americans as they are to Whites.

Racial Resentment and the 2020 Presidential Election

President Trump exploited both racist and racial-resentment sentiments during his term in office in much the same way he campaigned in 2016. In addition to appealing to racists, such sentiments attracted a larger base of people by playing on threats to Whites' interests posed by undeserving racial and ethnic minorities. The president's base did not have to be racist, but they possessed values that made racist sentiments tolerable. While much of Trump's expressions will be considered overtly racist, his sentiments used long-standing racial stereotypes that African Americans and other minorities were a threat to the "American way of life" or the status quo that benefited them.

A consideration of race or the belief that African Americans have a case for special consideration threaten historical narratives of Whites' benevolence. This came to light in President Trump's criticism of the *New York Times'* 1619 Project, a Pulitzer Prize–winning series examining different ways the legacy of slavery touches the daily lives of African Americans. For the president and many others, the 1619 Project distorted American history and indoctrinated American children into disrespecting the founding fathers. According to Trump, "The left has warped, distorted, and defiled the American story with deceptions, falsehoods, and lies. There is no better example than the *New York Times'* totally discredited 1619 Project," Mr. Trump said at the event. "This project rewrites American history to teach our children that we were founded on the principle of oppression, not freedom."

In this same vein, President Donald Trump eliminated racial sensitivity training in the federal workplace. The administration instructed federal agency leadership to begin identifying contracts for any training that contains concepts like white privilege and inherent bias so that they can begin ending such contracts. "We were paying people hundreds of thousands of dollars to teach very bad ideas and were frankly very sick ideas. They were teaching people to hate our country, and I'm not going to do that, I'm not going to allow that to happen," Trump said. Sensitivity training acknowledged the existence of racial prejudice and discrimination, and it distorted the view of Whites' compassion and goodwill.

President Trump vowed to preserve the legacies of Confederate statues, that paid homage to an era and individuals who defended racial prejudice discrimination. Support for repressive symbols became a defining moment for the president's defense of the racial hierarchy. The president referred to white nationalists who held a rally in Charlottesville in defense of Confederate monuments as "very fine people." Subsequently, President Trump signed an executive order directing federal law enforcement agencies to prosecute people who damage federal monuments and to withhold portions of federal funding to cities that don't protect statues from demonstrators.

Under President Trump's watch, several unarmed African Americans were shot and killed by the police. Some of the protests across the country turned into violent clashes with the police and the destruction of property. President Trump downplayed racial disparities in deaths by the police by maintaining a "Whites die too" posture. Calls for police reform were met with a double-down on police tactics. The president defended the killing of two protestors by a 17-year-old White teenager carrying an assault rifle at a demonstration in Kenosha, Wisconsin.

While reluctant to denounce White supremacists, the president's position on Black Lives Matter—an organization intended to bring awareness to the police brutality and the killing of unarmed black citizens—conveyed that claims of racial equality, even in the most obvious police situations, were antithetical to and challenged Whites' status, especially the police authority.

Regarding ameliorative policies, President Trump presided over a sweeping US government retreat on civil rights, voter suppression, housing discrimination, and police misconduct.

In response to President Trump, African Americans' resentment toward Whites likely increased during this time period. To African Americans, it was evident that the president was playing off racial stereotypes and challenges to the status quo to defend the existing racial hierarchy. The president reinforced his support for the status quo and racial hierarchy through numerous rallies he continued to hold after the election. African Americans will likely identify the Trumpian era in American politics as prima facie evidence that race is used to promote white privilege and black disadvantage. African Americans' resentment toward Whites is expected to increase because of President Trump and his broad base of support.

By the time of the 2020 presidential election cycle, President Trump had accumulated a record and persona that appealed to racists and Whites who were racially resentful toward African Americans. For all intents and purposes, people knew what they were getting. There was a record of racial and racist appeals and many liked it so much they were willing to accept uncouth sentiments and behavior, such as the president's demeaning behavior toward women, the denigration of science and scientists, and the politicization of mask-wear and social distancing during the pandemic.

President Trump continued to exploit racial stereotypes and the threat African Americans posed to the status quo in 2020. Most prominent in the 2020 election were Trump's direct appeals to White women in suburbs and "law and order." It was observed that many female voters had abandoned Trump and recoiled from his divisive language and disapproved of his handling of both race relations and the pandemic. But he tried to regain their support through a campaign of fear and racial stereotypes. Mostly through rally speeches and tweets, President Trump stoked fear about crime. President Trump indicated that Joe Biden would "abolish suburbs" and institute programs that would bring impoverished criminals into the suburbs, where they would destroy the "suburban lifestyle dream." According to McGowan (2017), the president's rhetoric was not about the actual suburbs, but such reference was meant to evoke an archetypal identity for a place historically rooted in the maintenance of racial segregation and white supremacy.

Playing on the threat of African Americans from George Wallace's and Barry Goldwater's playbook (Lopez 2014), "law and order" emphasized the lawlessness and unruliness of African Americans on the basis of the rioting and looting of peaceful protests in response to the killing of unarmed African Americans. The president referred to peaceful protesters as thugs and terrorists, while proceeding to activate active-duty military troops as a show of force.

Some of President Trump's racist and resentful rhetoric appeared in the first presidential debate. He decried anti-racism training in the debate, suggesting that such training "teaches people that our country is a horrible place, it's a racist place, and they were teaching people to hate our country." In perhaps the most memorable exchange in the debate, the president refused to condemn white supremacy. Instead, pressed by Mike Wallace and Joe Biden, he told the far-right group the Proud Boys to "stand back and stand by," before saying, "somebody's gotta do something about antifa and the left."

President Trump became more resolute on an already racially resentful persona in 2020. Racial prejudice and racial resentment toward African Americans should be at least as meaningful in 2020 as it was in 2016. In the end, President Trump lost a close race to Vice President Joe Biden. The hope was that Joe Biden would win by a wide margin, showing disapproval for mishandling the pandemic and a repudiation of racist, misogynistic, homophobic, and xenophobic sentiments, but the election was closer than many people expected. However, by most metrics, including the electoral votes (270) and the popular vote margin (51.3 percent), Biden's victory in 2020 was not unusually close compared to recent presidential elections. Biden's low vote margins in several states fueled speculations about different electoral outcomes.

Biden's victory does not reflect a repudiation of racial prejudice and racial resentment for African Americans and other minorities. The Trump administration is likely an indelible source of their resentment toward Whites. The closeness of the 2020 election threatened African Americans' sense of justice, as well as their faith in America, because it shows that Whites clung to racist and racially resentful sentiments, which advanced efforts in voter suppression, voter intimidation, misinformation, and threats of violence in the 2020 election. For example, 2020 Presidential Election Exit polling reported in the *New York Times* shows astonishingly high levels of support for Trump: 90 percent of White voters believed the criminal justice system treats all people fairly; 89 percent believed that racism in the US is not an important problem; 94 percent held an unfavorable view of Black Lives Matter; and 95 percent held unfavorable views of vice presidential candidate Kamala Harris (Andre et al. 2020).

Perhaps not to the extent of the election of Barack Obama in 2008, the election of Joe Biden reflects a "changing way of life" that will generate more racial prejudice and racially resentful sentiments. Racial resentment is likely to not disappear, but rather increase. The defeat of Donald Trump represents, to many of his supporters, the loss of White dominance and the rise of groups, such as African American women, with a different set of values that threatens the status quo.

As with the selection of Kamala Harris as the first African American and woman as vice president, Joe Biden can be expected to include more African Americans and women in prominent positions in his administration, which reflects a changing way of life in America that many Trump supporters fear most.

Racial Resentment and President Trump's Insurrection

On January 6, 2021, President Trump's supporters—White supremacists, right-wing extremists, and the racially resentful—invaded the Capitol Building in Washington, DC. Not since the British invasion in the War of 1812 had the Capitol Building and what it represents been so desecrated and defiled. Conspiracy theories and untruths propagated by President Trump and many prominent Republicans that the 2020 election was *stolen from him* and *the country needed to be taken back* fueled the insurrection. Ruthless Democrats, immoral African Americans, and other minorities were perceived as perpetrating the greatest crime in American history. The perceived theft of the 2020 election, effectively a repudiation of President Trump and his message, was perceived as the ultimate threat to the American way of life and White privilege. Shrouded in patriotism, racial resentment toward African Americans, racial prejudice, and White supremacy enabled an insurrection by rationalizing beliefs in a conspiracy theory—a belief that the 2020 election was stolen from President Trump.[1]

Before delving into the details of the insurrection, we note that President Trump's supporters, threatened by the perceived advancement of African Americans and other minorities, have shown a propensity across many dimensions to discount objective facts, minimize science, and believe in lies and conspiracy theories. Literally, President Trump's supporters saw their own survival, and Whites' survival, hinging on Trump's survival.

As we have argued throughout this book, while the focus is on racists, White supremacists, and right-wing extremists, one does not have to be racist in order to support or enable the insurrection.

The Kindling

President Trump began laying the foundation for election theft conspiracy theories several months before the 2020 presidential election, though it was dismissed as the rantings of a narcissist.[2] Even though he openly and repeatedly espoused that "if he lost the election, it would be due to election fraud," such claims would not become racialized until after the election. Following President Trump's loss to Joe Biden and his unwillingness to acknowledge his defeat, conspiracy theories attributed Trump's defeat to massive voter fraud and irregularities in big cities with large African American and Latino populations. Numerous lawsuits were filed, and eventually rejected, claiming voter fraud and attempting to invalidate votes of predominantly African American and Latino voters. Such conspiracy theories capitalized on and perpetuated harmful racial stereotypes of people of color violating democratic norms, and involvement in corrupt and fraudulent activities. Though Trump's messaging did not explicitly name African Americans, the implicit message was not just that the election was being stolen from him, but the election was being stolen by African Americans.

Attempting to substantiate the racial allegation, President Trump campaign's legal challenges concentrated on counties in battleground states with the large African American and Latino populations. For instance, in Wayne County, Michigan (including Detroit), the Trump team wanted this county to be tossed out because African Americans comprised nearly 80 percent of the population. It was believed that with Wayne County's black voters out of the picture, Trump would have won the electoral votes in Michigan. Ironically, no such anomalies were alleged by the Trump campaign in predominantly white suburban counties where Joe Biden won by large margins. This tactic became the basis for Trump's lawsuits – essentially hoping the court system would validate their beliefs about race with no evidence.

Milwaukee County (Wisconsin) was contested by the Trump campaign; about 27 percent of the county's population was African American and 15 percent was Hispanic or Latino. With Milwaukee County out of the picture, Trump would have won the electoral votes in Wisconsin. Similarly, the Trump campaign targeted Philadelphia County (Pennsylvania), where 43 percent of the population was African American and 15 percent was Hispanic or Latino. Other legal challenges were mounted in Georgia's Chatham County, where 41 percent of the population was African American, and Arizona's Maricopa County, where 31 percent of the population was Hispanic or Latino. In Nevada, the Trump campaign sought to have him named the winner, focusing attention on

Clark County, where nearly 32 percent of the population was Hispanic or Latino.

Despite the fact that lawsuits contesting the election were routinely rejected for lack of evidence, ultimately sustained by the Supreme Court, President Trump and prominent Republicans would not concede the election. President Trump fired the director of the Homeland Security agency, who announced there was "no evidence that any voting system deleted or lost votes, changed votes, or was in any way compromised."

The fact is that, after not showing up in 2016 at rates similar to the Obama era, African Americans and Latinos turned out to vote in unprecedented numbers in states that President Trump won in 2016. African Americans were targeted by voter suppression strategies like restricting registration, closing polling stations, and limiting early voting. African American voters were motivated by issues pertaining to racism and policing. According to a June 2020 Washington Post-Ipsos poll, 90 percent of African Americans said both racism and their treatment by law enforcement were important in how they voted. With these issues and the widely held belief among African Americans that Trump is a racist and on the wrong side of the police violence, African Americans overwhelmingly backed Biden and the first African American and first female vice president, Kamala Harris. Grassroots initiatives encouraged African American voters to cast their ballots despite barriers and the challenges created by the coronavirus pandemc.

Research on the motivations underlying the insurrection will be critical. As an initial attempt, Pape and Ruby (2021), examining court documents of those arrested in the Capitol Insurrection (N=193), showed that 89 percent of the suspects arrested had no connection to far-right militias or white nationalist organizations. Instead of representing "deep-red strongholds," more than half resided in battleground counties that Biden won. These individuals were ordinary citizens who were (our argument) sensitized by the conspiracy theory of the election being stolen by African Americans and believed that something needed to be done to stop the theft. This is consistent with our argument about how racial resentment and other non-prejudiced beliefs motivate ordinary citizens.

The repetition of conspiracy theories and untruths about voter fraud, legitimized by President Trump and prominent Republicans who were unwilling to acknowledge Joe Biden's victory, exacerbated deep-seated racial resentment among ordinary citizens who enabled the lie and the insurrection. Although the rationalization of conspiracy theories, beliefs in untruths about the election, and an unwillingness to acknowledge the outcome of the election were seen as harmlessly humoring and pacifying a narcissistic president, racial resentment, activated by a threat to the racial ordering of society, was a core enabler of beliefs in election fraud.

The Insurrection

The March to Save America, on the morning of the Electoral College's counting of the electoral votes on January 6, 2021, triggered pro-Trump supporters, right-wing extremists, and White supremacists.[3] However, a call to action came on December 23, 2020, as President Trump stated in a tweet:

> Statistically impossible to have lost the 2020 Election. Big protest in D.C. on January 6th. Be there, will be wild!

People traveled from around the country. Some came just to be part of what they envisioned as a historic event, while others clearly had in mind a full-blown takeover. It was revealed later that extensive planning and coordination by ring-wing extremist groups and White supremacists went into the insurrection.

President Trump and prominent supporters coaxed a massive crowd to march to the Capitol in protest of the Electoral College vote count after delivering a speech pushing unfounded claims that the election was rigged. With violent imagery and calls to fight, President Trump made his intentions clear:

> Republicans are constantly fighting like a boxer with his hands tied behind his back. It's like a boxer. And we want to be so nice. We want to be so respectful of everybody, including bad people. And we're going to have to fight much harder. . . .
>
> We're going to walk down to the Capitol, and we're going to cheer on our brave senators and congressmen and women, and we're probably not going to be cheering so much for some of them, because you'll never take back our country with weakness. You have to show strength, and you have to be strong.

Trump's order sent thousands of his supporters marching to the Capitol, overpowering law enforcement (Capitol Police), toppling barricades, and rioting inside the halls of Congress, leaving five people dead. Eventually, breaching the Capitol Building, sending congressmen and congresswomen scurrying for protection, insurgents looted congressional offices, while several others were able to breach the floors of the House and Senate searching for the Vice President, who earlier expressed to Trump that he did not have the authority to overturn electoral votes.

We cannot say with certainty whether everyone at the rally and the Capitol was motivated by White supremacist and right-wing extremist ideas. This book helps us understand how Trump's message about various threats and challenges to the status quo, articulated through his *Make America Great Again* slogan, appealed to the average non-racist person who saw their views as more political than racial. At the same time, however, they were not innocent bystanders to the insurrection and take-over. Bystanders are present at events but do not take an active role in the event; they are essentially chance spectators.

Those who were not participants in the storming of the Capitol, but attended the events of the day, were not there by chance. They were not tourists who randomly showed up at the rally, but rather they were motivated by President Trump to believe that the election was being stolen and that this indicated that life in America for Whites was changing for the worse. Reflecting racial resentment, these average citizens were there for a reason. Even though they may have not been motivated by the same values and sentiments of White supremacists and right-wing extremists, their resentment contributed to the righteousness of the crowd and enabled the insurrection. This is how beliefs about justice and deservingness backfire to compel ordinary citizen to commiserate with racists.

African American Point of View

African Americans found the pretext and conspiracy theories motivating the March to Save America abhorrent and repressive, especially given that it was built on a baseless conspiracy theory attempting to discredit their high turnout.

While dismayed by the insurgence, like most citizens, African Americans likely perceived hypocrisy and a racial double standard in President Trump's insurrection. It is not so much that the Capitol Building deserved to be infiltrated and that elected officials and law enforcement personnel deserved to die at the hands of White supremacists, right-wing extremists, and the racially threatened, but an African American perspective can be also expected to include feelings of vindication in seeing President Trump, prominent Republicans, and Trump's supporters revealed for who they really are. As a challenge to an ever-present attempt to ignore and minimize racial prejudice in American society, the racial origins of the insurrection are undeniable. This is a consequence of America's blind spot for right-wing extremism, racial prejudice, and White supremacy.

African Americans' sense of American hypocrisy stems from a variety of sources, such as referent cognitions (Folger 1986). Though not usually applied to race, African Americans' beliefs about justice stem from a mental comparison to what might happen to them in similar situations. It is likely that African Americans compared the insurrectionist treatment by the Capitol police to the treatment of peaceful protesters during George Floyd protests (murdered by the police in Minnesota) and Breonna Taylor (murdered by police) in the summer of 2020. The federal government's response was massive, extremely aggressive, and forceful. US Park law enforcements used grenade-launched chemical irritants and DC Police employed military crowd control tactics to corral and arrest protesters. Unmarked Bureau of Prisons riot control officers were deployed. A US Coast Guard helicopter was even used to try to disperse a crowd. Most memorably, federal police used tear gas to clear peaceful protesters out of Lafayette Square outside the White House so President Trump could walk to St. John's Church for a photo opportunity with a Bible in hand.

By contrast, when pro-Trump insurrectionists stormed the Capitol Building, they encountered a seemingly anemic defense by law enforcement, some of whom were captured on video moving aside barricades, storming and ransacking the Capitol, and even appearing to take a "selfies" with the mob.

The Aftermath

Following the restoration of order, Congress returned to session. Several Republican senators continued to question battleground states' counting of electoral votes, without evidence.

Though they vowed to return to the Capitol for inauguration, further attacks by Trump's supportors and right-wing extremists did not materialize, as the National Guard was fully deployed. Social media platforms terminated President Trump's use, which considerably quietened tensions among his supporters. Facilitated by cellphone video and photos of the insurrection posted online, the FBI began to arrest and charge insurrectionists.

President Trump was impeached by the House of Representatives and charged with "incitement of insurrection" over the deadly mob siege of the Capitol in the final days in office. The House voted 232 to 297 to impeach Trump; ten Republicans joined Democrats who said he needed to be held accountable and warned of a "clear and present danger" if Congress should leave him unchecked. The Senate trial occurred after Trump departed the presidency.

Trump departed office with his lowest approval rating ever, 29 percent, according to the Pew Research Center. Throughout four years of scandals and investigations, President Trump maintained a rating that rarely budged from a 10-point band between 35 and 45 percent. Nothing he could say, do, or tweet appeared to dramatically change public opinion of him. In addition, he made history as the first president to be impeached twice.

Joe Biden and Kamala Harris were inaugurated as planned.

While the insurrection did not overturn the 2020 election, many individuals continue to believe the election was stolen. Racial resentment toward African Americans will remain operative and readily accessible as a prime, enabling belief in conspiracy theories and right-wing extremism, and White supremacy among ordinary people whose self-concept reflects fair, just, egalitarian, and open-minded individuals. Legitimizing racial myths fueling racial resentment toward African Americans and minorities, such as those that gave rise to Trump's conspiracy theories, will unfortunately endure.

Acknowledgments

This book is the product of years of collaborative research between the two of us. Along the way, many colleagues, friends, and organizations have shaped our thinking, overtly, subtly, and through their scholarship. Research, in many ways, is a solitary process, but with the influence of so many people, we never felt alone. The preceding pages undoubtedly have imperfections, and we apologize in advance for any errors and omissions. If this book is successful, it is due in large part to our appreciation for collaborative scholarship, and the support we have received along the way.

We would like to acknowledge the generosity of the University of Delaware Statistical Teaching and Analytic Research Training (START) Program in the College of Arts & Sciences for supporting us as organizer (David) and lecturer (Darren) when the program was located in Warsaw, Poland. This physical environment and travels throughout much of Eastern Europe taught us about how normal everyday people became complicit in one of the most atrocious crimes committed against humanity. Many of the appeals in the 2016 presidential primaries in the United States sounded eerily similar to the appeals that many may have heard decades earlier in the places we visited. We saw it clearly. We saw what is at stake when people rationalize benign values and sentiments, such as justice, fairness, and deservingness, which align with anti-Semitic, racist, and dominant group beliefs. The University of Warsaw provided much appreciated intellectual space and exposure to scholars that aided in synthesizing our experiences.

We wish to thank those who supported our research and data collection over the years, including the University of Delaware Center for Political Communication and former director, Paul Brewer; Brian

Schaffner, Stephen Ansolabehere, Samantha Luks, and the Cooperative Congressional Election Study (CCES) Project; the Board of Overseers for the 2010 General Social Survey; Cindy Lou Bennett, director, University of Arkansas at Little Rock Survey Research Center; and Tyson King-Meadows and Kathie Stromile Golden, who organized the National Conference of Black Political Scientists team module for the 2010 CCES. University of Notre Dame undergraduate students Nick Attone and Angelle Henderson offered helpful insights. Also thanks to the former dean of Arts & Science at the University of Delaware, George H. Watson, and current dean, John Pelesko, for their support and release time for David to complete the project. Thanks to John L. Jackson, dean of the Annenberg School of Communication at the University of Pennsylvania, and the school's staff. David spent the 2019–2020 academic year as a Visiting Scholar at the Annenberg School, and they served as gracious hosts for our final meeting to complete the details of the manuscript.

We are grateful to James M. Jones, Mark Peffley, Karem Ozan Kalkan, Chris Federico, Phillip Munoz, Katherine Cramer, and Dave Campbell for reading and commenting on early drafts of the manuscript. We would also like to thank faculty and student audiences in the Research on Individuals, Politics & Society (RIPS) Lab at Vanderbilt University; the Political Behavior and Identities workshop at Duke University; Center for Mind, Brain, and Culture (CMBC) at Emory University; the social psychology and Center for Law and Social Sciences (CLASS) group at the University of Southern California; the Political Science Department at the State University of New York at Geneseo; the Racial Attitudes and Identities Network (RAIN) at Harvard University; and the ICPSR Summer Program in Quantitative Methods of Social Research (Race, Ethnicity, and Quantitative Methodology workshop and Blalock Lecture Series) at the University of Michigan.

Individually and collectively, we have benefited from the sage advice and supportive ear of colleagues. We would like to thank Jim Gibson, Paul Sniderman, Christian Davenport, Christopher Parker, Samuel Gaertner, Chris Federico, Nicholas Valentino, Roger Tourangeau, Maria Krysan, Larry Bobo, Patricia Moy, Camille Zubrinsky Charles, Cindy Kam, Taeku Lee, Vincent Hutchings, and the late James S. Jackson. Lastly, we thank the University of Chicago Press, and our partners at the Press, Charles Myers, Holly Smith, and Mary Corrado.

Darren: I feel advantaged by being quarantined with strong, assertive, and smart women. Thanks to my family, Karen Davis, Peyton Davis, and Quinn Davis, for tolerating my incessant complaints and insightful comments.

David: I appreciate the fore thinkers that influenced my work on the book, in particular, the work of Howard Schuman, Melvin Lerner, Carol Hafer, Norman Feather, Don Kinder, David Sears, James Sidanius, John Jost, Paul Sniderman, Stanley Feldman, Leonie Huddy, and Katherine Tate. Also, for their invested mentorship and professional guidance over the years, I thank Saundra Ardrey, Howard Bailey, Cynthia Jackson-Elmore, Richard Hula, Paula Kearns, Scott Keeter, Derek Avery, Patrick McKay, Gretchen Bauer, Joe Pika, Leland Ware, Ralph Begleiter, Deborah Hess Norris, Molly Brodie, Eric Olesen, and the late Lee Sigelman. I completed working on the book manuscript while a professor and senior associate dean at the University of Delaware (UD), and now hold an appointment as Dean of the Goldman School of Public Policy at the University of California, Berkeley. UD is an excellent creative space with a wonderful group of scholars, and I thank the entire campus for their support.

For their personal support, I thank my parents, Jean Wilson and the late Eton R. Wilson; my late grandparents Angela Wilson, Wilson Q. Welch, and Anne Stanback Welch; my aunt Jackie Welch Schlicher, her husband Mark, and Mary McKelvy Welch for their constant curiosity in politics; my sister, Natalie Wilson, and life brother, Samuel C. Watkins III, for their sibling love. Finally, thanks to my wife, Rosalind Johnson, and son, Dalind, for their love, patience, and tolerance.

Appendix: Description of Data

We use this appendix to describe our data and measures. The studies we have conducted over the years are diverse, containing convenience and random samples, multiple modes of data collection, and different wordings of questions. As we have noted in the text, these data in some form have aided in the creation of our racial resentment scale.

2007 University of Delaware Study

The data in the UD study come from a convenience sample of students who volunteered to participate in a mode of data collection experiment at the University of Delaware. Participants were solicited campus-wide, and had the option of choosing one of three consecutive days in October 2007 to take part in the survey. On each day of the survey, different groups of students arrived in a large auditorium and selected a random number that was preassigned to a data collection mode: web, paper-pencil, and clicker. Then students were taken to three separate locations to take their surveys.

The final sample consisted of 622 respondents, including 230 (37%), 262 (42%), and 130 (21%) who were surveyed through the paper-pencil, clicker, and web modes respectively.[1] In terms of racial backgrounds of the sample, 520 (84%) were White, 28 (5%) Black, 23 (4%) Asian, and 25 (4%) Latino. Pacific Islander and American Indian each had 3 (.5%) respondents from their respective groups, and 12 respondents (2%) said they belonged to some "other" race not listed. Eight (1%) respondents did not provide their racial background when asked. For measurement and theoretical reasons, we removed self-identified Black respondents and those who did not provide a race, bringing the final working sample to 574. Of this group, 393 (68%) were females and 175 (30%) males; 6 (1%) respondents provided no gender.

Racial Resentment Scale Items

Resent07: I resent all of the special attention/favors that African Americans receive, other Americans like me have problems too.

Resent08: African Americans should not need any special privileges when slavery and racism are things of the past.

Resent09: How concerned are you that the special privileges for African Americans place you at an unfair disadvantage when you have done nothing to harm them?

Resent10: For African Americans to succeed they need to stop using racism and slavery as excuses.

Responses for all except Resent09: Agree strongly (=4), Agree somewhat, Disagree somewhat, or Disagree strongly (=1); Resent09 responses: Very concerned (=4), Concerned, Somewhat concerned, or Not at all concerned (=1).

2008 Cooperative Campaign Analysis Project

We use survey data from the 2008 Cooperative Campaign Analysis Project (CCAP). The CCAP data contain a national sample of registered voters, stratified by political geography, and oversampled populations in "battleground" states.[2] The YouGov research firm collected the data online using a six-wave pre- (December [2007], January, March, September, October) and post-election (November) panel design.[3] The CCAP data consist of "common" and "team" content questions. The common content items constituted the first 10 minutes of the online self-administered questionnaire, and collaborating sponsors were allowed to fill the latter 10 minutes with customized questions. These team questions were placed in the latter portion of the survey to standardize questionnaire context across the waves. The data were collected in the two months—September and October—preceding the 2008 presidential election. The respondents in our working data participated in at least one of the waves as well as the baseline study when demographic information was collected. We include only self-reported non-Hispanic White respondents (September N=1,231 and October N=1,176).

Racial Resentment Scale Items

EXR1: I resent all of the special attention/favors that African Americans receive; other Americans like me have problems too.

EXR2: African Americans should not need any special privileges when slavery and racism are things of the past.

EXR3: The special privileges for African Americans place me at an unfair disadvantage when I have done nothing to harm them.

EXR4: For African Americans to succeed they need to stop using racism and slavery as excuses.

Responses for all items: Strongly agree (=4), Somewhat agree, Somewhat disagree, or Strongly disagree (=1).

2010 General Social Survey

The General Social Survey (GSS) is a nationally representative biennial survey conducted by the National Opinion Research Center (NORC). The 2010 cross-sectional data contain 4,901 respondents collected from face-to-face (n=4,036) and telephone (n=851) interviews[4] with a cross-section of US adults. The 2010 study was the first to fully implement a new sampling design containing cases collected in 2010 (n=2,044), as well as a group of individuals who were originally interviewed in 2006 (n=1,276) and 2008 (n=1,581), and who agreed to be reinterviewed for future studies. The racial resentment items were part of a larger module on intergroup relations, presented to individuals originally sampled two years earlier in 2008. This group consists of 1,581 respondents, including 1,122 non-Hispanic Whites, 223 non-Hispanic African Americans, 168 Hispanic persons, and 68 persons of some "other" race or ethnicity. Our working data for the 2010 GSS includes only the 1,122 non-Hispanic White respondents.

Racial Resentment Scale Items

NORACISM: African Americans do not need any special consideration because racism is a thing of the past.

RACRESNT: I resent any special considerations that Africans Americans receive because it's unfair to other Americans.

RACEXCUS: For African Americans to succeed they need to stop using racism and slavery as excuses.

Responses for all items: Strongly agree (=4), Somewhat agree, Somewhat disagree, or Strongly disagree (=1).

2011 University of Arkansas Little Rock Racial Attitudes Survey (UALR)

The UALR study contains responses from residents of Pulaski County, Arkansas. The data were collected via telephone interviews—dual frame (landline [88%] and cell phone [12%])—between September 8, 2011, and December 15, 2011. The survey was conducted by the UALR Institute of Government Survey Research Center, and interviews were conducted in both English and Spanish.

The study focused on the three largest racial-ethnic groups in Pulaski County: Whites, Blacks, and Hispanics. To achieve more accurate estimates of minority populations and make substantive cross-racial comparison, the researchers intentionally oversampled Black (n=398) and Hispanic (n=221) respondents, and when these groups are combined with White respondents (n=428), the working sample size is a total of 1,047 respondents. The researchers also "race-matched" interviewers and respondents; thus, Blacks, Whites, and Hispanics were interviewed by members of their self-reported racial-ethnic group. The study contained three of the Wilson and Davis (2011) racial resentment items, and were presented to non–African American respondents at the end of the survey. Our analyses include only the White respondents (N=428).

Racial Resentment Scale Items

Q44RES: I resent any special considerations that Blacks receive because it's unfair to other Americans.

Q45BL: Blacks do not need any special consideration because racism is a thing of the past.

Q46SUC: For Blacks to succeed they need to stop using racism and slavery as excuses.

Responses for all items: Strongly agree (=4), Agree, Disagree, or Strongly disagree (=1).

2011 National Black Catholic Study

The 2011 Religion and Politics Study was sponsored by researchers at the University of Notre Dame, and is designed to examine the political attitudes and behaviors of Catholics in America. Knowledge Networks (now GfK Knowledge Panel) conducted the study from July 2011 to August 2011, generating the non-probability sample from their online panel. Participants were selected using address-based sampling (ABS), a sampling frame that covers about 97 percent of US households. Samples were drawn from among active panelists using a probability proportional to size (PPS) weighted sampling approach. After the random representative samples were drawn, participants were required to complete the survey over the internet. We present the data only for White respondents (n = 1,098) who participated in the study.

Racial Resentment Scale Items

Q43_A: African Americans do not need any special consideration because racism is a thing of the past.

Q43_C: I resent any special considerations that Africans Americans receive because it's unfair to other Americans.

Q43_D: For African Americans to succeed they need to stop using racism and slavery as excuses.

Q43_E: Special considerations for African Americans place me at an unfair disadvantage because I have done nothing to harm them.

Q43_F: African Americans bring up race only when they need to make an excuse for their failure.

Responses for all items: Agree strongly (=5), Agree somewhat, Neither agree nor disagree, Disagree somewhat, or Disagree strongly (=1).

2012 University of Delaware Center for Political Communication (CPC) Study

The 2012 UD CPC data come from a telephone survey of a representative sample of 906 adults living in the continental United States.

The survey was administered by Princeton Survey Research Associates International (PSRAI), and data were collected by Princeton Data Source in May–June 2012, using a dual sampling frame consisting of both landline (n=551) and cell phone (n=355) respondents. The response rate was 12.5 percent (calculated using the American Association for Public Opinion Research's RR4, reflecting refusals as well as non-contacts). The contact and cooperation rates were 19 and 67 percent, respectively. The data are unweighted but contain weighted to correct known demographic discrepancies related to sex, age, race-ethnicity, region, education, count population density, and household size and phone lines. The sampling error for the full sample is ±3.9 percentage points. The final working data file contains 676 non-Hispanic White respondents.

Racial Resentment Scale Items

Q24a: I resent any special considerations that African Americans receive because it's unfair to other Americans.

Q24b: Special considerations for African Americans place me at an unfair disadvantage because I have done nothing to harm them.

Q24c: African Americans bring up race only when they need to make an excuse for their failure.

Responses for all items: Strongly agree (=4), Somewhat agree, Somewhat disagree, or Strongly disagree (=1).

2010, 2012, 2016, and 2018 Cooperative Congressional Election Studies (CCES)

Administered by YouGov, the CCES data come from a collaborative public opinion project, in cooperation with principal investigators at Harvard University, utilizing questionnaires developed by researchers across many universities, who have combined resources to create a large non-probability sample. The CCES provides participating researchers with ten minutes of "common content"—standard items asked of all respondents—and then ten minutes of specialized "team content." As is standard for the CCES, YouGov selected respondents for the 2010, 2012, 2016, and 2018 studies from a panel of adults over the age of 18. In each year, pre-election data were collected in October and post-election data were collected in November.

Each of the studies contains at least four of the Wilson and Davis (2011) racial resentment items. The items were presented only to non–African Americans respondents and came after the CCES common content questionnaire items. In 2012, there were two CCES studies containing the Wilson and Davis items; Wilson and Davis conducted the "team 1" study, and a group of researchers at the University of Delaware conducted the "team 2" study. The final working samples in our study comprised Whites (2010: N=1,052; 2012 [team 1]: N=1,125; 2012 [team 2]: N=1,100; and 2016: N=1,088). The 2016 CCES collected data from an additional sample of African American respondents (N=686).

2010 CCES Racial Resentment Items

NCB18. African Americans do not need any special consideration because racism is a thing of the past.

NCB20. I resent any special considerations that Africans Americans receive because it's unfair to other Americans.

NCB21. For African Americans to succeed they need to stop using racism and slavery as excuses.

NCB22. Special considerations for African Americans place me at an unfair disadvantage because I have done nothing to harm them.

NCB23. African Americans bring up race only when they need to make an excuse for their failure.

*Responses for all items: Strongly agree (=5), Agree, Neither agree nor disagree, Disagree, and Strongly disagree (=1).

2012 CCES Racial Resentment (Agree-Disagree) Items—Team 1 (Wilson and Davis) Study (Items in both Pre- and Post-studies)

WIL90B: I resent any special considerations that Africans Americans receive because it's unfair to other Americans.

WIL90C: For African Americans to succeed they need to stop using past racism and slavery as excuses.

WIL90D: Special considerations for African Americans place me at an unfair disadvantage because I have done nothing to harm them.

WIL90E: African Americans bring up race only when they need to make an excuse for their failure.

*Responses for all items: Strongly agree (=5), Agree, Neither agree nor disagree, Disagree, and Strongly disagree (=1).

2012 CCES Racial Resentment (Construct Specific) Items—Team 1 (Wilson and Davis) Study (Items in both Pre- and Post-studies)

WIL91A: How much special consideration should African Americans need because of past racism? (Responses: None [=1], A little, Some, Quite a bit, or A great deal [=5])

WIL91B: How different are problems caused by race from other problems that people have to deal with? (Responses: Not at all different [=1], A little different, Somewhat different, Very different, or Extremely different [=5])

WIL91C1: How much do you resent special considerations that Africans Americans receive? (Responses: None [=1], A little, Some, Quite a bit, or A great deal [=5])

WIL91C2: How much do you agree or disagree that any special considerations African Americans receive are unfair to other Americans? (Responses: Strongly disagree [=1], Disagree, Neither agree nor disagree, Agree, or Strongly agree [=5])

WIL91D: In order for them to succeed, how important is it for African Americans to stop using past racism and slavery as excuses? (Responses: Not at all important [=1], A little important, Somewhat important, Very important, or Extremely important [=5])

WIL91E: How often do African Americans bring up race in order to make an excuse for their failure? (Responses: Never [=1], Rarely, Sometimes, Very often, or Extremely often [=5])

2012 CCES Racial Resentment Items—Team 2 (CPC) Study (Items in both Pre- and Post-studies)

CPC19. Racial discrimination is no different from other everyday problems people have to deal with.

CPC20. I resent any special considerations that Africans Americans receive because it's unfair to other Americans

CPC21. For African Americans to succeed they need to stop using racism and slavery as excuses.

CPC22. Special considerations for African Americans place me at an unfair disadvantage because I have done nothing to harm them.

CPC23. African Americans bring up race only when they need to make an excuse for their failure.

*Responses for all items: Strongly agree (=5), Agree, Neither agree nor disagree, Disagree, and Strongly disagree (=1).

2012 CCES Racial Resentment (Construct Specific) Items—Team 2 (CPC) Study (Items in both Pre- and Post-studies)

WIL91A: How much special consideration should African Americans need because of past racism? (Responses: None [=1], A little, Some, Quite a bit, or A great deal [=5])

WIL91B: How different are problems caused by race from other problems that people have to deal with? (Responses: Not at all different [=1], A little different, Somewhat different, Very different, or Extremely different [=5])

WIL91C1: How much do you resent special considerations that Africans Americans receive? (Responses: None [=1], A little, Some, Quite a bit, or A great deal [=5])

WIL91C2: How much do you agree or disagree that any special considerations African Americans receive are unfair to other Americans? (Responses: Strongly disagree [=1], Disagree, Neither agree nor disagree, Agree, or Strongly agree [=5])

WIL91D: In order for them to succeed, how important is it for African Americans to stop using past racism and slavery as excuses? (Responses: Not at all important [=1], A little important, Somewhat important, Very important, or Extremely important [=5])

WIL91E: How often do African Americans bring up race in order to make an excuse for their failure? (Responses: Never [=1], Rarely, Sometimes, Very often, or Extremely often [=5])

2016 CCES Racial Resentment Items

WD1: I resent any special considerations that Africans Americans receive because it's unfair to other Americans.

WD2: For African Americans to succeed they need to stop using past racism and slavery as excuses.

WD3: Special considerations for African Americans place me at an unfair disadvantage because I have done nothing to harm them.

WD4: African Americans bring up race only when they need to make an excuse for their failure.

*Responses for all items: Strongly agree (=5), Agree, Neither agree nor disagree, Disagree, and Strongly disagree (=1).

2018 CCES Racial Resentment Items
UND380_2: Racial discrimination is no different from other everyday problems people have to deal with.

UND380_3: I resent any special considerations that African Americans receive because it's unfair to other Americans.

UND380_4 For African Americans to succeed they need to stop using racism and slavery as excuses.

UND380_5 I don't understand why race is any different from what other people have to deal with.

UND380_6 Special considerations for African Americans place me at an unfair disadvantage because I have done nothing to harm them.

UND380_7 African Americans bring up race only when they need to make an excuse for their failure.

*Responses for all items: Strongly agree (=5), Agree, Neither agree nor disagree, Disagree, and Strongly disagree (=1).

Appendix: Chapter 8

The Development of the African Americans' Resentment toward Whites Scale

Prior to collecting the data, we sought to identify a parsimonious set of items that measure African Americans' racial resentments toward Whites. We brainstormed content to create a list of items that would ostensibly touch on various dimensions of what African Americans might resent about Whites. These items ranged from beliefs about how Whites view and treat African Americans, to how Whites might view and judge their in-group members. We shared these items with colleagues and students, soliciting feedback and revising the list. We settled on 22 items to test in the Pilot Study and 20 items in the CCES. The items were worded as assertions that respondents could agree or disagree with on a 5-point Likert scale.

Study 1

The first study, which we call the "2016 Pilot Study," contains a national non-probability sample of non-Hispanic, self-reported, African American respondents recruited from the Federated Samples© opt-in online panel. Members of the Federated panel agree to take part in academic and market research surveys, and earn "reward points" for their participation.[1] We administered the online survey through the Qualtrics® web tool. Data collection took place between September 15 and September 26, 2016, with respondents participating through computer (49%), mobile phone (43%), and tablet (8%) devices. On average, respondents took approximately 12 minutes to complete the questionnaire. Importantly, the sample contains significantly more female (84.9%) than male (15.1%) respondents. The mean and median age in the sample are 42.6 (SD=14.7) and 41 years respectively. The median respondent income for the sample is between $40,000 to less than $50,000; and 43 percent of the sample are employed full or part-time, 37 percent are retired or disabled, 9 percent are students or homemakers, and 11 percent are unemployed. The sample is overwhelmingly Democrat (79%), with fewer independent (16%) or Republican (5%) partisans, and more respondents said they voted (68%) than did not (32%). The under-representation for African American males serves as our strongest concern; thus, we created a post-stratification weight based on gender to compare our results. None of the substantive findings were changed as a result of the gender weight; thus, we proceed forward with our non-gender-weighted sample. The final working sample includes 684 African American respondents.

Study 2

The second study is the 2016 CCES, which we have utilized throughout the book, and whose details can be found at the end of this appendix. The team module that we utilize from the 2016 CCES contained 686 non-Hispanic, self-reported, African American respondents. We collected the large sample for the express purpose of validating our African Americans' resentment scale on a national population. Like the 2016 Pilot Study, the CCES African American respondents are overwhelmingly more female (71.7%) than male (28.3%); however, weighting the data on gender, once again, did not alter the results. The mean and median ages for the respondents are 45.7 (SD=14.9) and 46 respectively. In terms of socioeconomic status, pluralities of respondents had earned a four-year degree or more (47%) and were employed full-time (48.8%), and the sample had a median family income of between $50,000 and less than $60,000. The sample was largely Democrat (70.4%), with smaller numbers reporting independent status (19.1%) or Republican affiliation (3.1%). The final working sample includes those 656 African American respondents who answered all of the draft items assessing resentment toward Whites.

Both of the studies were conducted online. To deal with any order effects, the online questionnaires randomized (up to) five items to appear on each web page—in a matrix format, with items listed vertically in rows and responses listed horizontally in columns—and also randomized the order in which the respondents saw each of the items.

Data Reduction

For both studies we included all items in a principal components "exploratory" factor analysis (EFA), with oblique (Oblimin) rotation, due to the correlated nature of the various dimensions of African Americans' racial attitudes. The principal components analysis is a data-driven statistical procedure that imposes no substantive constraints on the data; there are no restrictions on the pattern of relationships between observed and latent variables (Tabachnick, Fidell, and Ullman 2007). The estimated "structure" matrices from the principle components technique serve as the basis of our results, and we expect a single factor solution and item factor loadings >.500 (Comrey and Lee 1992).

The EFA model in the Pilot Study yielded four correlated factors accounting for 61% of the total variance explained by the variables. Partitioned, the first factor accounted for 43.7% (eigenvalue=9.6) of the variance, the second factor accounted for 7.8% (eigenvalue=1.7), the third factor accounted for 5.5% (eigenvalue=1.2), and the fourth factor 4.7% (eigenvalue=1.0). The EFA model in the CCES data yielded two correlated factors, accounting for 56.6% of the total variance explained in the variables; however, the first factor accounted for 47.3% (eigenvalue=9.45) and the second accounted for 9.3% (eigenvalue=1.86). All of the variables loaded on the first factor with values >.500 and none loaded on the second factor with this criteria. For both studies, we identified the strongest loading items, giving balance to an item's association with one or more of the three dimensions. We assessed the validity and reliability of various combinations of the items using additional statistical techniques; we share some of these results below, and settled on six items that were in the top ten Factor 1 loadings for both studies that also covered the core dimensions.

Table A8.1 provides the descriptive statistics for each item and the scale in both studies.

There is remarkable consistency across the studies in terms of the relative level of endorsement of the statements. In both studies African American respondents agreed most with BENEFIT and second most

TABLE A8.1. **Pilot Study 2016—Item Descriptive Statistics for African American Racial Resentment toward Whites Items**

2016 Pilot Study (N=684)	M	SD	Item-Total Correlations	EFA Factor Loadings
NOACCOUNT - White people get away with offenses that African Americans would never get away with. (RR_9)	4.39	.92	.69**	.80
BENFIT - White people are given the benefit of the doubt more than African Americans. (RR_10)	4.51	.84	.57**	.69
IGNORE - White people tend to ignore the effects of racism and discrimination. (RR_11)	4.21	.97	.71**	.81
DENY - I resent when White people deny the existence of racial discrimination. (RR_14)	4.10	1.11	.67**	.78
APATHY - White people do not go to great lengths to understand the problems African Americans face. (RR_18)	3.93	1.05	.67**	78
DISCREDIT - Even when African Americans work hard to succeed, White people still view them in lesser terms. (RR_19)	4.07	1.03	.72**	.81
Overall Composite Scale	4.20	.77		

2016 CCES Study (N=656)

	M	SD	Item-Total Correlations	EFA Factor Loadings
NOACCOUNT - Whites get away with offenses that African Americans would never get away with. (RR_9)	4.21	.96	.74**	.84
BENEFIT - Whites are given the benefit of the doubt more than African Americans. (RR_10)	4.34	.87	.77**	.85
IGNORE - Whites tend to ignore the effects of racism and discrimination. (RR_11)	4.07	.94	.70**	.80
DENY - I resent when Whites deny the existence of racial discrimination. (RR_14)	4.14	.95	.66**	.76
APATHY - Whites do not go to great lengths to understand the problems African Americans face. (RR_18)	3.90	.96	.68**	.78
DISCREDIT - Even when African Americans work hard to succeed, Whites still view them in lesser terms. (RR_19)	3.95	.98	.72**	.81
Overall Composite Scale	4.10	.76		

Note. *p<.05, **p<.01.

with NOACCOUNT, both serving the dimension of White privilege. The middle two items with regard to level of endorsement, for both studies, are IGNORE and DENY, both serving the dimension of responsibility denial. And the lowest two endorsed items across the studies are APATHY and DISCREDIT, both serving the dimension of deservingness and effort. When the six items are included in an EFA, they have strong factor loadings, reflecting very good internal validity, and their item-total correlations—estimates of the relationship with a composite scale of the items, excluding the specific item—are all well above .50 (i.e., $R^2 \geq .25$). Finally, the mean (M) statistics in table A8.1 average greater than 4 in each study, suggesting high levels of aggregate African Americans' resentment toward Whites. The totality of the statistical properties presented in table A8.1 give us strong confidence in the validity and reliability of our items.

Conceptual Strength

The items seem to work well together, but often racial measures can be strongly correlated but not conceptually strong when data and theory are combined statistically. How much certainty can we have that the data support the construct we propose? We analyzed a series of confirmatory factor analysis (CFA) models to assess whether our African Americans' Resentment toward Whites (AARTW) items form a valid measurement construct by way of "fit." We performed the CFAs using AMOS 24 (Arbuckle 2014), evaluating several established fit statistics: chi-square ($\chi 2$, which is sensitive to large sample size), the relative fix index (RFI), the normed fit index (NFI), the comparative fit index (CFI), and the root mean squared error of approximation (RMSEA). Acceptable model fit is associated with non-significant $\chi 2$ values, RFI >.90, NFI > .95, CFI > .95, and RMSEA < .08 (Bentler 1990; Meyers, Gamst, and Guarino 2006). We evaluated two models in both studies, one that included all six of the items as a single dimension, and another that structured the items as three latent dimensions—responsibility denial, White privilege, and deservingness/effort—that constitute African Americans' racial resentment as a second-order construct. Figure A8.1 shows the conceptual diagrams of each model for the two studies, including the standardized factor loadings for each of the items. The diagrams show that in both the single and multiple dimension models the items strongly correlated with

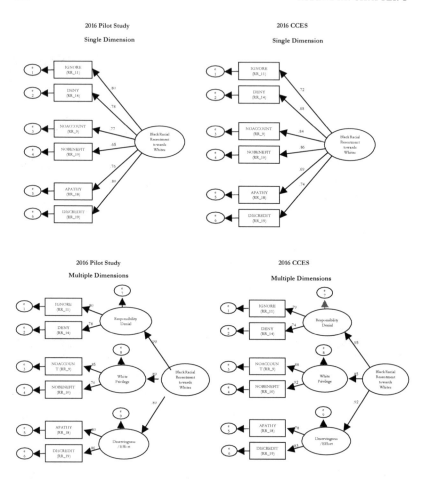

FIGURE A8.1. 2016 Pilot Study vs. 2016 CCES

the underlying African Americans' resentment construct, but the question is which structure is better in terms of fit.

Table A8.2 provides the summary statistics for the various models. The Cronbach Alpha statistics show strong reliability for both models, and the EFA results show there is a single factor explaining the variance in the items. The most vital evidence comes from the CFA model fit statistics. In both years, the single dimension model underperforms on most of the fit measures, but the multiple dimension model has excellent fit properties. All of the fit measures for the multiple dimension model,

TABLE A8.2. **Reliability and Validity Results for African Americans' Racial Resentment toward Whites Scale**

Measurement Statistics	2016 Pilot Study (N=684)		2016 CCES (N=656)	
	Single Dimension	Multiple Dimensions	Single Dimension	Multiple Dimensions
Cronbach Alpha	.868	–	.891	–
Responsibility Denial	–	.716	–	.734
White Privilege	–	.710	–	.895
Deservingness/Effort	–	.789	–	.783
EFA Model Results				
Eigenvalue	3.63	–	3.89	–
PCT variance explained	60.58	–	64.93	–
CFA Model Results				
NFI	.956	.997	.909	.996
RFI	.897	.989	.849	.990
CFI	.960	1.00	.913	.999
RMSEA	.048	.000	.179	.026
Chi-square	79.92 (df=9)	5.48 (df=6)	192.42 (df=9)	8.52 (df=6)
	$p<.01$	$p=.49$	$p<.01$	$p=.20$

across both studies, indicate an excellent match between the proposed model and the observed data. Notably, even the Chi-square statistic, which is extremely sensitive to sample size, meets the non-significance fit criteria. Thus, the six items constituting the AARTW scale are not randomly correlated, but instead form a coherent and conceptually sound scale.

Appendix: Question Wording
by Chapter

Chapter 2

American National Election Study (ANES) 1948–2016—Cumulative

ADMINISTRATIVE
VCF0004—Year of Study

CLASSIC RACIAL RESENTMENT

VCF9039—Generations of slavery and discrimination have created conditions
that make it difficult for blacks to work their way out of the lower class.

VCF9040—Irish, Italians, Jewish and many other minorities overcame prejudice and worked their way up. Blacks should to the same without any special favors.

VCF9041—It's really a matter of some people not trying hard enough; if African
Americans would only try harder they could be just as well off. (Reversed
coding)

VCF9042—Over the past few years, African Americans have gotten less than
they deserve.

GROUP THERMOMETERS
We'd also like to get your feelings about some groups in American society. When I read the name of a group, we'd like you to rate it with what
we call a feeling thermometer. Ratings between 50 degrees and 100 degrees mean that you feel favorably and warm toward the group; ratings

between 0 and 50 degrees mean that you don't feel favorably toward the group and that you don't care too much for that group. If you don't feel particularly warm or cold toward a group you would rate them at 50 degrees. If we come to a group you don't know much about, just tell me and we'll move on to the next one.

VCF0206—Blacks

VCF0207—Whites

VCF0211—Liberals

VCF0212—Conservatives

2016 Pilot Study

CLASSIC RACIAL RESENTMENT WORDING EXPERIMENT

Explicit Emotional Version

WRRv2_3. Irish, Italians, Jewish and many other minorities overcame prejudice and worked their way up. I resent when African Americans request special favors to do the same.

WRRv2_6. It angers me when African Americans claim that generations of slavery and discrimination have created conditions that make it difficult for them to work their way out of the lower class.

WRRv2_5. I resent the notion that over the past few years, African Americans have gotten less than they deserve.

WRRv2_4. It is really a matter of some people not trying hard enough. It angers me that African Americans do not try harder to be just as well off as Whites.

Standard Version

WRRv1_3. Irish, Italians, Jewish and many other minorities overcame prejudice and worked their way up. African Americans should do the same without any special favors.

WRRv1_6. Generations of slavery and discrimination have created conditions that make it difficult for African Americans to work their way out of the lower class.

WRRvi_5. Over the past few years, African Americans have gotten less than they deserve.

WRRvi_4. It is really a matter of some people not trying hard enough; if African Americans would only try harder they could be just as well off as whites.

Chapter 3

2012 CCES (Team A Content) (Pre/Post)

WHITE RESENTMENT TOWARD AFRICAN AMERICANS

WIL90B/ WIL990B. I resent any special considerations that Africans Americans receive because it's unfair to other Americans.

WIL90C/ WIL990C. For African Americans to succeed they need to stop using past racism and slavery as excuses.

WIL90D/ WIL990D. Special considerations for African Americans place me at an unfair disadvantage because I have done nothing to harm them.

WIL90E/ WIL990E. African Americans bring up race only when they need to make an excuse for their failure.

VIEWS ON EQUALITY

WIL3A. The United States would be better off if we cared less about how equal all people were.

WIL3B. In America, some people are just more deserving of success than others.

WIL3C. If people were treated more equally we would have fewer problems in America.

WIL3D. It is probably a good thing that in America certain groups are at the top and other groups are at the bottom.

AUTHORITARIAN BELIEFS

WIL2A. To compromise with our political opponents is dangerous because it usually leads to the betrayal of our own side.

WIL2B. In the long run the best way to live is to pick friends and associates whose tastes and beliefs are the same as one's own.

WIL2C. In this complicated world of ours the only way we can know what's going on is to rely on leaders or experts who can be trusted.

WIL2D. There are a number of people in this world who I have come to hate because of the things they stand for.

"SPECIAL LAWS" QUESTION WORDING EXPERIMENT (POST-ELECTION)

Experiment Variables

WIL901_treat—Treatment variable ("Laws" | "Special Laws")

WIL901_groupint—Group Treatment Variable ("Americans" | "African Americans")

Items (randomized ¼ WIL901a, ¼ WIL901b)

WIL901a. Question Text: How much do you support or oppose LAWS to protect the voting rights of [Group Treatment]?

WIL901b. How much do you support or oppose SPECIAL LAWS to protect the voting rights of [Group Treatment]?

2012 CCES (Team B Content)

WHITE RESENTMENT TOWARD AFRICAN AMERICANS (PRE/POST)

CPC20 / CPC920A. I resent any special considerations that Africans Americans receive because it's unfair to other Americans.

CPC21/ CPC921A. For African Americans to succeed they need to stop using racism and slavery as excuses.

CPC22/ CPC922A. Special considerations for African Americans place me at an unfair disadvantage because I have done nothing to harm them.

CPC23/ CPC923A. African Americans bring up race only when they need to make an excuse for their failure.

STATUS QUO THREAT

CPC3A. The American way of life is under attack.

CPC3B. Things are really out of control in the United States.

CPC3C. The United States of the past is a much better place than the United States of the future.

CPC3D. The United States is changing too fast.

CPC3E. Too many freedoms have made America its own worst enemy.

2016 CCES

WHITE RESENTMENT TOWARD AFRICAN AMERICANS

WD1: I resent any special considerations that Africans Americans receive because it's unfair to other Americans.

WD2: For African Americans to succeed they need to stop using past racism and slavery as excuses.

WD3: Special considerations for African Americans place me at an unfair disadvantage because I have done nothing to harm them.

WD4: African Americans bring up race only when they need to make an excuse for their failure.

MODERN RACISM

MR1: Discrimination against African Americans is no longer a problem in the United States.

MR2: It is easy to understand the anger of African Americans.

MR3: African Americans are too demanding in their push for equal rights.

MR4: African Americans should not push themselves where they are not wanted.

MR5: Over the past few years, African Americans have gotten more economically than they deserve.

CLASSIC RACIAL RESENTMENT

KS1: Irish, Italians, Jewish and many other minorities overcame prejudice and worked their way up. African Americans should do the same without any special favors.

KS2: Generations of slavery and discrimination have created conditions that make it difficult for African Americans to work their way out of the lower class.

KS3: Over the past few years, African Americans have gotten less than they deserve.

KS4: It's really a matter of some people not trying hard enough; if African Americans would only try harder they could be just as well off as whites.

STATUS QUO THREAT

WD3A. The American way of life is under attack.

WD3B. Things are really out of control in the United States.

WD3C. The United States of the past is a much better place than the United States of the future.

WD3D. The United States is changing too fast.

WD3E. Too many freedoms have made America its own worst enemy.

SOCIAL DOMINANCE ORIENTATION (RANDOMIZE ½ "EVERYONE/PEOPLE"; ½ "RACIAL GROUPS")

SD_FORM—Randomization variable for Social Dominance Item Experiment

SD1—Our society should do whatever is necessary to make sure that [everyone | racial groups] has an equal opportunity to succeed.

SD2—We have gone too far in pushing equal rights [for racial groups] in this country.

SD3—One of the big problems in this country is that we don't give [everyone | racial groups] an equal chance.

SD4—This country would be better off if we worried less about how equal [people | racial groups] are.

SD5—It is not really that big a problem if some [people | racial groups] have more of a chance in life than others.

2010 General Social Survey

WHITE RESENTMENT TOWARD AFRICAN AMERICANS (WRTA)

NORACISM: African Americans do not need any special consideration because racism is a thing of the past. (Strongly agree-Strongly disagree)

RACRESNT: I resent any special considerations that Africans Americans receive because it's unfair to other Americans. (Strongly agree-Strongly disagree)

RACEXCUS: For African Americans to succeed they need to stop using racism and slavery as excuses. (Strongly agree-Strongly disagree)

RACIAL STEREOTYPES ABOUT AFRICAN AMERICANS

WLTHBLKX: Socioeconomic status

(Now I have some questions about different groups in our society. I'm going to show you a seven-point scale on which the characteristics of people in a group can be rated. In the first statement a score of 1 means that you think almost all of the people in that group are "rich." A score of 7 means that you think almost all of the people in the group are "poor." A score of 4 means that you think that the group is not towards one end or another, and of course you may choose any number in between that comes closest to where you think people in the group stand.) Where would you rate Blacks in general on this scale?

WORKBLKX: Work-ethic

The second set of characteristics asks if people in the group tend to be hardworking or if they tend to be lazy.

(A score of 1 means that you think almost all of the people in the group are "hardworking." A score of 7 means that you think almost everyone in the group is "lazy." A score of 4 means that you think that the group is not towards one end or the other, and of course you may choose any number in between that comes closest to where you think people in the group stand.) Where would you rate Blacks in general on this scale?

INTLBLKX: Intelligence

Do people in these groups tend to be unintelligent or tend to be intelligent? (A score of 1 means that you think almost all of the people in the group are "unintelligent." A score of 7 means that you think almost everyone in the group is "intelligent." A score of 4 means that you think that the group is not towards one end or the other, and of course you may choose any number in between that comes closest to where you think people in the group stand.) Where would you rate Whites in general on this scale?

CONSERVATISM

POLVIEWS: We hear a lot of talk these days about liberals and conservatives. I'm going to show you a seven-point scale on which the political views that people might hold are arranged from extremely liberal (point 1) to extremely conservative (point 7). Where would you place yourself on this scale?

SOCIAL DISTANCE FOR RACIAL GROUPS

CLOSEBLK: In general, how close do you feel to blacks? (Not at all close–Very close)

CLOSEWHT: In general, how close do you feel to whites? (Not at all close–Very close)

RACIAL IDENTITY

RACIDIMP : How important is your racial identity to you? Would you say . . . (Very important–Not important at all)

COLORBLIND IDENTITY

COLBLIND: For the most part, I'm colorblind; that is, I don't care about what race people are. (Strongly agree–Strongly disagree)

ATTITUDES ABOUT RACE AND RACE RELATIONS

RACTIRED: I'm tired of hearing people talk about racial problems in the US today. (Strongly agree–Strongly disagree)

WHTADVNT: Whites are generally treated better than other groups in American society today. (Strongly agree–Strongly disagree)

RACNOBIZ: Maybe some racial minority groups do experience unfair treatment, but that's no business of mine. (Strongly agree–Strongly disagree)

RACCARE: How concerned are you personally about race relations? Are you very concerned, somewhat concerned, not very concerned, or not concerned at all? (Very concerned–not concerned at all)

AMELIORATION POLICY

HELPBLK: Some people think that African Americans have been discriminated against for so long that the government has a special obligation to help improve their living standards; they are at point 1. Others believe that the government should not be giving special treatment to Blacks/Negroes/African-Americans; they are at point 5. Where would you place yourself on this scale, or haven't you made up your mind on this? (The government has a special obligation to help improve their living standards—Agree with both—The government should not be giving special treatment to African Americans.)

HELPPOOR: I'd like to talk with you about issues some people tell us are important. Some people think that the government in Washington should do everything possible to improve the standard of living of all poor Americans; they are at point 1 on this card. Other people think it's not the government's responsibility, and that each person should take care of himself; they are at point 5. Where would you place yourself on this scale, or haven't you made up your mind on this? (The government in Washington should do everything possible to improve the standard of living of all poor Americans—Agree with both—Each person should take care of himself.)

HELPSICK: In general, some people think that it is the responsibility of the government in Washington to see to it that people have help in paying for doctors and hospital bills; they are at point 1. Others think that these matters are not the responsibility of the federal government and that people should take care of these things themselves; they are at point 5. Where would you place yourself on this scale, or haven't you made up your mind on this? (The government in Washington should see to it that people have help in paying for doctors and hospital bills—Agree with both—These matters are not the responsibility of the federal government and that people should take care of these things themselves.)

AFFIRMATIVE ACTION POLICY

AFFRMACT: Some people say that because of past discrimination, blacks should be given preference in hiring and promotion. Others say that such preference in hiring and promotion of blacks is wrong because it discriminates against whites. What about your opinion? Are you for or against preferential hiring and promotion of blacks? Do you favor preference in hiring and promotion strongly or not strongly? Do you oppose preference in hiring and promotion strongly or not strongly?

Chapter 4

CCES 2010, 2012, 2016, 2018

DEMOGRAPHICS (VARIABLE NAMES IN PARENTHESES)
Age (birthyr). In what year were you born? (Computed as difference between data collection year and birth year).

Gender (Gender). Are you male or female?

Education (educ). What is the highest level of education you have completed?

Income (faminc). Thinking back over the last year, what was your family's annual income?

Political Ideology (ideo5). In general, how would you describe your own political viewpoint?

Party Identification (pid3). Generally speaking, do you think of yourself as a Democrat, Republican, Independent, or Another (Other open [pid3_t]) party, or are you not sure?

Strength of Party Identification (pid7).

Political Interest (newsint). Some people seem to follow what's going on in government and public affairs most of the time, whether there's an election going on or not. Others aren't that interested. [How oftent] Would you say you follow what's going on in government and public affairs . . .

TEA PARTY FAVORABILITY (CCES 2010, CCES 2012)

CC424. Tea Party Opinion. What is your view of the Tea Party movement—would you say it is very positive, somewhat positive, neutral, somewhat negative, or very negative or don't you know enough about the Tea Party movement to say?

AFFIRMATIVE ACTION (CCES 2010, 2012)

CC327. Affirmative action programs give preference to racial minorities in employment and college admissions in order to correct for past discrimination. Do you support or oppose affirmative action?

IMMIGRATION (CCES 2010, 2012, 2016, 2018)

What do you think the US government should do about immigration? Select all that apply:

Border Patrols

CC322_4. Increase the number of border patrols on the US-Mexican border. (CCES 2010)

Deny Citizenship

CC322_6. Deny automatic citizenship to American-born children of illegal immigrants. (CCES 2012)

Police Profiling (CCES 2010, 2012)

CC322_5 / CC322_3. Allow police to question anyone they think may be in the country illegally.

Grant Legal Status (CCES 2010, 2012, 2016)

CC322_2. / CC322_1 / CC16_331_1. Grant legal status to all illegal immigrants who have held jobs and paid taxes for at least 3 years, and not been convicted of any felony crimes.

Deportation

CC16_331_7. Identify and deport illegal immigrants. (CCES 2016)

CC18_322f. Send to prison any person who has been deported from the United States and reenters the United States. (CCES 2018)

DACA policy

CC18_322b. Provide legal status to children of immigrants who are already in the United States and were brought to the United States by their parents. Provide these children the option of citizenship in 10 years if they meet citizenship requirements and commit no crimes. (DACA). (CCES 2018)

(CC18_322d_new). What do you think the US government should do about immigration? Do you support or oppose each of the following? . . . Grant legal status to DACA children, spend $25 billion to build the border wall, and reduce legal immigration by eliminating the visa lottery and ending family-based migration. (CCES 2018)

PRESIDENTIAL JOB APPROVAL

We'd now like to ask you some questions about the people who represent you in Washington DC and in your state. Do you approve of the way each is doing their job . . .

CC308a President Obama (CCES2010, CCES2012)

CONGRESS—JOB APPROVAL

CC16_308b. Do you approve or disapprove of the way each is doing their job . . . The US Congress (CCES 2016)

CC18_308b. Do you approve or disapprove of the way each is doing their job . . . The US Congress (CCES 2018)

SUPREME COURT—JOB APPROVAL

CC16_308c. Do you approve or disapprove of the way each is doing their job . . .
The US Supreme Court (CCES 2016)

CC18_308c. Do you approve or disapprove of the way each is doing their job . . .
The US Supreme Court (CCES 2018)

CANDIDATE PREFERENCE

Obama-Romney Vote (CC354b). For which candidate for President of the
United States did you vote? (CCES 2012)

Trump-Clinton Vote (CC18_317). In the election for US President, who did you
vote for? (CCES 2018)

2012 CCES (Team A Content)

Felon Voting Rights (WIL14). Do you think US citizens convicted of a felony,
currently now ON PROBATION should have the right to vote?

2016 CCES

MODERN RACISM (CCES2016-TEAM A CONTENT)

MR1: Discrimination against African Americans is no longer a problem in the
United States.

MR2: It is easy to understand the anger of African Americans.

MR3: African Americans are too demanding in their push for equal rights.

MR4: African Americans should not push themselves where they are not
wanted.

MR5: Over the past few years, African Americans have gotten more economically than they deserve.

2018 CCES

JUST-WORLD BELIEFS

UND381_1. Society is set up so that people usually get what they deserve.

UND381_3. Everyone has a fair shot at wealth and happiness.

SYSTEM JUSTIFICATION

UND381_2. We must work hard to defend and preserve the way things are.

UND381_4. Our values and beliefs are constantly under attack.

PERCEPTIONS OF RACE RELATIONS

CC18_422a. White people in the US have certain advantages because of the color of their skin.

CC18_422b. Racial problems in the US are rare, isolated situations.

WHITE IDENTITY

UND380_1. My racial identity is an important part of who I am.

GUN REGULATION POLICY

CC18_320a. On the issue of gun regulation, are you for or against each of the following proposals? . . . Background checks for all sales, including at gun shows and over the Internet.

REPEAL AFFORDABLE CARE ACT

CC18_327c. Thinking now about health care policy, would you support or oppose each of the following proposals? . . . Repeal the entire Affordable Care Act.

FEELINGS ABOUT ELECTING SPECIFIC CANDIDATES—EXPERIMENT

(DEM_FORM). Randomization Variable

Now, we'd like you to think about recent presidential election contests.

DEM6a. How good or bad is it that any eligible person can be elected president?

DEM6b. How good or bad is it that someone like Barack Obama can be elected president?

DEM6c. How good or bad is it that someone like Hillary Clinton can be elected president?

DEM6d. How good or bad is it that someone like Donald Trump can be elected president?

DEM6e. How good or bad is it that someone like Mitt Romney can be elected president?

Chapter 5

PREFERENCE FOR THE PAST (WD3C)

The United States of the past is a much better place than the United States of the future. (2016 CCES).

MAKE AMERICA GREAT AGAIN LIST EXPERIMENT (2016 CCES)

Randomization Variable for the Experiment (LIST1_Form).

List1a. Donald Trump frequently uses the slogan, "Make America Great Again." When Donald Trump says "Make America Great Again," how many of these things do you think he is referring to?

List1a.

1. When America held a stronger military presence in the world
2. When politicians followed the voice of their constituents
3. When government was not involved in regulating business
   (In the box below, please insert the number of things from the list that you think Donald Trump is referring to.)

List1b.

1. When America held a stronger military presence in the world
2. When politicians followed the voice of their constituents
3. When government was not involved in regulating business
4. When people knew their place and accepted responsibility
   (In the box below, please insert the number of things from the list that you think Donald Trump is referring to.)

List1c.

1. When America held a stronger military presence in the world
2. When politicians followed the voice of their constituents
3. When government was not involved in regulating business
4. When African Americans knew their place and accepted responsibility
   (In the box below, please insert the number of things from the list that you think Donald Trump is referring to.)

SOCIAL DOMINANCE ORIENTATION (RANDOMIZE ½ "EVERYONE/PEOPLE"; ½ "RACIAL GROUPS")

SD_FORM—Randomization variable for Social Dominance Item Experiment

SD1—Our society should do whatever is necessary to make sure that [everyone | racial groups] has an equal opportunity to succeed.

SD2—We have gone too far in pushing equal rights [(blank) | for racial groups] in this country.

SD3—One of the big problems in this country is that we don't give [everyone | racial groups] an equal chance.

SD4—This country would be better off if we worried less about how equal [people | racial groups] are.

Chapter 6

2012 CCES (Team B Content)

ECONOMIC BLAME EXPERIMENT

CPC51_CPC52_treat. Treatment Variable for Groups

CPC51. Question Text: How much do you blame _____ for any economic difficulties or hardships you might be having these days?

CPC52. Question Text: How much do you blame _____ for economic difficulties or hardships the nation is having?

CCES 2010 / 2012

CLIMATE CHANGE OPINION

CC321. From what you know about global climate change or global warming, which one of the following statements comes closest to your opinion?

1. Global climate change has been established as a serious problem, and immediate action is necessary.
2. There is enough evidence that climate change is taking place and some action should be taken.
3. We don't know enough about global climate change, and more research is necessary before we take any actions.
4. Concern about global climate change is exaggerated. No action is necessary.
5. Global climate change is not occurring; this is not a real issue.

TAX POLICY

CC18_325g. Would you support or oppose reducing the corporate tax rate from 39 percent to 21 percent?

Chapter 7

2016 CCES

POLITICAL THREAT EXPERIMENT

WD96. Rights and freedoms include things like free speech, voting, religious practices, and protections from unlawful searches and seizures. Do you think [Insert Target] poses an immediate threat to the rights and freedoms of ordinary citizens, or not?

1. Federal Government
2. President Obama
3. Congress
4. Supreme Court

SCHADENFREUDE TOWARD OBAMA EXPERIMENT

Randomization of Valence Experiment Variable (SCHAD_Form).

Please indicate how you generally feel about each of the following: Very happy to see, Happy to see, No Feeling, Unhappy to see, or Very unhappy to see . . .

SCHAD1A/1B. Barack Obama being identified as one of the [best | worst] presidents in history.

SCHAD2A/2B. Barack Obama's foreign policy [accomplishments | failures].

SCHAD4A/4B. The economic [successes | failures] under Barack Obama's leadership as president.

SCHAD5A/5B. The [successes | failures] of President Obama's healthcare legislation.

Chapter 8

2016 CCES

AFRICAN AMERICANS' RESENTMENT TOWARD WHITES

RR1. Whites have benefited more from their race than they are willing to admit.

RR2. I resent the fact that Whites think racism does not exist.

RR3. I get irritated when Whites claim they experience the same discrimination as African Americans.

RR4. Whites are given the benefit of the doubt more often than African Americans.

RR5. Whites do not see how their skin color gives them certain privileges that African Americans do not have.

RR6. I resent when Whites say they have worked hard for what they have in life.

RR7. Whites think they are more deserving of rights than African Americans.

RR8. I believe White people are always judging me negatively.

RR9. Whites get away with offenses that African Americans would never get away with.

RR10. Whites overlook that they tend to prefer their own group members.

RR11. Whites tend to dismiss the current effects of racism and discrimination on African Americans.

RR12. Most Whites would prefer to see African Americans fail.

RR13. On average, Whites do not give African Americans credit for their successes.

RR14. I resent when Whites deny the existence of racial discrimination.

RR15. Generations of White privilege have created conditions that make it difficult for African Americans to work their way out of the lower class.

RR16. If Whites would only try harder they could ensure African Americans are just as well off as Whites.

RR17. Without working very hard, Whites have gotten more than they deserve.

RR18. Whites do not go to great lengths to understand the problems African Americans face.

RR19. Even when African Americans work hard to succeed, Whites still view them in lesser terms.

RR20. When an African American is promoted over a White person, the White person will claim it's due to race.

WHITE PRIVILEGE

There are aspects of life where some Whites experience societal privileges beyond what is commonly experienced by non-White people under the same social, political, or economic circumstances. Look at the list below and please indicate the extent to which Whites are privileged in each of the areas on the list. Generally speaking . . .

Priv1. Whites have better chances to get housing loans than African Americans.

Priv3. Whites receive better treatment from medical providers.

Priv9. Whites are given lower sentences than Blacks for the same offenses.

Priv10. Whites are being paid higher than African Americans for the same job.

SUPPORT FOR DEMOCRATIC PRACTICES

The foundation of American democracy is based on a series of cherished ideas about how leaders should be elected. How much do you support or oppose each of the following ideas about democratic values:

DEM1. The notion of majority rule

DEM2. The practice of free and fair elections

DEM3. The rule of 1 person, 1 vote

OBAMA APPROVAL

CC16_320a. Do you approve of the way each is doing their job . . . President Obama

STATE POLICY PRIORITIES

State legislatures must make choices when making spending decisions on important state programs.

Would you like your legislature to increase or decrease spending on the four areas below?

CC16_426_1 Welfare

CC16_426_2 Health Care

CC16_426_3 Education

CC16_426_4 Law Enforcement

IMMIGRATION

What do you think the US government should do about immigration? Select all that apply.

CC16_331_1. Grant legal status to all illegal immigrants who have held jobs and paid taxes for at least 3 years, and not been convicted of any felony crimes.

CC16_331_3. Grant legal status to people who were brought to the US illegally as children, but who have graduated from a US high school.

LAW ENFORCEMENT & CRIMINAL JUSTICE

CC16_307. Do the police make you feel . . . Mostly safe, Somewhat safe, Somewhat unsafe, or Mostly unsafe.

CC16_334a. Do you support or oppose each of the following proposals? . . . Eliminate mandatory minimum sentences for non-violent drug offenders.

CC16_427_b. Thinking now about your local community, how would you grade the following . . . The police.

2016 Pilot Study

AFRICAN AMERICANS' RESENTMENT TOWARD WHITES

Q2_4 2. White people get away with offenses that African Americans would never get away with.

Q1_1 1. White people have benefited more from their race than they are willing to admit.

Q1_4 1. In most instances, White people are given the benefit of the doubt more often than African Americans.

Q3_1 3. White people tend to dismiss the current effects of racism and discrimination on African Americans.

Q4_3 4. White people do not go to great lengths to understand the problems African Americans face.

Q3_5 3. Generations of White privilege have created conditions that make it difficult for African Americans to work their way out of the lower class.

Q2_5 2. White people overlook that they tend to prefer their own group members.

Q3_2 3. Most White people would prefer to see African Americans fail.

Q2_3 2. I believe White people are always judging me negatively.

Q4_2 4. Most White people blame their professional shortcomings on African Americans.

Q3_3 3. On average, White people do not give African Americans credit for their successes.

Q2_2 2. White people think they are more deserving of rights than African Americans.

Q4_4 4. Even when African Americans work hard to succeed, White people still view them in lesser terms.

Q4_5 4. When an African American person is promoted over a White person, the White person will claim it is because of race.

Q4_1 4. If White people would only try harder, they could ensure African Americans are just as well off as Whites.

Q2_1 2. I feel resentful towards White people when they accuse African Americans of not working hard enough.

Q2_6 2. I feel resentful towards White people when they accuse African Americans of wanting to live off welfare.

Q1_6 1. I feel resentful toward White people when they say that racism against African Americans does not exist.

Q3_4 3. I resent when White people deny the existence of racial discrimination.

Q1_3 1. I get irritated when White people claim they experience the same discrimination as African Americans.

Q1_2 1. White people do not think racism exists anymore.

Q1_5 1. White people do not see how their skin color gives them certain privileges that African Americans do not have.

PRESIDENTIAL CANDIDATE SUPPORT

HORSERACE If the presidential election were being held TODAY, would you vote for the Republican ticket of Donald Trump and Mike Pence, for the Democratic ticket of Hillary Clinton and Tim Kaine, for the Libertarian Party ticket headed by Gary Johnson, or the Green Party ticket headed by Jill Stein?

FEELING THERMOMETER/SOCIAL DISTANCE

Feelings toward Whites (FTwht). Where 0 IS VERY COLD AND DISTANT, and 10 IS VERY WARM AND CLOSE, please indicate how you feel toward WHITE PERSONS in this country.

POLITICAL PREDISPOSITIONS

Ideology (Ideo). In general, would you describe your political views as . . . Very Conservative to Very Liberal.

Party Identification (PartyID). In politics TODAY, do you consider yourself a Republican, Democrat, Independent, or something else in the list below?

GROUP SOLIDARITY

Blkpol_3. How much do you agree or disagree with the following statements. Please read each carefully . . . African Americans should shop in African American owned stores whenever possible.

GROUP INFLUENCE

Blkinfl. How much influence do you believe that AFRICAN AMERICANS have in running the country?

GROUP LINKED FATE

Afamfate. How much is YOUR LIFE affected by what generally happens to African Americans in this country?

Notes

Chapter One

1. A Lexis-Nexis search of US newspapers and magazines from 1960 to 2020 shows a dramatic and monotonic increase in 2008 in headlines and articles mentioning White anger, racial resentment, political correctness, and Whites' disadvantage. We take this as an indicator of a growing concern among Whites of their perceived threat to their privilege, power, and status.

2. Data obtained from the 2016 American National Election Study.

3. Recent works by Hochschild (2016), *Strangers in Their Own Land: Anger and Mourning on the American Right*, and Metzl (2019), *Dying of Whiteness: How the Politics of Racial Resentment Is Killing America's Heartland*, detail catastrophic consequences of such beliefs. Whereas these works, perhaps prematurely, assume racial resentment is the best descriptor of Whites' sentiment toward politics today, our book establishes it empirically.

4. Another race-neutral analytical framework such as social dominance theory (SDT) offers tremendous insight into politics today (Ahmadian, Azarshahi, and Paulhus 2017; Choma and Hanoch 2017; Crowson and Brandes 2017; Pettigrew 2017; Womick et al. 2019), but such a framework has not been as widely adopted and available in political science as racial resentment. In fact, racial resentment has been the most prominent analytical framework for understanding racial prejudice for the past 30 years.

5. The term "racial resentment" itself became ingrained in our lexicon in the 1990s as journalists and politicians used it to depict David Duke's appeal among individual voters.

Chapter Two

1. The measurement of individualism items have consistently low psycho-metric properties (e.g., Feldman and Huddy 2005; Sears and Henry 2003). This might be part of the problem in investigating the role individualism plays in ra-cial resentment.

2. The latest version of this survey item (e.g., ANES 2008) replaces "Irish, Italians, Jews, and Other Minorities" with simply "Other Minorities." All items also replaced "Blacks" with "African Americans."

3. The following percentages of Blacks agreed or strongly agreed with the item: 1986–42.9% (n=156), 1988–52.8% (n=212), 1990–39.2% (n=125), 1992–49.1% (n=285), 1994–48.2% (n=195), 2000–46.0% (n=159), and 2006–44.2% (n=163).

Chapter Four

1. Measured on the traditional 7-point scale.

2. We are mindful that several scholars have proposed measures of both concepts with varying degrees of success. Due to space constraints in the 2018 CCES, we had to compromise between including one 4-item measure or at-tempting to measure both with two items. We decided that it was better to have at least two indicators of a just world and system justification. A belief in a just world is measured by two survey items: "Society is set up so that people get what they deserve" and "Our values are constantly under attack." System justification is also measured by two survey items: "We must work hard to preserve things as they are" and "Everyone has a fair shot at wealth and happiness."

3. In keeping with previous work, White identity is measured by a single item, "How often do you think about being White?"

4. Every generation can probably identify a president who falls short of ex-pectations, but such a moniker has been recently applied to President George H. W. Bush.

5. An important caveat in this research is that Conway et al. (2018) created a Left-Wing Authoritarianism scale (LWA) to reflect an appeal to liberal authori-tarian leaders as opposed to using the traditional Right-Wing Authoritarianism (RWA) measure.

Chapter Five

1. Extensive research has examined priming, framing, and persuasive mes-sages in political campaigns (Kenski and Jamieson 2017), though we are not aware of research on political slogans per se.

2. "Again" means to return to a previous position or condition in a specified or unspecified period or era. The exclusion of a specific time period gives the slogan power, coding, and deniability.

3. Aberbach and Walker (1970) showed that African Americans and Whites interpreted the "Black Power" slogan very differently. While the vast majority of Whites were hostile to the concept, interpreting it as illegitimate and vengeful, African Americans were almost evenly divided in their interpretations. Thus, political slogans may elicit different emotions among African Americans as well as across racial categories.

4. In a content analysis of the issues associated with *Make America Great Again* in Trump's tweets from June 1, 2014, to April 30, 2017 (n=1,084), we found that the slogan was not linked to any particular issue. Trump's use of the slogan in his tweets ranged from the economy, campaign appearances, endorsements, immigration, media criticism, and inauguration. No tweets were found that either implicitly or explicitly linked the slogan to a racial issue. During this period, 20 percent of Trump's tweets associated the slogan with polling results that mostly showed his increasing popularity. Results are available from the authors upon request.

5. This analysis is not included because our racial resentment measure was not included in the data.

6. It is important to note that we do not treat Whites' racial resentment the same as African Americans' racial resentment. African Americans' resentment toward Whites is a belief that Whites benefit unfairly from racial discrimination, which is perceived to keep African Americans relegated to a lower status. Chapter 8 is devoted entirely to this concept.

Chapter Six

1. This is in reference to a comparable analysis of attribution of responsibility for the state of the economy and the classic measurement of racial resentment using ANES data. For example, in the 2012 ANES, respondents were asked: "How much is [subject] to blame for the poor economic conditions of the past several years?" The targets under consideration were President Obama, former President Bush, Democrats in Congress, Republicans in Congress, Wall Street bankers, consumers who borrowed too much money, and mortgage lenders.

2. http://www.miamiherald.com/news/state/florida/article125325319.html#story link=cpy.

3. John M. Broder, "Obama Affirms Climate Change Goals," *New York Times*, November 18, 2008. http://www.nytimes.com/2008/11/19/us/politics/19climate.html.

4. These numbers were obtained from Gallup. http://www.gallup.com/poll/
1615/environment.aspx.

Chapter Seven

1. In our view of schadenfreude, the deservingness of misfortune holds no expectation of extreme or harsh acts, and the suffering need not have extended du-
ration. Also, the person experiencing schadenfreude does not need to know the
full consequence of the misfortune for the individual; they simply need to view
the misfortune as a deserved aspect of a prior injustice (e.g., getting an undeserved scholarship due to racial background). Thus, when we refer to misfortune, it is not only limited to violence, torture, imprisonment, death, natural di-
saster, or other crippling events; an "other" simply not getting what they hope to
get is enough (e.g., losing an election, having an initiative fail, being heckled).

2. There may be exceptions to the ability to reverse resentment. For example, one might learn about errors in the perceived facts (e.g., there was no cheating) or find out more details about another's circumstances (e.g., a person actually worked hard, but there was an error in the process of recording the effort).
The point is that the process of deservingness appraisal and resentment typically
occur in an automatic fashion through the use of cognitive shortcuts about a person, their attributes, or other facts related to a situation. Once one resents another, it is difficult to pull the resentment back.

3. We did not believe that respondents would comprehend the meaning of the
"status quo." So, we intentionally broadened the factors under threat to encompass aspects of the status quo.

4. We are mindful that such a procedure is somewhat arbitrary, though not any
more arbitrary than other procedures. As a result, we view the results as cursory.

5. Principal components factor analysis of the four items resulted in a highly
reliable scale; the analysis produced one factor with an eigenvalue of 3.33 and .83
explained variance. Each item loaded on the first factor at .87 or greater.

Chapter Eight

1. See Hagner and Pierce (1984) for a similar discussion regarding levels of
conceptualization.

2. We examined the extent to which these results were an aberrant feature
of the items or measure of racial resentment. The remaining individual racial
resentment items from table 8.1 were analyzed by comparing them to standard
demographic items. Overall, the results of these analyses similarly show that
the racial resentment items are uncorrelated to education, gender, income, age,

homeownership, and church attendance. There are only a few instances where some of those factors become positive and statistically significant. Thus, we find such analyses convincing and supportive of our inferences.

3. "In the past year, have you attended a local political meeting (such as school board or city council)?", "In the past year, have you put up a political sign (such as a lawn sign or bumper sticker)?", and "In the past year, have you worked for a candidate or campaign?" are used as indicators of political participation.

4. To measure the support for various policies, we used "Do you support increasing or decreasing state spending on welfare?", "Do you support increasing or decreasing state spending on health care?", "Do you support increasing or decreasing state spending on education?", and "Do you support increasing or decreasing state spending on law enforcement?"

5. We used the following survey questions to assess attitudes toward the police and criminal justice: "Do the police make you feel safe?", "Do you support or oppose the following proposal: eliminating mandatory minimum sentences for non-violent drug offenders?", "Do you support or oppose the following proposal: increasing prison sentences for felons who have already committed two or more serious or violent crimes?", and "How would you grade the local police?"

Chapter Nine

1. This was not the only conspiracy theory, to be sure. Many believed President Trump was a hero safeguarding the world from a "deep state" cabal of Satan-worshipping pedophiles, Democratic politicians, and Hollywood celebrities who run a global sex-trafficking ring, harvesting the blood of children for life-sustaining chemicals.

2. Claims of election fraud have been alleged by Republicans in previous elections. Thus, when Trump started to claim in the summer that mail-in ballots would lead to fraud and cost him the election, few Republicans objected. President Trump claimed that "millions voted illegally" costing him the popular vote in 2016, though no systematic fraud was discovered.

3. Convening the Electoral College was considered ceremonial. States' electoral votes had already been certified. Because there was no way to invalidate states electoral votes, the Capitol insurrection was viewed as coup de tete, an overthrow of America, and challenge to democratic governance.

Appendix: Description of Data

1. The three modes have roughly the same expected proportion of respondents ($\chi2[df=8]=7.5$, n.s.); however, males were more likely than females to be as-

signed to the paper-pencil mode ($\chi2[df=2]=8.5$, p<.05). This statistically significant result may be due to the paper-pencil mode's larger sample (i.e., it barely reaches statistical significance). A final validation check was run on a 7-point ideology scale, and the results reveal no significant differences in self-reported ideology across mode of data collection ($F[2,555]=.16$, n.s.).

To rule out mode effects we ran a comparison of means across each of the resentment measures. None of the scales—RRS ($F(2,545)=.74$, n.s.), MRS ($F(2,531)=1.1$, n.s.) or EXR ($F(2,551)=.71$, n.s.)—show statistically significant differences across the mode of data collection. Based on the accumulated findings of these tests we are confident that the three mode data sets can be combined to form a single file.

2. "Registered voter" identification is based on a self-report. The political geographic strata are early primary battleground (FL, WI, PA, IA, NH, MN, NM, NV, and OH) and non-battleground (all other) states. The sampling frame was designed by YouGov Polimetrix using target estimates based on the 2007 American Community Study (ACS) conducted by the Census Bureau. Sample targets were created within each stratum according to age, race, gender, education, and voter registration battleground/non-battleground state location. While the data contain sample design weights, our analyses are unweighted because of our experimental design and our focus on measurement.

3. The baseline study (wave 1) took place 12/17/07 to 1/3/08; wave 2 took place 1/24/08–2/4/08; wave 3 took place 3/21/08–4/14/08; wave 4 took place 9/17/08–9/29/08; wave 5 took place 10/22/08–11/3/08; and the post-election study (wave 6) took place 11/5/08–12/1/08.

4. Fourteen respondents did not have a code for their interview mode.

Appendix: Chapter Eight

1. Further information about the Federated panel is located at https://luc.id/federatedsample/.

References

Aberbach, Joel D., and Jack L. Walker. 1970. "The Meaning of Black Power: A Comparison of White and Black Interpretations of a Political Slogan." *American Political Science Review* 64: 367–388.

Adorno, Theodor W., Else Frenkel-Brunswik, Daniel J. Levinson, R. Nevitt Sanford, and Betty Aron. 1950. *The Authoritarian Personality.* New York: W. W. Norton Company.

Ahmadian, Sara, Sara Azarshahi, and Delroy L. Paulhus. 2017. "Explaining Donald Trump via Communication Style: Grandiosity, Informality, and Dynamism." *Personality and Individual Differences* 107: 49–53.

Alexander, Michelle. 2012. *The New Jim Crow: Mass Incarceration in the Age of Colorblindness.* New York: The New Press.

Allen, Richard L., Michael C. Dawson, and Ronald E. Brown. 1989. "A Schema-Based Approach to Modeling an African-American Racial Belief System." *American Political Science Review* 83: 421–441.

Allport, Gordon. 1954. *The Nature of Prejudice.* Reading, MA: Addison-Wesley.

Altemeyer, Bob. 1981. *Right-Wing Authoritarianism.* Winnipeg: University of Manitoba Press.

Andre, Michael, A. Aufrichtig, G. Beltran, M. Bloch, L. Buchanan, A. Chavez, N. Cohn, M. Conlen, A. Daniel, A. Elkeurti, A. Fischer, J. Holder, W. Houp, J. Huang, J. Katz, A. Krolik, J. C. Lee, R. Lieberman, I. Marcus, J. Patel, C. Smart, B. Smithgall, U. Syam, R. Taylor, M. Watkins, and I. White. 2020. "National Exit Polls: How Different Groups Voted." November 3. https://www.nytimes.com/interactive/2020/11/03/us/elections/exit-polls-president.html.

Andrich, David. 1978. "Application of a Psychometric Rating Model to Ordered Categories Which Are Scored with Successive Integers." *Applied Psychological Measurement* 2: 581–594.

Anonymous Authors. 2007. *The Big Book of Alcoholics Anonymous: The Story of How Many Thousands of Men and Women Have Recovered from Alcoholism*. 4th ed. New York: Benei Noaj.

Aquino, Karl, Americus Reed II, Stefan Thau, and Dan Freeman. 2007. "A Grotesque and Dark Beauty: How Moral Identity and Mechanisms of Moral Disengagement Influence Cognitive and Emotional Reactions to War." *Journal of Experimental Social Psychology* 43: 385–392.

Arbuckle, James L. 2014. Amos (version 23.0) [computer program]. Chicago: IBM SPSS.

Azevedo, Flavio, John T. Jost, and Tobias Rothmund. 2017. "'Making America Great Again': System Justification in the U.S. Presidential Election of 2016." *Translational Issues in Psychological Science* 3: 231–240.

Badaan, Vivienne, and John T. Jost. 2020. "Conceptual, Empirical, and Practical Problems with the Claim that Intolerance, Prejudice, and Discrimination Are Equivalent on the Political Left and Right." *Current Opinion in Behavioral Sciences* 34: 229–238.

Bai, Hui, and Christopher M. Federico. 2019. "Collective Existential Threat Mediates White Population Decline's Effect on Defensive Reactions." *Group Processes and Intergroup Relations* 23 (3): 136843021983976. Online.

Bandura, Albert. 1999. "Moral Disengagement in the Perpetration of Inhumanities." *Personality and Social Psychology Review* 3: 193–209.

Bandura, Albert. 2002. "Selective Moral Disengagement in the Exercise of Moral Agency." *Journal of Moral Education* 31 (2): 101–119.

Bandura, Albert. 2016. *Moral Disengagement: How People Do Harm and Live with Themselves*. New York: Worth Publishers.

Bandura, Albert, Claudio Barbaranelli, Gian Vittorio Caprara, and Concetta Pastorelli. 1996. "Mechanisms of Moral Disengagement in the Exercise of Moral Agency." *Journal of Personality and Social Psychology* 71: 364–374.

Bandura, Albert, Gian V. Caprara, Claudio Barbaranelli, Concetta Pastorelli, and Camillo Regalia. 2001. "Sociocognitive Self-Regulatory Mechanisms Governing Transgressive Behavior." *Journal of Personality and Social Psychology* 80: 125–135.

Banton, Michael P. 1987. *Racial Theories*. Cambridge: Cambridge University Press.

Barbalet, J. 1998. *Emotion, Social Theory, and Social Structure: A Macrosociological Approach*. Cambridge: Cambridge University Press.

Barbalet, Jack. 2001. *Emotion, Social Theory, and Social Structure: A Macrosociological Approach*. Cambridge: Cambridge University Press.

Barclay, Laurie J., Daniel P. Skarlicki, and S. Douglas Pugh. 2005. "Exploring the Role of Emotions in Injustice Perceptions and Retaliation." *Journal of Applied Psychology* 90: 629–643.

Bartels, Larry M. 2002. "Beyond the Running Tally: Partisan Bias in Political Perceptions." *Political Behavior* 24: 117–150.

Benegal, Salil D. 2018. "The Spillover of Race and Racial Attitudes into Public Opinion about Climate Change." *Environmental Politics* 27: 733–756.

Bentler, P. M. 1990. "Comparative Fit Indexes in Structural Models." *Psychological Bulletin* 107: 238–246.

Blum, Lawrence. 2002. *"I'm Not a Racist but . . .": The Moral Quandary of Race.* Ithaca, NY: Cornell University Press.

Blumer, Herbert. 1958. "Race Prejudice as a Sense of Group Position." *Pacific Sociological Review* 1: 3–7.

Bobo, Lawrence. 1983. "Whites' Opposition to Busing: Symbolic Racism or Realistic Group Conflict?" *Journal of Personality and Social Psychology* 45: 1196–1210.

Bobo, Lawrence D. 1988a. "Attitudes toward the Black Political Movement: Trends, Meaning, and Effects on Racial Policy Preferences." *Social Psychology Quarterly* 51: 287–302.

Bobo, Lawrence D. 1988b. "Group Conflict, Prejudice, and the Paradox of Contemporary Racial Attitudes." In *Eliminating Racism: Profiles in Controversy,* edited by P. A. Katz and D. A. Taylor, 85–114. New York: Plenum.

Bobo, Lawrence D. 1999. "Prejudice as Group Position: Microfoundations of a Sociological Approach to Racism and Race Relations." *Journal of Social Issues* 55: 445–472.

Bobo, Lawrence, and Vincent L. Hutchings. 1996. "Perceptions of Racial Group Competition: Extending Blumer's Theory of Group Position to a Multiracial Social Context." *American Sociological Review* 61: 951–972.

Bobo, Lawrence, and James R. Kluegel. 1993. "Opposition to Race-Targeting: Self-Interest, Stratification Ideology, or Racial Attitudes?" *American Sociological Review* 58: 443–464.

Bobo, Lawrence, and Mia Tuan. 2006. *Prejudice in Politics: Group Position, Public Opinion, and the Wisconsin Treaty Rights Dispute.* Cambridge, MA: Harvard University Press.

Bonilla-Silva, Eduardo. 2018. *Racism without Racists: Color-Blind Racism and the Persistence of Racial Inequality in America.* 5th ed. Oxford: Rowan and Littlefield.

Bothwell, Robert K., and John C. Brigham. 1983. "Selective Evaluation and Recall during the 1980 Reagan-Carter Debate." *Journal of Applied Psychology* 13: 427–442.

Boush, David M. 1993. "How Advertising Slogans Can Prime Evaluations of Brand Extensions." *Psychology & Marketing* 10: 67–78.

Brand, Jeffrey S. 1994. "The Supreme Court, Equal Protection and Jury Selection: Denying That Race Still Matters." *Wisconsin Law Review* 511–584.

Brandt, M. J., and C. Reyna. 2011. "Stereotypes as Attributions." In *Psychology of Stereotypes,* edited by E. L. Simon, 47–80. Hauppauge, NY: Nova.

Brezina, T., and K. Winder. 2003. "Economic Disadvantage, Status Generalization, and Negative Racial Stereotyping by White Americans." *Social Psychology Quarterly* 66: 402–418.

Brigham, John C. 1994. "College Students' Racial Attitudes." *Journal of Applied Social Psychology* 23:1933–1967.

Brown, M. W., and R. Cudeck. 1993. "Alternate ways of Assessing Model Fit." In *Testing Structural Equation Models*, edited by K. A. Bollen and J. S. Long, 136–162. Newbury Park, CA: Sage.

Brulle, Robert J., Jason Carmichael, and J. Craig Jenkins. 2012. "Shifting Public Opinion on Climate Change: An Empirical Assessment of Factors Influencing Concern over Climate Change in the U.S., 2002–2010." *Climatic Change* 114: 169–188.

Caldeira, Gregory A., and James L. Gibson. 1992. "The Etiology of Public Support for the Supreme Court." *American Journal of Political Science* 36: 635–664.

Callaghan, Karen, and Nayda Terkildsen. 2002. "Understanding the Role of Race in Candidate Evaluation." *Political Decision Making, Deliberation and Participation* 6: 51–95.

Campbell, Angus, Philip E. Converse, Warren E. Miller, and Donald E. Stokes. 1960. *The American Voter.* New York: John Wiley and Sons.

Campbell, Troy H., and Aaron C. Kay. 2014. "Solution Aversion: On the Relation Between Ideology and Motivated Disbelief." *Journal of Personality and Social Psychology* 5: 809–824.

Carmines, Edward G., Paul M. Sniderman, and Beth C. Easter. 2011. "On the Meaning, Measurement, and Implications of Racial Resentment." *Annals of the American Academy of Political and Social Science* 634: 98–116.

Carmines, Edward G., and James A. Stimson. 1980. "The Two Faces of Issue Voting." *American Political Science Review* 74: 78–91.

Carney, Riley K., and Ryan D. Enos. 2017. "Conservatism and Fairness in Contemporary Politics: Unpacking the Psychological Underpinnings of Modern Racism." Paper presented at NYU CESS Experiments Conference, New York.

Cassese, Erin C., Tiffany D. Barnes, and Regina P. Branton. 2015. "Racializing Gender: Public Opinion at the Intersection." *Politics and Gender* 11: 1–26.

Ceccarelli, Leah M. 1998. "Polysemy: Multiple Meanings in Rhetorical Criticism." *Quarterly Journal of Speech* 84: 395–415.

Chang, Edward C., and Edward H. Ritter. 1976. "Ethnocentrism in Black College Students." *Journal of Social Psychology* 100: 89–98.

Chen, Philip, and Ruchika Mohanty. 2018. "Obama's Economy: Conditional Racial Spillover into Evaluations of the Economy." *International Journal of Public Opinion Research* 30: 365–390.

Chester, David S., and C. Nathan DeWall. 2016. "The Pleasure of Revenge: Retaliatory Aggression Arises from a Neural Imbalance toward Reward." *Social Cognition and Affective Neuroscience* 7: 1173–1182.

Child, Dennis. 2006. *The Essentials of Factor Analysis*. 3rd ed. New York: Continuum International.

Choma, Becky L., and Yaniv Hanoch. 2017. "Cognitive Ability and Authoritarianism: Understanding Support for Trump and Clinton." *Personality and Individual Differences* 106: 287–291.

Chong, Dennis, and Reuel Rogers. 2005. "Racial Solidarity and Political Participation." *Political Behavior* 27: 347–374.

Cikara, Mina, and Susan T. Fiske. 2012. "Stereotypes and Schadenfreude: Affective and Physiological Markers of Pleasure at Outgroup Misfortunes." *Social Psychological and Personality Science* 3: 63–71.

Combs, David J. Y., Caitlin A. J. Powell, David Ryan Schurtz, and Richard H. Smith. 2009. "Politics, Schadenfreude, and Ingroup Identification: The Sometimes Happy Thing about a Poor Economy and Death." *Journal of Experimental Social Psychology* 45: 635–646.

Comrey, Andrew L., and Howard B. Lee. 1992. *A First Course in Factor Analysis*. 2nd ed. Hillsdale, NJ: Erlbaum.

Conway, Lucian Gideon, III, Shannon C. Houck, Laura Janelle Gornick, and Meredith A. Repke. 2018. "Finding the Loch Ness Monster: Left-Wing Authoritarianism in the United States." *Political Psychology* 39: 1049–1067.

Cose, Ellis. 1993. *The Rage of a Privileged Class: Why Are Middle-Class Blacks Angry? Why Should America Care?* New York: HarperPerenial.

Craig, Maureen A., and Jennifer A. Richeson. 2014. "On the Precipice of a 'Majority-Minority' America: Perceived Status Threat from the Racial Demographic Shift Affects White Americans' Political Ideology." *Psychological Science* 25: 1189–1197.

Cramer, Katherine J. 2016. *The Politics of Resentment: Rural Consciousness in Wisconsin and the Rise of Scott Walker*. Chicago: University of Chicago Press.

Cramer, Katherine. 2020. "Understanding the Role of Racism in Contemporary US Public Opinion." *Annual Review of Political Science* 23: 1–17.

Crawford, Jarret T., Shreya Vodapalli, Ryan E. Stingel, and John Ruscio. 2019. "Do Status-Legitimizing Beliefs Moderate Effects of Racial Progress on Perceptions of Anti-White Bias? A Replication of Wilkins and Kaiserm." *Social Psychological and Personality Science* 10: 768–774.

Cronbach, Lee. 1951. "Coefficient Alpha and the Internal Structure of Tests." *Psychometrika* 16: 297–334.

Cropanzano, Russell, and Robert Folger. 1989. "Referent Cognitions and Task Decision Autonomy: Beyond Equity Theory." *Journal of Applied Psychology* 74: 293–299.

Crowson, Howard Michael, and Joyce A. Brandes. 2017. "Differentiating between Donald Trump and Hillary Clinton Voters Using Facets of Right-Wing Authoritarianism and Social-Dominance Orientation: A Brief Report." *Psychological Reports* 120: 364–373.

Dalbert, Claudia. 2001. *The Justice Motive as a Personal Resource: Dealing with Challenges and Critical Life Events.* New York: Kluwer Academic/Plenum.

Dalbert, Claudia. 2009. "Belief in a Just World." In *Handbook of Individual Differences in Social Behavior,* edited by Mark R. Leary and Rick H. Hoyle, 288–297. New York: Guilford.

Danbold, Felix, and Yuen J. Huo. 2015. "No Longer 'All-American'? Whites' Defensive Reactions to Their Numerical Decline." *Social Psychological and Personality Science* 6: 210–218.

Darley, John M., and Thane S. Pittman. 2003. "The Psychology of Compensatory and Retributive Justice." *Personality and Social Psychology Review* 7: 324–336.

Davis, Darren W. 1995. "Exploring Black Political Intolerance." *Political Behavior* 17: 1–22.

Davis, Darren W. 2007. *Negative Liberty: Public Opinion and the Terrorist Attacks on America.* New York: Russell Sage.

Davis, Darren W., and Brian D. Silver. 2004. "Civil Liberties vs. Security: Public Opinion in the Context of the Terrorist Attacks on America." *American Journal of Political Science* 48: 28–46.

Davis, Darren W., David C. Wilson, and Patricia Moy. 2019. "Decoding Donald Trump's 'Make America Great Again' Slogan." Unpublished manuscript.

Dawson, Michael C. 1994. *Behind the Mule: Race and Class in African American Politics.* Princeton: Princeton University Press.

Dawson, Michael C. 2003. *Black Visions: The Roots of Contemporary African-American Political Ideologies.* Chicago: University of Chicago Press.

DeBell, Matthew. 2017. "Polarized Opinions on Racial Progress and Inequality: Measurement and Application to Affirmative Action Preferences." *Political Psychology* 38: 481–498.

De Cremer, David, Maarten J. J. Wubben, and Lieven Brebels. 2008. "When Unfair Treatment Leads to Anger: The Effects of Other People's Emotions and Ambiguous Unfair Procedures." *Journal of Applied Social Psychology* 38: 2518–2549.

De Quervain, Dominique J. F., Urs Fischbacher, Valerie Treyer, Melanie Schellhammer, Ulrich Schnyder, and Alfred Buck. 2004. "The Neural Basis of Altruistic Punishment." *Science* 305: 1254-1258.

Delgado, Richard, and Jean Stefancic. 1997. *Critical White Studies: Looking behind the Mirror.* Philadelphia: Temple University Press.

Denton, Robert E., Jr. 1980. "The Rhetorical Functions of Slogans: Classification and Characteristics." *Communication Quarterly* 28: 10–18.

Devine, Patricia G. 1989. "Stereotypes and Prejudice: Their Automatic and Controlled Components." *Journal of Personality and Social Psychology* 56: 5–18.

Devine, Patricia G., and Andrew J. Elliot. 1995. "Are Racial Stereotypes Really Fading? The Princeton Trilogy Revisited." *Personality and Social Psychology Bulletin* 21: 1139–1150.

Diedenhofen, Birk, and Jochen Musch. 2016. "cocron: A Web Interface and R Package for the Statistical Comparison of Cronbach's Alpha Coefficients." *International Journal of Internet Science* 11: 51–60.

Dovidio, John F., Nancy Evans, and Richard B. Tyler. 1986. "Racial Stereotypes: The Contents of Their Cognitive Representations." *Journal of Experimental Social Psychology* 22: 22–37.

Dovidio, John F., and Samuel L. Gaertner. 1986. "The Aversive Form of Racism." In *Prejudice, Discrimination and Racism*, edited by J. F. Dovidio and S. L. Gaertner, 61–89. Academic Press.

Dovidio, John F., Samuel L. Gaertner, and Adam R. Pearson. 2005. "On the Nature of Prejudice: The Psychological Foundations of Hate." In *The Psychology of Hate*, edited by Robert J. Sternberg, 211–234. American Psychological Association.

Druckman, James N., Erik Peterson, and Rune Slothuus. 2013. "How Elite Partisan Polarization Affects Public Opinion Formation." *American Political Science Review* 107: 57–79.

Eagly, Alice H., and Amanda B. Diekman. 2005. "What Is the Problem? Prejudice as an Attitude-in-Context." In *On the Nature of Prejudice: Fifty Years after Allport*, edited by John F. Dovidio, Peter Glick, and Laurie A. Rudman. Malden, MA: Blackwell.

Ellison, Christopher G., and Daniel A. Powers. 1994. "The Contact Hypothesis and Racial Attitudes among Black Americans." *Social Science Quarterly* 75:385–400.

Feagin, Joe R., and Melvin P. Sikes. 1994. *Living with Racism: The Black Middle-Class Experience*. Boston: Beacon Press.

Feather, N. T., 1996. "Reactions to Penalties for an Offense in Relation to Authoritarianism, Values, Perceived Responsibility, Perceived Seriousness, and Deservingness." *Journal of Personality and Social Psychology* 71: 571–587.

Feather, Norman T. 1999. "Judgments of Deservingness: Studies in the Psychology of Justice and Achievement." *Personality and Social Psychology Review* 3: 86–107.

Feather, Norman T. 2006. "Deservingness and Emotions: Applying the Structural Model of Deservingness to the Analysis of Affective Reactions to Outcomes." *European Review of Social Psychology* 17: 38–70.

Feather, N. T. 2008. "Perceived Legitimacy of a Promotion Decision in Relation to Deservingness, Entitlement, and Resentment in the Context of Affirmative Action and Performance 1." *Journal of Applied Social Psychology* 38: 1230–1254.

Federico, Christopher M., and Rafael Aguilera. 2019. "The Distinct Pattern of Relationships between the Big Five and Racial Resentment among White Americans." *Social Psychological and Personality Science* 10: 274–284.

Federico, Christopher M., and Jim Sidanius. 2002. "Racism, Ideology, and Affirmative Action Revisited: The Antecedents and Consequences of 'Principled Objections' to Affirmative Action." *Journal of Personality and Social Psychology* 82: 488–502.

Feinberg, Matthew, and Robb Willer. 2011. "Apocalypse Soon? Dire Messages Reduce Belief in Global Warming by Contradicting Just-World Beliefs." *Psychological Science* 22: 34–38.

Feldman, S. 1988. "Structure and Consistency in Public Opinion: The Role of Core Beliefs and Values." *American Journal of Political Science* 32:416–440.

Feldman, Stanley, and Leonie Huddy. 2005. "Racial Resentment and White Opposition to Race-Conscious Programs: Principles or Prejudice?" *American Journal of Political Science* 49: 168–183.

Feldman, Stanley, and Leonie Huddy. 2018. "Racially Motivated Reasoning." In *The Feeling, Thinking Citizen: Essays in Honor of Milton Lodge*, edited by Howard Lavine and Charles S. Taber. New York: Routledge.

Feldt, Leonard S., David J. Woodruff, and Fathi A. Salih. 1987. "Statistical Inference for Coefficient Alpha." *Applied Psychological Measurement* 11: 93–103.

Festinger, Leon. 1957. *A Theory of Cognitive Dissonance*. Evanston, IL: Row, Peterson.

Feygina, Irina, John T. Jost, and Rachel E. Goldsmith. 2010. "System Justification, the Denial of Global Warming, and the Possibility of 'System-Sanctioned Change.'" *Personality and Social Psychology Bulletin* 36: 326–338.

Firebaugh, Glenn, and Kenneth E. Davis. 1988. "Trends in Antiblack Prejudice, 1972–1988: Region and Cohort Effects." *American Journal of Sociology* 94: 251–272.

Flynn, James, Paul Slovic, and C. K. Mertz. 1994. "Gender, Race, and Perception of Environmental Health Risks." *Risk Analysis* 14: 1101–1108.

Folger, Robert. 1986. "A Referent Cognitions Theory of Relative Deprivation." In *Relative Deprivation and Social Comparison: The Ontario Symposium*, vol. 4, edited by James M. Olsen, C. Peter Herman, and Mark P. Zanna, 33–55. London: Psychology Press.

Folger, R., and D. P. Skarlicki. 1998. "When Tough Times Make Tough Bosses: Managerial Distancing as a Function of Layoff Blame." *Academy of Management Journal* 41: 79–87.

Forman, Tyrone A., and Amanda E. Lewis. 2006. "Racial Apathy and Hurricane Katrina: The Social Anatomy of Prejudice in the Post–Civil Rights Era." *Du Bois Review* 3: 175–2002.

Forman, Tyrone A., and Amanda E. Lewis. 2015. "Beyond Prejudice? Young Whites' Racial Attitudes in Post–Civil Rights America, 1976 to 2000." *American Behavioral Scientist* 59: 1394–1428.

Furnham, Adrian. 2003. "Belief in a Just World: Research Progress Over the Past Decade." *Personality and Individual Differences* 34: 795–817.

Furr, Michael R., and Verne R. Bacharach. 2014. *Psychometrics: An Introduction*. 2nd ed. London: Sage.

Gaertner, Samuel L., and John F. Dovidio. 1986. "The Aversive Form of Racism." In *Prejudice, Discrimination, and Racism*, edited by John F. Dovidio and Samuel L. Gaertner, 61–89. New York: Academic Press.

Gaines, Brian J., James H. Kuklinski, Paul J. Quirk, Buddy Peyton, and Jay Verkuilen. 2007. "Same Facts, Different Interpretations: Partisan Motivation and Opinion on Iraq." *Journal of Politics* 69: 957–974.

Gawronski, Bertram. 2012. "Back to the Future of Dissonance Theory: Cognitive Consistency as a Core Motive." *Social Cognition* 30: 652–668.

Gibbard, Allan. 1992. "Moral Concepts: Substance and Sentiment." *Philosophical Perspectives* 6: 199–221.

Gibson, James L. 2008. "Group Identities and Theories of Justice: An Experimental Investigation into the Justice and Injustice of Land Squatting in South Africa." *Journal of Politics* 70: 700–716.

Gibson, James L. 2009. *Overcoming Historical Injustices: Land Reconciliation in South Africa*. Cambridge: Cambridge University Press.

Gibson, James L. 2013. "Measuring Political Tolerance and General Support for Pro–Civil Liberties Policies: Notes, Evidence, and Cautions." *Public Opinion Quarterly* 77: 45–68.

Gibson, James L., and Michael J. Nelson. 2018. *Black and Blue: How African Americans Judge the U.S. Legal System*. Oxford: Oxford University Press.

Gilens, Martin, Paul M. Sniderman, and James K. Kuklinski. 1998. "Affirmative Action and the Politics of Realignment." *British Journal of Political Science* 28: 159–183.

Gini, Gianluca, Tiziana Pozzoli, and Shelley Hymel. 2014. "Moral Disengagement among Children and Youth: A Meta-analytic Review of Links to Aggressive Behavior." *Aggressive Behavior* 40: 56–68.

Goidel, Kirby, Wayne Parent, and Bob Mann. 2011. "Race, Racial Resentment, Attentiveness to the News Media, and Public Opinion toward the Jena Six." *Social Science Quarterly* 92: 20–34.

Goldman, Barry M. 2003. "The Application of Referent Cognitions Theory to Legal-Claiming by Terminated Workers: The Role of Organizational Justice and Anger." *Journal of Management* 29: 705–728.

Gomez, Brad T., and J. Matthew Wilson. 2006. "Rethinking Symbolic Racism: Evidence of Attribution Bias." *Journal of Politics* 68: 611–625.

Gonsalkorale, Karen, Jeffrey W. Sherman, and Karl Christoph Klauer. 2008. "Aging and Prejudice: Diminished Regulation of Automatic Race Bias among Older Adults." *Journal of Experiment Social Psychology* 45: 410–414.

Graham, Otis. L. 2015. *Presidents and the American Environment.* Lawrence: University Press of Kansas.

Grunwald, Michael. 2012. *The New New Deal: The Hidden Story of Change in the Obama Era.* New York: Simon and Schuster.

Hafer, Carolyn L. 2000. "Do Innocent Victims Threaten the Belief in a Just World? Evidence from a Modified Stroop Task." *Journal of Personality and Social Psychology* 79: 165–173.

Hafer, Carolyn L., and Laurent Begue. 2005. "Experimental Research on Just-World Theory: Problems, Development, and Future Challenges." *Psychological Bulletin* 131: 128–167.

Hafer, Carolyn L., and Alicia N. Rubel. 2015. "Long-Term Focus and Prosocial-Antisocial Tendencies Interact to Predict Beliefs in Just World." *Personality and Individual Differences* 75: 121–124.

Hagner, Paul R., and John C. Pierce. 1984. "Racial Differences in Political Conceptualization." *Political Research Quarterly* 37: 212–235.

Haines, Tim. 2016. "Bill Clinton: 'If You're a White Southerner,' You Know What 'Make America Great Again' Really Means." *Real Clear Politics*, September 7. Online source: https://bit.ly/2Cx6G3G.

Hair, Joseph F., Jr., William C. Black, Barry J. Babin, and Rolph E. Anderson. 2012. *Multivariate Data Analysis.* 7th ed. Upper Saddle River, NJ: Pearson.

Hajnal, Zolton. 2001. "White Residents, Black Incumbents, and a Declining Racial Divide." *American Political Science Review* 95: 603–617.

Halmari, Helena. 1993. "Dividing the World: The Dichotomous Rhetoric of Ronald Reagan." *Multilingua: Journal of Cross-Cultural and Interlanguage Communication* 12: 143–176.

Heider, Fritz. 1958. *The Psychology of Interpersonal Relation.* NY: John Wiley & Sons.

Henry, P. J., and Andrea Saul. 2006. "The Development of System Justification in the Developing World." *Social Justice Research* 19: 365–378.

Henry, P. J., and David O. Sears. 2002. "The Symbolic Racism 2000 Scale." *Political Psychology* 23: 253–283.

Hochschild, Arlie Russell. 2016. *Strangers in Their Own Land: Anger and Mourning on the American Right.* New York: The New Press.

Hochschild, Jennifer L. 1981. *What's Fair? American Beliefs about Distributive Justice.* Cambridge, MA: Harvard University Press.

Hoggett, Paul, Hen Wilkinson, and Phoebe Beedell. 2013. "Fairness and the Politics of Resentment." *Journal of Social Policy* 42: 567–585.

Huber, Gregory A., and John S. Lapinski. 2006. "The 'Race-Card' Revisited: Assessing Racial Priming in Policy Contests." *American Journal of Political Science* 50: 421–440.

Huber, Gregory A., and John S. Lapinski. 2008. "Testing the Implicit-Explicit Model of Racialized Political Communication." *Perspectives on Politics* 6: 125–134.

Huddy, Leonie, and Stanley Feldman. 2009. "On Assessing the Political Effects of Racial Prejudice." *Annual Review of Political Science* 12: 423–447.

Hughes, Michael. 1997. "Symbolic Racism, Old-Fashioned Racism, and Whites' Opposition to Affirmative Action." In *Racial Attitudes in the 1990s: Continuity and Change*, edited by Steven A. Tuch and Jack K. Martin, 45–75. Westport, CT: Praeger.

Hunt, Matthew O. 2000. "Status, Religion, and the 'Belief in a Just World': Comparing African Americans, Latinos, and Whites." *Social Science Quarterly* 81: 325–343.

Hunt, Matthew O., and David C. Wilson. 2009. "Race/Ethnicity, Perceived Discrimination, and Beliefs about the Meaning of an Obama Presidency." *Du Bois Review* 6: 173–191.

Hurwitz, Jon, and Mark Peffley. 2005. "Playing the Race Card in the Post–Willie Horton Era." *Public Opinion Quarterly* 69: 99–112.

Hurwitz, Jon, Mark Peffley, and Jeffrey Mondak. 2015. "Linked Fate and Outgroup Perceptions: Blacks, Latinos, and the U.S. Criminal Justice System." *Political Research Quarterly* 68: 505–520.

Hutchings, Vince L. 2009. "Change or More of the Same? Evaluating Racial Attitudes in the Obama Era." *Public Opinion Quarterly* 73: 917–942.

Hutchings, Vincent L., Nicholas A. Valentino, Tasha S. Philpot, and Ismail K. White. 2004. "The Compassion Strategy: Race and the Gender Gap in American Politics." *Public Opinion Quarterly* 68: 512–541.

Hutchings, Vince L., Hanes Walton Jr., and Andrea Benjamin. 2010. "The Impact of Explicit Racial Cues on Gender Differences in Support for Confederate Symbols and Partisanship." *Journal of Politics* 72: 1175–1188.

Iyengar, Shanto. 1989. "How Citizens Think about National Issues: A Matter of Responsibility." *American Journal of Political Science* 33: 878–900.

Jackman, Mary. 2005. "Rejection or Inclusion of Outgroups." In *On the Nature of Prejudice: Fifty Years after Allport*, edited by John F. Dovidio, Peter Glick, and Laurie A. Rudman. Malden, MA: Blackwell.

Jardina, Ashley. 2019. *White Identity Politics*. Cambridge: Cambridge University Press.

Johnston, Christopher D., Howard G. Lavine, and Christopher M. Federico.

2017. *Open versus Closed: Personality, Identity, and the Politics of Redistribution*. Cambridge: Cambridge University Press.

Jones, Philip Edward. 2014. "Revisiting Stereotypes of Non-White Politicians' Ideological and Partisan Orientations." *American Politics Research* 42: 283–310.

Jost, John T. 2020. *A Theory of System Justification*. Cambridge, MA: Harvard University Press.

Jost, John T., and Mahzarin R. Banaji. 1994. "The Role of Stereotyping in System Justification and the Production of False Consciousness." *British Journal of Social Psychology* 33: 1–27.

Jost, John T., Mahzarin R. Banaji, and Brian A. Nosek. 2004. "A Decade of System Justification Theory: Accumulated Evidence of Conscious and Unconscious Bolstering of the Status Quo." *Political Psychology* 25: 881–919.

Jost, John T., D. Burgess, and Christina Mosso. 2001. "Conflicts of Legitimation among Self, Group, and System: The Integrative Potential of System Justification Theory." In *The Psychology of Legitimacy: Emerging Perspectives on Ideology, Justice, and Intergroup Relations*, edited by J. T. Jost and B. Major, 363–388. New York: Cambridge University Press.

Jost, John T., Christopher M. Federico, and Jaime L. Napier. 2009. "Political Ideology: Its Structure, Functions, and Elective Affinities." *Annual Review of Psychology* 60: 307–337.

Jost, John T., Jack Glaser, Arie W. Kruglanski, and Frank J. Sulloway. 2003. "Political Conservatism as Motivated Social Cognition." *Psychological Bulletin* 129: 339–375.

Jost, John T., Brian A. Nosek, and Samuel D. Gosling. 2008. "Ideology: Its Resurgence in Social, Personality, and Political Psychology." *Perspectives on Psychological Science* 3: 126–136.

Journal of Blacks in Higher Education. 2019. The Racial Gap in Traditional High School Completion Rates. February 5. https://www.jbhe.com/2019/02/the-racial-gap-in-traditional-high-school-completion-rates/.

Kahan, Dan M., Donald Braman, John Gastil, Paul Slovic, and C. K. Mertz. 2007. "Culture and Identity-Protective Cognition: Explaining the White-Male Effect in Risk Perception." *Journal of Empirical Legal Studies* 4: 465–505.

Kam, Cindy D., and Camille D. Burge. 2018. "Uncovering Reactions to the Racial Resentment Scale across the Racial Divide." *Journal of Politics* 80: 314–320.

Kam, Cindy D., and Camille D. Burge. 2019. "Racial Resentment and Public Opinion across the Racial Divide." *Political Research Quarterly* 72: 767–784.

Kay, Aaron C., John T. Jost, Anesu N. Mandisodza, Steven J. Sherman, John V. Petrocelli, and Amy L. Johnson. 2007. "Panglossian Ideology in the Service of System Justification: How Complementary Stereotypes Help Us to Rationalize Inequality." *Advances in Experimental Social Psychology* 39: 305–358.

Kemper, Theodore D., and R. Collins. 1990. "Dimensions of Microinteraction." *American Journal of Sociology* 96: 32–68.

Kenski, Kate, and Kathleen Hall Jamieson, eds. 2017. *The Oxford Handbook of Political Communication.* New York: Oxford University Press.

Kinder, Donald R., and Lynn M. Sanders. 1996. *Divided by Color: Racial Politics and Democratic Ideals.* Chicago: University of Chicago Press.

Kinder, Donald R., and Howard Schuman. 2004. "Racial Attitudes: Developments and Divisions in Survey Research." In *A Telescope on Society: Survey Research and Social Science at the University of Michigan and Beyond,* edited by J. S. House, T. F. Juster, R. L. Kahn, H. O. Schuman, and E. Singer, 365–392. Ann Arbor: University of Michigan Press.

Kinder, Donald R., and David O. Sears. 1981. "Prejudice and Politics: Symbolic Racism versus Racial Threats to the Good Life." *Journal of Personality and Social Psychology* 40: 414–431.

Kluegel, James R., and Eliot R. Smith. 1986. *Beliefs about Inequality.* New York: Aldine De Gruyter.

Knowles, Eric D., Brian S. Lowery, and Rebecca L. Schaumberg. 2009. "Anti-Egalitarians for Obama? Group-Dominance Motivation and the Obama Vote." *Journal of Experimental Social Psychology* 45: 955–969.

Kopko, Kyle C., Sarah McKinnon Bryner, Jeffrey Budziak, Christopher J. Devine, and Steven P. Nawara. 2011. "In the Eye of the Beholder? Motivated Reasoning in Disputed Elections." *Political Behavior* 33: 271–290.

Kuklinski, James H., Michael D. Cobb, and Martin Gilens. 1997. "Racial Attitudes and the New South." *Journal of Politics* 59: 323–349.

Kuklinski, James H., Paul M. Sniderman, Kathleen Knight, Thomas Piazza, Philip E. Tetlock, Gordon R. Lawrence, and Barbara Mellers. 1997. "Racial Prejudice and Attitudes toward Affirmative Action." *American Journal of Political Science* 41: 402–419.

Lammers, Joris, and Matt Baldwin. 2017. "Past-Focused Temporal Communication Overcomes Conservatives' Resistance to Liberal Political Ideas." *Journal of Personality and Social Psychology* 114: 599–619.

Laurin, Kristin, Aaron C. Kay, and Gavan J. Fitzsimons. 2012. "Reactance versus Rationalization: Divergent Responses to Policies that Constrain Freedom." *Psychological Science* 23: 205–209.

Lavine, Howard, Christopher D. Johnston, and Marco R. Steenbergen. 2013. *The Ambivalent Partisan: How Critical Loyalty Promotes Democracy.* New York: Oxford University Press.

Leach, C. W., R. Spears, N. R. Branscombe, and B. Doosje. 2003. "Malicious Pleasure: Schadenfreude at the Suffering of Another Group." *Journal of Personality and Social Psychology* 84: 932–943.

Lebo, Matthew J., and Daniel Cassino. 2007. "The Aggregated Consequences of Motivated Reasoning and the Dynamic of Partisan Approval." *Political Psychology* 28: 719–746.

Leeper, Thomas J., and Rune Slothuus. 2014. "Political Parties, Motivated Reasoning, and Public Opinion Formation." *Political Psychology* 35: 129–156.

Lerner, Melvin J. 1965. "Evaluation of Performance as a Function of Performer's Reward and Attractiveness." *Journal of Personality and Social Psychology* 1: 355–360.

Lerner, Melvin J. 1980a. "The Belief in a Just World." In *The Belief in a Just World: Perspectives in Social Psychology*, edited by M. J. Lerner, 9–30. Boston: Springer.

Lerner, Melvin J. 1980b. *The Belief in a Just World: A Fundamental Delusion.* New York: Plenum Press.

Lerner, Melvin J., and Dale T. Miller. 1978. "Just World Research and the Attribution Process: Looking Back and Ahead." *Psychological Bulletin* 85: 1030–1051.

Lewis, Angela K. 2005. "Black Conservatism in America." *Journal of African American Studies* 8: 3–13.

Lewis, Angela K. 2013. *Conservatism in the Black Community: To the Right and Misunderstood.* New York: Routledge.

Lien, Pei-te, M. Margaret Conway, and Janelle Wong. 2003. "The Contours and Sources of Ethnic Identity Choices among Asian Americans." *Social Science Quarterly* 84: 461–481.

Lipsitz, George. 1998. *The Possessive Investment in Whiteness: How White People Benefit from Identity Politics.* Philadelphia: Temple University Press.

Livingston, Robert W. 2002. "The Role of Perceived Negativity in the Moderation of African Americans' Implicit and Explicit Racial Attitudes." *Journal of Experimental Social Psychology* 38: 405–413.

Lodge, Milton, and Charles S. Taber. 2013. *The Rationalizing Voter.* Cambridge: Cambridge University Press.

Loose, K., Y. Hou, and A. J. Berinsky. 2018. "Achieving Efficiency without Losing Accuracy: Strategies for Scale Reduction with an Application to Risk Attitudes and Racial Resentment." *Social Science Quarterly* 99: 563–582.

Lopez, Ian Haney. 2014. *Dog Whistle Politics: How Coded Racial Appeals Have Reinvented Racism and Wrecked the Middle Class.* New York: Oxford University Press.

Lublin, David. 1999. *The Paradox of Representation: Racial Gerrymandering and Minority Interests in Congress.* Princeton: Princeton University Press, 1999.

Lundberg, Kristjen B., B. Keith Payne, Josh Pasek, and Jon A. Krosnick. 2017. "Racial Attitudes Predicted Changes in Ostensibly Race Neutral Political Attitudes under the Obama Administration." *Political Psychology* 38: 313–330.

Mayrl, Damon, and Aliya Saperstein. 2013. "When White People Report Racial Discrimination: The Role of Region, Religion, and Politics." *Social Science Research* 42: 742–754.

McAlister, Alfred L., Albert Bandura, and Steven V. Owen. 2006. "Mechanisms of Moral Disengagement in Support of Military Force: The Impact of Sept. 11." *Journal of Social and Clinical Psychology* 25: 141–165.

McClosky, Herbert. 1958. "Conservatism and Personality." *American Political Science Review* 52: 27–45.

McConahay, John B. 1986. "Modern Racism, Ambivalence, and the Modern Racism Scale." In *Prejudice, Discrimination, and Racism*, edited by John F. Dovidio and Samuel Gaertner, 91–125. Orlando, FL: Academic Press.

McConahay, John B., Betty B. Hardee, and Valerie Batts. 1981. "Has Racism Declined in America? It Depends on Who Is Asking and What Is Asked." *Journal of Conflict Resolution* 25: 563–579.

McConahay, J. B., and J. C. Hough Jr. 1976. "Symbolic Racism." *Journal of Social Issues* 32: 23–45.

McConnaughy, Corrine M., Ismail K. White, David L. Leal, and Jason P. Casellas. 2010. "A Latino on the Ballot: Explaining Coethnic Voting among Latinos and the Response of White Americans." *Journal of Politics* 72: 1199–1211.

Mccright, Aaron M., and Riley E. Dunlap. 2011a. "The Politicization of Climate Change and Polarization in the American Public's Views of Global Warming, 2001–2010." *Sociological Quarterly* 52: 155–194.

Mccright, Aaron M., and Riley E. Dunlap. 2011b. "Cool Dudes: The Denial of Climate Change among Conservative White Males in the United States." *Global Environmental Change* 21: 1163–1172.

McDermott, Monica, and Frank L. Samson. 2005. "White Racial and Ethnic Identity in the United States." *Annual Review of Sociology* 31: 245–261.

McGirt, Ellen. 2016. "Why 'Make America Great Again' Is an Offensive Slogan." *Fortune*, October 21. fortune.com/2016/10/21/why-make-america-great-again-is-an-offensive-slogan/.

McGowan, Ernest. 2017. *African Americans in White Suburbia: Social Networks and Political Behavior.* Lawrence: University of Kansas Press.

Meertens, Roel W., and Thomas F. Pettigrew. 1997. "Is Subtle Prejudice Really Prejudice?" *Public Opinion Quarterly* 61: 54–71.

Melton, Marissa. 2017. "Is 'Make America Great Again' Racist?" *Voice of America News*, August 31. https://www.voanews.com/a/is-make-america-great-racist/4009714.html.

Mendelberg, Tali. 2001. *The Race Card: Campaign Strategy, Implicit Messages, and the Norm of Equality.* Princeton: Princeton University Press.

Metzl, Jonathan. 2019. *Dying of Whiteness: How the Politics of Racial Resentment Is Killing America's Heartland*. New York: Basic Books.

Meyers, Lawrence S., Glenn Gamst, and A. J. Guarino. 2006. *Applied Multivariate Research: Design and Interpretation*. Thousand Oaks, CA: Sage.

Monforti, Jessica Lavariega, and Melissa R. Michelson. 2014. "Multiple Paths to Cynicism: Social Networks, Identity, and Linked Fate among Latinos." In *Latino Political en Cicencia Poltica: The Search for Latino Identity and Racial Consciousness*, edited by Tony Affigne, Evelyn Hu-DeHart, and Marion Orr. New York: NYU Press.

Montada, Leo, Sigrun-Heide Filipp, and Melvin J. Lerner. 1992. *Life Crises and Experiences of Loss in Adulthood*. Hillsdale, NJ: Lawrence Erlbaum Associates.

Montada, Leo, Manfred Schmitt, and Claudia Dalbert. 1986. "Thinking about Justice and Dealing with One's Own Privileges: A Study of Existential Guilt." In *Justice in Social Relations*, edited by H. W. Bierhoff, R. Cohen, and J. Greenberg, 125–143. New York: Plenum Press.

Norton, Michael I., and Samuel R. Sommers. 2011. "Whites See Racism as a Zero-Sum Game That They Are Now Losing." *Perspectives on Psychological Science* 6: 215–218.

Nour, Kteily S., Jim Sidanius, and Shana Levin. 2010. "Social Dominance Orientation: Cause or 'Mere Effect'? Evidence for SDO as a Causal Predictor of Prejudice and Discrimination against Ethnic and Racial Outgroups." *Journal of Experimental Social Psychology* 47: 208–214.

Oliver, Eric J., and Tali Mendelberg. 2000. "Reconsidering the Environmental Determinants of White Racial Attitudes." *American Journal of Political Science* 44: 574–589.

O'Neil, Kevin, and Marta Tienda. 2010. "A Tale of Two Counties: Natives' Opinions toward Immigration in North Carolina." *International Migration Review* 44: 728–761.

Orey, Byron D'Andra. 2004. "Explaining Black Conservatives: Racial Uplift or Racial Resentment?" *Black Scholar* 34: 18–22.

Orlet, Christopher. 2008. "Inhuman Humanities." *American Spectator*, May 22.

Ortony, Andrew, Gerald L. Clore, and Allan Collins. 1988. *The Cognitive Structure of Emotions*. Cambridge: Cambridge University Press.

Pape, Robert A., and Keven Ruby. 2021. "The Capitol Rioters Aren't like Other Extremists." *Atlantic*. February 2, 2021. https://www.theatlantic.com/ideas/archive/2021/02/the-capitol-rioters-arent-like-other-extremists/617895/

Parker, Christopher Sebastian. 2021. "Status Threat: Moving the Right Further to the Right?" *Daedalus* 150: 56–75.

Peffley, Mark, and Jon Hurwitz. 1998. "Whites' Stereotypes of Blacks: Sources and Political Consequences." In *Perception and Prejudice: Race and Politics in the United States*, edited by M. Peffley and J. Hurwitz, 58–99. New Haven: Yale University Press.

Peffley, Mark, and Jon Hurwitz. 2010. *Justice in America: The Separate Realities of Blacks and Whites*. New York: Cambridge University Press.

Peffley, Mark, Jon Hurwitz, and Paul M. Sniderman. 1997. "Racial Stereotypes and Whites' Political Views of Blacks in the Context of Welfare and Crime." *American Journal of Political Science* 41: 30–60.

Peffley, Mark, and John T. Williams. 1985. "Attributing Presidential Responsibility for National Economic Problems." *American Politics Quarterly* 13: 393–425.

Perez, Efren O., and Marc J. Hetherington. 2014. "Authoritarianism in Black and White: Testing the Cross-Racial Validity of the Child Rearing Scale." *Political Analysis* 22: 398–412.

Perlmann, Joel. 1988. *Ethnic Differences: Schooling and Social Structure among the Irish, Italians, Jews, and Blacks in an American City, 1880–1935*. Cambridge: Cambridge University Press.

Perry, Pamela. 2007. "White Universal Identity as a 'Sense of Group Position.'" *Symbolic Interaction* 30: 375–393.

Peterson, Michael Bang, Martin Skov, Soren Serritzlew, and Thomas Ramsoy. 2013. "Motivated Reasoning and Political Parties: Evidence for Increased Processing in the Face of Party Cues." *Political Behavior* 35: 831–854.

Pettigrew, Thomas F. 1979a. "Racial Change and Social Policy." *Annals of the American Academy of Political and Social Science* 441: 114–131.

Pettigrew, Thomas F. 1979b. "The Ultimate Attribution Error: Extending Allport's Cognitive Analysis of Prejudice." *Personality and Social Psychology Bulletin* 5: 461–476.

Pettigrew, Thomas F. 2017. "Social Psychological Perspectives on Trump Supporters." *Journal of Social and Political Psychology* 5: 107–116.

Pew Research Center. 2016. "On Views of Race and Inequality, Blacks and Whites Are Worlds Apart." June 26. https://www.pewsocialtrends.org/2016/06/27/1-demographic-trends-and-economic-well-being/.

Pew Research Center. 2019. "Race in America 2019." Washington, DC: Pew Research Center.

Phillips, Kristine. 2017. "Trump Replies 'Make America Great Again!' to Tweet about His Attacks on African Americans." *Washington Post*, November 23. https://www.washingtonpost.com/news/politics/wp/2017/11/23/trump-replies-make-america-great-again-to-tweet-about-his-attacks-on-african-americans/?utm_term=.e342c15f8ddf.

Philpot, Tasha S., Daron R. Shaw, and Ernest B. McGowen. 2009. "Winning the Race: Black Voter Turnout in the 2008 Presidential Election." *Public Opinion Quarterly* 73: 995–1022.

Pietryka, M. T., and R. C. Macintosh. 2017. "ANES Scales Often Don't Measure

What You Think They Measure–An ERPC2016 Analysis" https://pie-try-ka .com/files/pdf/wp-pietryka-macIntosh-171214.pdf

Pratto, Felicia, Jim Sidanius, Lisa M. Stallworth, and Bertram F. Malle. 1994. "Social Dominance Orientation: A Personality Variable Predicting Social and Political Attitudes." *Journal of Personality and Social Psychology* 67: 741–763.

Pratto, Felicia, Lisa M. Stallworth, and Sahr Conway-Lanz. 1998. "Social Dominance Orientation and the Ideological Legitimization of Social Policy." *Journal of Applied Social Psychology* 28: 1853–1875.

Rasch, Geor. 1960. *Probabilistic Models for Some Intelligence and Attainment Tests*. Chicago: University of Chicago Press.

Rawls, John. 1971. *A Theory of Justice*. Cambridge, MA: Harvard University Press.

Redlawsk, David P. 2002. "Hot Cognition or Cool Consideration? Testing the Effects of Motivated Reasoning on Political Decision Making." *Journal of Politics* 64: 1021–1044.

Redlawsk, David P., Caroline J. Tolbert, and William Franko. 2010. "Voters, Emotions, and Race in 2008: Obama as the First Black President." *Political Research Quarterly* 63: 875–889.

Redlawsk, David P., Caroline J. Tolbert, and Natasha Altema McNeely. 2014. "Symbolic Racism and Emotional Responses to the 2012 Presidential Candidates." *Political Research Quarterly* 67: 680–694.

Reyna, Christine, P. J. Henry, William Korfmacher, and Amanda Tucker. 2005. "Examining the Principles in Principled Conservatism: The Role of Responsibility Stereotypes as Cues for Deservingness in Racial Policy Decisions." *Journal of Personality and Social Psychology* 90: 109–128.

Roberts, Robert C. 2003. *Emotions: An Essay in Aid of Moral Psychology*. Cambridge: Cambridge University Press.

Rokeach, Milton. 1960. *Open and Closed Mind: Investigations into the Nature of Belief Systems and Personality Systems*. New York: Basic Books.

Roos, J. M., M. Hughes, and A. V. Reichelmann. 2019. "A Puzzle of Racial Attitudes: A Measurement Analysis of Racial Attitudes and Policy Indicators." *Socius* 5: 1–14.

Ross, Lee D., Teresa M. Amabile, and Julia L. Steinmetz. 1977. "Social Roles, Social Control, and Biases in Social-Perception Processes." *Journal of Personality and Social Psychology* 35: 485–494.

Rudolph, Thomas J. 2003. "Who's Responsible for the Economy? The Formation and Consequences of Responsibility Attributions." *American Journal of Political Science* 47: 698–713.

Sanchez, Gabriel R., and Edward D. Vargas. 2016. "Taking a Closer Look as Group Identity: The Link between Theory and Measurement of Group Consciousness and Linked Fate." *Political Research Quarterly* 69: 160–174.

Schaffner, Brian A., and Cameron Roche. 2017. "Misinformation and Motivated Reasoning: Responses to Economic News in a Politicized Environment." *Public Opinion Quarterly* 81: 86–110.

Scheler, Max. 1992. *On Feeling, Knowing and Valuing.* Chicago: University of Chicago Press.

Schneider, Monica C., and Angela L. Bos. 2011. "An Explanation of the Content of Stereotypes of Black Politicians." *Political Psychology* 32: 205–233.

Schuman, Howard. 2000. "The Perils of Correlations, the Lure of Labels, and the Beauty of Negative Results." In *Racialized Politics: Values, Ideology, and Prejudice in American Public Opinion,* edited by David O. Sears, James Sidanius, and Lawrence Bobo. Chicago: University of Chicago Press.

Sears, David O. 1988. "Symbolic Racism." In *Eliminating Racism: Profiles in Controversy,* edited by Patricia A. Katz and Dalmus A. Taylor, 53–84. New York: Plenum.

Sears, David O., and Patrick J. Henry. 2003. "The Origins of Symbolic Racism." *Journal of Personality and Social Psychology* 85: 259–275.

Sears, D. O., and P. J. Henry. 2005. "Over Thirty Years Later: A Contemporary Look at Symbolic Racism." *Advances in Experimental Social Psychology* 37: 95–125.

Sears, David O., and Donald R. Kinder. 1971. "Racial Tensions and Voting in Los Angeles." In *Los Angeles: Viability and Prospects for Metropolitan Leadership,* edited by Werner Z. Hirsch, 51–88. New York: Praeger.

Sears, David O., and John B. McConahay. 1973. *The Politics of Violence: The New Urban Blacks and the Watts Riot.* Boston: Houghton Mifflin.

Sears, David O., Colette van Laar, Mary Carrillo, and Rick Kosterman. 1997. "Is It Really Racism? The Origins of White Americans' Opposition to Race-Targeted Policies." *Public Opinion Quarterly* 61: 16–53.

Shamay-Tsoory, Simone, Dorin Ahronberg-Kirschenbaum, and Nirit Bauminger-Zviely. 2014. "There Is No Joy like Malicious Joy: Schadenfreude in Young Children." *PLOS ONE* 9: 1–7.

Shankel, George E. 1942. *American Mottoes and Slogans.* New York: H. W. Wilson.

Shapiro, Thomas M. 2004. *The Hidden Cost of Being African American: How Wealth Perpetuates Inequality.* Oxford: Oxford University Press.

Sherif, Muzafer. 1937. "The Psychology of Slogans." *Journal of Abnormal and Social Psychology* 32: 450–461.

Sibley, Chris G., and Fiona K. Barlow, eds. 2016. *The Cambridge Handbook of the Psychology of Prejudice.* Cambridge Handbooks in Psychology. Cambridge: Cambridge University Press.

Sidanius, Jim, Erik Devereux, and Felicia Pratto. 1992. "Dominance Theory as Explanations for Racial Policy Attitudes." *Journal of Social Psychology* 132: 377–395.

Sidanius, J., and F. Pratto. 1999. *Social Dominance: An Intergroup Theory of Social Hierarchy and Oppression*. New York: Cambridge University Press.

Sidanius, Jim, Felicia Pratto, and Lawrence Bobo. 1996. "Racism, Conservatism, Affirmative Action, and Intellectual Sophistication: A Matter of Principled Conservatism or Group Dominance?" *Journal of Personality and Social Psychology* 70: 476–490.

Sidanius, J., F. Pratto, C. Van Laar, and S. Levin. 2004. "Social Dominance Theory: Its Agenda and Method." *Political Psychology* 25: 845–880.

Sides, John, Michael Tesler, and Lynn Vavreck. 2019. *Identity Crisis: The 2016 Presidential Campaign and the Battle for the Meaning of America*. Princeton: Princeton University Press.

Singer, Tania, Ben Seymour, John P. O'Doherty, Klass E. Stephen, Raymound J. Dolan, and Chris D. Firth. 2006. "Empathic Neural Responses Are Modulated by the Perceived Fairness of Others." *Nature* 439: 466–469.

Skarlicki, Daniel P., and Robert Folger. 1997. "Retaliation in the Workplace: The Roles of Distributive, Procedural, and Interactional Justice." *Journal of Applied Psychology* 82: 434–443.

Slothuus, Rune, and Claes H. de Vreese. 2010. "Political Parties, Motivated Reasoning, and Issue Framing Effects." *Journal of Politics* 73: 630–645.

Smith, Craig A., and Richard S. Lazarus. 1993. "Appraisal Components, Core Relational Themes, and the Emotions." *Cognition and Emotion* 7: 233–269.

Smith, Richard H. 2013. *The Joy of Pain: Schadenfreude and the Dark Side of Human Nature*. New York: Oxford University Press.

Sniderman, Paul M. 2017. *The Democratic Faith: Essays on Democratic Citizenship*. New Haven: Yale University Press.

Sniderman, Paul M., Richard A. Brody, and James H. Kuklinski. 1984. "Policy Reasoning and Political Values: The Problem of Racial Equality." *American Journal of Political Science* 28: 75–94.

Sniderman, Paul M., and Edward G. Carmines. 1997. *Reaching beyond Race*. Cambridge, MA: Harvard University Press.

Sniderman, Paul M., Gretchen C. Crosby, and William G. Howell. 2000. "The Politics of Race." In *Racialized Politics: Values, Ideology, and Prejudice in American Public Opinion*, edited by D. O. Sears, J. Sidanius, and L. Bobo. Chicago: University of Chicago Press.

Sniderman, Paul M., and Thomas Piazza. 1993. *The Scar of Race*. Cambridge, MA: Harvard University Press.

Sniderman, Paul M., Thomas Piazza, Philip E. Tetlock, and Ann Kendrick. 1991. "The New Racism." *American Journal of Political Science*. 35: 423–447.

Sniderman, Paul M. and Phillip Tetlock. 1986. "Symbolic Racism: Problems with Motive Attribution in Political Analysis." *Journal of Social Issues* 42: 129–150.

Soffen, Kim, and Denise Lu. 2016. "When Was America Great? It De-

pends on Who You Are." *Washington Post*, October 7, 2016. ttps://www
.washingtonpost.com/graphics/politics/2016-election/when-was-america
-great/?noredirect=on.

Solomon, Robert. 1993. *The Passions: Emotions and the Meaning of Life*. Indi-
anapolis: Hackett.

Spurgin, Earl. 2015. "An Emotional-Freedom Defense of Schadenfreude." *Ethi-
cal Theory and Modern Practice* 18: 767–784.

Steckler, George A. 1957. "Authoritarian Ideology in Negro College Students."
Journal of Abnormal and Social Psychology 54: 396–399.

Stoker, Laura. 1998. "Understanding Whites' Resistance to Affirmative Action:
The Role of Principled Commitments and Racial Prejudice." In *Perception
and Prejudice: Race and Politics in the United States*, edited by J. Hurwitz
and M. Peffley, 135–170. New Haven: Yale University Press.

Strobel, Alexander, Jan Zimmerman, Anja Schmitz, Martin Reuter, Stefanie
Lis, Sabine Windmann, and Peter Kirsch. 2011. "Beyond Revenge: Neural
and Genetic Bases of Altruistic Punishment." *Neuroimage* 54: 671–680.

Suhr, D. 2006. "Exploratory or Confirmatory Factor Analysis." Proceedings
of the 31st SAS Users Group International Conference, pp. 1–17. Cary, NC:
SAS Institute.

Tabachnick, Barbara, Linda S. Fidell, and Jodie B. Ullman. 2007. *Using Multivariate Statistics*. 5th ed. Boston: Allyn and Bacon/Pearson Education.

Taber, Charles S., Damon Cann, and Simona Kucsova. 2009. "The Motivated
Processing of Political Arguments." *Political Behavior* 31: 137–155.

Taber, Charles S., and Milton Lodge. 2006. "Motivated Skepticism in the Evaluation of Political Beliefs." *American Journal of Political Science* 50: 755–769.

Tajfel, Henri, and John C. Turner. 1979. "An Integrative Theory of Intergroup
Conflict." In *The Social Psychology of Intergroup Relations*, edited by William G. Austin and Stephen Worchel. Monterey, CA: Brooks/Cole.

Tarman, Christopher, and David O. Sears. 2005. "The Conceptualization and
Measurement of Symbolic Racism." *Journal of Politics* 67: 731–761.

Tate, Katherine. 1994. *From Protest to Politics: The New Black Voters in American Elections*. Cambridge, MA: Harvard University Press.

Taylor, Marylee C., and Matthew B. Schroeder. 2010. "The Impact of Hispanic
Population Growth on the Outlook of African Americans." *Social Science
Research* 39: 491–505.

Tedin, Kent L., and Richard W. Murray. 1994. "Support for Biracial Political Co-
alitions among Blacks and Hispanics." *Social Science Quarterly* 75: 772–789.

Tepper, Bennett J. 2000. "Consequences of Abusive Supervision." *Academy of
Management Journal* 43: 178.

Tesler, Michael. 2012a. "The Return of Old-Fashioned Racism to White Americans' Partisan Preferences in the Early Obama Era." *Journal of Politics* 75:
110–123.

Tesler, Michael. 2012b. "The Spillover of Racialization into Health Care: How President Obama Polarized Public Opinion by Racial Attitudes and Race." *American Journal of Political Science* 56: 690–704.

Tesler, Michael. 2016. *Post-Racial or Most-Racial? Race and Politics in the Obama Era*. Chicago: University of Chicago Press.

Tesler, Michael, and David O. Sears. 2010. *Obama's Race: The 2008 Election and the Dream of a Post-Racial America*. Chicago: University of Chicago Press.

Thamm, Robert. 1992. "Social Structure and Emotion." *Sociological Perspectives* 35: 649–671.

Thamm, Robert J. 2004. "Toward a Universal Power and Status Theory of Emotions." *Advances in Group Processes* 26: 189–222.

Tileagă, Cristian. 2016. *The Nature of Prejudice: Society, Discrimination, and Moral Exclusion*. New York: Routledge.

Tuch, Steven A., and Michael Hughes. 2011. "Whites' Racial Policy Attitudes in the Twenty-First Century: The Continuing Significance of Racial Resentment." *Annals of the American Academy of Political and Social Science* 634: 134–152.

Tumulty, Karen. 2017. "How Donald Trump Came Up with 'Make America Great Again.'" *Washington Post*, January 17. https://www.washingtonpost.com/politics/how-donald-trump-came-up-with-make-america-great-again/2017/01/17/fb6acf5e-dbf7-11e6-ad42-f3375f271c9c_story.html.

Turner, Jonathan H., and Jan E. Stets. 2005. *The Sociology of Emotion*. Cambridge: Cambridge University Press.

Tyler, Tom. R. 1997. *Social Justice in a Diverse Society*. Boulder, CO: Westview.

Tyler, Tom. R., and Johanne Maartje van der Toorn. 2013. "Social Justice." In *Oxford Handbook of Political Psychology*, edited by L. Huddy, D. O. Sears, and J. Levy, 627–661. 2nd ed. Oxford: Oxford University Press.

United States Sentencing Commission. 2017. "Demographic Differences in Sentencing: An Update to the 2012 Booker Report." https://www.ussc.gov/sites/default/files/pdf/research-and-publications/research-publications/2017/20171114_Demographics.pdf.

Vaca, Nicolas C. 2004. *The Presumed Alliance: The Unspoken Conflict between Latinos and Blacks and What It Means for America*. New York: Harper Collins.

Vaes, Jeroen, Maria Paola Paladino, and Chiara Magagnotti. 2011. "The Human Message in Politics: The Impact of Emotional Slogans on Subtle Conformity." *Journal of Social Psychology* 151: 162–179.

Valentino, Nicholas A. 1999. "Crime News and the Priming of Racial Attitudes during Evaluations of the President." *Public Opinion Quarterly* 63: 293–320.

Valentino, Nicholas A., and Ted Brader. 2011. "The Sword's Other Edge: Perceptions of Discrimination and Racial Policy Opinion after Obama." *Public Opinion Quarterly* 75: 201–206.

Valentino, Nicholas A., Vincent L. Hutchings, and Ismail K. White. 2002. "Cues That Matter: How Political Ads Prime Racial Attitudes during Campaigns." *American Political Science Review* 96: 75–90.

Van Assche, Jasper, Kristof Dhont, and Thomas F. Pettigrew. 2018. "The Social-Psychological Bases of Far-Right Support in Europe and the United States." *Journal of Community Applied Social Psychology* 29: 385–401.

Van Dijk, Wilco W., Jaap W. Ouwerkerk, Richard H. Smith, and Mina Cikara. 2015. "The Role of Self-Evaluation and Envy in Schadenfreude." *European Review of Social Psychology* 26: 247–282.

Vollum, Scott, and Jacqueline Buffington-Vollum. 2010. "An Examination of Social Psychological Factors and Support for the Death Penalty: Attribution, Moral Disengagement, and the Value-Expressive Function of Attitudes." *American Journal of Criminal Justice* 35: 15–36.

Vollum, Scott, Jacqueline Buffington-Vollum, and Dennis R. Longmire. 2004. "Moral Disengagement and Attitudes about Violence toward Animals." *Society & Animals* 12: 209–235.

Wakslak, Cheryl J., John T. Jost, Tom R. Tyler, and Emmeline S. Chen. 2007. "Moral Outrage Mediates the Dampening Effect of System Justification on Support for Redistributive Social Policies." *Psychological Science* 18: 267–274.

Wallsten, Kevin, Tatishe M. Nteta, Lauren A. McCarthy, and Melinda R. Tarsi. 2017. "Prejudice or Principled Conservatism? Racial Resentment and White Opinion toward Paying College Athletes." *Political Research Quarterly* 70: 209–222.

Watson, Elwood. 1998. "Guess What Came to American Politics? Contemporary Black Conservatism." *Journal of Black Studies* 29: 73–92.

Weaver, Vesla M. 2012. "The Electoral Consequences of Skin Color: The 'Hidden' Side of Race in Politics." *Political Behavior* 34: 159–192.

Weber, Christopher, and Christopher M. Federico. 2007. "Interpersonal Attachment and Patterns of Ideological Belief." *Political Psychology* 28: 389–416.

Weber, Christopher R., Howard Lavine, Leonie Huddy, and Christopher M. Federico. 2014. "Placing Racial Stereotypes in Context: Social Desirability and the Politics of Racial Hostility." *American Journal of Political Science* 58: 63–78.

Westacott, Emrys. 2016. "Why Trump's 'Make American Great Again' Nostalgia Is a Dangerous Political Tool." *Timeline*, https://bit.ly/2ExDmfU.

Wetts, Rachel, and Robb Willer. 2018. "Privilege on the Precipice: Perceived Racial Status Threats Lead White Americans to Oppose Welfare Programs." *Social Forces* 97: 793–822.

Wilkins, Clara L., and Cheryl R. Kaiser. 2014. "Racial Progress as Threat to the Status Hierarchy: Implication for Perceptions of Anti-White Bias." *Psychological Science* 25: 439–446.

Williams, Linda F. 1990. "White/Black Perceptions of the Electability of Black Political Candidates." *National Political Science Review* 2: 45–64.

Williams, Sarah. 1984. "Left-Right Ideological Differences in Blaming Victims." *Political Psychology* 5: 573–581.

Wilson, David C., and Darren W. Davis. 2009. "Measuring Explicit Racial Resentment: A Comparison of Old and New Concepts and Measures." Paper presented at the annual meeting of the American Political Science Association in Toronto, Ontario.

Wilson, David C., and Darren W. Davis. 2011. "Reexamining Racial Resentment: Conceptualization and Content." *Annals of the American Academy of Political and Social Science* 634: 117–133.

Wilson, David C., and Darren W. Davis. 2018. "The Racial Double Standard: Attributing Racial Motivations in Voting Behavior." *Public Opinion Quarterly* 82: 63–86.

Wilson, David C., and Tyson King-Meadows. 2016. "Perceived Electoral Malfeasance and Resentment over the Election of Barack Obama." *Electoral Studies* 44: 35–45.

Wilson, Thomas C. 1996. "Cohort and Prejudice: Whites' Attitudes toward Blacks, Hispanics, Jews, and Asians." *Public Opinion Quarterly* 60: 253–274.

Wojniusz, Helen K. 1979. "Racial Hostility among Blacks in Chicago." *Journal of Black Studies* 10: 40–59.

Womick, Jake, Tobias Rothmund, Flavio Azevedo, Laura A. King, and John T. Jost. 2019. "Group-Based Dominance and Authoritarian Aggression Predict Support for Donald Trump in the 2016 U.S. Presidential Election." *Social Psychological and Personality Science* 10: 643–652.

Wright, Benjamin D., and Geoffrey N. Masters. 1982. *Rating Scale Analysis.* Chicago: MESA Press.

Wright, Benjamin D., and Mark Stone. 1999. *Measurement Essentials.* 2nd ed. Wilmington, DE: Wide Range.

Yong, An Gie, and Sean Pearce. 2013. "Beginner's Guide to Factor Analysis: Focusing on Exploratory Factor Analysis." *Tutorials in Quantitative Methods for Psychology* 9: 79–94.

YouGov. 2016. *Cooperative Congressional Election Study: Clinton Leads Trump by 4.* November 7. https://today.yougov.com/topics/politics/articles-reports/2016/11/07/cces-2016.

Yzerbyt, V. Y., A. Rogier, and S. T. Fiske. 1998. "Group Entitativity and Social Attribution: On Translating Situational Constraints into Stereotypes." *Personality and Social Psychology Bulletin* 24: 1089–1103.

Index

Note: Italicized page numbers refer to figures and tables; such pages may also include regular text.

social dominance theory (SDT), 22–23
Solomon, Robert, 45
Sommers, Samuel R., 28
Sotomayor, Sonia, Limbaugh on nomination of, 200. *See also* Latinos; minorities, racial-ethnic/other
status quo: African Americans on, 30, 221, 227; climate change as threat to, 173–77, 180–81, 186; defending, 42–43, 228; desire to maintain, 31, 50, 76–77, 106; MAGA and, 140–43; Obama as threat to, 163, 165, 196–97, 199–200, 212–13, 248; political correctness as threat to, 142–43; threats to, 25–26, 27, 35–36, 43, 72, 78–80, 219; threats to, surveyed, 96–97, 288–89, 290; threats to, trigger Capitol Insurrection, 257–58; threats to, trigger White solidarity, 123–24. *See also* racial resentment; threat
stereotyping, negative: of African Americans, 18–21, 23, 42–43, 49, 52, 62, 70–71; and deservingness, 193–94, 212, 222, 244, 246; in election of 2020 (Trump), 256; formulations of, 53–54; of Obama, 208; as politicians, 197; racial resentment and, 28–29, 291; of Trump's opposition, 311n1. *See also* racial resentment; Whites
Stets, Jan E., 44
Supreme Court, US: approval of, 127–29; on DACA, 237; and political preferences, 127, 134–35, 257; as threat, *198–99*
surveys: on authoritarianism, 287–88; on equality, 287; on Obama as threat, *198*; on poor economic conditions, 167; on presidential candidates 2008–2016, 130–*31*; on racial resentment, *57*, *59*, *67*, *82*, *84*, *88*, 121–22, *225–27*, 268–76, 287, 288; on racial resentment, and climate change denial, 181–*82*; on racial resentment, of African Americans, 277–*80*, 281–*82*, *283*; on racial resentment, of Catholics, 271; on racial schadenfreude, 202; on threats to status quo, 96–97; on Trump's corporate tax breaks, 185–*86*
symbolic racism. *See* racism, symbolic
system justification: and climate change, 180–81, 188; prevalent among conservatives, 177–78; and racial resentment, 119–*20*; threats embodied in, 177

tax breaks, Trump's corporate, self-contradictory White support for, 184–*86*
Taylor, Breonna, 195, 260
Tea Party, *122*, 294. *See also* conservatism/conservatives; Republicans
Terkildsen, Nayda, 197
Tesler, Michael, 160
threat: Blacks pose to Whites, xi–xii, 14–15, 17, 25, 50, 186–87; Blacks pose to Whites, system justification theory and, 26–27; Blacks pose to Whites, triggers White solidarity, 123–24; Blacks pose to Whites, various presidents and, 131–32, 163; MAGA and, xiii, 15; Obama as, to Whites, xi–xiii, 17, 29, 123–24, 163, 186–87, 196–97, 248; political, 300; political correctness as, 142; to status quo, 25–26, 77, 78–79, 108, 140–43, 159; to status quo, climate change as, 173–77, 180–81; to status quo, triggers Capitol Insurrection, 257–58. See also *Make America Great Again* (MAGA) slogan; Obama, Barack; racial progress; racial resentment; status quo
Trump, Donald, 3, 34, 115, 234–35; birtherism of, 12; and Capitol Insurrection, 255–61; complaints about election of 2016, 311n2; and conspiracy theories, 255, 258; in election of 2020, 253–54; fuels threats to White status quo, 123–24, 251; impeachment of, 261; and MAGA, 140, 149–50, 158; and political correctness, xii, xiii, 143; as presidential candidate, 130–*31*, 206, 210; SDO supports, 125–26; on 1619 Project, 251; support for, and cognitive consistency vs. self-interest, 164–65; support for, by nonracists, 16–17, 257–59; support for, from Supreme Court and Congress, 128; tax-break policy of, 184–86, 248; unqualified for presidency, 129–*31*. *See also* Capitol Insurrection (2021); conservatism/conservatives; *Make America Great Again* (MAGA) slogan; Republicans